SPITFIRES
OVER
SICILY

The Crucial Role of the Malta Spitfires in the
Battle of Sicily, January – August 1943

BRIAN CULL

with

Nicola Malizia & Frederick Galea

GRUB STREET · LONDON

Published by Grub Street,
The Basement,
10 Chivalry Road,
London SW11 1HT

Copyright © 2000 Grub Street, London
Text copyright © Brian Cull

British Library Cataloguing in Publication Data
Cull, Brian
  Spitfires over Sicily: July-August 1943
  1. World War, 1939-1945 – Aerial operations
  2. World War, 1939-1945 – Campaigns – Italy – Sicily
  I. Title II. Malizia, Nicola III. Galea, Frederick
  940.5′42158

ISBN 1-902304-32-2

Typeset by Pearl Graphics, Hemel Hempstead

Printed and bound in Great Britain by
Biddles Ltd, Guildford and King's Lynn

BRIAN CULL is the author of the following Grub Street titles:

AIR WAR FOR YUGOSLAVIA, GREECE and CRETE 1940-41 with Christopher
  Shores and Nicola Malizia
MALTA: THE HURRICANE YEARS 1940-41 with Christopher Shores and
  Nicola Malizia
MALTA: THE SPITFIRE YEAR 1942 with Christopher Shores and
  Nicola Malizia
BLOODY SHAMBLES Volume 1 with Christopher Shores and Yasuho Izawa
BLOODY SHAMBLES Volume 2 with Christopher Shores and Yasuho Izawa
SPITFIRES OVER ISRAEL with Shlomo Aloni and David Nicolle
TWELVE DAYS IN MAY with Bruce Lander and Heinrich Weiss
WINGS OVER SUEZ with David Nicolle and Shlomo Aloni
249 AT WAR
THE DESERT HAWKS with Leo Nomis
HURRICANES OVER TOBRUK with Don Minterne

CONTENTS

Acknowledgements   iv

Foreword   v

Introduction and Preamble   1

Chapter I   Spitbombers: Malta on the Offensive, January-March 1943   7

Chapter II   Malta: The Thorn in Sicily's Side, April-May 1943   41

Chapter III   The Fall of Pantelleria, June 1943   63

Chapter IV   The Blitz on Sicily, 1-9 July 1943   93

Chapter V   D-Day: Invasion, 10 July 1943   121

Chapter VI   The Air Fighting Intensifies, 11-13 July 1943   133

Chapter VII   The Air Battle is Won, 14-31 July 1943   160

Chapter VIII   The End in Sicily: The German Dunkirk, August 1943   178

Appendix I   A Potted History of GCII/7   203

Appendix II   My First Day in Sicily, Flg Off Gordon Wilson RCAF   205

Appendix III   Malta's Spitfire IX – EN199   206

Appendix IV   Italian Documentation reference Flt Lt Les Gosling DFC RCAF   207

Appendix V   The Adventures of Flg Off Brendan Baker   208

Appendix VI   Spitfires Pilots Aerial Combat Claims & Credits, Malta and Sicily   209

Appendix VII   Spitfire Operational Losses & Pilot Casualties, Malta and Sicily   215

Appendix VIII   Spitfire Squadron Codes   218

Maps   219

Select Bibliography   222

Addenda to *Hurricanes over Tobruk*   224

Index   225

ACKNOWLEDGEMENTS

Poor health over the past year would have made this book difficult for me to complete on time had it not been for the wonderful support and understanding received from my wife, Val, which included helping with research at the Public Record Office, in addition to ensuring a continuous flow of sustaining beverages over a long period. I of course thank my two co-authors Frederick Galea and Nicola Malizia who have generously given their time and expertise, the latter sadly also not enjoying the best of health in recent times; many happy hours have been spent in the company of Frederick and his charming wife Val during our frequent visits to Malta. I wish to thank old friends Chris Shores and Tony Rogers for helping me out in my hour of need by conducting interviews and research on my behalf.

A number of veterans of the Sicily fighting have been most generous with their contributions. In particular, I wish to thank Raymond Baxter, journalist, broadcaster, TV celebrity and former fighter pilot with 93 Squadron for his contribution including the Foreword, while Wg Cdr Peter Olver DFC, who briefly commanded 244 Wing before becoming a prisoner of war, similarly provided his reminiscences, as did Jim Gray DFC, an American volunteer in the RAF who also flew with 93 Squadron. Mrs Teresa Ray-Tutt, widow of Sqn Ldr Blair White, who was killed in action just prior to the invasion, is to be thanked for making available a copy of her late husband's logbook, while three gallant Canadians who flew with 92 Squadron, Milton Jowsey DFC, Rex Probert DFC, and Gordon Wilson, also kindly provided anecdotes and photographs. However, sadly, many of the prominent fighter pilots featured in *Spitfires over Sicily* are no longer with us although, fortunately, several had published their memoirs which include references to the Sicily campaign, including Grp Capt Wilf Duncan Smith DSO DFC (*Spitfire into Battle*), Grp Capt Hugh Dundas DSO DFC (*Flying Start*), and Wg Cdr Colin Gray DSO DFC (*Spitfire Patrol*). My gratitude is also extended, as with all my books, to Mr Jack Lee, gentleman and scholar, himself a veteran of the Sicily campaign.

As will be discerned within, liberal use has been made of quotes appearing in Dr Jochen Prien's highly recommended *Jagdgeschwader 53 Volume Two*, which provides an excellent account of the main opponents of Malta's Spitfires during the period covered by this book, and I wish to record my gratitude to Dr Prien accordingly. Similarly, no study of the invasion of Sicily would be complete without reference to Colonel Carlo D'Este's masterly campaign history *Bitter Victory*, while Charles Whiting writes graphically about the tragic airborne operations in *Slaughter over Sicily*; many other interesting and related titles are to be found in the Select Bibliography.

My good friend and fellow historian Heinrich Weiss has been most helpful in providing details of Luftwaffe personnel, as has German historian Gerhard Stemmer, while Gianandrea Bussi has similarly contributed most generously regarding Italian personnel, as has Frank Olynyk, author of *Stars & Bars*, regarding American Spitfire pilots; long-standing friend and author Paul Sortehaug of New Zealand provided transcripts of interviews he had conducted, plus copies of combat reports and photographs relating to RNZAF pilots who flew Spitfires during the Sicily campaign. Others who have contributed in one way or another include my French friends Joss Leclercq and Bernard Baeza for information including translations regarding GCII/7, Mr Ted Shute regarding ASR matters, George Harding (ex-242 Squadron) of Hastings for the loan of photographs, Barry Baddock MA (for translations), Sonja Stammwitz (for translations), and Art Nicholson of Texas (for providing books and other documents). As ever, Flt Lt Andy Thomas kindly made available his wonderful photographic collection, while Chris Thomas expertly created another mini masterpiece for the dust jacket illustration. Mr Graham Davies of AHB again helped fill many gaps in the historical detail necessary for such a work as *Spitfires over Sicily*, for which I am grateful, as I am to Mrs P. Williams at PMC RAF Gloucester. The staff of the Public Record Office are to be thanked for their efficient and speedy service, as are the staff of the Bury St Edmunds Public Library. Last but not least, John Davies and his staff at Grub Street are to be thanked for another excellent production.

Brian Cull, Bury St Edmunds, January 2000

FOREWORD

Raymond Baxter
Fighter Pilot 93 Squadron 1943

This book provides a clinical account of a critical phase of the Second World War in Europe. Yet, although the importance of the invasion and conquest of Sicily must be self-evident, the subject has received surprisingly little attention in the plethora of books published since 1945, and which collectively must present the most comprehensive record and archive in the entire history of warfare. If only for this reason, Brian Cull and his colleagues are to be congratulated. But the fruits of their meticulous research have a peculiar significance. They provide an insight into the shape of things yet to come in the long and painful march to Berlin.

That tragic mistakes were made may be regarded as inevitable, but that many of those mistakes were to be repeated heightens the tragedy. Aspects of effective Anglo-American co-operation – or the lack of it – became apparent in Sicily, yet they were to persist through the near disaster of Salerno and thereafter. The over-ambitious airborne assaults and their incompetent execution resulted in the avoidable (and therefore doubly tragic) wastage of highly trained and gallant British soldiers – arguably a preview of Arnhem all those bitter months later.

The names and character of senior commanders destined to play key roles in what lay ahead emerge from the comparative obscurity of the North African campaign: Eisenhower himself, Patton, Coningham and Broadhurst, and the incomparable Bertram Ramsey who, having master-minded Operation *Dynamo* – the Dunkirk Evacuation of 1940 – was in supreme command of all Anglo-American naval forces at Salerno and ultimately Operation *Overlord*, the D-Day landings and the invasion of Normandy in June 1944.

But this book is concerned primarily with the air war over Sicily – the critical nature of which was defined by Montgomery on the eve of the invasion: "I am under no illusions as to the stern fight which lies ahead . . . We are going to embark on the land battle before we have won the air battle". In this context at least the Royal Air Force was brilliantly well served, as it had been in the Battle of Britain, by its wing and squadron commanders. Indeed, many of those in Sicily had already won their spurs in 1940 – Brian Kingcome, 'Sheep' Gilroy, Duncan Smith, 'Cocky' Dundas, and 'Wilfy' Sizer, for example. Having had the privilege of being led in the air by these men I can personally pay tribute to their excellence. Not only were they brilliant fighter pilots and tacticians, they were 'leaders' in every sense of the word. Those whom they commanded not only looked up to them with admiration, but with total loyalty, confidence and indeed affection.

And this brings me to mention the only 'missing ingredient' of this book. It leaves its readers to imagine for themselves, as clinical account follows cryptic comment, what it all really felt like. I can only speak for myself on behalf of my friends and comrades. Young as we were, we knew perfectly well that we were writing history. Churchill's description of this "strike at the soft under belly of Europe" inspired us, although we were not too sure about the "soft". The North African campaign had familiarised us to the living conditions of a forward fighter squadron in the Tactical Air Force. During our brief stay in Malta we revelled in the luxury of living 'indoors'. Once in Sicily it was back to the conventional army ridge-tent in the nearest olive grove. The tents were dug-out to a depth of about three feet to provide protection and increase headroom. Two or three to a tent – except the CO and Adjutant. We slept under a mosquito net in a bedroll (the crude forerunner of the modern sleeping bag) and army-type collapsible canvas camp beds.

In North Africa Coningham introduced the revolutionary concept of the Aircrew Mess shared by officers and NCO pilots. This consisted of marquees joined together – one the 'dining room' with trestle tables and benches, the other 'the bar' furnished with whatever may have come to hand. Showers were generally home-made and rudimentary. There was no NAAFI, no cinema and 93 Squadron at any rate never got one of the much publicised concerts by visiting 'stars'. We were our own enter-tainment. Feminine company – nurses perhaps from a field hospital within 20 miles, or US Red Cross girls – was so rare as to trigger a monumental party.

To those who have indulged in the deadly game of shooting, and being shot at, to kill – not just once or twice, but day after day – ideas and attitudes are never quite the same again. The experience engenders bonds of comradeship and mutual expectation and trust unmatched elsewhere, and only understood by those who shared it.

This book is a worthy tribute to the Sicilian Chapter.

January 2000

HOME THOUGHTS

Blue are the skies of Sicily
And green is the olive grove.
Brown are the hills of Sicily
Where the winding rivers rove.

But I'd rather the grey and windswept sky
Of the English Lakes when a storm is nigh.
I'd rather the green of Kentish trees
As orchards sigh to a summer breeze.
I'd rather the brown on shoulders of Shap
Where curlews call and foxes yap.

The stench of death in Sicily
And deaths in those heavenly skies;
There's burning heat in Sicily
And myriad flies on wounds and eyes.

But cool is the dew on an English lawn
When roses sleep and dreams are born,
Whilst a harvest moon with her silver light
Casts the spell of peace on an English night.
And softly on the fragrant air
The wings of love are hovering there.

Written by Raymond Baxter
in 1943

INTRODUCTION AND PREAMBLE

Malta had virtually stood alone since the opening days of the war in the Middle East and Mediterranean. The Regia Aeronautica launched its first raid against the little island on the morning of 11 June 1940, the day following Italy's declaration of war against Britain and France. To defend herself, Malta could boast no more than a handful of Fleet Air Arm Sea Gladiator biplane fighters, hurriedly taken out of storage, together with half a dozen volunteer RAF pilots, none of whom were trained fighter pilots. Within two weeks however, the first of what would eventually amount to several hundred Hurricanes had arrived from the United Kingdom, flown across war-ravaged Northern France to bases in Southern France from where the survivors of the initial small band of reinforcements headed out across the Mediterranean, via the North African coast, for Malta[1].

By the end of 1940 Malta had recorded 211 air raids; by the end of 1941 the total had reached 1,174. During 1942 the alarms were sounded on no fewer than 2,031 occasions as Axis bombers pounded the island almost at will until gradually more and more Spitfires reached Malta and fought to regain supremacy in the skies above – at great cost in lives and aircraft. But, as Maltese historian Philip Vella wrote:[2]

> "Nature's greatest gift to Malta, its rocky structure, was never put to better use than during the war years. Were it not for the strength of the Malta stone that minimised the effect of bombing and blast, besides rendering ineffective the use of incendiaries, the alarming tonnage of bombs dropped would have wiped out the island."

In April 1942 alone, an estimated 6,727 tons of bombs had fallen on Malta – an island the size of the Isle of Wight – more than any monthly tonnage dropped on England at the height of the Battle of Britain in 1940.

These raids emanated from Sicily, which had long been the thorn in Malta's side. Sicily had been the base for the might of the Regia Aeronautica before its sudden decline, and for a succession of Luftwaffe units including many of the élite Jagdgeschwadern, including Gruppen of JG27, JG53 and JG77. The RAF at Malta had periodically attempted to thwart Sicily's potency but it had always been a case of too few to make a difference. Attacks on Sicilian targets by Malta-based Blenheims, Wellingtons, Beaufighters and Hurricanes in 1941 were nothing but pinpricks, with catastrophic losses suffered by the Blenheims in particular. The offensive fared little better in 1942, survival of the island, its people and its garrison being uppermost. But the planned invasion by Axis forces did not materialise; a few gallant merchantmen weathered the fearful pounding by Axis air

---

[1] see *Malta: The Hurricane Years 1940-1941* by Christopher Shores and Brian Cull with Nicola Malizia; also *Malta: The Spitfire Year 1942* by the same authors.
[2] see *Malta: Blitzed But Not Beaten* by Philip Vella, who died in 1987. A personal friend of all three authors, he had been assisted in this notable work by Frederick Galea.

forces to keep the island supplied, and Spitfire reinforcements were flown in from aircraft carriers. Malta hung on, but 1942 had been a bad year for Malta and its people. Many civilians and servicemen lost their lives in the bombing.

It was at the height of the aerial assault on Malta – mid-1942, at the time when the Axis powers had designs on invading the island – that the idea of the Allies invading Sicily was initially discussed in London. With America throwing an ever increasing number of men and machines into the European and Mediterranean theatres of war, the Allied Command was confident of eventual victory, even though to the ordinary soldier, sailor and airman – British, Commonwealth, and now American – doing the actual fighting, victory seemed far away. German and Italian forces in North Africa were, by mid-1942, rampant in the Western Desert, forcing the Eighth Army back into Egypt as far as El Alamein. But there a stand was made and the tables turned, thus assuring ultimate British victory in North Africa. The Axis forces were speedily pushed back into Libya, then into Tunisia until their eventual surrender in May 1943. The tide had irrevocably turned.

A top level meeting was held at Casablanca in mid-January 1943 involving US President Roosevelt and Prime Minister Churchill, plus their Combined Chiefs-of-Staff, during which the proposed invasion of Sicily was the main topic of discussion although, initially, the British favoured taking Sardinia rather than Sicily. The British argued that Sardinia was less well defended and would offer a good base for the bomber offensive against Northern Italy, but the Americans countered that Sicily currently offered a greater threat to Allied convoys and tankers plying the Eastern and Central Mediterranean, and that the island would have to be taken eventually. The British Naval CoS concurred, adding that securing the Eastern Mediterranean would also make it unnecessary for Allied shipping to continue using the long Cape route to India. On 19 January, the decision was taken – Sicily would be the target for invasion as soon as the Tunisian Campaign was successfully concluded. The four main objectives would be (a) securing the Mediterranean line of communication (b) diverting German forces from the Russian front (c) increasing pressure on Italy (d) creating a situation in which Turkey could be enlisted as an active ally.

Following the successful conclusion to the Tunisian Campaign at the beginning of May 1943, the British promptly produced a plan whereby a British force would be assembled in the Middle East and an American one in North Africa. D-Day was set for 25 July 1943. General Dwight Eisenhower, who had ably conducted Operation *Torch* (the Allied invasion of North-West Africa) was made Supreme Commander with General Sir Harold Alexander as Deputy Commander. Admiral Sir Andrew Cunningham was appointed Naval Commander, and Air Chief Marshal Sir Arthur Tedder, Air Commander. The operation was given the codename *Husky*. The original plan called for General Sir Bernard Montomery's British 8th Army – the Desert Rats – to land between Gela and Avola to capture the south-eastern airfields plus the ports of Augusta and Syracuse, before taking Catania and the Gerbini airfields; the American 7th Army under General George Patton would simultaneously land at Sciacca and Selinunte from where they would capture Castelventrano airfield before taking Palermo, but Montgomery objected. He considered his troops would be so thinly dispersed that Axis reinforcements from the mainland would be able to easily drive a wedge between the British and American forces. He also argued that no provision had been made for the capture of Comiso and Ponte Olivo airfields, and that initially it would be of greater importance to capture airfields than ports. He eventually won the day, against much opposition from his equally arrogant American counterpart, Patton – who now began referring to Montgomery as 'the little limey fart' – and a new plan was devised. Both forces would instead concentrate on south and south-east Sicily, the US Western Naval Task Force under Vice-Admiral H. Kent Hewitt USN to land its forces between Licata and Scoglitti, the British Eastern Naval Task Force under Admiral Sir Bertram Ramsay RN, to be responsible for landings on the Pachino peninsula and the Gulf of Noto, but short of Syracuse. D-Day was changed to 10 July 1943. The die was cast.

All was not well in the Italian camp, however, where many prayed for a speedy end to the war which could only spell disaster for Italy. Among those instrumental in seeking an immediate termination of hostilities was the monarch, King Victor Emmanuel III, who had set himself the task of ridding the state of Italy's Fascist leader, Benito Mussolini – Il Duce – and his totalitarian régime. In a letter to the Duke of Acquarone in January 1943 he advised that he had "definitely decided to end the Fascist régime and dismiss Mussolini . . ." He was urged to implement the decision by Marshals Badoglio and Cavaglia, and influential Generals Carboni and Castello among others including Count Dino Grandi, who confided to the King's senior aide:

> "One must not have any illusions. Italy should attempt little by little to unhitch her wagon from that of Germany to make the crash less painful. I have always been a supporter of a policy of understanding with Great Britain, and within the limits of my power have always sought to oppose the thrust in the direction of Germany . . . On the home front, in face of the apathy of the great mass of the people, a general lack of confidence in their leaders, there is a resentment of many of the old Fascist elements . . . At any moment, in the face of military disaster, a political movement could take shape with a social basis which the Communists would at once exploit. Only the King at the right moment could restore things to their place . . ."

Tragically for the Italian people, their war would continue for many more months.

Practically every night during the period covered by this account Wellingtons from Malta and Libya carried out raids against targets in Sicily and on the Italian mainland, including Naples and even Rome. Other bombers, including USAAF Liberators, B-26s and B-17s operating from North African bases, undertook daily daylight raids against similar targets, escorted by armadas of P-38s and P-40s – and even American Spitfires. By May 1943, following the end of the Tunisian Campaign, the key Italian island of Pantelleria was subjected to intense bombing. There was brief stiff resistance by the Luftwaffe and Regia Aeronautica before it surrendered. Axis shipping continued to be hounded by Allied fighter-bombers and bombers, aided by Ultra reports of shipping movements. From Malta, anti-shipping Beaufighters helped to keep the Mediterranean open for Allied convoys. Even at night the Luftwaffe was not free to roam the skies around Malta, AI-equipped Beaufighters and newly arrived Mosquito night fighters taking a steady toll of those that dared. The Mosquitos also began intruder operations over Sicily, causing havoc among nocturnal air traffic and road transport, while enemy movement was closely monitored by Malta's photo-reconnaissance Baltimores and Spitfires, the latter in particular photographing Sicily's airfields, in company with the USAAF's F-5 Lightnings (the PR version of the P-38), and thereby keeping a constant eye on the arrival of reinforcements.

It was the efforts of all these diversified units which helped to achieve the Allied successes of 1943 in the Mediterranean – but this is the story of Malta's Spitfires, which also started taking the war to the enemy in 1943. As the year progressed, larger and larger fighter sweeps were flown over southern Sicily, combined with audacious Spitbomber attacks on airfields and other important military targets. By the beginning of 1943 the whole pattern of the war had changed for Malta. Whereas in mid-1942 it had been impossible to safely disperse one squadron of Spitfires on the island, six months later the five resident squadrons could be securely dispersed, albeit in fortified anti-blast aircraft pens constructed by soldiers, airmen and civilians; while, within a year, no fewer than 25 Spitfire squadrons would be assembled on the island and neighbouring Gozo in preparation for the invasion of Sicily. By mid-1943, Spitbomber attacks were practically the order of the day, while RAF fighters dominated the air by sheer numbers alone. Air supremacy had yet to be achieved, however, for whenever the Luftwaffe rose to the challenge, Malta's Spitfires invariably came off second best. The Luftwaffe's mighty Bf109G easily out-performed the Spitfire V and it would not be until the more powerful Spitfire IX was in widespread use with Malta's squadrons that parity was restored and eventually, by early July 1943, Malta's Spitfires were able to make a magnificent contribution to the invasion of Sicily.

* * *

At the beginning of 1943 the state of play was:

MALTA: RAF Spitfire Squadrons, 1 January 1943:

126 Squadron RAF Luqa	Sqn Ldr J.R. Urwin Mann DFC
185 Squadron RAF Hal Far	Sqn Ldr B.E.G. White
229 Squadron RAF Krendi	Sqn Ldr T. Smart DFC
249 Squadron RAF Krendi	Sqn Ldr E.N. Woods DFC
1435 Squadron RAF Luqa	Sqn Ldr W.A. Smith DFC

In addition, 69 Squadron operated a flight of PR Spitfire IVs under the command of Sqn Ldr R.C. Mackay DFC.

The Station Commanders were in the main until recent times operational fighter pilots, two of whom took every opportunity to fly operational sorties with their squadrons, as will be noted:

Grp Capt W.K. Le May OBE	OC RAF Luqa (Grp Capt W.H. Merton OBE from 23 January)
Wg Cdr J.M. Thompson DFC	Wing Commander Flying
Grp Capt W.A.J. Satchell DSO	OC RAF Takali (Grp Capt G.Y. Tyrrell MC from 8 February)
Wg Cdr S.B. Grant DFC	Wing Commander Flying
Wg Cdr P.P. Hanks DSO DFC	OC RAF Hal Far
Wg Cdr M.M. Stephens DSO DFC	Wing Commander Flying
Wg Cdr F.H. Tyson OC	RAF Krendi
Wg Cdr A.V.R. Johnstone DFC	Wing Commander Flying

THE REGIA AERONAUTICA
AERONAUTICA della SICILIA (Sicily-based)

53°Stormo CT, Sciacca	Col Ciro Aiello
153°Gruppo	Magg Andrea Favini
372^Squadriglia MC202	Cap Bruno Zavadlal

373^Squadriglia MC202	Cap Cesare Marchesi
374^Squadriglia MC202	Cap Natale Veronesi
3°Gruppo Aut CT, Chinisia	Magg Aldo Alessandrini
153^Squadriglia MC200	
154^Squadriglia MC200	Cap Giuseppe Tovazzi
155^Squadriglia MC200	
157°Gruppo Aut CT, Castelvetrano	Magg Elio Fiacchino
357^Squadriglia MC200	
379^Squadriglia MC200	
384^Squadriglia MC200	

In addition, 377^Squadriglia Aut CT was based at Palermo with CR42s under Cap Luciano Marcolin, and 76^Squadriglia (detached from 7°Gruppo, 54°Stormo CT) under Cap Pietro Calistri at Castelvetrano for naval escort duties, also with CR42s, while 164^Squadriglia under Cap Adriano Porcu (detached from 161°Gruppo CT) was at Reggio di Calabria, on the toe of mainland Italy, with MC200s, MC202s and D.520s for the protection of the Messina Strait and Italian naval forces. The Dewoitwine D.520s were former Vichy French aircraft taken over by the Regia Aeronautica to help offset its serious shortage of fighter aircraft.

AERONAUTICA della SICILIA (Pantelleria-based)

1°Stormo CT	Col Alfredo Reglieri
6°Gruppo	Magg Luigi Di Bernardo
79^Squadriglia MC202	Cap Edoardo Baldini
81^Squadriglia MC202	Cap Guido Beggiato
88^Squadriglia MC202	Ten Giorgio Falchi
17°Gruppo	Magg Pericle Baruffi
71^Squadriglia MC202	Cap Aldo Felici
72^Squadriglia MC202	Cap Pio Tomaselli
80^Squadriglia MC202	Cap Clizio Nioi
53°Stormo CT	
151°Gruppo	TenCol Antonio Giachino
366^Squadriglia G50bis	Ten Piero Veneziani
367^Squadriglia G50bis	Cap Giuseppe Costantini
368^Squadriglia G50bis	Cap Mario Ferrero

Aeronautica della Sicilia's fighter strength, as at 1 January 1943, totalled 177 MC202s, 64 MC200s, 35 G50bis and 17 CR42s, of which less than half were serviceable at this date. There were also 38 bombers (18 SM84s, 15 Z1007s and five BR20Ms) based at Palermo, Castelvetrano and Sciacca:-

10°Stormo BT under the overall command of Col Ettore Pasquinelli, which comprised 30°Gruppo Aut BT (Magg Giuseppe Noziglia), 32°Gruppo Aut BT (Magg Carlo Alberto Capitani), and 33°Gruppo Aut BT (TenCol Ercole Savi), all equipped with the Z1007bis; and 25°Gruppo Aut BT (TenCol Giorgio Agnati) with

SM84s. In addition, 202^Squadriglia BT was equipped with BR20M night bombers (Ten Giorgio Commini), and 173^Squadriglia RST (Cap Edoardo Agnello) with CR25s and Ca314s. ASR and local maritime reconnaissance was the duty of 170^, 186^ and 189^Squadriglie based at Augusta (83°Gruppo RM commanded by Magg Ugo Maiorani), and 144^ and 197^ Squadriglie of 85°Gruppo RM (Magg Francesco Romano) at Marsala, the seaplane squadriglie equipped with a mixture of Z501s, Z506Bs and Fiat RS14s. The Z1007bis-equipped units (10°Stormo BT plus 33°Gruppo Aut BT, together with the attached 173^Squadriglia RST) returned to mainland Italy on 18 January in preparation for conversion to the Ju88.

THE LUFTWAFFE

The Luftwaffe had maintained a presence on Sicily since early 1941, when Fliegerkorps X established a force of Bf109s, Bf110s, Ju88s, He111s and Ju87s which almost overwhelmed the defenders of Malta, but the island held on. By the summer of that year nearly all the German units had withdrawn to participate in the Russian campaign, returning in December to again inflict much damage to the island's Hurricanes, the onslaught continuing until the summer of 1942. There was one final blitz in October 1942 before the Germans admitted defeat. Malta could not be bombed into submission. III/JG53 had participated in the assault during the first half of 1942 before moving to North Africa, its position taken by II Gruppe. III/JG53 returned to Sicily in November 1942, having added 113 victories to the 61 it had claimed between January and May 1942 over Malta.

FLIEGERKORPS II (Süd) – Sicily-based:

3/JG53	Bf109G	Trapani	Hptm Wolfgang Tonne
III/JG53			Maj Franz Götz
7/JG53	Bf109G	Trapani – moved to Catania mid-January	Hptm Winfried Pufahl
8/JG53	Bf109G	Trapani – moved to San Pietro mid-January	Oblt Karl Leonhard
9/JG53	Bf109G	San Pietro	Oblt Hans Röhrig
III/ZG26	Bf110C	Trapani	Hptm Georg Christl
II/NJG1	Ju88C	Comiso	Hptm Dr Horst Patuschka

II Fliegerkorps' fighter/fighter-bomber establishment at this stage was 60 Bf109Gs and 77 Bf110Cs, plus about 14 Ju88C night fighters. The bomber force totalled about 260 mainly Ju88s and was based at Comiso, Gerbini and Catania, and included I/KG26 (equipped with He111s), III/KG26, III/KG30, II/KG76, II/KG77 and elements of KG60, while 2(F)/122 provided reconnaissance capability with its Ju88Ds based at Trapani. In addition, there were also eight Gruppen of Luftwaffe transport aircraft employed mainly on the Sicily-Tunisia airbridge operating out of Trapani: KGzbV1, 2, 102, 105, 300, 400, 600 and 800 with about 500 Ju52/3ms, Ju90s, FW200s and Me323s operating in conjunction with Italian transport squadrons of the SAS (Servizio Aerei Speciali): 18°, 44°, and 48° Stormi TM with 140 SM75s, SM81s, SM82s, and Fiat G.12s.

CHAPTER I

SPITBOMBERS: MALTA ON THE OFFENSIVE

January to March 1943

"Whether the tactical value derived from these [Spitbomber] raids was great, is difficult to say, but it was most certainly of great morale value to the squadrons and indeed the entire Maltese population to feel that the RAF were once again on the offensive." [1]
Wg Cdr Sandy Johnstone DFC, Krendi Wing Leader January-March 1943

On the first day of 1943, Flg Off Pat O'Brien of 185 Squadron wrote in his diary:

"New Years Day. Well, I think I can say that – all being well – I should be able to see dear old Glasgow again this month, and the sooner the better. I'm brassed off with Malta."

He, like many other fighter pilots currently on the island, had experienced the fierce October battles – and had survived. He, like many others, wanted to go home. Next day he wrote:

"Did a sweep to Lampedusa and Linosa but saw nothing. Went in at sea level. Its a long stretch of water and it wouldn't be a nice place for engine trouble to develop. Had a chat with the CO about going back to Britain. Cheesed off with this bloody place."

The opening two days of 1943 proved relatively peaceful for Malta's Spitfire pilots. Routine standing patrols, combined with an unsuccessful search by a section from 126 Squadron for the crew of a missing Wellington, resulted in a Spitfire of 229 Squadron sustaining repairable damage when it crashed on landing following a patrol. The pilot was unhurt. The tempo changed somewhat the following morning (3 January) when, at 0730, a single He111 – probably from I/KG26 – approached Malta from the south-west at low altitude, but did not cross the coast. Its track had however been detected by radar and patrolling Spitfires from 126 and 185 Squadrons were warned of its presence, the four aircraft from the former unit sighting the intruder some ten miles off the coast, flying at 3,500 feet. The Heinkel was pursued but only Sgt L.G. Barnes RCAF (EP205/MK-Y) was able to get into firing position before the Spitfires were forced to return to Malta due to running low on fuel. When last seen the bomber was streaming smoke and flying very low over the sea. 185 Squadron's Flt Lt R.E. Atkinson was scrambled to offer assistance but was recalled when it was believed the bomber had crashed into the sea north of Gozo; it was credited to Sgt Barnes as probably destroyed. Eight more Spitfires from 185 Squadron were scrambled at intervals between 0830 and 0850 in readiness to counter further intrusions but no raids materialised.

---

[1] see *Where No Angels Dwell* by Air Vice-Marshal Sandy Johnstone.

This was a period of reorganisation for the Luftwaffe and Regia Aeronautica on Sicily, following the reversal of fortunes for the Axis forces in North Africa, although the Bf109G-equipped III/JG53 – which had returned to Sicily from that theatre in late November – was far from idle since its main task at this time was to provide escort for large numbers of heavily-laden transports – Ju52/3ms, Ju90s, FW200s and giant six-engined Me323s of the TransportGruppen, plus SM75s, SM81s, SM82s and Fiat G.12s of the SAS, usually 50 to 60 aircraft at a time – conveying urgently needed supplies and fuel from Trapani to Tunis or Bizerte for the hard-pressed Afrika Korps which had been pushed back to the Tripoli area of Libya, a duty shared with the Bf110s of III/ZG26 which were more suited for the job. On arrival in Tunisia the Messerschmitts would be refuelled before they escorted the transports back to Sicily. They also occasionally escorted reconnaissance aircraft to Malta but seldom flew offensive sorties in the vicinity of the island, the offensive role in the area having been taken over by Malta's Spitfires.

Three Spitfires of 126 Squadron took off just after midday on 4 January as escort to four Beaufighters of 227 Squadron which were tasked to carry out an anti-shipping sweep in the area Pantelleria-Sousse-Kuriat-Linosa. No shipping was seen but at 1440 six Ju88s of I/KG76 were sighted east of Sousse flying at between 200 and 300 feet above the sea, the Beaufighters giving chase at wave-top height while the Spitfires provided cover. Two of the Ju88s were claimed damaged by the Beaufighters. Another was attacked and damaged by one of the Spitfires flown by Plt Off W.J. Hibbert RCAF, although his aircraft (BR591/MK-D) was hit by return fire as were two of the Beaufighters. All three damaged aircraft made it back to Malta safely, as did the Ju88s back to their base, one bomber pilot having been wounded in the action. During the day four Spitbombers of 249 Squadron led by Sqn Ldr Woods targeted the landing ground on the island of Lampedusa, the escort led by Krendi's new Wing Leader, Wg Cdr Sandy Johnstone, and included one Spitfire flown by Wg Cdr Tyson, the new Station Commander (who occasionally flew night sorties over Sicily in a Hurricane, dropping urgently needed supplies to agents). No aircraft were seen on the landing ground where the bombs were seen to explode without causing any tangible damage. Next day (5 January), 249 Squadron despatched four Spitbombers to attack Comiso airfield, Wg Cdr Grant leading the escort. One bomb was observed to achieve a direct hit on a building and another exploded among buildings on the southern edge of the aerodrome. Two more fell near the runway and two others burst in front of a Ju88 which was circling, apparently preparing to land. A Bf109G was sighted and attacked halfway between the aerodrome and the coast but without effect while, on returning to Krendi, Flt Sgt N. Bage crash-landed EP140/T-M although the aircraft was not badly damaged.

On the morning of 6 January, 16 Spitfires drawn equally from 229 and 249 Squadrons patrolled the Cape Scalambri-Comiso area at between 17,000 and 20,000 feet, hoping to draw up the fighters, but the only enemy aircraft observed were two which orbited several thousand feet above, and these made no attempt to interfere. A second sweep covering the Gela and Comiso area carried out by eight of 229 Squadron during the early afternoon met with similar disappointment, but it was a different story when, at 1405, six Spitfires of 249 Squadron departed for a sweep over southern Sicily, where eight enemy fighters identified as three Bf109Gs and five MC202s attacked the formation from astern, hitting two of the Spitfires. Flg Off J.A.N. Dawkins' aircraft (AB465/T-R) was seen to go down emitting white smoke but apparently under control. Although his colleagues believed that he would survive a force-landing, Dawkins was in fact killed. Of the incident, newly arrived

Plt Off I.F. Kennedy RCAF – known as 'Hap' to his friends – wrote:

> "There were some Messerschmitt pilots at Comiso who were masters of the hit and run tactic. They would attack from high above, usually directly out of the sun, at high speed, one very quick pass only, then disappear, impossible to catch. If the victim was lucky, he could bale out; if not, there wasn't a word. So it was with Jack Dawkins. The yellow-nosed ME109 flashed between us, and black crosses on pale blue wings disappeared far below. Perhaps one second had elapsed. Not a word from Jack, his aircraft leaving a long trail of smoke." [2]

Eight Spitfires of 185 Squadron led by Wg Cdr Prosser Hanks, Hal Far Station Commander, set off at 1545, four of these tasked to bomb Lampedusa aerodrome, over which they arrived at 1630. One bomb was seen to burst in the south-east corner in front of an aircraft which appeared to be about to take off. Another was seen to explode among buildings on the north-east corner. Flak was intense but none of the Spitfires was hit. Meanwhile, the other section led by Sqn Ldr Blair White (EP473/GL-M) attacked two E-boats sighted ten miles north of Lampedusa above which were two MC202s flying at 2,000 feet. Flt Sgt G.D. Billing RCAF (EP520) recalled:

> "In the Linosa area we attacked two E-boats. They were escorted by Macchi 202s. I attacked two and saw strikes but broke off to return to Malta as low on petrol."

While Flg Off O'Brien noted:

> "B Flight did a sweep in the Lampedusa area and shot up a couple of E-boats. They were attacked by two Macchi 202s and Withy shot one up. Thinks he destroyed it – claimed a probable."

The Macchi attacked by Flg Off H.F. Withy (EP791) was last seen losing height rapidly, but was not observed to crash. 153°Gruppo reported that one of its Macchis flown by Ten Mario Prosperpio of 374^Squadriglia crashed between Giarre and Riposto during an escort mission, but whether this was the aircraft attacked by Withy is unclear. Early next morning (7 January), sections from 185 and 229 Squadrons again carried out sweeps in the Lampedusa-Linosa-Pantelleria area. No enemy aircraft were sighted in the air but on Lampedusa aerodrome four large twin-engined and one possible tri-motor aircraft were seen, plus a number of small vessels in the harbour. These were not attacked but on returning to Malta a reconnaissance Spitfire was despatched to take photographs, which subsequently revealed six SM81s and four unidentified fighters on the landing ground, and two ASR-type launches in the harbour. Four bomb-carrying Spitfires of 185 Squadron led by Wg Cdr Stephens (BR109/GL-W) were despatched to attack these aircraft, five others including the CO, Sqn Ldr White, acting as top cover. One of the Spitbombers was flown by Flg Off O'Brien:

> "Did a sweep on Lampedusa this afternoon. I was Red 3 to Wg Cdr Stephens and we were the bombers. The weather over the target was very poor and we

---

2 see *Black Crosses off my Wingtip* by Sqn Ldr I.F. Kennedy.

dive bombed through the cloud. I saw some bombs fall in the sea as I went down. There was quite a bit of flak but no one was hit. We got split up and came home independently. Wingco saw some fires burning. Quite a bit of fun."

A little earlier in the day Sqn Ldr Woods had led five Spitbombers of 249 Squadron to attack a sulphur-producing factory at Licata, where a number of large explosions were seen and one Spitfire (BR463) suffered flak damage, causing it to hit a bowser on landing back at Krendi. Although an undercarriage leg collapsed, the pilot was unhurt. 249 Squadron now received a new CO, Sqn Ldr M.G. MacLeod RCAF arriving from 229 Squadron to take over from Sqn Ldr Woods who was posted to Air HQ. At the same time Plt Off W.J. Cleverly was promoted to command A Flight vice tour-expired Flt Lt Robin Seed, who was awarded the DFC. Flt Lt John Lynch, an American from California, had taken command of B Flight from Flt Lt F.E. Fowler who had become sick.

Lampedusa aerodrome was again the target for 185 Squadron on the morning of 8 January, three Spitbombers (a fourth having returned early with oil pressure problems) attacking at 1000. Two bombs were observed to explode in the south-west corner and one in the centre of the aerodrome. Considerable light and heavy accurate flak was experienced although none of the Spitfires was hit. During the day six of 126 Squadron and eight of 229 Squadron also carried out sweeps in the Lampedusa area but failed to locate any enemy aircraft. During the morning of 9 January several enemy aircraft were detected approaching Malta but none crossed the coast. Patrolling Spitfires failed to make any sightings. Later in the day two Spitfires of 126 Squadron were despatched to search for an overdue PR Spitfire, landing just three minutes after the errant aircraft had touched down.

Four Spitfires of 229 Squadron were scrambled at 0910 on 10 January to investigate a twin-engined aircraft reported ten miles south of Malta, only to find that it was a 69 Squadron Baltimore flying at 2,000 feet. An hour later four Bf109Gs crossed the coast at about 23,000 feet, at a time when the only Spitfire airborne was an aircraft of 1435 Squadron on an air test. Shortly thereafter, eight Spitfires of 185 Squadron set out to attack Gela, as noted by Flg Off O'Brien:

"Went on a sweep. Red Section led by Keith [Capt Kuhlman SAAF, A Flight commander] were bombers. I was Red 3. Len [Flg Off Cheek] led the escort. Weather was pretty good. We slightly overshot our target, Gela, and the bombing was very poor. I saw two lots of bombs fall just off the aerodrome. Our approach messed things up and we couldn't get a decent dive on it. A couple of little jobs [Bf109s] were up and followed us back. We didn't see them but one of them jumped Len's section and Matt Reid [Plt Off M.J. Reid RCAF] got shot up although he was able to land OK [his aircraft EP791 was hit by four cannon shells in addition to machine-gun fire]. There was a certain amount of finger trouble − but most of all a hell of a lot of R/T interference which messed things up completely. Len's R/T was u/s. [Sgt] Thorogood [EP187] got a squirt at a 109 and claims a damaged. This all happened only five-ten miles north of Malta."

185 Squadron was also active during the afternoon, eight aircraft visiting Lampedusa once again. The aerodrome was partly obscured by cloud and results of the bombing were unobserved. Although greeted by considerable amounts of flak, none of the Spitfires were hit. On the return flight to Malta two unidentified aircraft were observed following at a distance but no interception occurred. Meanwhile,

four Spitfires of 1435 Squadron were despatched to search for a missing 69 Squadron Baltimore, overdue from a sortie to the Messina Straits area. Next day (11 January) a Spitfire of 126 Squadron was ordered to continue the search, the pilot locating wreckage including what was thought to be an aircraft hatch. But of the crew there was no sight. 69 Squadron suffered a further loss when one of its PR Spitfire IVs, BS500 flown by Plt Off J.A. Frazer RAAF, failed to return from a morning sortie to the Corfu-Valona area. Two Spitfires of 229 Squadron were sent to search for the missing pilot, as was an ASR Flight Swordfish and an HSL, but nothing was found. Similar lack of success was the outcome of a continued search by a PR Beaufighter. During the day Spitfires patrolled over an incoming convoy. At 1550, a Ju88 was sighted north-west of the convoy and pursued by four of 1435 Squadron for 40 miles before it escaped in cloud. A patrol from 229 Squadron was later vectored onto another snooper south-east of the convoy although they were unable to sight it. The convoy was not attacked.

Poor weather hampered operations over the next two days, although Spitbomber raids against Lampedusa aerodrome by 185 Squadron, and the harbour at Sciacca by 249 Squadron, were undertaken on 12 January, with mainly unobserved or unimpressive results. Flg Off O'Brien participated in the attack on Lampedusa:

> "Did a sweep on Lampedusa again. I led the bombers and Keith [Capt Kuhlman] was escort. Weather around Malta was pretty duff but OK around target. I made my attack out of the sun, diving from 17,000 feet down to about 10,000 feet. Accidentally released my bombs too soon and saw them splash in the sea, followed by another two. Took violent evasive action as quite a lot of flak was coming up. My section didn't follow me out as they were all at different heights. Saw two below and managed to get one of them to join up with me. Flew home pretty low and hit Malta OK. Six enemy little jobs [fighters] were up but did not contact them."

Next day O'Brien recorded in his diary:

> "Dozens of parcels for ex-pilots were sorted out today and we split them up between the present pilots. We each got about 300 cigarettes and some sweets. Unfortunately, most of the parcels were months old and the sweets and cakes were very musty and most of them not fit for eating. Learned that Flt Lt Bob Seed of 249 was stood down today and expects to leave tonight. Lucky type. He came out with Keith and me. We are about the only ones left now of the August mob."

Flg Off O'Brien finally received the news he was waiting for, he and Capt Kuhlman being stood down pending a flight back to the UK. Flg Off H.A. Knight, a South African in the RAF, was promoted to command A Flight vice fellow South African Keith Kuhlman.

185 Squadron was back over Lampedusa on the morning of 14 January, five Spitbombers led by Sqn Ldr White (BR109/GL-W) dive-bombing from 9,000 feet, the majority of the bombs falling just north of the west-end of the runway although two were seen to explode near two large transport aircraft, believed to have been Ju52s, parked in the north-east corner of the aerodrome. The attack was repeated by 185 Squadron at 1600, on this occasion the sections led by Wg Cdr Hanks and Sqn Ldr White (EP701/GL-B). Two aircraft dive-bombed from north to south while three others bombed in a V formation from north to east. The pilots reported

accurate and heavy flak although none was hit. Malta was alerted during the morning when several Bf109Gs crossed the coast at 20,000 feet. The guns opened up and patrolling Spitfires were warned of their presence. One Spitfire of 1435 Squadron, flying some way behind the others of its section, was attacked by two Messerschmitts but Flg Off J.G. Torney (EP619/V-I) was able to turn and fire a burst at one as it swept by. At about the same time the 126 Squadron section sighted two Messerschmitts ten miles west of Malta flying northwards but they were too far away to intercept.

Lampedusa was again visited by 185 Squadron on 15 January, but none of the Spitfires were carrying bombs on this occasion. As they approached the island they were greeted by intense and fairly accurate AA fire. Coastal defence guns also opened up and their heavy shells were seen bursting in the water. The Spitbombers were back next day (16 January), heavy AA fire deterring accurate bombing. Ten Spitbombers (six/249, four/229) bombed factories north-east of Pachino in the morning, when at least two direct hits were claimed on one building and three hits on another. Fires broke out and thick, black smoke was observed to gush forth from one factory chimney. Ten of the escort – from the same two units – joined in the attack and strafed buildings with their cannons and machine-guns. Tents and a W/T station south of Pachino was also strafed. Another of the Spitfires attacked two aircraft identified as Bf109s on Pachino airfield and saw pieces fly off, but it was believed these were possibly dummies. Wg Cdr Johnstone led the escort:

> "One after the other the bombs rained down on the target area, dropping at regular intervals and exploding with frightening velocity. At least three made direct hits on the factory, sending tons of masonry hurtling through the air to join the twisted metal of the gutted machinery. As the last bomber began its dive I swooped down to ground level with my eleven [*sic*] escorting companions and raced in on the scene of destruction, raking the smoke and flames with cannon and machine-gun fire. I swept towards the wreckage of the factory and saw the large double doors gaping invitingly from a portion of the building still left standing. Quickly, I lined up with the black cavern and fired rapid burst through the opening. As I pulled back on the stick to lift the Spitfire above the smoke, there were clear indications that my fire power had struck home. There were signs of a large explosion and judging from the clouds of steam, followed by dense black smoke which billowed from the tall chimney and burst from several of the factory windows, I was certain that I had hit a massive boiler. Out of the corner of my eye I saw a small donkey, hitched to a tiny cart, take to its heels and make off at a furious pace down the road to Pachino, leaving nothing behind it but swirling clouds of dust. The unfortunate animal must have been struck on the behind by a stray bullet as it stood quietly beside the building." [3]

Owing to the excessive speed which the Spitbombers had achieved during this dive-bombing attack, several of the pilots experienced the indignity of their seats collapsing under the strain of pulling violently out of the dive, as recalled by Sgt Don Nicholson of 249 Squadron:

> "The collapsed seat incident was really the result of several things. Firstly, the Spitfire was not designed to be a dive-bomber, although I eventually

---

[3] see *Where No Angels Dwell*.

worked out a most efficient method of using it as such. Secondly, we started our dive from much too great a height, causing our speed of dive to build up at an alarming rate, and because of my concentration of the target area, the high speed went virtually unnoticed resulting in a failure to trim the aircraft properly. The sudden release of the bombs over the target caused the aircraft to flip out of the dive with tremendous G force causing me to black out – and the bolts holding the seat to sheer. As a result I was forced to stand on the rudder pedals in order to see ahead. This was not too bad flying more or less straight and level but caused a few problems coming in to land. However, all was well and I landed safely."

A Sunderland flying boat of 230 Squadron piloted by Flt Lt A.M. Todd set out from Kalafrana during the early afternoon of 17 January, to search for a missing Beaufighter of 227 Squadron. Escort was provided by eight Spitfires, four each from 126 and 229 Squadrons although one of the former had to return early owing to engine trouble. The Spitfires carried out searches at sea level, firstly to the east of Cape Bon, then on to Keliba before entering the Gulf of Hammamet, where two dinghies were eventually sighted by a pilot of 126 Squadron. The Sunderland was contacted, alighted nearby and picked up both airmen. At this stage two Bf109Gs appeared but were chased away by the escort. By now several of the Spitfires were getting desperately low on fuel, Sgt Tony Williams (EP460/X-Z) radioing to say he was baling out. He was somewhat luckily plucked from the sea by the Sunderland, as Flt Lt Archie Todd's subsequent report revealed:

"As we were preparing to take off [having picked up the Beaufighter crew] a Spitfire was seen to dive into the sea about half a mile on the starboard bow, and the pilot was sighted in his parachute the same distance ahead. We taxied over in that direction and for a short time after we were guided by his parachute billowing on top of the water. This, however, soon sank, and when we arrived we could not see anything of the pilot. It was beginning to get dark and the swell made it difficult to spot the man in the water. We taxied round for some minutes, and had the pilot not raised his arm when he was on top of a swell, we would have failed to locate him even though at the time he was less than 30 yards away. I again got down wind and approached slowly, finally cutting all motors and allowing the aircraft to drift up to him. We had considerable trouble in getting rid of his parachute and found him most difficult to get aboard owing to the weight of his wet clothing and the large amount of equipment in his Mae West."

Meanwhile, the 229 Squadron section leader Flt Lt A.R. Chaplin (BR562/X-R) informed his section that he was heading for the North African coast owing to his fuel situation, ordering his companions to return to Malta. South African-born Arthur Chaplin[4] was not seen again and was presumed to have been lost when his aircraft ditched some miles short of the coast. As this drama was being enacted out to sea, four Spitbombers (three/126, one/1435) paid a visit to Lampedusa. While three released their bombs from between 14,000 feet and 16,000 feet, Sqn Ldr Urwin Mann (EP330/MK-J) of 126 Squadron released from 10,000 feet and then continued his dive, strafing buildings and aircraft seen on the airfield.

---

[4] On 27 December 1942, Flt Lt Chaplin had shot down a Bf109G of III/JG53 which had been on a weather reconnaissance over the Malta area. Uffz Ludwig Laue of 7 Staffel, who was killed, was the Gruppe's first battle casualty since its return to Sicily from North Africa.

Lampedusa was again the target for Spitbombers of 185 Squadron on the morning of 18 January, five aircraft plus three from 126 Squadron dive-bombing the aerodrome at 1140. Bombs were seen to explode at either end of the runway, two more fell across the centre and two others in the western perimeter. Targets in Sicily were the order of the afternoon, eight Spitbombers (five/249, three/229) escorted by two dozen fighters from the same units attacking the power station at Porto Empedocle. Two direct hits on the power station were observed, four more on adjacent buildings. Flt Lt Seed led the 249 Squadron section, his last sortie from Malta. On the return flight two of the escort strafed a small vessel of about 2-3,000 tons outside the harbour, causing debris to fly off its deck. Meanwhile, three Spitbombers from 185 Squadron were over Sicily seeking targets of opportunity, as noted by the Squadron diarist:

> "In the afternoon a new dimension was started for us by Wg Cdr Hanks [EP701/GL-B] who, with Sqn Ldr White [BR109/GL-W] and Flt Lt Atkinson [BR534], paid a '0' feet visit to Sicily with Spitbombers, and pranged a passenger train good and proper, afterwards shooting up the engine."

The train was located leaving Pozzallo station and was attacked in line astern by all three. Two bombs straddled the locomotive, two straddled the tender and two exploded just ahead of the train, which was then strafed by all three. The pilots reported that it was last seen enveloped in steam and smoke and was undoubtedly destroyed.

Offensive sweeps were carried to the west of Malta – between Sicily, Tripoli and the Tunisian coast – during the day (19 January) a total of 23 Spitfires sorties being flown, mainly by 249 Squadron, but no enemy shipping or aircraft were sighted. Lampedusa received its daily visit, three Spitbombers of 126 Squadron bombing and strafing the dispersal area and adjacent buildings, while at dusk two of 229 Squadron carried out an unsuccessful search in conjunction with an ASR Swordfish and an HSL from Malta for the crew of a missing US Liberator. That evening Malta's Spitfires entered a new phase of the intruder war, single aircraft from 126 and 1435 Squadrons being despatched at hourly intervals to search for targets of opportunity by moonlight. The first two aircraft returned with their bomb loads intact including AR560/JMT flown by Wg Cdr Thompson, the pilots having been unable to find suitable targets, but one from 1435 – BR161/V-E flown by Flt Lt W.C. Walton – headed for Comiso at 2000 and successfully released its two bombs over the aerodrome where explosions were seen on or near buildings. An hour later Flt Lt J.H. Long RCAF (EP573/MK-I) of 126 Squadron observed a double-engined train travelling between Chiaramonte, Palazzola and Vizzini. Following a strafing attack, both engines were seen to be enveloped in steam and smoke. Earlier in the day 185 Squadron lost one of its aircraft (EP701/GL-B) when Sub Lt E.F. Pratt RNZNVR of the RNAS, recent recipient of the DSC for his work flying Albacores and Hurricanes on ASR and intruder sorties from Malta, crashed into the sea during a practice flight. It was assumed that he had been dazzled by the sun while flying at low level.

185 Squadron now turned its attention to Sicily, six Spitbombers led by Wg Cdr Stephens and Sqn Ldr White (BR109/GL-W) attacking a road bridge between Rosolini and Noto just after 0700 on 20 January. Two bombs were seen to burst at the foot of the bridge and two on the actual road. A railway engine in the sidings at Noto was strafed and believed seriously damaged, while four signal boxes, a warehouse and engine shed were also attacked. A goods train sighted on the line

between Pozzallo and Ispica was strafed and was last seen with steam gushing out of the engine and one truck on fire. As the last two aircraft departed the target area they were followed by two MC202s for about 20 miles which opened fire from long range. The Spitfires turned and returned fire, also at long range, but without obvious results. During the afternoon 16 Spitfires from 1435 Squadron escorted Beaufighters on a shipping search between Lampedusa, Mahdia and Kerkennah, sighting a single aircraft believed to have been a Ju88 but it made off before it could be engaged. 185 Squadron was again active at dusk, six Spitbombers departing at half-hourly intervals to attack the railway junction between Pozzallo and Cape Passero. Various targets of opportunity at Noto were also strafed including warehouses, railway sidings, railway trucks and engines. Flt Lt Hal Knight alone bagged two trains with cannon and machine-gun fire. Two lorries seen with their lights on were given a burst of machine-gun fire as the Spitfires sped overhead on their way home. Sqn Ldr White (BR109/GL-W) reported bombing Noto junction and station but, shortly after this sortie, he went down with a severe bout of influenza, Sqn Ldr J.D. Ashton DFC arriving from Air HQ to take temporary command of the Squadron.

At 0715 next morning (21 January) two Spitfires flown by Flt Lt A.R. Stewart (EP717/V-D) and Plt Off D.J. Hawkins (EP721/V-X) of 1435 Squadron strafed two schooners sighted two miles west of Cape Rossello. Strikes were seen on each vessel but the pilots were unable to observe results as they had to dodge the masts as they pulled up from their wave-top level attack. After lunch the Spitbombers set off from their bases, four from 229 and five from 249 Squadrons with appropriate escort, attacking a barracks at Licata, while four others from 229 and four from 126 Squadron bombed Gela. Two Bf109Gs were sighted at 15,000 feet 20 miles north-west of Gozo by returning aircraft but no contact was made. Wg Cdr Thompson (AR560/JMT), who led the bombers, noted: "Bombs in north-west of aerodrome – played with two 109s north of Gozo." With the onset of darkness, six Spitbombers (three each from 126 and 1435 Squadrons) set out on intruder sorties at half-hourly intervals. One pilot from 1435 Squadron spotted an enemy aircraft showing its lights near Vizzini and chased this towards Catania, where it was lost in the mountains. Others strafed M/T, while bombs were dropped on Gela aerodrome and railway stations near Flordia and Ragusa. All returned safely, the last landing at 2110. Among aircraft photographed by PR Spitfire IVs during the day were two giant BV222 flying boats moored at Taranto, where 16 Z506Bs and 11 Z501s were also observed.

Licata railway station and sidings was the target for 185 Squadron on the morning of 22 January, six Spitbombers accompanied by four fighters taking off at 0630, one of the former returning early. A train was attacked near Licata, one bomb seen to explode near the engine which blew its tender off the track. Other bombs burst among buildings in the station area but strafing was hampered by many people seen on the roads in the fields. The aerodrome at Lampedusa was again targeted, three Spitbombers from 126 Squadron sighting four large aircraft in north-west dispersal area and six to eight smaller ones on the southern edge of the airfield, but their bombs exploded without apparent effect on the eastern perimeter. Throughout the day sections of Spitfires from 185, 249 and 1435 Squadrons carried out offensive sweeps over both Lampedusa and southern Sicily without sighting any enemy aircraft. Intruder sorties continued after dark, a total of ten bomb-carrying Spitfires from 126 and 185 Squadrons including one flown by Wg Cdr Stephens venturing over south-east Sicily and attacking targets of opportunity including M/T at Noto, buildings near Licata, a railway bridge south-west of Caia

Benado and warehouses at Rosolini. Plt Off S.S. Williams of 185 Squadron visited Syracuse by mistake and there shot out a searchlight trying to pick up his aircraft. On returning to Malta at about 1900 one Spitfire pilot observed two enemy fighters off Licata, but no attack was made.

185 Squadron was busy again next morning (23 January), three Spitbombers attacking a passenger train sighted in Marzamemi station but the bombs missed and fell instead on the track. They also strafed a railway station between Scicli and Pozzallo and an armoured car near Pachino, although this did not stop. Two aircraft from 1435 Squadron were also active over southern Sicily, strafing a hutted army camp near Rosolini and two signal boxes between Noto and Rosolini, while Sqn Ldr Urwin Mann (ER647/MK-J) led another section, from 126 Squadron, to the Agrigento-Licata area and reported:

> "Flak going in and coming out. Shot up two transport, two lorries [full of troops]. Met Ju52 coming out but last of petrol and bad weather prevented from pressing home attack."

Shortly thereafter, two more Spitbombers from 249 Squadron patrolled an area ten miles west of Gela to east of Licata without finding any suitable targets. The leader then decided to bomb a railway bridge but his bombs hung-up owing to an electrical fault and he was obliged to return to Malta, escorted by his No2. The last of the intruders from 1435 Squadron returned shortly before midnight, pilots claiming damage to the pier at Gela, bombs on Comiso aerodrome and an attack on a car sighted on the Gela to Comiso road.

First off on the morning of 24 January were two Spitfires of 1435 Squadron, the pilots briefed to attack targets in the Noto area. On arriving in the specified area, a train was seen approaching the town from the south; this was duly strafed and was left shrouded in steam, apparently seriously damaged. The 1435 Squadron section was followed closely by four Spitbombers of 185 Squadron led by Flt Lt Knight (BR109/GL-W) which were to bomb the railway junction at Canicatti but, at 0740, when still over the sea, they were attacked from astern by four Bf109Gs from III/JG53, as noted by Flg Off O'Brien:

> "Our ex-Flight went on a Rhubarb this morning and were jumped by four 109s and jettisoned their bombs. In the mêlée Harold [Flt Lt Knight] damaged a 109 but three of our kites were shot up (not seriously). [Flt Sgt] Vance put up a black and is to pay a long visit to the Middle East (so I hear). I'm afraid Vance would never be any good to any squadron – he always knows best. He was even heard to say I was doing OK, the Wingco buggered things up'. What can you do with a type like that? A Yank, of course![5] Len's section had an encounter with a Ju88 but although they put one engine on fire they only claim a probable."

The Ju88, from II/KG30, was flying northwards at sea level when sighted by the rear cover section and was attacked by Canadians Flg Off E.G. Lapp (EP554) and Flt Sgt C.J. Carmody (EP471). Although damaged and with its pilot wounded, the

---

[5] Flt Sgt Fred Vance, from Washington DC, who had previously served with 121 Eagle Squadron in the UK, was indeed posted to the Middle East, where he joined 112 Squadron flying Kittyhawks and participated in the closing stages of the Tunisian Campaign; in July he returned to Malta for the invasion of Sicily and was subsequently killed in action (see Chapter VI).

Junkers was nonetheless able to reach its base and land safely. One of the Messerschmitt pilots claimed a Spitfire shot down in this action, apparently reporting that it crashed near Augusta, but none was lost. The power station at Porto Empedocle was the main target for 11 Spitbombers (seven/249, four/229) at 1415, bombs seen to explode on buildings near the station and on the nearby railway line but low cloud prevented clearer observation of results. Four of the escort from 229 Squadron joined in strafing attacks, two receiving minor flak damage. During the day Wg Cdr Thompson took up a newly arrived Spitfire VIII (EP404) on a test flight, and noted: "Clipped-wing Spit test. ME109s seen near the island, unable to engage – too high."

The clash with 185 Squadron had been the first serious engagement with Malta's Spitfires for the Messerschmitt pilots of III/JG53 since their return to Sicily from North Africa towards the end of December, as noted by Lt Jürgen Harder in a letter to his family:

> "We fly only air defence, very rarely to Malta. I am now getting 8 Staffel, which is without a Kapitän and is supposed to be brought up to scratch again. Every day I am at the airfield [San Pietro] from six in the morning until six in the evening; I direct operations, now and then fly myself when enemy aircraft are reported, and train the young pilots." [6]

With 8 Staffel operating from San Pietro, as was 9 Staffel, Hptm Pufahl's 7 Staffel moved to Catania from where it was mainly employed on convoy escort duties. During one of these escort missions in conjunction with aircraft from 8 Staffel, two Marauders were claimed shot down but one pilot was also lost in the action. The Italians were also shuffling their units at this time, all the Z1007bis-equipped units transferring to the mainland for conversion to the Ju88, their place being taken by eight squadrons equipped with SM84s: 18^ and 52^Squadriglie from 27°Gruppo BT, and 10^ and 19^ Squadriglie from 28°Gruppo BT, moving into Palermo, while 262^ and 263^Squadriglie from 107° Gruppo Aut BT, and 278^ and 281^Squadriglie from 132°Gruppo Aut AS transferred to Castelvetrano and Gerbini respectively. During this period the Italian Commando Supremo had ordered the withdrawal of the bulk of its air force from Tripolitania and, as a consequence, some 180 aircraft – of which half were fighters (81 CR42s, 12 MC200s, two MC202s), the remainder comprising Z1007bis bombers, SM79s torpedo-bombers plus a variety of reconnaissance machines – arrived at Trapani between 7-19 January for onward flight to the mainland.

The first pair of Spitfires from 126 Squadron which returned from a Rhubarb over south-eastern Sicily on the morning of 25 January had failed to find any suitable targets, but a second pair flown by Flt Lt H.S. Jackson (AB526/MK-P) and Plt Off J. Hodges (BR387/MK-A) which had departed half an hour later, at 0935, achieved greater success. At Marzamemi they encountered a passenger train, strafing the engine and two goods wagons; the boiler apparently blew up, engulfing the train in steam while the goods wagons were set on fire. A number of military lorries sighted on a road north of Licata were also attacked, one of which ran off the road. Another, full of soldiers, was strafed near Agrigento, the occupants seen to spill out onto the road. A Ju52/3m which was sighted by Jackson flying at 300 feet east of Licata was attacked full beam from 200 yards. It dropped down to deck level and took refuge under a heavy AA barrage but was not seen to crash owing

---

[6] see *Jagdgeschwader 53 Volume Two* by Jochen Prien.

to the evasive action taken by the Spitfire. During the day Sqn Ldr Ashton led a section of 185 Squadron through cloud over Lampedusa to check if any aircraft could be located on the aerodrome. None were seen and the Spitfires were greeted by intense AA fire as they sped across the island although they emerged unscathed. Two other sections from 185 Squadron sighted Messerschmitts but no engagement ensued, as noted by Flt Sgt Jerry Billing:

> "We were over Sicily at 27,000 feet, two sections of four Spitfires, when we spotted 12 ME109s who split and began to stay out of range. We tried to turn into them a few times but they avoided the hassle. We continued to ease our way towards the coast and homeward and, to our surprise, the 109s simply turned northwards towards Palermo, not wanting any part of a fight that day." [7]

The following morning (26 January) four Spitbombers from 1435 Squadron carried out an attack on the aerodrome, when bursts were seen among buildings on the eastern perimeter and near gunposts. One Spitfire suffered a hang-up although it was able to successfully jettison its bombs on the way home. Two others from 1435 Squadron visited south-eastern Sicily and attacked a train sighted travelling northwards from Noto, leaving this shrouded in smoke and steam, but later sweeps by 126 and 1435 Squadrons failed to find any suitable targets. Two more trains were damaged by a pair of Spitfires from 1435 Squadron on 27 January, one near Noto and the other stationary at Avola station. With the lack of aerial targets over south-eastern Sicily, the island's rolling stock had become the main target for the marauding Spitfires during daylight hours, while 23 Squadron's Mosquitos and the Beaufighters of 89 Squadron had taken over the role of night intruders, a task for which they were better suited.

Four Spitbombers from 126 Squadron set out for specific targets in south-east Sicily at 0540 on the morning of 28 January. Sqn Ldr Urwin Mann (EP330/MK-J) was tasked to bomb Gela station, Flg Off R.E. Green and Sgt R.B. Hendry RNZAF were to attack Licata station and a barracks just outside Gela, while Flt Lt Long (AB526/MK-P) was detailed to release his bombs over Comiso aerodrome, where about 70 Ju88s were known to be present, although widely dispersed. Having dropped his bombs, Sqn Ldr Urwin Mann sighted a twin-engined aircraft which he believed to have been a Me210 – possibly an aircraft from 2(F)/122 operating out of Sardinia – flying at 300 feet east of Gela. He climbed to make a head-on attack, reporting strikes on its starboard engine and fuselage. It was last seen at 100 feet, losing height, but was not observed to crash; of the sortie he noted:

> "Gela station bombed, blew up railway line. Engaged a ME210. Shot out starboard engine. [At] 300 feet encountered considerable light flak. Short of petrol – returned to base."

The success of the operation was marred by the failure of Flt Lt Jack Long to return from his sortie to Comiso. On his return to Malta and after his aircraft had been refuelled and rearmed, Sqn Ldr Urwin Mann carried out an hour-long search for his missing flight commander, but to no avail; the Canadian was later reported to have been shot down and killed, the victim of flak. A larger offensive sweep was carried out by a dozen Spitbombers (eight/249, four/229) during the late morning,

---

[7] see *A Knave Among Knights in their Spitfires* by Jerry Billing.

warehouses at Scicli being the target. Two aircraft from 229 Squadron suffered engine problems en route, one returning safely to Malta but Sgt Don Goodwin RCAF (EP691/X-A) was obliged to bale out before reaching the coast. Meanwhile, the remaining bombers carried out the attack, all bombs observed to burst within the target area except two which apparently fell on the railway line to the north of Scicli. Three of the escort also participated in the follow-up strafing attack. Following the return of the Spitbombers, ten aircraft of 126 Squadron were ordered off to search for the missing pilot but saw nothing, although a later search by four of 1435 Squadron succeeded in locating the pilot about 40 miles north of Malta. Flt Lt P.W.E. Heppell DFC, leading the section, was warned of the approach of Messerschmitts and ordered two of his companions to drop down to sea level while he and the other provided cover. At 1140 two Messerschmitts were sighted heading northwards, while two more veered towards the two low flying Spitfires. Having been warned of their approach, Sgts M.R. Sharun RCAF (EP444/V-T) and G.A. Cameron RCAF (EP833/V-R) turned towards their assailants and each fired short bursts, reporting seeing strikes on one of the Messerschmitts as it flashed past. Meanwhile, HSL107 was on its way from St Paul's Bay, as recalled by its Master, Plt Off K. Baker, in his subsequent report:

"When just reaching position Spitfire was sighted bearing NW from the launch, very low down on the horizon. Contact was established, the signals received on the launch being very weak and indistinguishable. Spitfire was requested to come closer but apparently message was not understood. Spitfire sent a further message, also not understood by the launch, and then ceased to orbit and left for the island, still exceptionally low. Launch closed to estimated position. Nothing seen. After search five miles, another Spitfire was sighted. It approached, waggled its wings and veered off. Launch immediately set off to follow. Unable to make VHF contact with Spitfire. After proceeding for three miles, contact was made with Spitfire. Following a message from the launch, he proceeded to dive on the object in the water.

At 1255 sighted oil patch just off port bow. At 1257 sighted pilot in water off starboard bow; distance half a mile. At 1300 picked up pilot, no dinghy. Pilot got aboard with difficulty, being in a very exhausted condition, suffering severely from cramp. Stripped off his Mae West and jacket and carried him to wardroom. The remainder of his clothes were cut away and work commenced on his body to try to get his circulation going again as rapidly as possible. Resistance of pilot at this time seemed very low. Forced a few drops of brandy down his throat on two occasions and fortunately caused him to be sick each time, which may have been a good thing as he brought up sea water. After about 45 minutes' hard rubbing and massage, pilot said he felt warmer and would like to sleep. Covered him with ample number of blankets. No further action taken until we arrived back alongside jetty at 1357 when Medical Officer took charge."

Sgt Goodwin was taken to hospital suffering from exposure. On recovery he admitted that he had almost given up hope of rescue. He had attempted to inflate his dinghy prior to releasing his parachute, which began to sink, so let go of the dinghy to release the parachute, thereby losing the dinghy which promptly sank. Although he made several dives in an attempt to recover the dinghy he was unable to do so, swallowing a lot of water in the process. He was lucky to have survived his ordeal.

A lone Spitbomber from 126 Squadron set off at 0540 on the morning of 29 January, the pilot releasing his bombs on a railway viaduct east of Noto. He was followed by eight of 185 Squadron on a sweep of the Rosolini-Pozzallo-Marzamemi-Pachino area, but no aircraft were sighted. A similar but smaller sweep by four more from the same unit in the afternoon also returned empty handed. 69 Squadron suffered the loss of another Spitfire IV (BR424) when Flt Lt R.C. Hill failed to return from a mid-morning photographic reconnaissance sortie to Taranto and Messina. It transpired that his aircraft had been intercepted by two Bf109Gs of 8/JG53 from San Pietro and shot down by Uffz Friedrich Scheer for his first victory. Flt Lt Hill, a South African, survived the crash and was picked up by Italian soldiers. It was recorded that when he was presented to the two pilots involved in shooting him down he refused to shake hands since neither was an officer.

The power station at Avola was the target for 11 Spitbombers (seven/126, four/1435) on the morning of 30 January, one bomb seen to score a direct hit while others burst nearby. A second power station situated two miles north of Avola was also attacked, as was a signal box and a railway bridge. One Spitfire did not drop its bombs owing to an electrical fault, seemingly an ever increasing problem, which caused the loss of a 1435 Squadron aircraft involved in an afternoon attack on Lampedusa. Two Spitbombers attempted to attack six SM79s sighted in the north-west corner of the aerodrome but one of Flt Lt Heppell's bombs failed to release. On announcing his predicament to Ops, he was ordered to bale out of AR561/V-J just off Kalafrana, which he did at 1720, covered by his colleague Plt Off R.L. Wood, and was promptly picked up by an alerted HSL166. He subsequently reported:

> "My Spitfire was carrying two 250-lb instantaneous bombs with rod attachments, one of which hung-up when over the target – Lampedusa. I heard a bang when making a stall turn over the target and this may have caused it. On the way back to base Red 2 told me that my starboard bomb was hung-up. I returned to base intending to drop it on Filfla. The bomb did not come off so I asked Red 3 to look at it and was informed that the tail of the bomb was off and the rear end of the bomb was hard against the mainplane, causing the rod and nose to point downwards. As landing was impossible, I decided to bale out. I climbed to 6,000 feet about one mile off Kalafrana to the south, the rescue launch being out off Delimara Point. I attempted to jettison the hood but although the starboard side cleared, the port side stuck. I pulled it off from the outside and had to hammer very hard at the hood to release it. I then released straps and R/T. Ran west to east towards the launch and when above it, trimming nose down, rolled over onto my back, and was halfway out when the aircraft dived and held me in. I grabbed the stick and righted the aircraft, returning to the cockpit. I then took off oxygen mask which had blown up, obscuring my vision, regained height and tried the same procedure. My parachute caught in the faring behind the pilot's head position and my shoulders were against the aerial mast. The aircraft was again diving and I think that I kicked the stick forward because I suddenly dropped out. I was turning head over heels in the air and pulled the rip-cord after dropping about 500 feet. I looked around and saw the launch a little way behind me and as I was facing downwind, remained that way. I blew up my Mae West and turned parachute release to 'red' position. As I hit the water and submerged, I pressed the release and kicked. When I surfaced, I was entirely free of parachute, which was drifting

away. The launch picked me up within two minutes. The aircraft, after I left, continued in its dive and plunged into the sea 200 feet from the launch, the bomb exploding immediately. I heard the explosion and felt the concussion from it 3,000 feet up. The people in the launch did not have effects from it. Beyond feeling bruised about the legs and ribs, I did not receive any injury."

The air alarm was sounded twice at Malta during the day, the first just after 1000 when a dozen enemy aircraft were reported approaching at 22,000 feet. Eight patrolling Spitfires, four each from 229 and 249 Squadrons, were warned and vectored to the east and north of the island but no sightings were made, although AA fired at two enemy aircraft seen flying at 21,000 feet off Grand Harbour. The second warning went off at 1430 on the approach of enemy fighters, four of 185 Squadron sighting two Bf109Gs at 14,000 feet north of the island, some 20 miles south of Cape Scalambri. Flg Off Len Cheek (AB532) and Sgt G.C. Warcup (EP471) carried out diving attacks from astern and fired at long range but made no claims.

The month ended with an escort to eight anti-shipping Beaufighters by eight Spitfires drawn from 126 and 185 Squadrons, which departed Malta just after 1000. Off Sousse the Beaufighters sighted three schooners and three flak ships and attacked the former while the Spitfires circled overhead at 15,000 feet. Heavy AA fire was experienced from the shore, two Beaufighters being shot down before six Bf109Gs appeared and shadowed the remaining strike aircraft although they did not attempt to engage. The six surviving Beaufighters and their escort returned safely to Malta. Four Spitfires from 185 Squadron which carried out a sweep over south-eastern Sicily at about the same time also reported sighting Messerschmitts near Pozzallo but since they were heading northwards they were not engaged. Late in the afternoon four Spitfires from 1435 Squadron were scrambled to locate and escort four US Liberators of the 376th Bombardment Group which had been engaged on a bombing mission to Messina, where at least ten Bf109Gs and one FW190 had intercepted. One of the Liberators was badly damaged but had managed to keep pace with the other three, all four being located some 75 miles south-east of Malta and escorted to Luqa, where they landed safely.

A remarkable flight apparently took place about this time, as recalled by Wt Off Ron Hind of 185 Squadron, who was recovering from being shot down during the October fighting:

"I was walking to Valetta – at least, trying to cadge a lift. Suddenly behind me I heard a voice asking if I would like a lift. I waved my arm and turned around to be confronted by Air Vice-Marshal Sir Keith Park, who was of course being driven in his open-air car [an MG tourer]. After *asking* me to put my hat on, he wanted to know if the men were pleased with the extra bread ration that he had managed to obtain. He then went on to ask me how long I had been in Malta. After being questioned about my experiences I was asked why I wasn't commissioned as it would enable me to help the newer arrivals in that capacity. I pointed out that as a Warrant Officer my pay was 17/6d per day whereas a Pilot Officer would earn only 10/6d per day. I remember him kind of smiling at this but was quickly asked what other kites I had flown. The Blenheim was mentioned. I had previously flown Blenheims at the training school at Jurby, Isle of Man.

In the not too distant future I found myself commissioned and called to Headquarters, with others, for another meeting with the AVM, and Wg Cdr Prosser Hanks [Station Commander at Hal Far], when I was 'selected' to go to Luqa to take off in a Blenheim and get special photographs of Catania aerodrome, where there were large crates arriving. They wanted to find out precisely what the crates contained and it had to be a low-level flying job when conditions were favourable. I have no doubts that there were more suitable pilots and more experienced to fly a Blenheim. Why was I selected? Put it down to a stroke of fate! As far as I can remember, it was believed at the time that the large crates being unloaded at Catania contained gliders. The day and the time of opening of the crates was made known to our top brass. It was decided to photograph these crates, opened if possible, at the time of the supplied information.

Conditions as I recollect for that time of the year were excellent and I don't believe on the whole there was much cloud cover. I had with me a navigator, gunner and a chap from the photographic unit. Due to a miscalculation on my part, we came in too low and we had to land! Low flying was required to photograph the required objectives, but no landing was planned! A black on my part! Thank goodness the wind was in the right direction. Having landed we had to continue up the runway, right up to the airport control tower. The anti-aircraft guns on the aerodrome and the ME109s on the ground made one feel apprehensive and we wanted to take off as soon as possible. Of course we had to stop to allow the photographer to take photographs and, would you believe it, nobody took any notice of us. Having taken the photographs we had to turn round and taxi down the aerodrome before taking off, and still there was absolutely no movement of note but, when we were almost over the control tower, all hell let loose. We were caught up by ME109s near Malta, but our Spits protected us enabling a safe return, except for bullet holes in the fuselage. The photographs apparently were what were expected."

Recent photographs of Catania taken by PR Spitfires had revealed the presence of a number of interesting aircraft including one five-engined, twin-fuselage Heinkel which was believed to be in use for towing giant Me321 gliders on the Sicily-Tunisia airbridge run. During one reconnaissance sortie at the beginning of February, a PR Spitfire IV from 69 Squadron was intercepted by two fighters near Messina but successfully evaded and returned to Malta unscathed. A few days later the Spitfire Flight was enlarged to become 683 Squadron under the command of Wg Cdr Adrian Warburton DSO DFC, the celebrated reconnaissance pilot.

February saw a continuation of the almost daily Spitbomber sweeps, four from 126 Squadron visiting Lampedusa on the first day of the month, while a further quartet from the same unit returned from a sweep over Sicily next day with their bombs intact, having been unable to find any suitable targets. Better success was achieved on the morning of 3 February when a dozen Spitbombers drawn equally from 229 Squadron led by Sqn Ldr Smart and 249 Squadron led by Sqn Ldr MacLeod bombed railway stations and warehouses near Pozzallo. One direct hit was seen on a building following which a considerable amount of debris erupted into the air. As the bombers completed their runs, the escort dived down to strafe in their wake. Wg Cdr Thompson, who led the show in AR560/JMT, noted: "Near misses on power station, direct hits on admin buildings." In the afternoon four from 1435 Squadron attacked the power station at Cassibile. Bombs were seen to explode among buildings although one aircraft was unable to release its bombs. The pilot flew out to sea and subsequently managed to jettison them before returning inland to strafe a railway bridge. On returning from an early morning sweep over south-eastern Sicily on 4 February, when a number of Bf109Gs were sighted between Scicli and Pozzallo although no engagements ensued, the engine of Plt Off T. Nesbitt's 185 Squadron aircraft (BR107) failed and he baled out some 15 miles north-east of Grand Harbour at 0900. Four of 126 Squadron were scrambled to circle over him in the water until HSL166 arrived to pick him up some 40 minutes later. Of the incident, Tom Nesbitt later reported:

"I undid my harness, R/T and oxygen tubes and tried to jettison the hood. It didn't, so I opened it in the normal way and undid the side door. Rolling the aircraft over, I was either thrown out or fell out in a satisfactory manner. Floating down, I swung but managed to check this by pulling the shroud lines. It was rather cold in the air, and the loss of one boot made it worse. Nearing the water I inflated my Mae West. As I struck the water I hit the release and the parachute harness fell as the water closed over me. That was due more to the waves rather than sinking below the surface. I found that the Mae West was sufficient to keep me afloat but trod water to warm me up, and lost my other boot in doing so. Pulling the dinghy to me, I undid the fasteners and started to pull out the whole dinghy as it was. This was impossible as something was lashed about half way from the bottom and holding the end tight. Deciding that half a dinghy working was better than a whole dinghy deflated, I took the pin out of the CO_2 bottle and turned the wheel tap. The free end inflated but no amount of persuasion would free the other end, so I gave up and after many attempts clambered half onto the inflated portion. I then saw that a cord wrapped around the dinghy was causing all the trouble. I tried to cut this with my knife but lost this as my hands were numb. So I gave it all up and just lay across the inflated portion, half in and half out of the water, the bottom half becoming very cold.

As Spitfires had been circling all this time, I knew that it was only a matter of a short time before the HSL arrived, and I calculated that I would be out of there in about 30 minutes. Just about then I began to vomit as a result of swallowing a lot of sea water and fluorescene which had come out as soon as I touched water. Even though feeling pretty ill, I decided not to use any of the tablets in the emergency rations until it was really necessary. After about 30 or 40 minutes the HSL came up and seemed to find me without any trouble, probably helped by the whistle which I was blowing. They took me and my dinghy aboard, and after undressing me put me to bed in warm, dry clothes, complete with hot water bottle. I slept most of the way back to Kalafrana slipway where I was taken off and sent to SSQ. There a hot bath was provided followed by hot 'Ovaltine'. Transport was arranged to take me back to Hal Far to see the Squadron doctor who pronounced me more or less fit, but in need of two or three days' rest."

Cloud cover over the Gela area prevented accurate bombing by four Spitbombers of 1435 Squadron led by Wg Cdr Thompson on the morning of 5 February, the pilots releasing in a position estimated to be over Comiso aerodrome. Visibility was better over south-eastern Sicily next day (6 February), four from the same unit carrying out a low-level sweep between Gela and Licata where Plt Off E.G. Kleimeyer RCAF and Sgt W. Hart shot up signal boxes along the railway track and attacked a train west of Gela, which stopped in a cloud of steam and smoke, while Flt Lt N.H.D. Ramsey and Plt Off R.J. Taggart RCAF strafed a goods train south of Noto which was also left in a cloud of steam. Two more from 1435 Squadron set out in the afternoon to repeat the good work, Flt Lt Heppell and Sgt F.W. Thomson destroying a railway engine in Cassibile station before flying to Syracuse, where however, no suitable targets were seen so they returned to the scene of their earlier success and carried out a further attack. In between these small-scale offensive operations, two Spitfires from 126 Squadron were despatched to search for a wayward Halifax, successfully locating it 15 miles south of Filfla and escorting it to Malta.

At 0745 on the morning of 7 February, two Spitbombers of 249 Squadron piloted by Flt Lt Lynch (BR373/T-N) and Plt Off Hap Kennedy (EP519/T-C) took off for a sweep of the Gela-Licata area. About eight miles west of Gela they sighted a train with six or seven coaches and carried out an attack, the two bombs released by Lynch scoring direct hits on the engine while those dropped by his companion fell just wide of the target. Both then strafed before flying southwards where they patrolled over the sea before re-crossing the coast ten miles west of Gela. Following a valley due north at deck level, they encountered a Ju52/3m flying at 1,500 feet just north of Riesi. Overtaking the lumbering transport aircraft, they climbed to attack. Lynch set fire to its port engine while Kennedy attacked from astern and below, scoring hits on the fuselage. The crippled machine, with flames spreading along the fuselage, made a slow left-hand turn and then dived into the ground in flames on a hillside about 15 miles north-east of Licata. Kennedy later commented:

> "As Flight Commander, he [Lynch] had the privilege of attacking first, and he set one engine on fire before I had a crack at it. I knew that he was generous to share it with me." [8]

Next day (8 February) two Spitbombers from 249 Squadron again flew a sweep over Gela and Licata, commencing at 0715. During this operation Flg Off George Newberry's aircraft (BR373/T-N) was hit by machine-gun fire when over Gela. Hurriedly releasing his bombs, he force-landed the crippled machine between a road and the railway line ten miles west of the town, but was able to inform his leader, Flt Lt Cleverly, over the R/T that he was unhurt. He was soon taken prisoner. On returning to Malta, Cleverly discovered that his own aircraft (BR177/T-E) had also been hit by ground fire. Eight more Spitfires, these from 185 Squadron and led by Flt Lt Hal Knight, departed shortly thereafter to carry out a sweep of Comiso-Ragusa-Noto, where little of note was discerned but, as the formation withdrew, two groups of three and two Bf109Gs were sighted at 25,000 feet near Cape Scalambri, heading southwards. At this crucial stage Flt Sgt Cornelius Carmody reported that his aircraft (EP473) had developed engine problems, his companions providing close escort as two of the Messerschmitts made a number of ineffectual attacks. Nearing Malta the ailing Spitfire gradually lost height and eventually hit the water in a shallow dive some 20 miles north of St Paul's Bay. The Canadian pilot was not seen to bale out. On receiving news of the downed aircraft, a dozen more Spitfires from 249 and 126 Squadrons were scrambled to search for the missing pilot, but no sighting was made. Apparently only two Bf109Gs from III/JG53 were involved in this action, not five as reported, flown by Lt Harder and Uffz Scheer of 8 Staffel, the former believing that he had been responsible for the loss of the Spitfire:

> "A nice thing happened to me today: No33, another Spitfire, was painted on

---

[8] see *Black Crosses off my Wingtip*.

my tail. I moved in on three Spitfires without being noticed, simply by tagging along in the midst of a gaggle of 18 [*sic*] Spitfires. There was no danger, for I kept my tail clear and approached out of the sun. I closed in to 150 meters behind three Tommies and I was about to knock down the first one when they noticed me. But they got such a terrific shock that two of them collided as they broke into me. One immediately went straight down and crashed into the water, while we unfortunately lost sight of the other, as the entire band now turned towards us two. One victory and not a shot being fired, the enemy had done it all – brought down by 'ramming' also counts as a victory." [9]

A new unit was established at Luqa on 8 February, 683 Squadron being formed from B Flight of 69 Squadron under Wg Cdr Warburton. For the Spitfire PR pilots there was very little change, their potentially dangerous, often lone, unescorted, reconnaissance sorties over Sicily and southern Italy were to continue as before.

Bad weather hampered operations during the ensuing few days, the only incident of note occurring on 11 February when Canadians Flg Off L.C. Gosling (EP669/X-C) and Flt Sgt S.H.K. Goodyear (EP641/X-J) of 229 Squadron sighted a Z506B seaplane on the water just off the south-eastern coast of Sicily. They dived down and carried out a thorough strafing, which set it on fire. It was left sinking. No survivors were seen. With an improvement in the weather next day (12 February), 1435 Squadron sent two Spitfires flown by Flt Lt Heppell and Sgt Mush Sharun to the Noto area. While flying at deck level they sighted a train approaching Noto from the south, attacking this and scoring hits on the engine and tender with cannon fire before it entered a tunnel, attacking again as it emerged from the other end. Although strikes were seen along its entire length, it kept going and reached the station at Noto. No further attacks were made owing to intense light AA fire, which damaged Heppell's aircraft (AR565/V-C) although he was able to fly back to Malta and make a safe landing. The same unit was active on the morning of 13 February, eight aircraft carrying out a sweep over Pozzallo and some 20 miles inland, but no enemy aircraft were encountered. There was a larger operation in the afternoon when ten Spitbombers (six/249 led by Sqn Ldr MacLeod, four/229 led by Sqn Ldr Smart) escorted by six fighters from the latter unit led by Wg Cdr Johnstone, bombed a quarry near Pachino and a chemical factory at Marzamemi. Much damage was believed to have been inflicted to buildings in both target areas, a fire being observed on the west side of the factory. Following this operation, Air Vice-Marshal Park sent a message to the Krendi Wing:

"AOC congratulates the Krendi Spitfire Wing on the successful bomb and cannon attack on chemical factory in Sicily. Next to destroying enemy aircraft, these bombing attacks are of the greatest importance in preparing the way for the Mediterranean offensive."

During the course of an otherwise uneventful sweep over the Gela-Comiso area next morning (14 February) by 126 Squadron – which had just taken delivery of the first three Spitfire IXs (EN146, EN200 and EN287) to reach the island – Flg Off Alex Vale suffered a heart-stopping moment as noted by an annotation in his logbook: "Engine went cuckoo over Comiso. Got it back OK. Was I scared!!" 229 Squadron suffered a loss on 15 February when Flt Sgt Sandy Goodyear (EP641/X-J) failed to return from a bombing attack on warehouses and railway junctions at

---

[9] see *Jagdgeschwader 53 Volume Two*.

Scicli during the afternoon. The Canadian was the pilot of one of the 15 Spitfires from 126, 185 and 229 Squadrons involved in the operation which achieved successful results; the four Spitbombers from 185 Squadron were led by the new CO, Sqn Ldr H.A. Crafts RNZAF[10], a former 229 Squadron flight commander, those from 229 Squadron by Sqn Ldr Smart, while Flt Lt Jackson led the 126 Squadron contingent. A second Spitfire from the latter unit crashed on landing on returning to Krendi, although the pilot was not injured. Four more Spitfires were despatched to search for the missing pilot and patrolled the area south of Sampieri but no sightings were made. In fact, Goodyear, a 21-year-old from Newfoundland, was killed. Fellow Canadian Flt Sgt Jerry Billing participated in the dive-bombing operation, and recalled:

> "Ahead of me was a black cloud – or wall – of ack-ack. I knew I had to go through it so I jammed on full throttle and went screaming for earth. About 1,000 yards ahead of me was another Spit going like a streamlined sack of shit, not attempting a pullout. I glanced at my altimeter – it read 8,000 feet – and I was having a hell of a lot of difficulty holding my dive. Seeing that I couldn't drop my bombs on the target, I spiralled a bit and released my two bombs on the corner of a quiet little village, opening up with my cannons at the same time. I noticed the Spit on my port strike the ground, followed by a brilliant explosion. I didn't know what happened to him, probably hit by flak. I found out later it was a chap I'd trained with in Canada, Goodyear, his home Newfoundland." [11]

Having fired at coastal defences as he crossed the coast on the return journey, Billing then spotted a submarine close to the shore:

> "I opened fire. His return fire was early and inaccurate. I could see his tracer coming towards me. They appeared to come in a long, slow pattern, then all at once – zip! They would pass. My bullets struck the conning tower, I saw one sailor blown off the deck and into the sea as I went zooming across the sub, very low. And I kept very low for a considerable distance, out of his firing range. I then climbed and banked for another attack. My speed was less this time so I started firing at approximately 600 yards and saw something explode within the tower. Climbing away I looked over my shoulder and saw the smoking craft." [12]

A fruitless sweep by eight Spitfires from 249 Squadron followed on 16 February, although one pilot reported sighting 30-plus small vessels, yellow and oblong-shaped, about one mile off the coast just south of Catania. A further patrol was sent to investigate but were unable to locate the vessels. On the way back to Malta Flt Sgt Jack Hughes' aircraft (EP708/T-U) developed engine problems and he diverted to Luqa, where an emergency landing was made. 1435 Squadron sent four Spitbombers to attack Comiso aerodrome in the morning, although one was obliged to return early owing to engine problems. The remaining three dive-bombed

---

[10] Sqn Ldr Howard Crafts, while waiting to transfer from Gibraltar to Malta in October of the previous year, had flown Spitfires with the *ad hoc* Gibraltar Defence Flight. On one occasion, he and his No2 had intercepted a Ju88 which they seriously damaged and which eventually crash-landed at Melilla in Spanish Morocco. This was the only success achieved by the Defence Flight.

[11/12] see *A Knave Among Knights in their Spitfires*.

hangars near where a number of twin-engined aircraft were seen to be dispersed, but no results were observed except for bomb bursts in the general area. The Squadron sent two more Spitfires, fitted with long-range tanks, to search for transport aircraft reported operating off the east coast of Sicily. When at sea level some 15 miles off Catania, Sqn Ldr Bill Smith (EP257/V-W) and Plt Off J.N. Kirkman (EP915/V-U) spotted two Z1007bis flying eastwards at 1,500 feet. Smith climbed and made a head-on attack on one, followed by a beam attack, scoring hits along the fuselage and stopping the port engine. Kirkman then attacked the same aircraft, which was then flying at sea level, but was hit by return fire. The crippled Spitfire was seen to climb steeply with black smoke pouring from its engine. Kirkman called over the R/T to announce that he was making for the coast near Catania but baled out near some fishing boats about two to three miles offshore. He was subsequently rescued from the sea by an Axis ASR craft and became a prisoner of war. Meanwhile, the seriously damaged Cant, an aircraft from 33°Gruppo, crash-landed at Catania and was totally destroyed although the crew survived.

Poor weather again effectively curtailed large-scale offensive operations for the next seven days, only a few sorties being flown during this period. Two Spitfires from 1435 Squadron flew an unsuccessful sortie to the Cassibile area on 20 February, while, on the night of 22 February, an unusual sortie was carried out by a Hurricane, possibly the last operational one still on the island. Its pilot, Wg Cdr Innes Westmacott DFC, had commanded a flight of Hurricane intruder/night fighters at Malta a year earlier, and during the day had been practising dive-bombing with the Hurricane (BG771) in preparation for a nocturnal mission over Sicily; of his flight, he recalled:

> "Intruder, south-east Sicily, one hour, 35 minutes. Nearly 10/10th cloud. Bombed cement factory at Francofonte for want of anything better. Returned early due to bad weather. Found out later that this target was not Francofonte!"

126 Squadron put up a dozen aircraft to carry out a diversionary sweep over southern Sicily in support of US B-24s from North Africa bombing Messina on 23 February. The Spitfires patrolled Noto-Ragusa-Comiso-Gela at between 22,000 and 26,000 feet without sighting enemy aircraft. A reconnaissance Spitfire was sent to photograph Pachino landing ground where one of the American bombers had force-landed; two small aircraft were also sighted on the airfield. The PR Spitfire IVs continued to fly daily sorties over Sicily and the mainland, one aircraft returning with flak damage sustained over Palermo, while another brought back pictures showing a total of 73 Ju88s at Comiso of which half a dozen were deemed to be unserviceable; the photographs also showed at least 20 single-engined fighters, a couple of Go242s, a Z1007bis and a Fi156. With this juicy target in mind, four Spitbombers from 1435 Squadron led by Wg Cdr Thompson, with four Vs as close escort and three IXs from 126 Squadron as top cover, were despatched to attack the aerodrome on the morning of 25 February. Bombs were released from 16,000 feet, three bursts being noted close to eight poorly dispersed aircraft in front of a hangar. As the Spitfires headed for home, a warning was received of enemy fighters in the vicinity but none were seen. Four aircraft from 185 Squadron covered the withdrawal, three Messerschmitts being sighted 35 miles north of Grand Harbour heading south at 17,000 feet, but these dived away as the Spitfires approached. During the afternoon a dozen Spitbombers led by Sqn Ldr Smart (229 Squadron) and Sqn Ldr MacLeod (249 Squadron) attacked a factory at Pozzallo, but definite results were unobserved although eight

bombs were seen to explode in the target area.

Wg Cdr Thompson and Sqn Ldr Urwin Mann led a dozen Spitbombers from 126 and 1435 Squadrons to bomb a factory at Marzamemi during the afternoon of 26 February, Wg Cdr Tyson leading the escort. Four direct hits and four near misses were recorded while other bombs fell near the power house and on the nearby railway line. Four of 249 Squadron provided rear cover and while flying at 22,000 feet, 40 miles north of Malta, were jumped by two Bf109Gs, one of which shot down Sgt Tony Notley. His aircraft (AR559/T-W) fell into the sea in flames, the 38th victim of Oblt Franz Schiess[13], the new Staffelkapitän of 8/JG53:

> "I took off with my Kazmarek (wingman) and soon we were in a battle with four Spitfires. There were only two of us, but we took them by surprise and they didn't spot us until one of them was already going down on fire – and were satisfied with that and a fine introduction to my Staffel, as well as a birthday gift. No38 for me, again over Malta." [14]

Two aircraft from 229 Squadron flown by Plt Off M.W. Frith and Sgt L.A. Taylor took off to search for the missing pilot but they saw only a small patch of oil in the sea in the area of impact. They were then diverted to intercept enemy aircraft 20 miles north of Malta but none were sighted.

Next day (27 February), Sqn Ldrs Crafts and Smart each led six Spitbombers from their respective units (185 and 229 Squadrons) to attack the power station and seaplane base at Syracuse yet again, when a direct hit was observed on a seaplane hangar while other bombs fell on railway yards south of the power station. Two bombs were seen to explode within 50 yards of two seaplanes, one of which was taxying. Moderate flak was experienced but none of the Spitfires was hit. Photo-reconnaissance Spitfires later brought back evidence of the success of the attack, which showed that a small vessel of about 200 tons had been sunk on the west side of the main jetty, together with much bomb damage to stores assembled alongside the railway sidings. By now the newly arrived Mosquitos of 23 Squadron were well into carrying out nocturnal intruder operations over western and eastern Sicily, and Pantelleria, and had begun taking a toll of enemy aircraft endeavouring to operate from bases within their reach.

Shortly after dawn on the last day of the month (28 February), four Spitfires from 185 Squadron were airborne to search for an overdue Wellington, believed to be somewhere off Linosa. The bomber was located successfully and escorted back to Malta. Forty-five minutes later six Spitbombers from 126 Squadron led by Flt Lt Jackson, escorted by four fighters led by Sqn Ldr Urwin Mann, took off to bomb Comiso aerodrome. Bombs were seen to burst between hangars and the runway, on a hangar and other buildings, the pilots observing ". . . a big fire with large clouds of black smoke . . ." as they departed. Four Spitfires from 249 Squadron covered their withdrawal but no enemy aircraft were seen. During the afternoon the power station at Cassibile was targeted by a dozen Spitbombers (six/185, six/249), bombs being released through the overcast. Spitbombers were out again in the early evening, eleven from 126 and 1435 Squadrons flying to Pozzallo where bombs were released through low-lying cloud. Three of the Spitfires dropped down

---

[13] Oblt Schiess, who had fought over Malta during some of the major air battles of 1942, raised his score to 67 before he was killed in action over Italy on 2 September 1943.
[14] see *Fighters over Tunisia* by Christopher Shores, Hans Ring and William Hess.

through the cloud and carried out a low level bombing run against factory buildings, two near misses being noted. Moderately accurate flak followed them but scored no hits. On the way back to Malta, one pilot observed a vessel, which he thought was a submarine, with small boats around it.

At the end of the month, AIRHQ Malta issued an assessment of the current situation in Tunisia and Malta's perceived future role in the Mediterranean:

"Air tactics in the Mediterranean are converging to a central point. That point is the 100 mile stretch of sea between Sicily and Tunisia. The aim of our strategy is air control of the Mediterranean, enabling our Navies and supply fleets to pass from Gibraltar to Suez without hindrance from the air, enabling our armies ultimately to strike across the inland sea at the vulnerable underbelly of Europe. The Eastern Mediterranean is now clear. Our fighters are providing a continuous fighter umbrella from Alexandria to Malta and no convoy has been appreciably interfered with by the enemy air force. The Western Mediterranean is also clear, enabling our armies in Algeria and Tunisia to be supplied through Gibraltar, but it is not yet possible for convoys to pass under the umbrella from Gibraltar via Malta right through from air bases on either side of the Sicilian Straits. These Straits and the territory on either side of them are therefore the main focus of our air activity today. Our immediate task is to close them to enemy shipping and thus to deprive the Axis forces in Tunisia of their supplies. For this task our main striking base is Malta. Certain advantages lie with the enemy. His sea route is a short one and can be covered by night. He has a large percentage of his European air force based in Sicily, which he aspires to convert into an air fortress rivalling Malta. He has additional air bases on Pantelleria and Lampedusa, commanding the Straits. Despite these advantages our torpedo bombers and submarines are exacting a heavy toll of shipping in the narrows. Our medium and heavy bombers, especially those of the USAAF are battering Tunisian, Sicilian and Italian supply ports, sinking ships at their moorings. This toll will become heavier as we are able to concentrate more of our air forces on this task. It will fall with relatively greater weight upon the enemy as his forces are swelled by the arrival of Rommel's retreating army, dependent on a decreasing number of ports for their supply. At first the enemy supplemented his seaborne troops and supplies with air transports. Malta's Beaufighters shot them down. Sicily countered with fighter escorts. Malta countered with long-range Spitfires to cover the Beaufighters. Thus supply by air has been appreciably checked. While Malta strikes at harbours and shipping with her broadsword, her rapier thrusts swiftly and continuously at land-lines of communications on either side of the Straits. By day fighter bombers strike at towns, aerodromes, railway centres, factories, power stations and supply ports. By night intruders prowl along the railway lines of Sicily and Southern Italy in the moonlight, sweeping down to ground level to destroy whole trains with a few quick blasts of cannon fire. These aircraft are Mosquitos brought from England to Malta under a crack squadron commander to help complete the rout of the Axis armies in the Mediterranean. The Mosquito is Britain's latest and deadliest offensive air weapon, which recently carried out the first daylight raid on Berlin. Thus does our tactical air plan unfold as it unfolded before the Battle of Alamein, first indirect attack on the enemy, via his supplies, then direct attack in conjunction with the Army. It will be the

Army's task, with air preparation and assistance, to eject the Axis from
Tunisia as they ejected him from el-Alamein. It will be the Air Force task,
in conjunction with the Navy, to pursue him to death or captivity in the
desert wastes. Then all three elements will unite for the final thrust into
occupied Europe."

By the end of February the first elements of II/JG27 had begun arriving in Sicily
from Germany where it had re-equipped with the latest Bf109G-6, 4 Staffel landing
at Palermo, and was joined shortly thereafter by 5 Staffel which flew into Trapani
to where 4 Staffel had since moved. A few days later 6 Staffel would join them,
although it transferred to San Pietro where III/JG53 was based. Hptm Ferdinand
Vögl assumed command of II/JG27 until the arrival of Maj Gustav Rödel, the
Geschwaderkommodore. The Gruppe suffered its first casualty since its return to
Sicily when Lt Johann Kuttner of 4 Staffel was killed in a flying accident shortly
after his arrival. Another unfortunate accident about this time involved Uffz Heinig,
a ferry pilot who was delivering a replacement Messerschmitt to Catania. As he
approached Catania he saw some children playing on a beach between Messina and
Taormina, and to show that he had seen them he dived so low that one of the
children was struck by a wing and killed. The distraught pilot was court-martialled,
lost his rank and was given a two-year prison sentence. During this period the Regia
Aeronautica commenced strengthening its forces in Sicily when the four squadriglie
of 12°Gruppo began arriving at Sciacca with MC200 fighter-bombers, while the
first three of the new MC205Vs of 17°Gruppo flew to Pantelleria for operations.
The Bf109Gs of II/JG27, a Gruppe which contained a number of highly experienced
ace pilots, were soon to start taking a toll of Malta's SpitfireVs.

Photographs taken by 683 Squadron Spitfire IVs also showed an increase in the
number of Ju88s at Comiso, news which prompted a raid by a dozen Spitbombers
from 126 and 1435 Squadrons on the afternoon of 1 March, Wg Cdr Thompson
leading the show, while a further eight fighters from 126 and 229 Squadrons flew
top cover. Sqn Ldrs Urwin Mann and Smith led their respective formations into
attack but results were not observed, due once again to low cloud. The 229
Squadron quartet encountered four Bf109Gs over the coastline at 22,000 feet, and
attacked, but the Messerschmitts evaded and dived away northwards, a similar
experience to that of the 126 Squadron escort although they managed to carry out
a head-on attack against the two Messerschmitts they encountered but without
observed result.

Earlier in the day, at 0800, Flt Lt Withy had led eight Spitfires from 185
Squadron on a sweep of the Scicli-Ragusa-Noto area at 25,000 feet. Shortly before
0900 they encountered three Bf109Gs from II/JG27 between Ragusa and Noto,
2,000 feet above. Flt Sgt J.M. Maffre (BR380) climbed and fired a short burst at
one from 250 yards, seeing strikes on its starboard wing before it evaded and dived
away. As the rest of the formation crossed the coast, the engine stopped of the
aircraft (BR534) flown by Flt Sgt Johnny Miller, leaving him no choice but to bale
out into the sea some 32 miles north of Grand Harbour. Flt Sgt Jerry Billing was
involved in the action:

> "During the mêlée Johnny Miller received a hit in his motor and he had to
> bale out. His parachute opened in order, but he had some difficulty opening
> his inflatable rubber dinghy. The Hun at this point had pulled out of the area,
> so I kept circling Miller. Realizing his situation, I undid my parachute and
> harness and snapped off my dinghy, opened my hood and threw my dinghy

to him in the water. He was not able to open mine either. Withy threw him his as well. Johnny was picked up, waterlogged, some hours later, and we found out that he simply forgot to pull the safety pin on the CO_2 bottle!" [15]

The rescued pilot later reported:

"I was flying on a sweep over south-east Sicily with seven other fighters of 185 Squadron. At 0850, while at 23,000 feet and 15 miles inland over Sicily, I was about to participate in an attack on three ME109s when my engine cut without warning. Having tried unsuccessfully to re-start the engine, I released my harness and began to glide towards base. When down to 5,000 feet, I attempted to jettison hood but was unable to do so. I therefore slid it back and turned the aircraft over. My parachute got wedged by the handle of the hood, but I managed to get free and after a short drop, found the toggle and the parachute opened. On my way down I removed my gloves and boots and turned the quick-release box. Immediately my feet touched the water I released my parachute.

When in the water I first freed the dinghy from its cover and, when it was free of the parachute, pushed lever on the Mae West to operate the CO_2 bottle, which did not function properly. I then tried to inflate the dinghy, but did not know that the valve locking-pin had to be removed. As the dinghy was a dead-weight tending to drag me down, I undid the quick-release on my Mae West and let the dinghy go free. I then tried to inflate the Mae West by mouth, but was only able to do so partially on account of the sea swell and the effort required. I noticed that I was being circled by aircraft and a Spitfire (piloted by Flt Lt Withy) dropped a dinghy about 35/40 yards away from me. I managed to reach it but either owing to the force of the impact or that it had caught on the IFF aerial, it was ripped. As it was partly open with a certain amount of air inside, I locked my feet around it to obtain extra buoyancy, but it sank after about five minutes.

I was rescued by the HSL [HSL107] at about 1030. I do not think I could have kept afloat more than 15 minutes longer, as my partially inflated Mae West kept me very low in the water, of which I drank large quantities. I was exhausted by swimming, and struggling after the second dinghy demanded a great effort. I was also getting very numb, owing to the low temperature of the water."

Although Miller's report makes no mention of being attacked by Messerschmitts, Uffz Hans Jürgens of 5/JG27 reported shooting down a Spitfire off Pachino at 0845, while Lt Heinz Schlechter of 6 Staffel claimed a second, although this was not confirmed.

Four Spitfires from 185 Squadron led by Plt Off J. Tarbuck paid a visit to Lampedusa on the morning of 2 March, their task to carry out a reconnaissance of the airfield and harbour. Five large twin-engined aircraft and a dozen small coastal craft were sighted and, on reporting these sightings on their return to Hal Far, four Spitbombers and an equal number of escort departed for the same location. Flt Lt Knight led the dive-bombing attack on the aerodrome and three bombs were seen to burst on the northern perimeter. Only slight AA fire was experienced and none of the attacking aircraft was hit. 683 Squadron lost one of its Spitfires during the

---

[15] see *A Knave Among Knights in their Spitfires*.

morning when Flg Off P.L. Hanson-Lester was forced to bale out of BS496 into the sea when its engine caught fire off Hal Far. Four Spitfires of 1435 Squadron on a practice flight were diverted to the area and saw Hanson-Lester descending on his parachute. They circled him until the rescue launch, HSL128, arrived and plucked the badly burned pilot to safety. Skippering the launch was the Marine ASR unit's CO, Flt Lt G.R. Crockett:

> "A Spitfire pilot on a test flight developed engine trouble, and soon his plane burst into flames. Rolling it over, he managed to bale out all right and, though he was burnt and his clothes were on fire, his parachute opened safely to deposit him in the sea about four miles south-west of Benghaisa Point. I picked him up in HSL128 just under ten minutes after he had landed in the water, and it was a lucky thing for him that we were so prompt as he was in a pretty bad way from burns and was not even wearing a Mae West because he was only up on a serviceability test in the Spitfire . . . the rescue of this badly burnt Spitfire pilot brought our total number of rescues up to 197."

Sqn Ldr Smith set off on an offensive sweep of the Comiso area at 0815 on 3 March at the head of four 229 Squadron Spitfires. When flying at 25,000 feet, six miles south of Comiso at 0840, six Bf109Gs of II/JG27 were sighted at about the same height. In a disastrous encounter, Plt Off Larry McDougall RCAF was immediately shot down by Fw Bernhard Schneider of 6 Staffel, his aircraft (EP717/X-D) crashing in flames, while Sgt E.E. Vine managed to bale out of his aircraft (AR565/X-C), probably also the victim of Schneider who claimed a second Spitfire west of Pozzallo for his 16th victory; McDougall was killed and Vine was taken prisoner, having drifted down to land on a beach. Meanwhile, both the other Spitfires had suffered damage, Plt Off Taggart baling out of BR161/X-E and coming down in the sea 35 miles north of St Paul's Bay, probably the victim of Obfw Emil Clade of 5 Staffel, another ace pilot whose score had now reached 15. A shocked Sqn Ldr Smith brought his damaged aircraft (EP658/X-F) back safely to Krendi. Sections of Spitfires were scrambled to locate and protect Taggart, who was seen to climb into his dinghy, while HSL107 was despatched from St Paul's Bay to effect a rescue. Three of eight Spitfires from 185 Squadron thus scrambled returned early with various problems, the remaining five sighting the downed pilot in his dinghy 12-15 miles off Cape Scalambri, which was also the object of attention for a Ju88 which was seen approaching from the south. It circled the dinghy but was chased away by Plt Off Williams (BR498) who opened fire from 350 yards closing to 150 yards, although no strikes were seen before the Ju88 disappeared overland. Relays of Spitfires took up protective patrolling until Taggart was safely picked up at 1020, and then escorted the launch back to Malta, as recorded by the fortunate pilot:

> "At about 0840, while flying as Red 4, we were attacked by ME109s six miles south of Comiso. I was hit in the oil cooler by a cannon shell. I might have been able to get home, but I tried to pursue the 109 and my engine showed signs of trying to seize up. I went in to a spin and recovered at about 16,000 feet. I was still over Sicily, and realising that I had to bale out, I flew south to bale out over the sea. I stopped my airscrew and called up for a fix. By opening the door and rolling the aircraft on its port side I crawled out on to the mainplane and over the trailing edge. This was at about 6,000 feet, two miles south of the coast. In coming down I drifted further off the coast.

When I hit the water, my parachute did not release. However, I rolled on to my back and released it by means of the box. There was no trouble inflating the dinghy and I climbed into it in the approved manner.

About half an hour later, Spitfires appeared and I attracted them by means of my signal cartridges. They then patrolled over me. One Ju88 appeared at '0' feet and made one circuit. A Spitfire chased it away into Sicily, firing at close range. I did not see any strikes. About half an hour later another Ju88 appeared from Sicily at about 500 feet. It flew towards me and did two circuits above me. The Spitfires attacked and shot it down into the sea about five miles north of me. The rescue launch then appeared and came straight towards me. This was only one hour forty minutes after baling out."

The rescue of Taggart was the ASR unit's 200th success, two members of a Beaufighter crew having been picked up by HSL166 earlier in the morning. It was a section from 249 Squadron that had shot down the Ju88 – B3+BB of Stab I/KG54, and possibly the same aircraft as encountered by 185 Squadron earlier. Led by Plt Off B.J. Oliver RNZAF (EP833/T-F), who initially attacked the Ju88 from astern, the others followed as recalled by Plt Off Hap Kennedy, who was leading the second pair:

"The leader of our section of four aircraft went in to attack but the fire coming at him was so strong, he broke away. His No2 [Sgt W.J.B. Stark, EP706/T-U] went in next and was shot down but managed to bale out. I was No3. The 88 was at 700 feet so I elected to go under him at sea level, and attacked from underneath at high speed, setting his starboard engine on fire. I broke straight up, but he got me in the tail even though I was going at 400 mph, and I came home with half a dozen holes in the Spit [EP343/T-V]. Because the 88 was on fire, the No4 [Sgt D.E. Cruse] did not attack. The [pilots] from 229 Squadron who were relieving us saw the scrap and when we got back to Malta, the Intelligence Officer decreed that the No3 aircraft had in fact shot down the 88 because 229 Squadron had reported whoever had attacked third was the one who had destroyed it.'" [16]

Despite this decision, Kennedy was apparently awarded only one third share of the destroyed Ju88, from which one crew member was seen to bale out, but too late, hitting the water with a partially-opened parachute. Oblt Anton Vögl and his crew – Uffz Klaus Unterecker, Uffz Georg Sareiter and Uffz Hermann Wessels – were all reported missing, presumed killed. Having successfully rescued Plt Off Taggart, HSL107 was directed to search for Sgt Stark, as recorded by the launch commander, Flt Lt E.G. Price, in his log:

"At 1010 a Ju88 was sighted at about 500 feet and [began] circling boat quarter mile radius, clockwise direction. Aircraft were heard on R/T to mention this machine. One minute later Spitfires shot this machine down in flames. A few minutes later two aircraft were sighted approximately three miles to the northward, orbiting position. 1028 – pilot sighted in dinghy dead ahead, distance about one and a half miles. Launch rapidly closed distance and at 1034 was alongside. Pilot (Plt Off Taggart) brought aboard, fit and cheerful, and following a rub down and a change into dry clothes he was quite well.

---

[16] see *Black Crosses off my Wingtip*.

> 1055 – message passed through escorting Spitfire for launch to proceed to position 23 miles Grand Harbour. Course was immediately set for this position. 1120 – two Spitfires were sighted two miles south-west of launch. Contact was established by R/T and information passed that they were orbiting a second airman in the water, in Mae West, no dinghy. Reached this position and picked up second pilot (Sgt Stark, 249 Squadron) at 1145. This airman very cold and slightly shocked, having been in the water for approximately one hour. He rapidly revived following applications of hot blankets, hot water bottles and a dose of brandy. Sgt Stark stated that a parachute cord fouled his dinghy as he opened the control valve of the bottle and while attempting to clear the cord he forgot to turn off the control valve, with the result that the dinghy received too much air in one place and split. Launch proceeded back to base."

The pilots of the circling Spitfires, having observed Stark's plight, had dropped their own dinghies but they fell too far away for Stark to retrieve one. The launch had arrived in the nick of time. Four more Spitfires from 249 Squadron were sent to provide cover and to escort the launch back to Malta, but one of these (EP140/T-M) crashed on landing when it hit an obstruction on the runway, tipped onto its nose, injuring its pilot, Sgt Ron Meadows. The morning of woe for Malta's Spitfires was to continue shortly after midday, when nine Messerschmitts were observed flying over the island at great height, apparently on reconnaissance. On the approach of the intruders, eight Spitfires from 185 Squadron led by Flt Sgt Jerry Billing (EP471) were scrambled to investigate and, at 1230 when 20 miles north of St Paul's Bay, at least five Messerschmitts were seen heading north at 20,000 feet. As the Spitfires climbed to intercept, the Messerschmitts turned and dived on them out of the sun. Billing wrote:

> "When at 17,000 feet, and climbing, the section was jumped out of the sun by five ME109s. I broke to the left. I fired at two, seeing strikes on wing-root area of one and tail of second, and was about to make another break when petrol started streaming in my face. Cannon and machine-gun bullets tore through my aircraft, blowing large holes in my wings, exploding my motor and ruining my controls. Glycol or gas, probably both, and oil as well, drenched my face and body. I reached for my goggles, only to find they had just been torn from my helmet by a passing bullet – a bullet also tore across my left sleeve and glove, exposing my bare hand. Being completely blinded I could make no attempt to get my aircraft back to base so decided to bale out. I had been flying with my hood open, so I undid my harness, pushed the stick forward and was thrown clear. My helmet, retained by the oxygen mask, was torn off. After a free drop of about ten seconds, I pulled the rip-cord and the parachute opened with a severe jolt. Being head down, my neck got rather a wrench. On the way down I got rid of my gloves and boots [owned previously by the late Flt Sgt Carmody], inflated my Mae West, undid dinghy cover and gave a twist to release box of parachute. Just before my feet touched water I released the parachute and held my nose. On coming to the surface I drew the dinghy towards me with the lead, pulled the dinghy from its cover, withdrew pin from valve and turned on the CO_2. The dinghy inflated upside down but I turned it over without difficulty. As I was going to get in, I found that my legs were entangled in parachute cords. I kicked myself free, lifted up the dinghy to empty it of water and got in by the narrow end with the aid of the loop handles. I then recovered the paddles but had to cut the cord which had got caught up

in the parachute cords. Spitfires circled around until the HSL [HSL166] picked me up about 1325. My knees and thighs had got grazed getting out of the aircraft and my neck was stiff and painful from the jolt of the parachute opening but otherwise I was none the worse." [17]

A second Spitfire, BR194 flown by Flt Sgt George Mercer, was also hit, sustaining severe damage to one wing and the undercarriage. Despite the difficulty of the situation, Mercer made a successful one-wheel landing at Hal Far. The Messerschmitts were again from II/JG27, and again Fw Schneider was involved, claiming two further Spitfires shot down, one at 1226 and the second four minutes later, although Lt Heinz Schlechter also claimed one, his first confirmed victory. An expensive day for Malta's Spitfire units – five aircraft shot down with two pilots missing, plus two more seriously damaged.

Following the drubbing on 3 March, fortunately there was relatively little employment for Malta's Spitfire pilots during the following ten days or so; escorting two RN destroyers was the main task on 4 March, while Flt Lt Heppell and Plt Off Wood of 1435 Squadron carried out an offensive sweep over south-eastern Sicily during the afternoon of 6 March, hunting for trains. Having crossed the coast near Sampieri, they came across a stationary train in a small station which they attacked with cannons and machine-guns, reporting that the engine appeared to blow up and was last seen enveloped in a cloud of black and grey smoke. On the return flight they were diverted to locate a wayward Hudson, which they found ten miles east of Malta and escorted it to the island. Convoy patrols occupied most of the squadrons during the day. Next day (7 March) saw 16 Spitfires from 229 and 249 Squadrons carry out a sweep of the Comiso area without attracting an aerial opposition. The highpoint of operations on 9 March were Spitbomber raids by pairs of aircraft from 249 Squadron, one pair attacking two boathouses near Torre Vendicari south of Avola. Bombs fell close to the target and demolished both buildings. A second pair bombed a railway bridge and signal box about 18 miles south of Scicli, where one direct hit was recorded on the bridge. The signal box was strafed as were a number of stationary trucks. Earlier in the day Flg Off Ron Green and Sgt A.J. Greenwood RAAF located a B-17 which had lost it way and escorted it to base. The photo-reconnaissance Spitfire IVs of 683 Squadron continued to operate daily flights to various locations in Sicily and the Italian mainland, generally achieving their tasks without undue interference but, on this date, Flg Sgt Clayton Peacock RCAF (BS364) failed to return from an afternoon sortie to the Taranto-Naples-Messina area.

At 0920 on the morning of 11 March, Wg Cdr A.D.J. Lovell DFC, who had recently taken over the Krendi Wing from tour-expired Wg Cdr Johnstone, and Sqn Ldr MacLeod of 249 Squadron set out to attack targets of opportunity in the Comiso area. They flew at sea level to a point 15 miles south of Pozzallo, turned westwards and crossed the coast ten miles south-west of Comiso. At 0945 a goods train was sighted about five miles inland which both attacked, causing the engine to belch smoke. No enemy aircraft were sighted nor AA fire experienced by Wg Cdr Lovell, but Sqn Ldr Malcolm MacLeod failed to return, his aircraft (EP519/T-C) apparently crashing into the sea. He was 249 Squadron's first (and only) CO to be killed in action. Flt Lt John Lynch was promoted to take his place, while Flt Lt K.B.L. Debenham, a Battle of Britain veteran, arrived from 185 Squadron as the new flight commander.

---

[17] see *A Knave Among Knights in their Spitfires*.

Messerschmitts were again evident on 12 March when 16 Spitfires from 185 and 126 Squadrons carried out sweeps just off the coast of south-east Sicily during the early afternoon. As Sqn Ldr Urwin Mann led his formation from 126 Squadron to patrol Cape Scalambri, one section was bounced by a single Bf109G. None of the Spitfires was hit but they were unable to catch the Messerschmitt as it pulled away after the attack. A few minutes later the other section, flying at 27,000 feet, saw two more German fighters some 5,000 feet below and attempted to repay the compliment. One Messerschmitt disappeared from the action by diving away while the other was engaged by two Spitfires which opened fire, but without tangible results.

At 0640 on the morning of 13 March, Flt Lt Cleverly led four of 249 Squadron to search for two Beauforts missing from night operations in the Gulf of Castellammare. Although they patrolled the area for some time no sightings were made. Later in the morning Wg Cdr Lovell led 16 Spitfires from 229 and 249 Squadrons, half of which were armed with bombs, to attack a factory and railway yards at Ragusa, where bombs were seen to fall in the target area. All Spitfires returned safely. Another force of eight Spitbombers escorted by an equal number of fighters from 126 and 1435 Squadrons set out for Sampieri the following morning, but no suitable targets were seen so they flew out to sea, then re-crossed the coast west of Pozzallo and released their bombs through low cloud. Results were not observed. Later eight Spitfires drawn from 126 and 249 Squadrons escorted an incoming convoy, while a PR Spitfire IV joined two Baltimores searching for a missing Baltimore which failed to return from a shipping search between Naples and Sicily; one crewman was located in his dinghy and was rescued in the early hours of the following morning. Another PR Spitfire, AB310 flown by Flg Off L.R. Philpotts, was attacked by four fighters, tentatively identified as Re2001s and Bf109s, during a reconnaissance mission over the ports and harbours in Sicily and southern Italy. He successfully evaded and returned safely to Luqa with his photographs. Trains were attacked by sections of Spitbombers over the next two days, followed by an attack on Lampedusa by 126 and 1435 Squadrons where bombs were dropped on the airfield, Comiso being similarly visited by 249 Squadron. Results from all these attacks were considered negligible. Comiso was raided again on 17 March, this time by 126 and 1435 Squadrons, heavy accurate flak being experienced although all Spitfires returned safely; as did Sgt R.M. Snowden of 683 Squadron, whose Spitfire (BR656) was chased by four Messerschmitts during a reconnaissance sortie to Messina.

Next day (18 March), Flg Off Kleimeyer, a Canadian of 1435 Squadron, led Sgt Wilbert Hart on a sweep over south-eastern Sicily, specifically hunting for trains. At 0805 south-west of Avola they sighted a north-bound train with engines at both front and rear. Two attacks by each aircraft resulted in clouds of smoke and steam engulfing the target, which Hart then attacked again, his aircraft (AR556/V-C) apparently sustaining some damage. When about six miles south of Cape Passero, on the return flight, Hart suddenly informed his leader that he would have to ditch. To the watching Kleimeyer, this was apparently successfully achieved but when he flew low over the scene only the cockpit cover and a dinghy paddle could be seen. Despite a search, Sgt Hart, a 32-year-old from Bolton, was not found and had presumably gone down with his aircraft. Small-scale sweeps continued but often the Spitfires returned without finding suitable targets, and mostly without opposition. However, on 20 March, when Wg Cdr Thompson led an attack on a factory near Pozzallo, one of the Spitbombers suffered damage by AA fire and another from bomb blast splinters although both returned safely. Not so fortunate were two Spitfires of 185 Squadron which took off at 1445 for a sweep over south-east Sicily, since neither returned. Flt Lt Henry Withy, the section leader, believed his aircraft (EP571) to have been hit by AA fire as its engine seized and he was obliged to bale out into the sea. As his companion, Flt Sgt Johnny Miller (BR109/GL-W), circled overhead to provide protection for his dinghy two Bf109Gs of 6/JG27 appeared and Fw Bernhard Schneider shot down the Canadian into the sea, his 19th victory and fifth Malta Spitfire for the month. As soon as news of the action reached Malta one of the two newly arrived RN Walrus amphibians[18] attached to the ASRU, W3012 crewed by Lt(A) R.D. Pursall RNVR and L/Air P. Garrett-Reed, was despatched to search for the missing pilots, but only Flt Lt Withy was rescued. He later reported:

> ". . . I noticed my constant speed was not working, and that my oil gauge was off the clock. I told Flt Sgt Miller and started climbing and got about 1,500 feet over the sea, then I called Control. During his acknowledgement, my engine stopped completely, so I quickly told the Controller I was baling out and jumped at approximately 1,000 feet. By opening the door, trimming fully forward, and standing on the seat, I had no difficulty getting out. Flt Sgt Miller orbited me while I got into my dinghy, which worked perfectly though my Mae West did not inflate. Though I saw no firing over Sicily, I believe the machine must have been hit by machine-gun fire as everything was in order prior to taking off.
>
> The cloud base was about 1,500 feet and after about 15 minutes I saw two ME109s approaching from the west. My No2 saw them as they turned to get up-sun of him, and a short dogfight ensued which took them above cloud. Shortly after this I saw a Spitfire come down in a slow, flat spin. I did not see the aircraft actually hit the water, though am certain it did so. There was no sign of a parachute. It is entirely due to Flt Sgt Miller remaining to give an accurate fix on me that I was picked up, and I feel that he is entitled to this recognition.
>
> After some time I heard aircraft engines and saw to the east four Spitfires [from 249 Squadron] and a Walrus. I fired one of my distress signals. They immediately turned towards me, and the Walrus landed and picked me up. While on the water a ME109 attacked the Walrus, not hitting it but the necessary evasive action damaged the port wing float. Owing to a heavy swell (about eight feet) take off was very difficult and was successful only on the third attempt. As I was only six to eight miles off the enemy coast, the pilot and crew of the Walrus did an excellent job, and needless to say, I am extremely grateful."

Whilst the rescue was in progress, more Messerschmitts appeared, as recalled by one of the circling 249 Squadron pilots, Sgt Ken Browne (BP869/T-Z):

> "We circled the Walrus at about 1,000 feet or so. I did not realise that my R/T was not working until one colleague flew close by me, apparently trying to warn me of enemy aircraft above. Before I could take action, i.e. pull into a tighter turn, I was hit (I think) by a single cannon shell in the port wing, right where the oil cooler was situated."

---

18 Two Walrus amphibians, W3011 and W3012, had recently arrived at Malta for ASR duties on detachment from 701 Squadron based at Beirut; W3011 was damaged in a landing accident at Hal Far at the end of April.

Browne's assailant was apparently Hptm Wolfgang Tonne of 3/JG53; Browne continued:

> "I headed for Malta but only got five or six miles when the engine seized up and the prop stopped dead. I was too low to bale out, so had to ditch – a bit dicey in a Spitfire. By good luck I managed to get the tail down first, to help break the impact, and only got a bad knock on the forehead from hitting the reflector sight due to the sudden deceleration and the effect of Newton's law of motion. I managed to get out complete with parachute and K-type dinghy pack before the plane sank – about 30 seconds or so. I then detached the dinghy and blew it up with the CO_2 bottle provided. The parachute sank. Then, after some difficulty, I managed to get in."

Another of the escort, Flg Off Bill Locke, a 20-year-old Canadian from Newfoundland (in BR345/T-W) also failed to return and was apparently shot down by Hptm Paul Sommer, a Danish pilot of II/JG27 who, together with his wingman, had arrived on the scene. In the skirmish Flg Off D.A.S. Colvin (EP712/T-C) and Flt Sgt Jack Hughes (EP201/T-D) believed they jointly damaged one of the attackers. Of the action, Sgt Don Nicholson recalled:

> "The shooting down of Ken Browne was once again the result of being jumped by 109s. They really were very efficient at this type of attack – a dive out of the sun, a quick burst of fire and away. Partly our own fault of course as we were perhaps too intent on watching the Walrus pick up the pilot from his dinghy."

Train busting continued on 22 March, Flt Lt Heppell's 1435 Squadron section attacking a mixed passenger/goods train near Sampieri in the morning, and left it belching smoke. Ten minutes later the same quartet attacked the engine of a goods train, which was seen to explode in clouds of smoke and steam. During the same mission two other Spitbombers led by Sqn Ldr H.F. O'Neill, the new CO, bombed a factory near Sampieri, reporting all four bombs on target. Next day Flt Lt Heppell flew another sortie during the late afternoon, he and Sgt T.G. Atkinson following the railway line from Rosolini to Ispica until they found a train which was attacked. It was left enveloped in steam and smoke.

The Luftwaffe put in a limited appearance again on 25 March, high-flying Messerschmitts being reported over Malta at 0830. Seven Spitfire Vs of 229 Squadron were scrambled, followed by three IXs of 126 Squadron and at 0905 three Bf109s were sighted 20 miles north of the island, flying northwards at 24,000 feet, and five minutes later a further eight were seen at 22,000 feet. Flg Off Les Gosling (EP606/X-P) engaged one and it was last seen diving away, pouring glycol, Gfr Wolfgang Körn of II/JG27 baling out into the sea about ten miles off the coast of Sicily. One of 126 Squadron's Spitfires was also shot down, Flg Off Bruce Stovel RCAF (EN200/MK-Q) baling out of his burning aircraft about six miles north-east of Grand Harbour. The slightly burned Canadian pilot was quickly rescued by a Maltese fishing boat before being transferred to HSL128, while a section of 185 Squadron patrolled overhead. Gfr Körn, the downed German pilot was also plucked from the sea, and he may have been responsible for shooting down Stovel's aircraft before falling to Gosling since no other German pilot appears to have made a claim in this action. The crew of an ASR Do24 out searching for Körn thought they had found their man when a dinghy was sighted, but this turned out to be the missing 249 Squadron pilot, Sgt Ken Browne, who had been bobbing up and down in his dinghy off the Sicilian coast for five days:

> "Unfortunately, the emergency rations were missing from the dinghy, so I had nothing to eat or drink. On 25 March, a Dornier 24 flying boat flew overhead. It landed, the crew no doubt thinking I was their man. When they came alongside they said 'Ach, Englander', and I thought they might leave me, but they took me aboard and treated me very well – put me in a rescue suit (a sort of track suit) and gave me soda water laced with brandy. I was taken to a Luftwaffe sick quarters in Syracuse, where I was fed well, and young German airmen came along to practice their English on me. I learned that I had been shot down by a Messerschmitt 109G, the latest of that mark and certainly one up on the older Spit VBs we had in Malta. After a week they transferred me to a Luftwaffe-run hospital at Catania as I was suffering from the effects of exposure and dehydration. While there I got pally with a NCO ME109 pilot."

The increased German fighter activity may have been triggered by the shooting down of a Ju88 by the Canadian pair Flg Off Hap Kennedy (EP343/T-V) and Flt Sgt Dean Kelly (BR110/T-A) of 249 Squadron some 10-15 miles south-west of Porto Empedocle earlier in the morning, at 0905. Kennedy's subsequent report revealed:

> "I was leading Tiger Blue Section on a search for a missing Wellington crew. We flew at 100 feet and just after turning onto reciprocal course at 0900 about 10 miles south-west of Porto Empodocle, I sighted an aircraft on our left, flying south-west at 100 feet. Immediately turning head on, I passed over the aircraft identifying it as a Junkers 88. I made one quarter astern attack, firing three bursts totalling five seconds, from 300 to 50 yards, setting on fire the port engine of the enemy aircraft. As I broke away I saw my No3, Flt Sgt Kelly, attacking the 88 which became completely enveloped in flames. Blue 2 did not attack unnecessarily. The Ju88 crashed into the sea about 15 miles south-west of Porto Empedocle. There were no survivors."

The Messerschmitts were back later in the morning and 18 Spitfires, which were airborne on a sweep over the Comiso area, were recalled and ordered to intercept but only eight from 229 Squadron made any sightings, although the enemy fighters were too far away for interception. Two IXs from 126 Squadron had also been scrambled and climbed to 37,000 feet over the island, from which height they spotted eight Messerschmitts about 10,000 feet below, but were unable to engage. Flt Sgt W.S. Lewis was the third 683 Squadron reconnaissance pilot in ten days to be intercepted by enemy fighters when three Bf109s attacked his Spitfire (BS358) over the southern Italian coastline, but he, too, was able to evade and escape and return safely to Luqa.

After the excitement of the previous day, 26 March was rather an anti-climax. Although all Spitfire squadrons despatched offensive patrols during the day, only a section of IXs from 126 Squadron sighted enemy aircraft, four Messerschmitts flying east of Scalambri at 26,000 feet during the afternoon. Wg Cdr Thompson (EN295) managed to close on one of the diving Messerschmitts and fired a deflection burst at 250 yards but no result was observed. A returning aircraft (EP652) of 185 Squadron crashed on landing at Hal Far and was slightly damaged;

the pilot, Sgt D.H. Warr, was unhurt. After the intensive and almost continuous fighting in Tunisia, some of the German pilots found Sicily almost too quiet for their liking. One of these, 8/JG53's commander, Oblt Franz Schiess, wrote home:

> "Every day the same. Off with the Staffel and back again in the evening. Real Malta weather – never stops raining. But it doesn't stop flying. I'll be glad to be back in Africa, where one leads an organised life – flying several times daily and with the chance of some action. Only one contact with the enemy here, when I shot one down. Naturally I feel annoyed that the 40th success eludes me. It holds up my leave, but I don't want to come home without my decoration. Still, that last one will come!" [19]

Two Spitfires from 229 Squadron joined an ASR Swordfish and three FAA Albacores on the morning of 27 March in a search for a missing Wellington, which failed to return from a night sortie. No sighting was made. Later two Spitfires from 1435 Squadron were scrambled to search for a dinghy reported five miles out to sea in the Gozo-Comino area but again no sighting was made. The aircraft (EP122/V-L) flown by Flt Sgt Percy Stratford crashed on Gozo due to engine problems – "he was fortunate enough to put his aircraft down on a small rock not much bigger than the Spitfire" – but suffered a broken arm and leg and damage to his face. Since the Spitfire was severely damaged it was pushed over the cliff edge into Dwerja Bay. Another four aircraft from the same unit carried out a sortie over south-east Sicily, sighting a passenger train approaching Pozzallo from the west. This was attacked with bombs and cannon but no results were observed.

Following a very quiet day on 28 March, the next day saw eight Spitfires from 126 Squadron, four carrying bombs, set off for a sweep over southern Sicily but saw no suitable targets and all returned with bombs intact. A further four from the same unit joined Beaufighters providing cover for an incoming convoy. No enemy aircraft were observed by these patrols but shortly thereafter four more IXs from 126 Squadron were scrambled when radar reported the approach of enemy aircraft. Having climbed to 36,000 over Grand Harbour, two Bf109s were sighted 6,000 feet below by the Spitfire pilots who immediately carried out a diving attack but the Messerschmitts disappeared into thick haze and were lost from sight. The penultimate day of the month again proved to be a quiet one, as did the last one (31 March) even though 126, 185, 249 and 1435 Squadrons all despatched mini sweeps over southern Sicily throughout the daylight hours, they still could not entice Messerschmitts nor Macchis to challenge them.

Towards the end of the month six twin-engined, twin-boom F-5 Lightning (the unarmed version of the P-38) photo-reconnaissance aircraft of the USAAF's 3rd Photographic & Mapping Group arrived at Luqa from Tunisia, tasked to sortie over Sicily in advance of the invasion. One aircraft was written off on arrival and two days later the detachment's CO failed to return from the unit's first PR sortie. Fliegerkorps II (Süd) in Sicily also received reinforcements when the Bf109Gs of 7 and 9 Staffeln of III/JG27 flew in to San Pietro from Kastelli in Crete, under the overall command of Hptm Frank-Werner Rott. Their task was twofold; to provide additional air defence for the south-eastern corner of Sicily together with the occasional offensive foray over Malta; and to provide escort and protection for ships and aircraft on the Sicily-Tunisia run. They now joined elements of II/JG27, III/JG53, II and III/ZG1 and III/ZG26 in these duties.

---

[19] see *Fighters over Tunisia*.

CHAPTER II

MALTA: THE THORN IN SICILY'S SIDE

April-May 1943

" . . . the Malta pilots seemed to be young and inexperienced, and not inclined to dogfight . . ."

Comment by Oblt Günther Hannak, Staffelkapitän of 7/JG27, following his capture after crash-landing his Messerschmitt at Luqa on 5 May 1943

Twelve months earlier – on 1 April 1942 – Malta had witnessed the start of the Easter mini blitz against its airfields, when many of those on the ground, let alone those who took to the air, believed their days were numbered. The intervening twelve months had seen a remarkable turnaround in Malta's fortunes and 1 April 1943 came and went like almost any other day during this period – routine patrols with very little enemy activity. Two Spitfires from 229 Squadron carried out an afternoon patrol at sea level just off the coast east of Cape Passero without encountering any enemy aircraft, while, at about the same time, four from 249 Squadron scrambled when radar picked up a plot south of the island but again no sightings were made.

There was a little excitement on 2 April when two Spitbombers from 249 Squadron led by Flt Lt Debenham were despatched at 1635 to attack a factory at Cassibile. Having released their bombs, scoring direct hits, Plt Off W.J. Costello RNZAF was intercepted by two Bf109Gs. As he turned to face his attackers, his aircraft (BR177/T-E) was hit in the starboard wing but nearby cloud enabled him to escape further damage and he was able to return safely to Luqa, where a creditable landing was made without the aid of brakes and flaps. Earlier in the day three pairs of Spitbombers had attacked the railway siding at Rosolini, a railway bridge north of Licata, and a power station at Marzamemi, all sorties flown without interference from enemy fighters. Two scrambles by sections of Spitfires during the morning of 3 April came to nothing, although enemy aircraft were sighted five miles north-east of Grand Harbour during the second of these. Climbing to 18,000 feet the section from 1435 Squadron observed vapour trails of four aircraft flying north at between 25,000 and 27,000 feet, though they were unable to make further sightings, while three Spitfires of 126 Squadron on an army co-operation exercise were diverted to intercept but again to no avail. At the same time 126 Squadron's CO, Sqn Ldr Urwin Mann, was carrying out an air test in ER647 and he was similarly warned of enemy aircraft in the area, but, as he noted in his logbook: "No joy, me much too low – Jerry, he much too high." It was the turn of 683 Squadron's CO, Wg Cdr Warburton, narrowly to escape being shot down during a sortie to Taranto. At least one enemy fighter intercepted his Spitfire (EN338), opening fire from astern but from long range, and Warburton was able to evade and escape without damage.

A dozen Spitbombers drawn equally from 126 and 1435 Squadrons set out at 1100 on the morning of 4 April, with the seaplane base at Syracuse as their primary target, where a squadron of E-boats was also harboured. Four Spitfire IXs from 126 Squadron led by Flt Lt Jackson provided top cover. One aircraft was obliged to return early with engine problems, jettisoning its bombs safely before landing, while the remainder carried out their attacks from 16,000 feet down to 8,000 feet. Four bombs were observed to explode within 100 yards of the E-boat base, and others among an assemblage of seven seaplanes and flying boats including one six-engined BV222. Explosions were also seen among buildings near the railway sidings. Heavy and light AA fire was experienced from a ship in the harbour and from shore batteries although none of the attacking aircraft was hit. Three more IXs from 126 Squadron covered the Spitbombers and their escort as they returned to Malta.

A Wellington on a test flight crashed into the sea near the rocky islet of Filfla, just short of the Dingli Cliffs during the afternoon. Two Beaufighters and a Spitfire were immediately despatched to provide cover as HSL128 headed for the scene. As the aircraft circled above, their crews could not have known of the drama unfolding in the sea below, as recorded in the fragmented report of one of the survivors:

> "Aircraft struck water at approx 100 knots . . . Pilot thrown through perspex windscreen. Plane sank in 20 to 30 seconds. On pilot calling 'I can't swim', 2nd pilot swam 25 yards for rubber cushion, giving same to pilot. S/E [radar] Op yelled 'I can't swim either'. 2nd pilot swam 25 yards, grabbed S/E Op by tunic collar, held him for a few minutes, but released to remove shoes (submerging at the same time). Regained hold on S/E Op who had swallowed water, and attempted to place him face uppermost but as both were sinking, again let go to remove other shoe. Regained hold, attempting to swim toward the coast two to three miles distant. Released S/E Op once more to discard tunic . . . arm entangled in tunic. S/E Op sank out of reach [drowned]. [Meanwhile] W/Op grabbed [unconscious] passenger by collar, passenger's face in water. Rear gunner swam over and took passenger by tunic collar . . . W/Op then placed passenger between knees, kicked off shoes, partially removed tunic . . . meanwhile, passenger slid down out of reach [drowned]. Sighted launch, yelled and waved . . . when launch within about 200 yards, [it] turned towards them. Launch crew threw lines, 2nd pilot and W/Op grabbed same. Rear gunner, further away, was pulled in by member of crew who dived in and life-saved him as he was too exhausted to help himself. Launch then picked up pilot . . ."

Both the rear gunner and the pilot were rescued by a deckhand aboard HSL128, who dived in to pluck both from almost certain death. Indeed, the pilot was brought aboard apparently drowned, but after artificial respiration had been applied he vomited and showed signs of life, and eventually recovered. Many an airman owed his life to the gallant actions of the crews of the rescue launches.

The power station at Porto Empedocle was the target for a dozen Spitbombers (six/229 led by Sqn Ldr Smart, six/185 led by Flt Lt Knight) in the early afternoon of 5 April, while four fighters provided cover. Bombs were seen to burst near the power station and railway sidings, and among factory buildings. Pilots reported light and heavy AA fire to be generally inaccurate. All returned safely. On three occasions during the day sections of Spitfires were scrambled as enemy reconnaissance flights were detected approaching Malta but none of these were intercepted, while an early morning search by four Spitfires from 185 Squadron led by Flt Lt Withy for a missing Wellington failed to locate any signs of wreckage or the crew.

At 1203 on 6 April the air raid siren was sounded at Malta when a small number of unidentified aircraft were tracked approaching from the north, four IXs from 126 Squadron being scrambled to join five Spitfires of 229 Squadron and four IXs of 185 Squadron engaged in practice flying. Four Messerschmitts were seen crossing the coast over Grand Harbour, the 229 Squadron formation being ordered to climb to 20,000 feet south of the island while the 185 Squadron section climbed to 18,000 feet to the north, sighting the Messerschmitts 10,000 feet above. They continued climbing but were unable to make contact. Meanwhile, the four IXs from 126 Squadron led by Flt Lt Jackson (EN142/MK-W) had reached 26,000 feet and were ten miles north-west of Grand Harbour when they encountered eight Messerschmitts flying south-east at 29,000 feet. The Bf109Gs from III/JG27 split into two formations, one group being pursued by the IXs to within 15 miles of Cape Scalambri before Jackson opened fire. He saw strikes on the fuselage and cowling of Uffz Erich Dreyer's 9 Staffel aircraft, then saw a big puff of black smoke changing to white as the stricken aircraft dived almost vertically. Plt Off G.G. White RNZAF (EN290/MK-G) gained on a second Messerschmitt and opened fire from 300 yards but without visible results. As the IXs returned to Malta, a section from 1435 Squadron took off to search for signs of the German fighter, patrolling off Cape Scalambri at 10,000 feet but failed to notice any activity. Uffz Dreyer was in fact killed when his aircraft dived into the sea five miles off Pozzallo. The fighter-bombers were out again in the afternoon, eight drawn from 229 Squadron (Sqn Ldr Smart) and 249 Squadron (Sqn Ldr Lynch) bombing a factory and the railway sidings at Ragusa. Low haze over the target prevented accurate observation of the bombing although some were seen to explode near the railway station. No enemy aircraft were observed by the attacking aircraft, the escorting fighters led by the new Wing Leader, Wg Cdr John Ellis DFC, a Battle of Britain veteran, or by those from 249 Squadron covering the withdrawal.

At 0615 on 7 April two 249 Squadron Spitfires set out to sweep south of Sciacca; when 40 miles south-west of this point at 0700, flying at sea level, a Ju88 was sighted one mile ahead, flying eastwards. Sqn Ldr Lynch (EP829/T-N) made a starboard rear quarter attack, firing a four-seconds burst with both cannon and machine-gun fire. Pieces flew off the bomber (F1+6R of III/KG76) and it dived into the sea in flames, Oblt Hans Merden and his crew perishing in the crash. Shortly after midday two Spitfires of 229 Squadron, one carrying bombs, set out to attack buildings at Cala Bernardo, but both bombs missed the target. On the return flight a small coastal craft was sighted a mile off the coast, heading southwards, four Spitbombers from 126 Squadron led by Sqn Ldr Urwin Mann being despatched to attack this with four others providing escort. Flying at sea level, landfall was made two miles south-west of Pozzallo. The formation then turned eastwards and flew two miles off the coast to Cape Passero before flying northwards to Cala Bernardo, where tragedy struck Sgt Tom Pennock, whose aircraft (EP567/MK-B) was seen to hit the sea with one wing before it disappeared beneath the waves; the pilot did not survive. The others returned to Malta having not sighted the coaster. During the evening two Spitfires of 185 Squadron together with a Beaufighter night fighter were scrambled on the approach of an unidentified aircraft, which turned out to be friendly. There was a repeat of this incident the following evening (8 April). Earlier in the day three pairs of Spitfires carried out offensive sweeps, but the only one of note occurred during mid-morning when two aircraft from 229 Squadron flown by Flg Off W.D. Idema and Plt Off K.B. Robinson set out to attack Agrigento power station. En route they sighted a stationary train in a railway station five miles inland from Porto Empedocle and decided to attack this instead. Two bombs fell near the engine and in the ensuing strafing attack, strikes were seen on both engine and tender. A second train was also strafed and strikes were registered along its coaches. On the return journey two bombs were aimed at a railway bridge some two miles from the coast, which burst about 30 yards from the target.

One of 249 Squadron's Canadians was lost due to engine problems on 9 April. Flt Sgt Wally Yaholnitsky's aircraft (BR131/T-O) plunged into the sea about eight miles off Cape Scalambri during an afternoon sweep after he had reported that his engine was malfunctioning. A companion saw him bale out and clamber into his dinghy, but when the remainder of the Spitfires carried out a low-level sweep he was not located. The rescue craft sent out to search for him returned without making a sighting. Later, however, his body was recovered from the sea and interred in Malta's Capuccini Naval Cemetery. Next day (10 April) it was the turn of the Luftwaffe to lose one of its aircraft to Malta's Spitfires, when 185 Squadron's Flt Lt Withy (EP791) and Flg Off R.C. Schuren (BR375), an American in the RCAF, carried out an early morning sweep in the Pantelleria area. At 0720 while flying at 200 feet they sighted a Ju88 about 10-15 miles north-east of Pantelleria, some 50 feet below. Withy attacked on the port quarter from 300 yards, firing two short bursts of cannon fire with no apparent result, as the bomber circled to get into the sun. Meanwhile, Schuren had climbed to 1,000 feet from where he dived and attacked on the port quarter, closing to dead astern and opened fire from 400 yards. He then made a second attack from 300 yards, closing to 200 yards, and observed strikes on the cockpit following which there was a flash and the hood fell off. At the same time Withy was attacking from the starboard and set both engines on fire. The Ju88 was seen to pull up, bank to port and dive straight into the sea. There had been considerable return fire from the rear and dorsal turrets and one of the Spitfires had taken a hit in the engine, although it was able to return safely.

Four Spitfires from 1435 Squadron missed a similar opportunity in the same area the following day (11 April). Having sighted a twin-engined aircraft flying at sea level one mile north of Pantelleria, they lost it when it turned back overland. Other patrols despatched to the Pantelleria-Lampedusa area failed to locate any enemy activity. Three sections from 229 Squadron were also out in the morning, one section having been despatched to locate a friendly aircraft with engine trouble, the others searching for signs of two Wellingtons missing from night operations. There were no sightings. Spitbombers were again active over south-eastern Sicily during the afternoon, eight from 185 and 1435 Squadrons raiding Biscari aerodrome. With a further eight Spitfires flying close escort and four IXs of 126 Squadron as high cover, the bombers crossed the Sicilian coast five miles south-east of Gela at 23,000 feet, before diving down to 11,000 feet and releasing their bombs. Explosions were seen in and near the southern dispersal area but no tangible results were observed, nor was any enemy aerial opposition encountered. Flg Off G.H.E. Maloney RCAF of 683 Squadron had a lucky escape following a round robin sortie which encompassed Catania, Gerbini, Gela, Biscari, Comiso and Pachino, before he headed towards Naples, where his Spitfire was pursued by a dozen FW190s which he managed to outdistance.

Sqn Ldr O'Neill led four Spitfires of 1435 Squadron on an early morning, long-range sweep between Sicily and Pantelleria next day (12 April), meeting a Ju88 at sea level some 10 miles south-west of Cape Granitola. The Spitfires gave chase,

O'Neill (EP658/V-F) and his No2, Sgt W.N. Harrison (EP834/V-Q), both opening fire from about 450 yards and seeing strikes on the bomber before the engagement was broken off over the Sicilian coast. Meanwhile, a Walrus of the ASR Flight was out searching for the crew of a missing Beaufort, three Spitfires of 1435 Squadron providing escort. Comiso aerodrome was the specified target during the afternoon for eight Spitbombers (four/229 led by Sqn Ldr Smart, four/249 led by Wg Cdr Ellis) while eight fighters from the two squadrons provided escort, one of which had to return early owing to engine problems, a second escorting it back to Malta. The fighter-bombers meanwhile found Comiso obscured by cloud and instead attacked railway sidings and factory buildings at Pozzallo. Half the bombs were seen to explode within the designated area, the remainder falling harmlessly in the harbour. Accurate light flak was experienced during the attack although none of the aircraft were shot down. However, when about 15-20 miles south of Pozzallo on the return flight, Sqn Ldr Tommy Smart was heard to call over the R/T: "Its off the clock – I am going to bale out." A few seconds later he was seen to bale out of his Spitfire (EP716/X-A) from 800 feet and hit the sea with his parachute streaming behind him. His companions circled the scene but were not able to locate him. A second Spitfire had been hit during the bombing attack although it was able to land safely. It would seem that Bf109Gs from III/JG27 were in the area, although not spotted by the Spitfire pilots, since Oblt Günther Hannak, 7 Staffel's Kapitän, claimed two Spitfires shot down for his 46th and 47th victories. If this was the case, then it would seem that he was responsible at least for the loss of 229 Squadron's CO. At 1705 two Spitfires from 229 Squadron took off to search for Sqn Ldr Smart but when 45 miles north-east of Malta the pilots saw a rescue launch being attacked by four Bf109s. Flt Lt R. Brown (EP669/X-C) climbed and attacked one of the Messerschmitts, firing three short bursts before it evaded and disappeared. He made no claim but Y Service later confirmed that a Bf109 had been damaged in this engagement. Ten minutes later two more Bf109s were seen at 3,000 feet and although they attacked the launch, HSL128, they failed to hit it; the skipper, Flt Sgt L.G. Head, recalled:

> "Three runs were made by the fighters but on each attack the launch manoeuvred away from the incoming shells and bullets and the enemy fighters failed to score a hit."

There was further action next day (13 April) following an afternoon raid on the aerodrome at Pantelleria by eight Spitbombers from 229 and 249 Squadrons led by Wg Cdr Ellis. Approaching from the south out of the sun the fighter-bombers released their bombs from 10,000 feet, six being seen to explode among four tri-motor transports believed to have been Ju52/3ms. Others were observed to burst near the entrance to an underground hangar. As the Spitbombers left Pantelleria, a single Macchi attacked one of 229 Squadron's aircraft, EP842/X-D flown by Plt Off J.M.W. Lloyd, from above and behind, inflicting damage to its starboard elevator before being chased away by another. A few minutes later, Flg Off Les Gosling (EP606/X-P) in one of the escorting Spitfires sighted a Macchi, possibly the same aircraft, at 6,000 feet some three miles south-east of the island and made a stern attack, firing three two-seconds bursts and closing to 50 yards. Strikes were noted on the fuselage behind the cockpit and the Macchi dived away. Seven Spitfires of 126 Squadron were airborne to cover the return of the Spitbombers, Flg Off Alex Vale (ER647/MK-Z) also reporting contact with the Macchis, one of which he claimed damaged. Although identified as MC202s, the fighters

encountered were in fact the new MC205Vs from 17°Gruppo which had just come
into service. Six of the new aircraft had scrambled on the approach of the Spitfires,
the pilot involved in attacking the 229 Squadron aircraft apparently reporting that
his victim crashed into the sea, thus recording the MC205V's initial victory.

At Luqa during the morning, it proved to be unlucky 13th for two pilots in
particular when a PR Spitfire – BR656 of 683 Squadron flown by Plt Off L.M.
Gilchrist – swung on landing and crashed into a stationary Spitfire IX
(EN146/MK-X) in which Sqn Ldr Urwin Mann was sitting, awaiting permission to
take off. 126 Squadron's CO suffered burns to his face and arms when his aircraft
burst into flames, and he was rushed to hospital, as was Gilchrist, who was
severely burned. Since their burns required specialist treatment both were
evacuated by air to the UK, command of 126 Squadron passing to the senior flight
commander, Flt Lt Hugh Jackson, who was promoted accordingly. The next two
days were relatively quiet, four long-range Spitfires from 185 Squadron flying an
early morning sweep on 14 April to within five miles of Malita di Porto Salvo on
the toe of mainland Italy. Two single-engined fighters were sighted at a distance
north of Syracuse but no engagements developed. Next day a total of 28 Spitfires
from 126, 185, 249 and 1435 Squadrons were airborne in relays between 1135 and
1400 on offensive sweeps over south-eastern Sicily as diversion for US bombers
raiding Catania. The Spitfires overflew the aerodromes and harbours within their
range but saw no enemy activity. Reconnaissance Spitfire IVs from 683 Squadron
and F-5 Lightnings from the USAAF's 3rd Photographic & Mapping Unit also
flew sorties over the target area.

There was an escalation in aerial activity on 16 April, stirred up by the approach
of two RN destroyers – HMS *Palladin* and *Pakenham* – heading for Malta from
the north-west following an attack on an Italian convoy, a total of 29 Spitfire
sorties being flown during the morning. At 0610, a Ju88 from II/KG76 was sighted
by patrolling Spitfires from 229 (now led by the newly promoted Sqn Ldr Heppell,
formerly of 1435 Squadron) and 1435 Squadrons flying at 1,500 feet about ten
miles west of Empedocle. The eight Spitfires climbed and attacked in line astern,
Sqn Ldr Heppell (EP702/X-E) leading the attack with Flg Off Idema (EP264/X-
X), Plt Off Robinson (EP448/X-A) and Plt Off J.A. Collis (EP305/X-Y). Three
from 1435 Squadron led by Sqn Ldr O'Neill (EP658/V-F), with Plt Off L.A.
Stewart (EP290/V-M) and Sgt Thomson (EP834/V-Q), followed closely on their
tails, all pilots reporting hits on the unfortunate aircraft which turned on its back
and dived into the sea, its starboard engine a mass of flames. A second Ju88 –
F1+BS of 8/KG76 flown by Htpm Heinrich Oldendorf, the Staffelkapitän – was
sighted at 0730 flying at low level by four Spitfires from 249 Squadron, about 15
miles off the coast near Sciacca. The Spitfires climbed and attacked in turn
although the leader failed to manoeuvre into position to open fire. By the time he
had turned to make a second run, the bomber, with its port engine on fire, had
levelled out and ditched in the sea. Return fire was experienced from both dorsal
and ventral positions, Flg Off Hap Kennedy's aircraft (EP712/T-C) sustaining
some damage, as he later reported:

> "I was Tiger Red 3, airborne at 0645 to escort a destroyer off Granitola,
> proceeding to Malta. We flew at deck level and sighted a destroyer off
> Sciacca. When approaching it, we saw a Ju88 flying east at 800 feet which
> we immediately engaged. I climbed and attacked second, firing four bursts
> totalling eight seconds of cannon and MG from starboard and port quarters
> astern, observing strikes on the port engine and port wing tank of the Ju88.

There was accurate return fire and my aircraft was ineffectively hit in the oil tank. The Ju88 was partly on fire at this time and with Red 2 [Plt Off Oliver, EP188/T-Y] and Red 4 [Plt Off Costello, BR565/T-T] attacking, it ditched in the sea quickly. We didn't wait to see if there were any survivors, but escorted the destroyer towards Malta until relieved by Spitfires of 229 Squadron. Returned to base at 2,000 feet. Landed at 0915."

Having again been hit by return fire, Kennedy later ruefully recalled his encounters with Sicily-based Ju88s:

"I had attacked three Ju88s, a German bomber with excellent rear gunners, and on each occasion all of them had put holes in my Spit before they went down into the sea." [1]

The demise of the two Ju88s was witnessed by the pilots of five MC202s of 151°Gruppo and nine MC200s from 54°Stormo, who were en route to Pantelleria from Sicily. The Italians reported seeing the first Ju88 fall into the sea in flames, and the second with two Spitfires on its tail. They attacked and claimed to have shot down one of the Spitfires into the sea. In fact, it was Sqn Ldr Heppell's aircraft which was hit, bullets smashing into his instrument panel and holing his port wingtip. Heppell and his No2, Plt Off Robinson, turned to face their attackers, Heppell seeing his fire entering the Macchi on its starboard side from cockpit back to tail. Robinson also reported seeing strikes on one at which he fired. Both were credited with damaging their opponents but, unbeknown to them, one of the Macchis crashed into the sea. Meantime, the 1435 Squadron patrol encountered three of the MC200s – apparently those flown by Ten Torselli, Sottoten Pozzoli and Serg Aldo Barbaglio of 160^Squadriglia – but identified by the RAF pilots as G.50s, which were flying at 3,000 feet. One was attacked by Sqn Ldr O'Neill, who reported scoring hits on its fuselage and tail before it made off for land at high speed. The other two Macchis then encountered Sqn Ldr Heppell's damaged Spitfire limping back to Malta, one carrying out an attack which wounded him in the thigh, chest and arm. The Italian pilot reported that the Spitfire had been set on fire but, despite this exaggerated claim and his wounds, Heppell was able to fly back to Luqa and land safely. Serg Barbaglio later related that the three Macchis had also sighted some twin-engined aircraft – presumably Beaufighters – escorting the convoy, while Spitfires patrolled above. Barbaglio fired at two of the twin-engined aircraft and reported that one left the formation trailing grey smoke, but was then attacked by a Spitfire which he managed to evade by diving towards the sea and safely reached Sciacca, only to find that his companions were missing. Both, however, had landed their damaged machines at Pantelleria, from where they were flown back to Sciacca aboard an SM82.

At 0755, four Spitfires from 185 Squadron saw a yellow smoke float and three people in the water clinging to what appeared to be a raft, and were presumed to be the crew of the Ju88 shot down by 249 Squadron. They signalled the position to the nearby destroyer although the German airmen were not picked up. A few minutes later a FW190 was sighted five miles south of Cape Granitola, flying eastwards at 1,000 feet. Flt Lt Withy (EP791) and Plt Off L.M. McKee (EP709) attacked from 400 yards, seeing strikes on its starboard wing root. The FW190 took evasive action by diving away but when at 400 feet it was attacked by Sgt C. Cross

---

[1] see *Black Crosses off my Wingtip*.

(EP520) with unobserved results before it finally disappeared in thick haze. As a result of these actions, Vice-Admiral Malta sent a message of appreciation to Air Vice-Marshal Park:

> "I am extremely grateful for the fighter cover this morning. It undoubtedly stopped *Paladin* being attacked."

The AOC responded accordingly:

> "Many thanks for your message of appreciation which has been passed to the fighter squadrons. They will be pleased to learn that their patrols kept all enemy aircraft attacks from destroyer."

The following two days were relatively quiet, eight Spitbombers from 185 and 229 Squadrons raiding the seaplane base at Syracuse and a nearby chemical factory during the early afternoon of 17 April. No enemy aircraft were encountered by the fighter-bombers or their escort, while bombs were seen to fall within the target areas. An evening raid against Biscari aerodrome was mounted by a further eight Spitbombers from 126 and 1435 Squadrons. At least four bombs fell on the aerodrome and a further four in the southern dispersal area. Next day (18 April), eight Spitbombers from 229 and 249 Squadrons visited Ragusa where a factory and the railway sidings were bombed. Explosions were seen to erupt among buildings and near misses on four oil tanks in the factory area. All aircraft returned safely from these operations which saw a complete lack of aerial opposition. The only other incident of note on 18 April was the rescue of four members of a ditched Wellington from their dinghies by an ASR Walrus amphibian (W3012 flown by Lt(A) Pursall) from Malta, which had been escorted to a position near the island of Linosa by four Spitfires of 249 Squadron. Flg Off Hap Kennedy was the first to sight the three dinghies, in which the downed airmen had survived since the night of 14/15 April, and directed the Walrus to make a successful landing and rescue.

With the defeat of the Axis armies in Tunisia, the Germans and Italians endeavoured to airlift as many of their troops back to Sicily as they possibly could, employing large numbers of Ju52/3ms, SM75s, SM82s and giant six-engined Me323s in this task. With Allied air supremacy in the area, the risks were high. On 10 April, American P-38 pilots had claimed 18 Ju52/3ms out of an estimated 50 encountered over the Sicilian Strait, together with eight of the escorting fighters, while later that same day a further air convoy had been intercepted by another group of P-38s which claimed 11 Ju52/3ms and two of the escort. Next day a further 21 Ju52/3ms plus six of the escort were claimed by P-38s in the same general area. On 18 April, US P-40s initially claimed an amazing 145 Ju52/3ms and their escorts shot down, this figure being whittled down to a still incredible 75 after scrutiny of individual claims.

It was the turn of South African Kittyhawks of 7SAAF Wing to join the turkey shoot on 19 April, claiming 13 Ju52/3ms and two SM82s out of a large formation encountered near Pantelleria. Malta's Spitfires effectively missed out in the slaughter of the transports, although on this latter date two from 229 Squadron, fitted with long-range tanks, had encountered the air convoy north of Pantelleria just before the South Africans struck. Mistakenly identifying them as Ju52/3ms, Plt Off Max Lloyd (EP842/X-D) and Sgt Rainald Salzman (EP790/X-K), approached two stragglers flying at sea level. Lloyd raked one, an SM82, from astern, following which it ditched in the sea. The crew were seen abandoning their sinking aircraft, and were later rescued by an Axis craft. Meanwhile, Salzman saw numerous strikes on the fuselage of his victim, a Fiat G.12, and set its port engine on fire. The stricken transport dived into the sea. No survivors were seen. A little earlier two other Spitfires from 229 Squadron flown by Flg Off Les Gosling (EP606/X-P) and his No2, Sgt A.J. Clayton (EP955/X-V), had met two Ju88s flying at 1,000 feet as escort to two flak ships, some 15 miles north-west of Pantelleria. Gosling attacked one of the bombers from astern, strikes being seen all over it and the port wing fuel tanks caught fire before it dived into the sea. He then attacked the second Ju88 from the port quarter, closing to line astern while Sgt Clayton did the same from the rear port quarter. Numerous strikes were seen and its starboard engine was set on fire. After jettisoning six external bombs, the bomber crashed into the sea in flames just after two of the crew baled out. Both aircraft were from III/KG76. Following these latest successes, the AOC sent a message to Krendi Wing:

> "Well done 229 Squadron. The destruction of four enemy aircraft this morning without any losses is excellent proof of straight shooting and good team work on the part of all pilots who were in combat."

A sortie by two Spitbombers from 249 Squadron during the morning was frustrated by poor visibility, but a larger strike in the afternoon by six from 126 Squadron led by Sqn Ldr Jackson and five from 1435 Squadron led by Wg Cdr Thompson achieved a measure of success. The power station complex at Cassibile was again the target, where one bomb was seen to burst in the middle of a workshop, causing a column of smoke, while others were seen to explode near the power station. A Spitfire from 1435 Squadron strafed a building east of the target from which light flak had been experienced, and there was also light ground fire from the ridge on the north side of the valley. A Spitfire of 126 Squadron suffered minor damage but was able to return safely. A dozen Spitbombers (six/185 led by Flt Lt Knight, six/229 led by Flt Lt Brown) with four fighters as close escort and four more as rear cover, targeted the power station and other installations at Porto Empedocle the following afternoon (20 April). Most of the bombs fell in the target area, some exploding near the power station, others near factory buildings and railway sidings. Light and heavy flak was experienced and again one Spitfire, a 229 Squadron aircraft, was slightly damaged. A long-range patrol by four Spitfires of 1435 Squadron next morning (21 April) sighted the remains of a ditched transport aircraft, believed to have been a Ju52/3m, between Pantelleria and Sicily. Only the tailplane was visible. Small-scale sweeps were carried out by flights of Spitfires during the day, none of which made contact with enemy aircraft. Four from 229 Squadron sighted an unidentified aircraft approaching from the north, which turned out to be friendly, and then, on returning to Malta at the end of their patrol, they were vectored onto another unidentified aircraft five miles west of Gozo which was also friendly. One of 683 Squadron's Spitfire IVs was sent to search for signs of a missing Baltimore during the late afternoon, joining two other Baltimores in this task, but saw nothing.

Shortly after dawn on 22 April, two long-range Spitfires from 249 Squadron were airborne, tasked to carry out a sweep along the east coast of Sicily as far as the Lipari Islands, where aerial activity had been reported. At 0700, an aircraft identified as a Ju52/3m was seen five miles off Riposto, flying south-west at sea level. Flg Off Hap Kennedy (AB535/T-Z) attacked and destroyed this transport which was in fact an SM82 of SAS. Thirty minutes later three Ju52/3ms were sighted south of Alicudi, flying westwards also at sea level, and these were also shot down, two by Sqn Ldr Lynch (EP829/T-N) and the other by Kennedy. All four fell in flames, as recorded by the latter in his subsequent report:

"I was Tiger Green Two, airborne 0610 on a long-range offensive sweep. We flew at deck level north-east around Cape Passero, then turned north up the east Sicilian coast. When we were opposite Riposto, about ten miles offshore, I sighted an aircraft flying south at deck level between us and the shore. I attacked immediately, identifying it as a Ju52, and after a one-second burst from port quarter astern (cannon and MG) setting the port engine on fire, the enemy aircraft dived into the sea. No survivors. We then continued north at deck level to Taormina, where we turned and climbed north-west overland, going down to deck level when we reached the sea again at Lipari Islands. We proceeded north-west to Alicudi, just south of which I sighted three more aircraft flying west at sea level. We overtook these, identified them as Ju52s, and I attacked one of them, firing a one-second burst of cannon and MG from port quarter astern, setting the port engine of the Ju52 on fire and it immediately crashed in the sea. Tiger Green One, Sqn Ldr Lynch, destroyed the other two Ju52s similarly. There was no return fire, no evasive action and no escort with any of the Ju52s. We then turned south, climbing hard to 22,000 feet over Sicily and returned via Comiso to Malta. Landed 0825."

In the afternoon a dozen Spitbombers from 229 and 249 Squadrons, plus their escort, led by Wg Cdr Ellis again raided the Syracuse seaplane base. Direct hits were claimed on factories and warehouses and, as one pilot remarked, ". . . the base became a mass of flames while smoke rose to 1,000 feet". Although heavy and medium AA fire was experienced none of the Spitfires was hit. There followed a further Spitbomber raid shortly thereafter, when five from 126 Squadron (Sqn Ldr Jackson) and six from 1435 Squadron (Sqn Ldr O'Neill) bombed dispersed army huts a few miles east of Pozzallo. Poor visibility obscured observation of the results of the attack. The main task for the Spitfires on 23 April was protection for a convoy approaching from the south, relays of aircraft flying escort throughout the morning. There were no incidents during these patrols.

Following a relatively quiet day on 24 April, 249 Squadron despatched two long-range Spitfires on an offensive sweep over eastern and north-eastern Sicily early next morning, meeting a twin-engined aircraft identified as a Ca313 (possibly a Ca311 of 87^Squadriglia OA) flying at 700 feet and patrolling over half a dozen small craft west of Cape Milazzo. The Spitfire leader, Sqn Ldr Lynch (EP829/T-N), immediately made a quarter head-on attack, seeing strikes on the fuselage. He then attacked from astern, causing pieces to fly off and a fire started in the starboard engine. A further attack set the port engine ablaze and the stricken aircraft dived into the sea in flames. The pilot of the other Spitfire, Flt Sgt Cruse, fired one burst from long range with unobserved results. No survivors were seen. Later in the morning a dozen Spitbombers drawn from 126 and 1435 Squadrons, with an escort provided by four IXs, bombed a factory, the railway sidings and a power station at Marzamemi. Arriving over the target at 1130, the Spitbombers dropped 20 250-lb bombs and three direct hits were observed on the main factory building and on a shed alongside, while further explosions were seen near the power station and the railway line, which resulted in flames and columns of smoke rising to a great height. Fairly intense light flak was experienced although none of the Spitbombers was hit.

A further fighter-bomber raid was launched next morning (26 April), when the seaplane base at Augusta was attacked by a dozen Spitbombers (six/229, six/185) while four more acted as top cover, and a further four as rear cover. Bombs were seen to fall on the submarine base and E-boat berths and among oil tanks. Although heavy and medium flak was experienced, this was late and inaccurate. Other Spitfires carried out sweeps between Cape Granitola and Pantelleria, and in the Sicilian Narrows, but no sightings were made. Lampedusa aerodrome was the target for a dozen Spitbombers from 229 and 249 Squadrons during the afternoon of 27 April, when bombs were seen to fall among transports believed to be SM81s dispersed on the west side of the airfield. Another burst was seen within 50 yards of a large aircraft, possibly a Fiat G.12, on the southern side. Top cover Spitfires sighted a single unidentified fighter over the target area at 20,000 feet but no contact was achieved before it disappeared out to sea. Earlier in the day, a patrol from 185 Squadron spotted two small unidentified vessels close to the coast of Pantelleria but no attack was carried out due to poor visibility in the area.

249 Squadron added to its laurels on 28 April, when two Ju52/3ms were shot down during an early morning sweep by Sqn Ldr Lynch (EP829/T-N) and Plt Off A.F. Osborne (AB535/T-Z). Having taken off at 0535 for a sweep along the Sicilian coastline, the two long-range Spitfires encountered the first Ju52/3m at sea-level five miles north of Cape Cefalu. Lynch attacked from the rear quarter with a four-second burst, seeing strikes on the fuselage and centre section; the transport started to steam petrol from its starboard engine and headed for the coast, but suddenly dived into the sea. Osborne then spotted another Ju52/3m a mile further out to sea, and made a full beam to quarter astern attack, gaining strikes on its fuselage. Lynch then joined in the attack, and saw his fire hitting the windscreen and fuselage before Osborne fired a second burst from the port quarter, following which it followed its companion into the sea. On their return to Malta, Lynch reported:

"As soon as my Junkers crashed, I went off to see how my No2 was doing. I found him attacking his Ju52 and we finished it off together."

These two victories were assessed to be the 1000th and 1001st aircraft shot down by Malta-based units since the start of the war. Soon after they landed from this historical flight, Sqn Ldr Lynch received a congratulatory message from the AOC:

"Congratulations to your Squadron on destroying the thousandth Bosche shot down by the Royal Air Force, Malta. The Squadron has kept its magnificent record."

Shortly thereafter, four long-range Spitfires from 229 Squadron sighted a 2,000-ton vessel about ten miles south-west of Cape Granitola, and nearby a stationary destroyer. Neither of these vessels was attacked but their location was reported to Ops, Beaufighters being sent out to deal with them. Soon after midday, a force of Spitbombers (nine/1435, three/126) was despatched to bomb targets at Syracuse, the majority of the bombs being aimed at the E-boat base. Direct hits were claimed on the wharves and it was believed a vessel was hit and set on fire. Another force of Spitfires (eight/249, four/229) was sent to patrol over south-eastern Sicily to provide a diversion for US bombers raiding the Messina Ferry docks, but no enemy aircraft were seen. It was a different story for the bomber force however, the raid being challenged by five MC205s, four D.520s and two MC200s of 161°Gruppo over the target area, the Italian pilots claiming five of the B-24s shot down and probably a sixth.

Sixteen miles south-west of Cape Granitola, a large, two-masted schooner was sighted by two long-range Spitfires of 126 Squadron on the morning of 29 April, Flg Off John Hodges (ER647/MK-Z) attacking with cannon and machine-gun fire. A fire was seen to erupt, followed by an explosion with flames and debris to mast height. The second Spitfire did not attack as the schooner was soon burning fiercely and members of the crew were seen jumping overboard. During mid-afternoon four patrolling Spitfires of 185 Squadron were vectored onto an unidentified aircraft approaching the island, which turned out to be friendly. The month ended relatively quietly for Malta's Spitfires, the only incidents occurring when four from 185 Squadron located two destroyers between Cape Bon and Pantelleria. The warships opened fire but the Spitfires easily evaded and returned with their sighting report. These may have in fact been Royal Navy vessels, 249 Squadron being ordered to send four aircraft to provide escort as they later approached Grand Harbour from the west. Two hours later, four more aircraft from 249 Squadron took off for a sea-level sweep along the east coast of Sicily. Near Marzamemi a stationary submarine was sighted and attacked by Flt Sgt Dean Kelly, whose cannon-fire appeared to have had little effect. One of the Spitfires, EP188/T-Y, flown by Flt Sgt Don Cruse, failed to return and was last seen as the section turned into the coast at Marzamemi, where in fact it crash-landed, the pilot being taken prisoner. Although no enemy aircraft had been seen, it would seem likely that Cruse was shot down by a Bf109G of II/JG27 since Fw Josef Brändle reported shooting down a Spitfire east of Cape Gallo.

The Germans continued to reinforce Sicily and, during the month II/ZG1 arrived with its Bf110s from the Eastern Front, joining the Geschwader's Me210-equipped III Gruppe at Palermo, from where the Bf110s of III/ZG26 were also operating. In addition to air and sea convoy escort duty, the twin-engined Zerstörer were required to defend the Palermo area from ever increasing attacks by USAAF bombers from North Africa. Another unit to arrive was I/SchG2, which flew in from Tunisia, where it had operated Bf109Es in the ground-attack role, but was now hastily re-equipped with FW190 fighter-bombers at its new base, Gerbini.

May opened quietly for Malta's Spitfires, the only offensive operation being carried out by two aircraft of 126 Squadron flown by Flg Off Alex Vale (AB536) and Plt Off J.R. Le Jeune (AR595) who encountered a goods train with six trucks near Marzamemi. Strikes were seen on the trucks and the engine, which came to a stop, enveloped in steam. Two neighbouring signal boxes were also strafed and set on fire, while a military car was similarly attacked before the Spitfires returned home. Four sorties were flown by the PR Spitfires covering the harbours of Naples, Taranto, Reggio, Messina, Palermo, Trapani, Augusta, and Syracuse. One PR aircraft, flown by Flt Sgt Snowden, developed engine trouble on returning to Malta, four Spitfires from 1435 Squadron being sent to escort it back to Luqa, where it landed safely. Next day was even quieter and not one offensive sortie was flown, but on 3 May a total of 19 Spitbombers from 185, 229 and 249 Squadrons, escorted by four fighters from the latter unit, took-off at 1810 to raid Lampedusa aerodrome, where 36 bombs were dropped around the perimeter, in the centre of the aerodrome, and along the north side, but results were unobserved owing to the haze over the target area. Intense and accurate flak was experienced, but none of the aircraft were known to have suffered damage although one of 229 Squadron crashed on landing, the pilot of which was shaken but unhurt. PR Spitfires and F-5 Lightnings were again very active and covered the majority of aerodromes and harbours in Sicily and south-eastern Italy.

The latest convoy reached Malta on 4 May, the squadrons flying 50 protective sorties during the day without incident, and no enemy aircraft were encountered. Later in the afternoon, however, four Spitfires of 185 Squadron were vectored to intercept an enemy aircraft which approached Malta from the north, obviously a reconnaissance machine from Sicily, but this turned back five miles from the coast. The Spitfires were unable to engage. Two Spitfires from the same unit had earlier been despatched to search for an overdue PRIV of 683 Squadron, but it transpired that the pilot, Flt Sgt Snowden, had overshot Malta owing to the thick haze over the island and had landed instead at Castel Benito on the Libyan coast. Next day, Flt Lt M.G. Brown RCAF flying Spitfire PRXI EN263[2] on a sortie to Palermo, was attacked by four Bf109s but these were "easily evaded."

Flights of Spitfires patrolled over Grand Harbour throughout the daylight hours of 5 May as cover for the convoy. At 1240 the alarm was sounded when a number of enemy aircraft – Bf109s – were reported approaching from the north, then crossed the island at great height, obviously on reconnaissance. Three patrolling Spitfires of 185 Squadron were vectored to intercept but failed to make contact. Meanwhile, AA batteries engaged the Messerschmitts as they came within range, gunners believing their shooting to be spot on when one of fighters was seen to leave the formation, trailing smoke. This was Oblt Günther Hannak's 7/JG27 aircraft (apparently a brand new aircraft still bearing its delivery call sign, GP+12) which had, according to Hannak, sprung an oil leak. With smoke filling his cockpit, Hannak glided his aircraft down to Luqa, where he made a successful wheels-up landing, the 47-victory ace and Staffelkapitän becoming a prisoner. His interrogation officer later wrote:

> "The P/W took off with nine other aircraft of his Staffel from Biscari at about 1225 to carry out a reconnaissance over Malta. P/W was the Staffelkapitän and led the formation. He was flying an aircraft belonging to another member of his Staffel as his own aircraft was unserviceable. The aircraft GP+12 had been flown to Biscari earlier the same morning. The formation flew more or less due south and made landfall approximately over Comino at about 22,000-24,000 feet. It was at this point that P/W noticed that his cockpit was filling with smoke and oil was splashing on his windscreen. He estimated his speed at this time at 500kph. The aircraft continued crossing the island and when over the sea P/W realised it was hopeless to continue. He jettisoned his cockpit cover, which also carried away his oxygen mask, and he had a temporary black-out. When he came to he had lost height and was at about 16,000 feet. He then cut the engine and circled over the sea. Finding that his engine would no longer work, he picked the largest aerodrome he could see and glided down with wheels up. P/W states that he saw a small formation of Spitfires below him as he came in over the island. They were climbing but he does not think they saw him. At no time was P/W's aircraft hit by AA fire, so far as he is aware."

Hannak also commented that the Malta pilots seemed to be young and inexperienced, and not inclined to dogfight. He had formed this impression after

---

[2] The Spitfire PRXI was an unarmed version of the IX modified to carry cameras, a type just reaching Malta.

having flown over the island about ten times. On the other hand he admitted that the AA defences were formidable. The Messerschmitt suffered only minor damage and was subsequently repainted in full RAF colours – while another Luftwaffe ace had been removed from the war.

As dawn broke on 6 May, four Spitfires of 185 Squadron took off on an offensive patrol and, at 0725, they came across an F-boat about 15 miles south-west of Marettimo. All four aircraft attacked with cannon and machine-gun fire, reporting strikes on the stern and amidships, and when it was left it appeared to be listing to starboard. On the way home one Spitfire (EP554) developed engine trouble and Flt Sgt George Mercer baled out into the sea 30 miles north of Gozo. The Canadian was picked up by HSL107 from Malta, as he later reported:

> "When about 35 miles from base glycol started to pour out of my exhaust, so I began to climb steeply, keeping coop-top closed as a protection against the glycol. At 2,000 feet glycol was nevertheless pouring into my face so I decided to jettison the coop-top and bale out after having trimmed the aircraft nose-heavy. I rolled aircraft to the right and fell out without trouble. After a few seconds drop I pulled the rip-cord, but the shroud lines became entangled with my left foot which made the parachute stream instead of opening. Pulling myself up the shroud lines, I was able to slacken them and free my foot. The parachute then opened. I was not wearing flying boots but walking shoes. On the way down, when nearing the sea, I threw down my gloves hoping they would help to indicate my height, and gave the parachute release a twist. I hit the water feet first, went over on my back and released the parachute. Feeling for my dinghy, I found that the dog-lead was broken, having probably been caught up on the seat adjustment lever. As I had not inflated my Mae West, I was able to submerge and recover the dinghy. The cover was ripped off easily and the dinghy inflated upside down. I had no difficulty in righting it and climbing in. The other three Spits circled around the dinghy until the HSL arrived about one and a quarter hours later."

The skipper of HSL107, Flt Lt E.G. Price, commented:

> "Pilot came aboard smoking a cigarette. No injuries. He was taken below and warmed up with hot drinks etc. Launch returned to base arriving back alongside at 1053. No snags encountered. Everything went like clockwork."

While the rescue was in progress, 16 Spitfires from 229 and 1435 Squadrons flew an offensive patrol over southern Sicily, keeping an eye on Comiso in particular, as a diversion for a raid by US bombers. No enemy aircraft were sighted. Four IXs of 126 Squadron were despatched at 0910 to provide withdrawal cover for the sweep, meeting four Bf109Gs flying at 20,000 feet near Comiso. The Messerschmitts were engaged, Flt Lt Ron Green (EN287/MK-F) observing strikes on one which he claimed damaged. Flights of Spitfires continued to provide patrols over the convoy in Grand Harbour, twice being vectored to investigate aircraft approaching from the north but no contacts were made. Another patrol, from 1435 Squadron, was ordered to locate and escort a US B-24 of the 343rd Bombardment Squadron which was in difficulties following a bombing raid on Reggio di Calabria. The damaged bomber was sighted 15 miles north of Gozo flying at 15,000 feet, and escorted to Luqa, but it was apparently unable to manoeuvre to carry out a landing and continued flying south, losing height. The pilot managed to ease it into an easterly turn and eventually ditched 500 yards offshore near Kalafrana. On ditching, the bomber broke up but nine of the crew were able to escape to be rescued by HSL128 and Seaplane Tender ST338. The latter craft, skippered by Flt Sgt Ted Shute, arrived at the floating wreckage and started to pick up survivors, some from the sea and others from the top of the aircraft but it was found that one member of the crew was trapped inside the fuselage. Shute then attempted to roll the aircraft over by gradually increasing power on both engines of his craft, but was unable to do so. At that moment, HSL128 (Flt Sgt Head) arrived and picked up another three of the survivors; nine men were saved and one was lost.

Two Spitfires of 229 Squadron fitted with long-range tanks set out just after 0630 on the morning of 7 May, Flg Off Les Gosling (EP720/X-E) and his No2 Sgt F. Stevenson briefed to carry out an offensive patrol over the Sicilian Narrows. An hour into the patrol, while flying at deck level, they spotted a Fi156 Storch about ten miles south-west of Marsala at about 15,000 feet. Climbing rapidly to engage, Gosling closed in and fired a short burst of cannon fire (eight rounds), following which the German aircraft burst into flames and dived into the sea. No evasive action nor return fire was seen, and there were no survivors. The Storch was apparently making the long ferry flight from Tunisia, and was piloted by Uffz Karl Kulla of II/JG77. This was just one of a stream of Axis aircraft evacuating to Sicily, a Ju52/3m carrying Hptm Erich Irps of Stab/JG53 and two officers of I Gruppe also being lost over the sea. Two Spitfires from 126 Squadron which attempted to carry out another offensive patrol in the early afternoon were forced to return owing to unsuitable weather.

Two Spitfire pilots of 126 Squadron, Flt Lt J.D. Keynes and Sgt Greenwood, were unlucky next day (8 May) when they narrowly missed engaging "a large unidentified aircraft" seen during a patrol between Marsala and Marettimo. As they manoeuvred to get into position they lost sight of the aircraft – probably another Ju52/3m, or even a Me323 – which was flying at sea level. There were no other sightings and the disappointed duo returned to Malta. Patrols from 229 and 185 Squadrons intercepted unidentified aircraft during the day, one in the morning and the other in the afternoon, both of which turned out to be friendly. Flt Sgt Jerry Billing and Plt Off Tom Nesbitt of 126 Squadron were also scrambled on the approach of a reconnaissance Ju88, which was reported south of Filfla, but heavy cloud prevented any contact being made.

Twenty-four Spitbombers drawn from 185, 229 and 249 Squadrons escorted by eight fighters set out to bomb the power station at Porto Empedocle at 1450. Many bombs were seen to burst immediately south of and around the power station, and several more on the buildings just east and west of the target, while others were seen to explode on the railway lines and two near misses were observed on E-boats in the harbour. Fairly intense AA fire was experienced but none of the Spitfires was hit, and no enemy aircraft were seen. During the early evening a Beaufighter crew radioed Malta advising they were in trouble. Four Spitfires of 185 Squadron were diverted to locate the distressed aircraft, arriving in time to see the crew bale out about 40 miles east of Malta. Both crewmen were seen to be dragged by their parachutes before being lost from sight. The Spitfires searched until relieved by others from 229 Squadron. Wreckage of an aircraft, an empty dinghy and an oil patch were all that could be seen. A search by an HSL failed to find any sign of the crew.

There was a further Spitbomber mission on 9 May, a dozen from 229 (now commanded by Sqn Ldr Blair White) and 249 Squadrons attacking the sulphur refineries at Licata shortly after midday, also targeting the railway station and sidings. A direct hit was observed on the east end of the railway bridge over the

River Salso, and others fell among the railway installations and between the refineries. There was little AA opposition and none from the Axis air force. Earlier, Spitfire patrols were alerted on the approach of an estimated nine enemy aircraft, five Bf109s being sighted over the eastern end of Malta at 23,000 feet but no contact was made. A Spitfire (EN188) of 4 Air Delivery Unit en route to Malta from North Africa failed to arrive, and it was learned later that the pilot had become lost in bad weather, flown too far north and missed both Malta and Sicily, and eventually crashed near Naples. Aircraft from Malta searched for signs of wreckage in vain, as did HSL128, unaware that it had strayed many miles off course.

Early next day (10 May), two Spitfires flown by Sqn Ldr Lynch (JK465/X) and Flg Off H.C. Holmes (AB535/T-Z) of 249 Squadron took off on an offensive sweep along the east coast of Sicily. At 0700 two Z506Bs were seen five miles east of Riposto, flying north-east at 500 feet. The two seaplanes of 186^Squadriglia RM flown by Cap Antonio Blengini and Sottoten Amedeo Fiorillo had just taken off to escort a Fiat RS14 on an anti-submarine patrol when intercepted by the two Spitfires, which were flying at deck level. The Spitfire pilots jettisoned their long-range tanks, climbed, and then carried out individual attacks from dead astern. Both seaplanes dived into the sea in flames[3]. Immediately afterwards a third seaplane was sighted approaching from the south-west at 500 feet and was identified as another Z506B, but was it fact the RS14 of 170^Squadriglia RM flown by Serg Magg Sergio Residori. Sqn Ldr Lynch turned in behind it and attacked with cannon and machine-gun fire, closing to 100 yards, following which it caught fire and spun into the sea with the loss of the crew[4]. Shortly afterwards a Ju52/3m was seen at deck level, heading south-west, and Flg Off Holmes made a stern attack but his cannons jammed. Lynch then carried out a port rear quarter attack whereupon the transport aircraft dived into the sea in flames. Before its demise, Lynch observed return fire from the side windows of the doomed machine. The action was not yet over, since three Bf110s were then seen in the vicinity, flying at 1,000 feet, and Lynch made a port rear quarter attack on one. At this crucial stage one cannon jammed and he expended all his remaining machine-gun ammunition on the Messerschmitt, observing numerous strikes on its port wing and port side of the fuselage. It was last seen heading for the coast, losing height and may have been the aircraft flown by Oblt Ferdinand Glanz of III/ZG1, who was reported to have been wounded in an action north-east of Catania.

Four Spitfires of 185 Squadron were airborne at 1115 to search for a dinghy reported south of Filfla, which they located. An HSL was directed to the position but the dinghy was found to be empty. Biscari was the target for eight Spitbombers of 126 and 1435 Squadrons, escorted by seven fighters, during the early afternoon. At least 14 bombs were seen to burst in the middle of the aerodrome and near the dispersal areas. As the formation set course for home they were trailed by six Messerschmitts but these did not make any serious attempt to intercept, four Spitfires of 126 Squadron acting as withdrawal cover. Wg Cdr Warburton, the CO of 683 Squadron, was again in the thick of the action, his Spitfire PRXI (EN263)

[3/4] Z506B (186-1, MM45398) was crewed by Cap Blengini (pilot), Sottoten Luigi Gay (co-pilot), 1°Av/Radio Emanuele Liso, Av/Mot Antonio Bettuzzi, and Av/Arm Giuseppe Trapani; and Z506B (186-2, MM45469) by Sottoten Fiorollo (pilot), M.llo Pasquale Vincenzetti (co-pilot), Ten Vascello Capponi (Chief Observer 83°Gruppo RM), Av/Mot Pasquale Rossano, Av/Radio Angelo Alula, and Av/Arm Angelo Lanna; while the RS14 (170-3, MM35675) was crewed by Serg Magg Residori (pilot), Serg Antonio Bergami (co-pilot), Av/Mot Alberto Barroni, Av/Radio Giovanni Zacco, and Av/Arm Simone Pellegrino; there were no survivors.

being intercepted by four MC202s off Cape Bon, although he was able to escape their advances. The previous day he had similarly avoided being intercepted by a fighter while over Sicily.

With Tunisia now completely in Allied hands, all remaining Axis air units had withdrawn to various bases across the Mediterranean, and all three Gruppen of JG53 were back in Sicily; Hptm Friedrich-Karl Müller's I Gruppe moved to Catania, Stab (Obstlt Baron Günther von Maltzahn) and II Gruppe (Maj Gerhard Michalski) to Comiso, while III Gruppe remained at Sciacca under Maj Franz Götz. The only other Luftwaffe fighter units currently on the island were Stab JG27 (Maj Gustav Rödel) and II/JG27 divided between Trapani and Palermo under Hptm Werner Schroer, and 7 and 9 Staffeln of III/JG27 at San Pietro (8/JG27 had recently moved to Crete). Malta's mainly inexperienced Spitfire pilots again faced a formidable challenge had they but known the capabilities and reputations of their new adversaries, many of whom were amongst the top-scoring pilots of the Mediterranean theatre of operations.

11 May saw another escort for US bombers raiding Catania, a total of 47 Spitfires from all five squadrons being airborne between 1055 and 1345. The first wave of bombers was met over Cape Passero, the second wave being contacted 20 miles west of Syracuse. Escort was provided until the bombers were 50 miles into their homeward journey, one flak-damaged B-24 being escorted by a section of 1435 Squadron Spitfires to Luqa, where it crash-landed with a wounded crewman on board. About a dozen enemy fighters were sighted in small groups and 1435 Squadron had inconclusive combats with two MC202s just before reaching Catania, and a single Bf109G shortly after turning for home. Two more Messerschmitts attempted to attack the damaged B-24, the rear gunner of which claimed hits on both the attacking aircraft. During these skirmishes one Spitfire was shot down with the loss of Jamaican-born Flg Off Ron Martin (EP833), probably the victim of one of the Macchi pilots. 1435 Squadron despatched a further four Spitfires to search for their missing pilot, but nothing was seen. The US Ninth Air Force sent a congratulatory message to the AOC Malta following this operation:

> "Sincere thanks for fighter escort which is first time in the history of this Command that we have received such support. All crews were enthusiastic and said that presence of your fighters gave them confidence and contributed greatly to success of mission."

Another Spitfire pilot was lost next day (12 May), Sgt James Yates of 185 Squadron falling victim to AA fire during an offensive patrol by four of 185 Squadron who strafed a goods train seen at Lazzaro, south of Reggio di Calabria. The locomotive was left in flames and the whole train was seen to be burning fiercely as the Spitfires departed. Only three rendezvoused, and during a search for their companion, the missing aircraft (EP709) was seen burning in the sea off Lazzaro; the body of the 20-year-old from Tadworth in Surrey was recovered from the sea and buried at Catania. Later, 16 Spitfires of 229 and 249 Squadrons carried out low-level sweeps over Cape Scalambri, Comiso, Avola, Noto and Cape Passero, while three more from 126 Squadron provided top cover. Two enemy fighters were seen but could not be intercepted.

Malta's Spitfires again provided cover for a US Ninth Air Force raid on Sicily, the B-24s attacking Augusta harbour during the early afternoon of 13 May. A total of 42 Spitfires drawn from 126, 229, 249 and 1425 Squadron were airborne to rendezvous with the bombers, although three were obliged to return early. Close escort was provided from Cape Passero to the target area and to 50 miles east-south-east on the return journey. Several enemy fighters were observed at different times but none attacked the bombers until 1400, two Bf110s approaching when the formation was about 15 miles east-south-east of Augusta. These were engaged by Flg Off Alex Vale (EN287/MK-F) of 126 Squadron who scored hits on both aircraft as they dived away. Next day (14 May) it was the turn of the Spitbombers to take up the offensive, eight from 185 Squadron and three more from 126 Squadron departing Malta at 1455 to bomb Comiso, six fighter providing close and rear cover. The target area was covered in cloud but there were sufficient gaps for the Spitbombers to release their bombs, bursts being observed in the centre of the runway. One aircraft of 185 Squadron returned early to Hal Far with engine trouble, Plt Off M.B. Zobell RCAF jettisoning his bombs over the sea but one hung up, this detonating on touch down, causing the Spitfire (BR194) to crash-land. The Canadian pilot survived the harrowing experience without injury, but 15-year-old Vincent Carabott from Zejtun, who was working nearby, was seriously injured by the bomb explosion. Enemy fighters were reported as the raid withdrew and the high cover IXs of 126 Squadron were vectored to the St Paul's Bay area but no sightings were made. On returning from one of these operations the wing of Flg Off Vale's aircraft (JK139/MK-A) hit a Maltese labourer, Carmelo Mifsud from Qormi, who was working on the runway at Luqa; he died in hospital next day. A second labourer, 17-year-old Joseph Testa, also from Qormi, was seriously injured. These incidents involving Maltese civilians injured by landing Spitfires were the only ones recorded at Malta for the whole year of 1943 – and, strangely, both occurred on the same day.

The ensuing few days were fairly routine for Malta's Spitfires: seven of 185 Squadron with long-range tanks fitted escorted four Beaufighters to the Pantelleria-Cape Granitola area on 15 May but no sightings were made; later, sweeps over the Cape Passero, Comiso, Gela, Cassibile and Cape Scalambri areas brought a similar lack of targets. Next day (16 May) nine Spitbombers visited Pozzallo where bombs were seen to burst amongst buildings and huts to the east of the town. There was only slight AA fire and no fighter opposition. Defensive patrols were occasionally alerted to approaching aircraft but no sightings were achieved, while a dinghy search ten miles south of Kalafrana resulted in only an oil patch being investigated. There occurred some excitement for four Spitfire pilots of 1435 Squadron on 17 May during an early morning sweep along the east coast. They thought their luck was in when they sighted what they took to be a Z506B over shipping in the harbour at Augusta and immediately gave chase, but did not attack when the seaplane – in fact, an RS14 of 170^Squadriglia – was recognised as an ASR machine by its red crosses and white paintwork. However, soon afterwards a tank landing craft full of troops was seen in the harbour, and this was strafed. Hits were observed all over the craft and a fire broke out in its stern area. Although flak was experienced from both the craft and shore batteries, none of the Spitfires was hit. Two small sweeps on 18 May again produced no reaction from enemy fighters. The only action during the day resulted when three Spitfires of 126 Squadron led by Sqn Ldr Jackson escorted a PR aircraft of 683 Squadron to Pantelleria. A small vessel of about 500 tons was sighted just south of the island and was thoroughly strafed by Plt Off Geoff White (EP444/MK-D) and left in flames. Constant heavy and light AA was experienced from shore batteries but none of the Spitfires were hit. Another PR Spitfire, BS358 flown by Plt Off G. Craig, carried out a reconnaissance of Naples harbour where it was attacked by two FW190s but managed to escape undamaged.

126 Squadron was again involved in a successful operation on the morning of 19 May, two Spitfires flown by Plt Offs White (AB536/MK-J) and Le Jeune (JG869/MK-B) strafing a coaster south of Cassibile just before crossing the coast, where they immediately encountered a goods train. This was also attacked with cannon and machine-gun fire, the locomotive being left enveloped in smoke and steam. A lorry was then sighted travelling down a road north of Marzamemi, which was given a burst of cannon fire, forcing it to stop. Two more Spitfires, these from 249 Squadron and carrying bombs, visited Canicatti in the afternoon. One bomb was seen to burst among trucks in the railway yard, the other apparently scoring a direct hit on the outer support arch of a railway bridge. Due to heavy cloud in their designated target area, two other Spitbombers from the same unit were forced to return with their bombs intact, which they jettisoned near Filfla before landing. Shortly before dusk, the alarms sounded at Malta when two aircraft were reported approaching from the south-west, these eventually crossing the south coast of Gozo at deck level. They were believed to be Me210s. Four patrolling Spitfires of 185 Squadron were in the area but in poor visibility were unable to intercept.

The Luftwaffe at last put in an appearance when eight Spitbombers, drawn equally from 185 and 229 Squadrons, bombed Comiso during the late afternoon of 20 May. Bombs were seen to explode in the centre of the runways and among buildings and, as the last aircraft departed, a fire was seen 800 yards west of the centre of the aerodrome from which huge columns of dark grey smoke were rising. As the Spitbombers withdrew, four Bf109Gs dived on them but broke away without pressing home the attack although one aircraft of 229 Squadron returned with bullet holes in its wings, another with flak damage; neither of the pilots, Flg Off Idema and Sgt E.R. Davies, was wounded. The escorting fighter Spitfires from 185, 229 and 1435 Squadrons sighted the Messerschmitts but were not able to engage.

Shortly after dawn on 21 May the air raid siren was sounded at Malta as enemy aircraft were detected approaching from the north. Twenty Spitfires – eight each from 229 and 1435, plus four from 249 – were scrambled at 0555, meeting 36-plus FW190 fighter-bombers of II/SchG2 with a Bf109G escort from I and II/JG53 north of the island at 19,000 feet, but some of these managed to evade the interception and crossed the coast to dive-bomb Hal Far and Takali. For the first time since December 1942 bombs fell on Malta. At Hal Far six bombs fell on the aerodrome destroying three FAA Albacores and one Spitfire, damaging a second Spitfire and causing superficial damage to a paint store and a Nissen hut. Two naval ratings were badly injured. At Takali the damage was less severe, four bombs falling on the aerodrome which caused slight damage to a Beaufighter. There were no civilian fatalities although one Maltese was injured. Several bombs fell harmlessly into the sea south-east of Gozo. Meanwhile, in the air, battle was joined. One section of 229 Squadron climbed to 24,000 feet and intercepted one formation of raiders 50 miles north of the island, causing them to break, while the other section engaged 16 FW190s about ten miles to the north. Flt Lt A.G. Russell (JK428/X-A) reported shooting down one and damaged a second; Flt Sgt Williams (ES233/X-X) also claimed one shot down, and yet another was damaged by Flt Sgt H.S. Wells (EP698/X-N). Sgt Davies (EP843/X-F) and Sgt P.S. Jennings (ER305/X-Y) meanwhile tangled with the Messerschmitt escort, each claiming one damaged although both Spitfires sustained slight damage in return; Jennings also claimed a FW190 damaged. JK366/X-C flown by Sgt Taylor was also slightly damaged, while EP842/X-D crashed and exploded on land east of Zejtun although its pilot, Plt Off John Collis, baled out safely from 4,000 feet and landed in a field. He had just attacked a FW190 from astern and, as his victim took evasive action, the Spitfire's engine cut. However, he may have been the victim of Uffz Hermann Witt of 5/JG53 who claimed a Spitfire shot down. Both sections of 1435 Squadron engaged the escort but inconclusively, as the Meserschmitts avoided combat. The 249 Squadron section attacked one group of six FW190s flying at 9,000 feet north of the island, Sgt R. Keating (EP833/T-F) reporting strikes on one before it evaded and dived away, although another 249 Squadron pilot, Flg Off John Beatson RAAF, noted: "Four FW190s off Gozo. Intercepted badly and they got away easily." But there were losses and two FW190s failed to return, both Obfw Otto Sorg of 5 Staffel (WkNr50188) and Fw Herbert Cornrade losing their lives, while a third fighter-bomber (WkNr55988) crashed at Catania with a wounded pilot, Lt Werner Fowé, also of 5 Staffel. A Messerschmitt of 2/JG53 also failed to return, Uffz Breiling being reported missing in Black 6 (WkNr15295), presumably the victim of either Sgt Davies or Sgt Jennings. The alarm was sounded again at 0937 when a further small formation of enemy fighters approached from the north – possibly searching for the missing pilots – but these turned away before crossing the coast. Four Spitfires of 249 Squadron were airborne and vectored in their direction. Two unidentified fighters were seen at 9,000 feet about six miles north of Gozo but contact was lost due to the haze.

The Luftwaffe reacted again next day (22 May), when eight Spitbombers of 1435 Squadron led by Sqn Ldr O'Neill attacked Gela's satellite landing ground at Ponte Olivo during the evening, bombs being seen to fall near buildings on the northern end. The escorting Spitfires from 126 and 1435 Squadrons, including six IXs led by Wg Cdr Thompson providing top cover, were engaged by an estimated 20 Bf109s and FW190s as the raid withdrew. Two Spitfires of 126 Squadron were shot down by Obfw Herbert Rollwage (his 38th victory) and his wingman, Fw Theo Reiter (his first), both of 5/JG53, 21-year-old Northumbrian Flt Sgt James Rennolds (JK816/MK-K) being killed while Flg Off John Hodges (EN142/MK-W) was able to bale out; the latter was seen to get into his dinghy about ten miles north of St Paul's Bay, over which one of his colleagues maintained cover until relieved by four from 185 Squadron. Meanwhile, Flt Lt Keynes (JK672/MK-E) of 126 Squadron gained some degree of revenge when he shot down Obfw Karl Marten (WkNr15292) of 5 Staffel; although wounded, Marten was able to bale out successfully off the Sicilian coast and was rescued from the sea by an Axis craft. Newly commissioned Canadian Plt Off Lem Barnes (JK139/MK-A) claimed a second Messerschmitt as damaged, while Plt Off R.H. Pearce (EP652/MK-D) reported hits on another. As the Spitfires returned to Malta, HSL107 was on its way out to rescue Hodges, who recalled:

> "When I was 15 miles west of St Paul's Bay my engine started to give trouble and I climbed to 3,000 feet. The engine then stopped. I took off my helmet and undid my straps, slid the hood back and turned the machine over onto its back, at 120mph. As I fell out the dinghy pack caught on the hood. The machine started to go down vertically and I managed to kick myself free and forced myself out at 1,500 feet. The parachute opened straight away. I saw my aircraft go in underneath me. While going down I had to blow up my Mae West because the CO_2 bottle did not work. I released my harness just as I hit the water and inflated my dinghy easily. I had difficulty getting into the dinghy because my left leg was caught in the parachute shrouds. I had six two-star cartridges which I let off at intervals. The rescue launch saw four and came straight to the spot and picked me up after I had been 25 minutes in the water."

After all the excitement of the previous two days, there followed a relatively quiet period for Malta's Spitfires, although small-scale forays by Messerschmitts and FW190s continued against the island. Seven Spitfires of 126 Squadron were scrambled on the morning of 23 May on the approach of intruders, Flg Off F. Cattermoul engaging a FW190 at which he fired an ineffective burst. Others patrolled off St Paul's Bay but no further contact was made and no raid on Malta materialised. Later, in the afternoon, four more from 126 Squadron led by Flt Lt Ron Green were scrambled, meeting two Bf109Gs north of Gozo. These were pursued but could not be caught, and were probably decoys for two others which attacked Plt Off Geoff White's aircraft JK650, as he ruefully recalled:

> "They came in fast from above – it was their favourite tactic. There was some AA fire below me and I was distracted by this. A 109 was behind me, fortunately firing at long range, and this stuff was exploding way down in front of me. I collected five bullets from him which was pretty fortunate because I wasn't taking any avoiding action until I suddenly saw his tracer coming past me. And then I dived. My radiator was hit and so I 'lost' my engine before I got down to the ground . . ."

The New Zealander was indeed fortunate since it would seem that his assailant was no less an ace than Hptm Friedrich-Karl Müller, Gruppenkommandeur of I/JG53, who claimed a Spitfire shot down for his 117th victory. Shortly thereafter, a dozen Spitbombers (six/229, six/249) set out to raid Lampedusa, where bombs were released over the aerodrome. Heavy AA prevented results being observed.

24 May passed with not much excitement apart from defensive patrols, one of which was vectored onto four Bf109s ten miles north of Gozo although there was no contact. Later, in the afternoon, another patrol chased five Messerschmitts in the same general area but again without success. Next day (25 May), the intruders were more daring, four FW190s crossing over Gozo. A patrol from 126 Squadron attempted to intercept but without joy. Two more unidentified aircraft were seen over St Paul's Bay at 1850, two sections each of two aircraft being scrambled by 185 Squadron, one led by Sqn Ldr Crafts, the other by Flt Lt Henry Withy. As the Spitfires climbed, Withy's aircraft (JK463) was seen to spin away and then dive into the sea ten miles north of Grand Harbour, leaving only wreckage and an oil patch. His loss was believed caused by oxygen failure.

The US Ninth Air Force carried out a further raid against eastern Sicily on 26 May, B-17s targeting Messina. MC205Vs of 1°Stormo rose to meet the heavy bombers and their escorting P-38s, as did MC202s and D.520s of 161°Gruppo from Reggio di Calabria, the Italian fighters claiming 15 victories. Bf109Gs and FW190s also engaged, claiming a further eight for the loss of two Messerschmitts, two FW190s, and, according to Italian records, a He115 flying low over the eastern coast which was surprised by the American fighters and duly shot down. Other US bombers attacked Comiso, Gela and Biscari, 126 Squadron providing six Spitfires as high escort. Led by Sqn Ldr Jackson (BS557/MK-C), the Spitfires encountered some Bf109s at 20,000 feet, one of which the CO attacked only to have his cannons jam. He then fired at a second with machine-guns only but no result was seen. A patrol from 185 Squadron also sighted Messerschmitts but they were too distant to engage.

With the US heavy bombing offensive well under way against the main airfields and other important targets in Sicily, there was scant employment for the Spitbombers and routine defensive patrols continued for the remainder of the month. Few enemy aircraft ventured over Malta although the occasional blip on the radar screens caused Spitfires to be scrambled or patrols to be diverted, albeit without contact. Even the odd small-scale offensive sweep over south-eastern Sicily failed to gain any response. Only on the last day of the month did it seem that some trade would be coming the way of the Spitfire patrols when a 36-plus raid approached from the north-west at 1830. On nearing Malta, the raid split into smaller groups, several of which crossed the coast. Eight Spitfires, four each from 185 and 229 Squadrons, were scrambled to intercept, and a further eight on patrol (four/229, four/1435) were vectored to engage. The 229 Squadron patrol sighted three unidentified fighters heading east over the island at 25,000 feet, then three FW190s appeared at 27,000 feet, Flg Off Les Gosling firing two short bursts at one before they dived away. The 185 Squadron quartet sighted four unidentified fighters at 27,000 feet between St Paul's Bay and Grand Harbour but they were too far away to engage. Similarly, the other 229 Squadron patrol saw four unidentified fighters 3,000 feet above them but again there was no contact. A few bombs were dropped by the raiders, most of which fell harmlessly into the sea but one fell on Valetta causing slight damage.

Aeronautica della Sicilia had at last received reinforcements in the guise of a number of the potent Bf109Gs from its German ally. During the middle of the month the first 'Italian' Messerschmitts had arrived when 150°Gruppo Aut CT commanded by Magg Antonio Vizzotto flew in, its three squadriglie (363^, 364^, and 365^) led by Cap Mario Bellagambi, Ten Giuseppe Giannelli and Ten Fausto Filippi, respectively. The Gruppo had initially trained on Bf109Fs, losing four of its pilots in accidents. More Bf109Gs were to follow, II/JG53 handing over 23 of its aircraft to Magg Aldo Alessandrini's 3°Gruppo Aut CT (153^, 154^, and 155^Squadriglie) at Comiso, the occasion being filmed by German propaganda photographers. JG53, however, could not spare pilots to serve as instructors and the Italians "were left more or less to their own devices, since no organised training course was planned. During the next three days the 3°Gruppo alone was involved in three crashes during conversion training, one with fatal results."[5] With the Italians now operating Bf109Gs, there were other changes afoot among Sicily's air defenders and, at the end of the month, the Messerschmitts of 7 and 9 Staffeln of III/JG27 transferred to Tanagra, north-west of Athens, where they were reunited with 8 Staffel before moving to Argos in the Peloponnese for duties over the Aegean.

---

[5] see *Jagdgeschwader 53 Volume Two*.

CHAPTER III

THE FALL OF PANTELLERIA

June 1943

"During the defensive action against the bombing attack on the Straits of Messina the fighter element failed in its task. One pilot from each of the fighter wings taking part will be tried by court-martial for cowardice in the face of the enemy."

Reichmarschall Göring to Sicily's Jagdgeschwadern, 25 June 1943

June opened quietly for the defenders of Malta, though the first Spitfire patrol was airborne at 0445 providing escort for incoming shipping and protection to those already in harbour. These patrols continued throughout the day and were not called into action until late afternoon when, at 1800, a raid comprising at least 22 fighters and fighter-bombers was detected approaching the island at between 25,000 and 30,000 feet. Three IXs of 126 Squadron were airborne and were ordered to intercept, while four Vs of 1435 Squadron and four IXs of 185 Squadron were scrambled to assist. The Messerschmitts crossed the coast and dropped four bombs which fell into the sea north-east of Grand Harbour, one section of three fighter-bombers being sighted by the 126 Squadron patrol, Plt Off Lem Barnes (EN532/MK-W) closing to 400 yards from dead astern on one as he fired, observing white smoke issuing from it as it turned on its back and dived towards the sea following his attack. He fired several further bursts, the Messerschmitt emitting clouds of black and white smoke as it levelled out at 2,000 feet, a height at which Barnes broke off his attack. He claimed it as probably destroyed; a Messerschmitt of III/JG53 was reported to have belly-landed near Comiso but whether as a result of this combat is not clear. Meanwhile, other Spitfire sections were unable to engage the departing raiders and one aircraft of 1435 Squadron, ES313/V-B flown by Plt Off Ken Chandler RCAF, developed engine trouble and crashed into the sea, the pilot having safely baled out five miles north of St Julian's Bay, although not without some difficulty:

"I rolled the aircraft onto its back. I started to fall out. One of the parachute shoulder straps caught on the hood which I had neglected to jettison. I could not reach the part which was caught as the speed of the fall made it impossible for me to raise my hands. About ten or fifteen seconds passed before I could wrench myself free. Suddenly, I found I was free. I pulled the ripcord and as I felt the jerk of the parachute, I saw my aircraft diving far below me. When I was six feet above the water I released my parachute. My dinghy remained attached to my Mae West which I had forgotten to inflate. However, my Mae West kept me afloat until I could inflate my dinghy. The water was calm and warm. Meanwhile, the rest of my section was circling my position."

A nearby minesweeper was promptly on the scene as were two ASR launches:

> "The minesweeper lowered a boat which started to pull towards me, but two
> HSLs arrived, converging on me. One [HSL166] threw a line, which I
> caught and I was pulled alongside and helped aboard. I was in the water for
> only about ten minutes."

The raiders returned next day (2 June), 21-plus being reported approaching Grand
Harbour at 1820, two Spitfires of 229 Squadron's standing patrol being vectored
onto them while eight more (four/229 and four/126) were scrambled. The original
pair spotted three of the fighter-bombers at 22,000 feet when 30 miles north of the
island, Sgt Salzman (JK428/X-A) making a head-on attack on one which dived
away without apparently being hit. A second Messerschmitt was seen attempting a
diving attack but this was evaded. By this time the 126 Squadron section had
sighted about a dozen scattered fighters, identified as Messerschmitts, FW190s and
Reggianes, about ten miles north of Gozo, Flg Off Alex Vale (EN402/MK-R)
gaining hits on a Bf109G before it escaped southwards; Vale annotated the relevant
logbook entry accordingly: "Y Service made it a probable", although it has not
been possible to ascertain the identity of his opponent. The 229 Squadron section
also sighted three fighters north of the island but were unable to engage.

The Luqa Wing now had a new Wing Leader, Wg Cdr W.G.G. Duncan Smith
DSO DFC having arrived from the UK at the end of May, replacing Wg Cdr
Thompson who had come to the end of his operational tour. On the morning of 3
June, Wg Cdr Duncan Smith (flying AR560 which still carried its previous owner's
markings, JMT) and 1435 Squadron's CO, Sqn Ldr O'Neill (JK282/V-U) set off at
0800 to escort a PR Spitfire flown by Wg Cdr Warburton to Syracuse. Having
uneventfully achieved their brief, O'Neill observed a schooner off Cassibile which
was duly strafed. It was the turn of Malta's fighters to go on the offensive, Wg Cdr
Duncan Smith leading 23 Spitfires – eight each from 229 and 249 Squadrons, plus
seven IXs of 126 Squadron – on a sweep over the Comiso area. South of Cape
Scalambri at 1210, while flying at 25,000 feet, at least six Bf109Gs of 5/JG53 were
encountered and engaged by 126 Squadron, Sqn Ldr Jackson (EN402/MK-R) and
Plt Off Geoff White (BS557/MK-C) each claiming one destroyed, while three
others were claimed damaged by the Wing Leader (JK650/JMT), Sgt C. Clay
(EN390/MK-G) and Sgt Jock Davidson (JK611/MK-M). One Messerschmitt was
shot down, that flown by Uffz Herbert Stracke who baled out of Black 7
(WkNr18097) over the sea and was drowned. In return, one of the Spitfires was
claimed shot down by Fw Theo Reiter. Of the action, Wg Cdr Duncan Smith wrote:

> "Leading 126 Squadron round Comiso, and not finding any enemy fighters,
> I re-crossed the Sicilian coast; then, climbing hard to 12,000 feet, turned the
> Squadron back inland again. As I expected, the ME109s were following us
> out so we had a splendid jump on six of them. I got in two good bursts at the
> leader, knocking several bits off his tail and port wing, and my No2
> damaged another. Other pilots destroyed two 109s and damaged two more.
> This success was the reward of a planned variation in our normal tactics." [1]

The Luftwaffe retaliated in force next day (4 June), a 35-plus fighter sweep being
detected approaching Malta from the north at 0745, but these did not cross the

---

[1] see *Spitfire into Battle* by Grp Capt W.G.G. Duncan Smith DSO DFC.

coast. Three sections of Spitfires were patrolling as the raiders approached, although one of 185 Squadron's IXs was obliged to return early, leaving the remaining three to engage a formation of Bf109Gs from I/JG53 escorting a number of FW190s of III/SKG10 at 26,000 feet, 10-15 miles north-east of Zonqor Point. The leader, Flt Lt Hal Knight (EN533/GL-N), closed to within 50 yards of one Messerschmitt which became enveloped in smoke and went down in flames. A patch of oil was seen on the surface of the sea some 15-20 miles north-east of Grand Harbour where it was believed the fighter had crashed. His victim was almost certainly Uffz Hans-Wilhelm Ellers of 1/JG53 whose aircraft (White 3/WkNr18082) failed to return from this sortie. Meanwhile, Sgt W.A. Cruickshank (EN404/GL-W) made a stern attack on a second Bf109, closing to 200 yards, and saw numerous strikes on its wings and fuselage before it fell away, apparently out of control. He was credited with its probable destruction, probably the aircraft (Yellow 6/WkNr18064) flown by Oblt Heinz-Günther Hennig of 3 Staffel who, despite being wounded, managed to reach Comiso safely where an emergency landing was successfully achieved. A patrol of 126 Squadron Spitfires also met five Messerschmitts – apparently from 4/JG53 – about ten miles north of Grand Harbour, Sgt E.A. Riseley (JK139/MK-A) damaging one. Flt Sgt J.E. Staples (JK611/MK-M) saw two more on the tail of his leader, Flt Lt John Keynes, attacked and forced them to break away but it was too late to save Keynes whose aircraft (EN532/MK-W) crashed into the sea, the 59th victim of Oblt Fritz Dinger. Staples then engaged two more Bf109s and saw strikes on the port wing and tailplane of the one he attacked before it escaped at low level. A rescue launch covered by a section from 126 Squadron was sent out to search for the missing 29-year-old pilot from Surrey, but to no avail – only an empty dinghy was sighted in the area of the combat. Some two hours later, Sqn Ldr White (JG838/X-W) led eight Spitfires of 229 Squadron to patrol off Grand Harbour when hostile aircraft were reported approaching. Two FW190s were sighted at 19,000 feet north of the harbour, the CO attacking one of these from astern before making a pass at the other. Although no hits were claimed, the Squadron recorded that "other souces" – presumably the Y Service – later confirmed damage to one of the intruders.

The first elements of 322 Spitfire Wing began arriving from Tunisia during the day, 81 Squadron landing at Takali led by newly promoted Wg Cdr C.F. Gray DFC, the new Wing Leader, while 322 Wing's former Wing Leader, newly promoted Grp Capt P.H. Hugo DSO DFC, was appointed OC Wing. The other four squadrons followed, 152 commanded by Sqn Ldr F.W. Lister, 154 by Sqn Ldr A.C.G. Wenman, 232 by Sqn Ldr C.I.R. Arthur, a Canadian in the RAF known as 'Duke', and 242 led by the Acting CO, Flt Lt G.F. Silvester, while Sqn Ldr W.M. Whitamore DFC arrived to take command of 81 Squadron. To make room for the new arrivals, 185 Squadron left Hal Far, its birthplace, and moved to Krendi, the move coinciding with the arrival of a new CO, Sqn Ldr I.N. MacDougall DFC relieving Sqn Ldr Crafts who was tour-expired. The new CO recalled:

" . . . I joined 1435 Squadron on 10 May and after about a month with that Squadron I took over 185, which was then at Hal Far and was equipped with Spitfire IXs. These were the first to arrive at Malta, I think, and they were a great improvement on the Spitfire Vs with which the other squadrons were equipped. By then, the days of the great blitzes on Malta were over. The Germans were licking their wounds after being thrown out of North Africa and most of their aerial activity consisted of reconnaissance, to see what the Allies would do next, and limited fighter opposition to the American heavy bomber raids which were building up in frequency against targets in Sicily and southern Italy. We had to leave Hal Far and form a Wing with 229 and 249 Squadrons at Krendi. This was an airfield on the southern side of the island, which had been hewn out of the side of a hill. There were bad crosswinds, the runways were narrow and the two 'home' squadrons turned out to watch us land. They had had a fair number of accidents and they looked forward to seeing 185 disgrace itself. But all the 185 pilots were very much on their mettle and both on our arrival and for the next week or so flew carefully and broke nothing. But eventually they relaxed and we had the same frequency of accidents as the other two squadrons."

At the same time as 185 Squadron received its new CO, Flt Lt McKee was promoted to lead B Flight and Flt Lt T.W. Wilmot DFM arrived to take over A Flight. 152 Squadron received some sad news when Sqn Ldr Lister was informed that a vehicle carrying some of his NCO pilots had crashed while making its way to the debarkation port in Tunisia, resulting in the deaths of three and minor injuries to five others, although the latter would all soon rejoin the Squadron at Malta.

The advance elements of another Spitfire Wing – 244 – also began arriving, Wg Cdr Peter Olver DFC leading 145 Squadron (Sqn Ldr L.C. Wade DFC, an American in the RAF with 22 victories, two shared) and 601 Squadron (Sqn Ldr J.S. Taylor DFC, 14 victories, two shared) to Luqa, from where it was to operate in preparation for the forthcoming invasion. The arrival of Wing's other components, 92, 417 RCAF and 1SAAF Squadrons, was imminent; all were veterans of the Desert fighting. With so many Spitfires now assembled at Luqa, the resident squadrons – 126 and 1435 – moved to the new strip at Safi and consequently became the Safi Wing under Wg Cdr Duncan Smith.

At 1345 on 5 June, four Spitfires of 229 Squadron led by Flt Lt Les Gosling were despatched to search for a missing Spitfire, JK310 of 232 Squadron, overdue on its flight from Tunisia, which was reported to have crashed on the small island of Linosa after its pilot, Plt Off Edward Cam, had advised Malta that his engine had cut. Orbiting the island at 4,000 feet and finding no ground opposition, the Spitfires dropped down to deck level and soon located the wrecked aircraft, which was minus one wing, but there was no sign of the pilot, who had in fact been taken prisoner. As they overflew the north-west corner of the island, one of the pilots reported suspected machine-gun fire from a blockhouse-type building, the leader ordering two of his section to strafe it before all four returned to Malta. Wg Cdr Ellis led the Krendi Wing comprising 23 Spitfires drawn from 185, 229 and 249 Squadrons on an offensive sweep over south-east Sicily on the morning of 6 June as a diversion for US Liberators which were carrying out raids in the Catania area. Three or four FW190s were sighted near Vittoria but these were soon lost from sight and no other enemy aircraft were encountered. During the mid-afternoon, 16 Spitfires from 185, 249 and 1435 Squadrons were patrolling when 15-plus Bf109s were sighted over Zonqor heading north-east at 31,000 feet. Flg Off Matt Reid (EN401) of 185 Squadron attacked one with five short bursts from rear quarter and astern but was unable to observe any tangible result. He then followed another Messerschmitt for about ten miles when he saw Flt Sgt G.R. Nadon RCAF (EN404/GL-W) attack one at 28,000 feet. The Canadian fired a long burst from astern, closing to 200 yards. Strikes were seen on its starboard wing root, following which the Messerschmitt rolled over and went into a spiral dive, emitting black smoke. Nadon was credited with its probable destruction and also fired at two others, though without observing any result.

An alert was sounded at Malta just after 0815 on 7 June when 12-plus enemy fighters crossed the coast at 30,000 feet on reconnaissance. Eight Spitfires were on patrol and a section from 185 Squadron spotted one unidentified fighter at 25,000 feet, diving away northwards. It was not pursued. A second alert was sounded at 1424 on the approach of at least two fighters, but these also evaded a section of patrolling Spitfires. The siren went again at 1612 when a formation of nine fighters was detected approaching from the north-east although these did not cross the coast. In the other direction eight Spitbombers of 1435 Squadron led by Wg Cdr Duncan Smith, with six IXs of 126 Squadron as cover, bombed factory buildings and railway sidings at Pozzallo. Explosions were seen among warehouses. During the raid, top cover was informed of enemy fighters in the Comiso area, aircraft returning from reconnaissance over Malta, but these were not sighted.

Six IXs of 126 Squadron carried out an offensive sweep early on the morning of 8 June, crossing the Sicilian coast between Sampieri and Pozzallo at 24,000 feet and patrolled the Comiso area. Although they failed to draw up any fighters from the airfield, eight were seen off Cape Scalambri heading eastwards at low level, while a further 15 Bf109s were sighted up-sun. However, these failed to attack and the Spitfires returned safely to Malta. The Messerschmitts were probably part of the formation II/JG53 which attacked four Spitfires of 229 Squadron 15 miles south of Cape Scalambri at 0855, damaging two including that flown by Sgt J.D. McKenzie (JK646/X-V), who turned for home, losing height and glycol and eventually baled out ten miles north of St Paul's Bay, from where he was picked up by HSL107 after 25 minutes in the water. Maj Michalski, the Gruppenkommandeur, and Uffz Hermann Witt of 5 Staffel each claimed a Spitfire destroyed in this action. Two further air raid alerts were sounded at Malta, one just before midday when nine fighters approached, including at least three FW190s, and the other during early evening when about six Bf109s were sighted off Zonqor Point. Although Spitfires were up on both occasions, no engagements occurred. Meanwhile, 683 Squadron's Flt Sgt Lewis (EN412) narrowly avoided becoming a victim of the Messerschmitts when he was jumped by two when photographing over Messina. Having evaded these, he safely returned to Malta despite a faltering engine.

9 June proved to be a relatively busy day for Malta's Spitfires, seven from 126 and 249 Squadrons being airborne when two unidentified high-flying fighters approached Gozo shortly after dawn but, although sighted high above the 126 Squadron patrol, were not engaged. Later in the day, a total of 16 patrolling Spitfires drawn from 81, 126 and 154 Squadrons were alerted to the possibility of a raid, although this did not materialise. Two IXs of 81 Squadron had returned early due to various problems and a third (EN254) crashed on landing, although the pilot, Sgt H.L. Theobald, was unhurt. At midday no fewer than 40 Spitfires took to the air (twelve/229, twelve/249, nine/185 including seven IXs, and seven IXs of 126), all fitted with medium-range fuel tanks, as escort to US Liberators tasked to bomb Catania and Gerbini airfields. The Spitfires of 126 Squadron, when over Catania at 22,000 feet, saw ten Bf109s, five FW190s and six MC202s some five miles out to sea, preparing to attack the bombers. The Spitfires climbed to engage but the enemy fighters declined combat and dived away. At 1325, when returning to Malta, another formation of fighters was sighted south of Cape Passero by 126 Squadron and Sqn Ldr Jackson (EN295/MK-P) led an attack on these, chasing a Macchi down from 24,000 feet to sea level, firing several bursts and observing strikes on its starboard wing before it evaded and escaped. 185 Squadron also sighted enemy fighters but no engagements developed. Although there were no reported combats for the Spitfire pilots apart from that in which Sqn Ldr

Jackson was involved, Fw Reiter of 5/JG53 nonetheless claimed a Spitfire shot down at 1300. Meanwhile, other Spitfires covered the bombers as they departed Sicily, escorting to Malta three with engine problems and two with flak damage. One of the latter crash-landed at Luqa, its crew suffering injuries during the process. Returning Spitfire pilots reported that the American bombing appeared good, bursts being seen all over both target areas – among aircraft dispersal area and pens, while fires could be seen burning at Gerbini from some 30 miles distant. In fact, at Gerbini all the SM79s of 279^Squadriglia AS were destroyed or seriously damaged. As dusk approached, three unidentified aircraft approached Malta from a northerly direction but did not cross the coast. Three Spitfires of 249 Squadron, scrambled to investigate, failed to sight the intruders.

Gela was the target for ten Spitbombers (six/249, four/185) on the morning of 10 June but, to the attacking pilots, the aerodrome seemed deserted. Two bombs were observed to explode on the south-west end of the runway. Covering Spitfires from 185 and 249 Squadrons similarly reported a lack of activity and all returned safely to Malta. It was the turn of 152 Squadron to supply the fighter-bomber force – eight aircraft led by Grp Capt Hugo – which departed Malta at 1600 to bomb buildings and the marshalling yards at Pozzallo, where two direct hits were reported on a road running east to west from the town. Escorting Spitfires from 81 and 242 Squadrons returned without incident, although one of the former (EN204) had crashed on take-off from Takali, Sgt M.J. O'Grady RAAF suffering minor head injuries when his aircraft hit a truck, then ploughed through two buses just outside 152 Squadron's dispersal before landing on top of one of the latter unit's Spitfires (ER787), which burst into flames. Airmen working on the Spitfire had a narrow escape, all suffering minor burns. The sirens were sounded at Malta at 1455 when three Bf109s approached from the north, crossed the coast over Gozo and turned towards Hal Far before heading out over Grand Harbour, pursued by four Spitfires of 185 Squadron's standing patrol. One of the Messerschmitts was a reconnaissance machine of 2(H)/14 flown by Lt Friedrich Zander, while escort was provided by Obfw Rollwage and Fw Reiter of 5/JG53; the latter recalled:

> "We had just made the turn to stay with the reconnaissance aircraft during its photo run when Rollwage called out a warning. He had spotted 'Indians' above us. The pilot of the reconnaissance Messerschmitt responded with an irritated 'ja, ja' and then he made a half-roll and dive in order to shoot his pictures from a much lower altitude. We stayed with him but unfortunately so did the Spitfires and the reconnaissance machine was shot down as we retired." [2]

Zander had fallen victim to 185 Squadron's Flg Off Hap Kennedy (EN533/GL-N):

> "We were at 31,000 feet. They were perhaps four miles away and already losing height in a wide sweeping turn to starboard over Grand Harbour. They straightened out on a northerly course with their noses down, and I knew they would be exceeding 400 mph. I had the throttle open and I rolled over and headed on a course to cut the angle toward the 109s, which had separated a little. I could see that I was gaining on the nearest 109. We were down to 5,000 feet and our dive had become quite shallow. I could see the Sicilian coast a few miles ahead. Now I was within range at 300 yards, and I let him have a good squirt. The first strikes were on the port radiator from

---

[2] see *Jagdgeschwader 53 Volume Two*.

which white smoke poured, indicating a glycol leak. I knew I had him before the engine broke out in heavy black smoke. At that moment a good burst of tracer went over my starboard wing, quite close to the fuselage. I skidded hard to port, then broke around. But there was no 109, only two Spitfires coming toward me. I thought the nearest inexperienced pilot mistook me for a 109. It happened not infrequently." [3]

Apparently unaware of his mistake, Kennedy's No2, fellow Canadian Plt Off Red Sinclair (EN403/GL-A), claimed to have fired at the Messerschmitt and was subsequently awarded a share in its destruction. Kennedy's report added:

"The ME109 was confirmed by Intelligence as destroyed as they learned that the pilot had baled out ten miles south of Pozzallo." [4]

Four patrolling Spitfires of 249 Squadron were vectored towards at least four enemy fighters which approached within ten miles of Gozo at about 1745 but no contact was made. Four more intruders were detected at 1953. A dozen airborne Spitfires from 81, 232 and 249 Squadrons were unable to carry out an interception although the 81 Squadron section pursued one to just south of Sicily before breaking away. Three IXs of 185 Squadron, again led by Flg Off Kennedy (EN468/GL-J), enjoyed greater success when scrambled at 1650 and were vectored north of Pozzallo where they sighted an ASR Do18 of 6 SeenotStaffel – obviously searching for the missing Messerschmitt reconnaissance pilot, Lt Zander[5] – escorted by a single MC202 which was orbiting 1,500 feet above the rescue machine. Kennedy called Ops for advice and was ordered not to attack the flying boat, whereupon the Spitfires promptly gave chase to the Macchi. Kennedy again takes up the story:

"Red Three, Flt Sgt [A.L.] Sinclair [EN349/GL-C], was closest to the Macchi and attacked first and got in some strikes. I had a good crack from 200 yards. It began to smoke. It was going down. I broke off the engagement as the enemy aircraft was in a gentle dive, engine on fire at about 1,000 feet about six miles off the coast. We were still a few miles off the coast at 1,000 feet. We turned around to head south for Malta. I passed quite close to the Dornier flying boat going in the opposite direction. I knew that there was a custom of chivalry about air/sea rescue operations. That was why I had called Ops. I also knew that the invasion of Sicily was imminent and that some of our boys might be down in the water in the next couple of weeks. But I had mixed emotions as I looked through the perspex for a fleeting second at the pilot of the Dornier." [6]

Sgt P.H.P. Roberts RAAF (EN404/GL-W) fired his guns in anger for the first time when he also opened up on the Macchi, as he later noted "Squirted at 202 but no hits". The third alert of the day was sounded at 1953 when four aircraft approached Malta from the north-west. A dozen Spitfires, four each from 81, 232 and 249 Squadrons, were airborne and the 232 Squadron section sighted three of the fighters at 20,000 feet off Gozo but they dived away before they could be engaged.

[3/4] see *Black Crosses off my Wingtip*.
[5] Despite an intensive search Lt Zander was not found and was presumed to have drowned.
[6] see *Black Crosses off my Wingtip*.

The 81 Squadron quartet also gave chase to the enemy but broke away just south of Sicily and returned to Malta. Due to the increase in the number of Spitfires now resident on the island, some shuffling of units took place to accommodate these, with 1435 Squadron moving from Krendi to the newly constructed airfield at Safi during the day, joining there 126 Squadron which had just moved in. The Station Commander, Wg Cdr Innes Westmacott DFC, a former Malta Hurricane fighter pilot, was there to greet them.

The Fall of Pantelleria

Following the surrender of Axis forces in Tunisia on 13 May, the next stage of the Allies' plan was put into action – the aerial assault against, and ultimate capture of, Pantelleria. Malta's squadrons were not to be directly involved, the main assault being launched by heavy and medium bombers of the NWAAF and A-36A and P-40 fighter-bombers, while escorts to the bombers were provided by P-38Gs, P-40s and US Spitfires of the 31st and 52nd Fighter Groups, the latter units based on the Tunisian coast at Korba under the command of Lt Col Fred M. Dean and Lt Col George W. West respectively. The American Spitfire pilots had performed admirably during the Tunisian fighting, the 31st FG having amassed over 60 victories and the 52nd FG even better with at least 86 in little over five months. Initially, the 52nd was required to provide air defence of Tunis and Bizerta, claiming three raiders in three days (two of these, a Fw190 and a Bf109, were credited to 1/Lt Sylvan Feld, thereby raising his score to nine), leaving the 31st to escort the bombing missions against Pantelleria.

By 6 June, Axis fighters were beginning to put in an appearance as the American bombers relentlessly targeted the fortified island, the Messerschmitts of III/JG53 claiming three Bostons shot down (in fact RAF Baltimores of 18 Squadron), while II/JG27 claimed a Spitfire (credited to Fw Heinrich Steis of 4 Staffel, his 15th victory) and a P-40 for the loss of a Bf109G of 6 Staffel (Lt Hans Nitzsche killed). The Spitfire attacked by Steis was apparently that flown by 2/Lt Frederick O. Trafton of the 308th FS of the 31st FG, who, nonetheless, survived the ordeal. Four MC200s of 3°Gruppo escorted by 21 MC202s from 151° and 153°Gruppi operating from Palermo failed to find the Allied invasion ships approaching from the west and returned with their bombs intact. Next day, III/JG53 claimed a P-40 and a P-38 but lost two of its own aircraft although both pilots survived; II/JG27 also claimed a P-40 but lost two Messerschmitts, one from each of 4 Staffel (Lt Hans-Ulrich Kornstädt PoW) and 6 Staffel (Fw Albin Dörffer PoW). One of the American Spitfire pilots, 1/Lt Robert M. Lupton Jr of the 309th FS, claimed a FW190 damaged during the day. Next day (8 June), there occurred a clash between a dozen Italian Bf109Gs of 150°Gruppo and a formation of MC200s of 3°Gruppo, each mistaking the other for the enemy. One 'Spitfire' was claimed by a Macchi pilot, but one Macchi was shot down into the sea by a Messerschmitt, while another formation of six Bf109Gs of 150°Gruppo, together with 23 MC202s from 151° and 153°Gruppi and 11 MC205V of 1°Stormo, flying a *caccia libera* mission (*Freie Jagd*, free chase) engaged in combat US Spitfires and P-38s which were escorting bombers, six Spitfires and one Lightning being claimed shot down for the loss of two MC202s and their pilots, 368^Squadriglia's CO, Cap Mario Ferrero, and M.llo Elio Cesari, plus two other Macchis severely damaged.

It was not until 9 June, however, that the American Spitfires engaged in major mortal combat. After an aircraft of the 308th FS flown by 1/Lt McMann was shot down off Pantelleria in the morning by a Bf109G (363-7) of 363^Squadriglia flown by Ten Ugo Drago, other pilots from the 308th were sent out to search for signs of their missing colleague (who was later rescued by an Allied craft), these intercepting a mixed force of an estimated 16-20 MC202s – in fact, there were 14 Macchis of 151°Gruppo plus four Bf109Gs of 150°Gruppo. Four Macchis and one Messerschmitt were claimed without loss, a stunning victory for the Spitfires, with Capt Thomas B. Fleming, who was leading, and 1/Lts Edwin Dalrymple, Royal N. Baker, Walter J. Overend and Merritt C. Wolfe claiming one apiece. Two Macchis were actually lost, both Cap Bruno Veronesi, the Gruppo commander, and Sottoten Antonio Crabbia baling out safely, as did the Messerschmitt pilot, Ten Drago, who had just claimed a second Spitfire shot down, another being claimed by Ten Giovanni Chiale. All three downed Italian pilots were later flown back to Palermo aboard an SM81. Among the US P-40 units in action this morning was the 99th FS, the first all-Negro unit within the USAAF, which was attached to the 33rd FG at Fardjouna (Tunisia) for operations; two of its pilots, 1/Lt Spann Watson and 1/Lt Willie Ashley, each claimed a FW190 damaged to open the Squadron's score.[7]

During the afternoon, while escorting B-24s in company with P-38s of the 1st FG, the 308th FS again became involved in combat, this time engaging Bf109Gs of II/JG27 and I/JG53. The Americans reported meeting an estimated 36 Axis fighters and claimed three shot down, one by Capt Fleming for his second victory of the day, another by 1/Lt Overend, also his second of the day, and the third by 1/Lt Alvin D. Callender. Another was damaged by 1/Lt Adrian A. Davis, while the Spitfire flown by 1/Lt Gordon Rich was hit and damaged, necessitating the pilot to bale out into the sea from where he, too, was later rescued, being picked up from his dinghy by an RAF Walrus. The Messerschmitt pilots meanwhile claimed five P-38s and one B-24 shot down, one pilot of 1/JG53 failing to return, Fw Marian Mazurek in White 16 (WkNr15266) of 1/JG53, a 35-victory ace, apparently falling victim to B-24 gunners.

But even greater success was to follow for the Spitfires next day (10 June) when three Bf109Gs and two FW190s were claimed in the morning. Messerschmitts of II/JG27, operating from Trapani, attempted to intercept a formation of B-26s and P-40s. In a disastrous operation for the defenders, II/JG27 lost nine aircraft[8] and their pilots to the combined fire of Spitfires of the 307th FS and P-40s of the 325th FG; 1/Lt John H. White claimed a FW190 and a Bf109, Capt William C. Bryson a FW190, 1/Lt Roland F. Wootten Jr a Bf109, 1/Lt John K. Conley a Bf109, 1/Lt Charlie F. Fischette a Bf109, he and Wootten sharing a probable. 1/Lt Jerry D. Collinsworth probably destroyed another, and damaged a FW190. In return, Lt Willy Kientsch of 6 Staffel claimed two Spitfires (his 31st and 32nd victories) and Fw Heinrich Steis of 4 Staffel a third (his 16th victory), while Hptm Werner Schroer, Kommandeur of II Gruppe, reported shooting down a B-26 and two P-40s in two separate actions, thereby raising his score to 80; pilots of II and III/JG53 claimed a further four P-40s and a B-26; one Messerschmitt of II/JG53 was damaged and force-landed near Modica. II/SchG2 reported that two of its FW190 fighter-bombers had been shot down by Spitfires off Pantelleria with the loss of Fw Walter Koch of 6 Staffel and Uffz August Lutter of 7 Staffel, both of whom were killed.

---

[7] The 99th Fighter Squadron would have to wait until 2 July before chalking up its first victory, when 1/Lt Charles B. Hall reported shooting down a FW190 over Sicily during a bomber escort mission.

[8] 4 Staffel lost Lt Erich Buschek, Uffz Meinhard Mondry, and Uffz Fritz Stumpf; 5 Staffel lost Lt Hans Lewes; and 6 Staffel lost Lt Wilhelm Kuetgens, Uffz Friedrich Cziossek, Uffz Helmut Hefter, Uffz Robert Karlsböck, and Fw Erwin Sinnwell – all of whom were posted missing.

The MC202s of 151°, 153° and 161° Gruppi were similarly decimated when they attempted to engage an evening raid by B-24s and B-26s, seven of the Macchis[9] falling to the Americans for the loss of one Spitfire, although this was reported to have been erroneously shot down by a P-40s of the 99th Fighter Squadron. The downed Spitfire pilot, 1/Lt George Gooding of the 307th FS, was not seen to bale out and his aircraft crashed into the sea. For the 309th FS, Maj Frank A. Hill shot down one Macchi, while others were claimed by Capts Carl W. Payne and Berry Chandler, and 1/Lts Dale E. Shafer Jr (who also reported being attacked by a P-40), Robert O. Rahn, and Donald J. Keith, while 1/Lt James R. Swiger claimed a Messerschmitt. In addition, 2/Lt Leonard H. Meldeau claimed a FW190 probable, and Capt John H. Paulk damaged another Messerschmitt. Italian pilots claimed two Spitfires, one P-38, one B-24 and six B-26s in this action.

The amazing run of victories continued on 11 June, the 31st claiming five Bf109s and two FW190s in two actions during the day – one apiece by Capts Bryson and Collinsworth (FW190) of the 307th, two by 1/Lt Fischette (plus a third damaged) and another by 1/Lt John White (FW190), also of the 307th, and two more by 1/Lts Baker and Derwood K. Smith of the 308th – all achieved for the loss of one Spitfire flown by 1/Lt Monroe P. Smith, who was killed, although three were claimed by JG53 pilots, one by Fw Martin von Vacano of 8 Staffel (his second victory) in the morning, and two in the afternoon battle by Oblt Wilhelm Klein of 1 Staffel (his sixth) and Oblt Franz Schiess of 8 Staffel (his 54th); two Messerschmitts of II Gruppe were lost, Lt Walter Hofmann being posted missing in Black <+1 (WkNr18054) while the other pilot survived a crash-landing near Cape Granitola, in which his aircraft (WkNr15299) was wrecked; a third pilot, from 6 Staffel, made a wheels-up landing at Trapani. These latest victories raised the 31st FG's score for the three-day period to no fewer than 27 MC202s, FW190s and Bf109Gs, mainly the latter. Spitfires of the 52nd FG joined in the action, 1/Lt Robert E. Armstrong Jr of the 4th FS shooting down a FW190 – apparently an aircraft of II/SchG2 flown by Lt Arthur Liedtke of 5 Staffel – which attempted to attack shipping of the invasion fleet; Liedtke was killed. Later, seven Bf109Gs of 150°Gruppo and nine MC202s of 53°Stormo provided escort for nine MC200s and FW190s attacking the shipping, but no losses were reported by the Italians on this occasion. Another unit of Spitfires operating with the USAAF was also active in the area of Pantelleria during the afternoon, when the newly re-formed GCII/7 of the embryonic Free French Air Force met Bf109Gs and FW190s, one of the latter being claimed by Sgt-Chef Louis Kann in co-operation with two American pilots (although the USAAF later denied him a share in the destruction of the fighter-bomber), while Adjt Constantin Feldzer reported meeting a lone Ju88 which he also claimed shot down. Of his recollections of this day, Feldzer later wrote:

> "The weather was very fine, with a cloud layer between 10,000 and 13,000 feet, over which the show of hundreds of planes crossing each other in a ballet shining in the sun, with no enemy planes in view, was somewhat deceiving. 13,000 feet below, a few Italian fishermen were praying to Madonna to give us a quick victory as they had had no drinking water for eight days. They didn't give a damn to whom would possess the island. Their only concern was to get drinking water, Fascist or not. GCII/7 had

---

[9] The missing pilots were Ten Giancarlo Celle of 151°Gruppo; Cap Domenico Bevilacqua, M.llo Paolo Franchi, Serg Rino Nava of 153°Gruppo; and Ten Giuseppe Marazio, Sottoten Iolando Soprani, M.llo Giuseppe Ravasio of 161°Gruppo.

despatched a dozen planes, and circling over these clouds for an hour made one sleepy rather than eager for action. That's how one's attention drops and trouble arrives. For take-off, we had switched on the belly tank, enabling us to drop it in case of combat, keeping the wing tanks full. When the belly-tank was empty, a red light flashed to signal the pilot to switch on the other tanks. That day, bad luck. The bulb of the red light had blown! The engine coughed for a few seconds, then silence. I tried the starter. Nothing. Gliding over a cloudy sea one hundred kilometres from the coast is not as poetic as one would imagine. The most efficient way to restart was to dive vertically, winding the propeller. The engine coughed, sprayed a few puffs of smoke and began to run smoothly."

As he broke cloud coming out of the dive, he suddenly saw below at about 1,000 feet a single Ju88 flying towards Sicily:

"What luck! It was gift of God on a blue tray, an incredible and wonderful gift which came after all I had endured for six months. Thank God for giving me three human lives and a fucking bomber! It was mine, this Ju88. I just had to make a slight change in the course of my dive, so it was no longer a dot in the sky but a plane growing in the middle of my gunsight. Just one correction in the course of my flight. Wait a split second to be sure not to miss, and with my body shaking I fire one long burst with all my guns – the plane shakes and the smell of cordite invades the cockpit. Just time to see the explosion, and I was already 300 feet below and well in front of the blazing Ju88 . . .[10]

On this date P-40 Warhawks of a second Free French unit, GCII/5, flew a total of 54 sorties in co-operation with the American fighter-bomber squadrons.

Thirty-three-year-old, Russian-born Adjt Constantin Feldzer had flown Bloch 152s with GCIII/10 during the Battle of France in 1940, when he claimed a Bf109 shot down. After fleeing to Algeria just before the French capitulation, he and others attempted to reach Gibraltar by sea but were captured and imprisoned. Released in 1942 following the Allied landings, he resumed flying and was posted to the newly reformed GCII/7; he later flew with Normandie-Niémen, the French volunteer group which served on the Eastern Front where he was shot down and spent the remaining months of the war as a POW.[11]

One of the first war correspondents to reach Pantelleria was Alex Clifford of the *Daily Mail*, who graphically recalled events leading up to the surrender and the chaos of the moment:

"Preliminary bombing of the island began on 9 May, and each day that passed saw a stepping-up of aerial and naval bombardment. One by one the little houses of Pantelleria village were pounded into dust. Jetties were smashed, roads blocked. A water distilling plant was broken, and it became more and more difficult to distribute supplies. The 15,000 troops on the

---

[10] GCII/7 (7th Escadrille of Groupe de Chasse II) commanded by Cmdt Adam was the first of recently re-formed Free French units to be equipped with Spitfires, and was attached to the RAF's 245 Coastal Wing at Sidi Ahmed but had moved up to Utique airfield between Tunis and Bizerta for this operation (see Appendix I).

[11] see *On Y Va!* by Constantin Feldzer.

island had to spend most of their time crowded into tunnels and trenches and the huge subterranean hangars on the airfield. The civilian population scattered to isolated houses on the hillsides."

After the Allied invasion force was sighted, and having contacted Rome with the news that he was no longer able to withstand the assault, Admiral Gino Pavesi, who commanded the island's garrison, radioed Malta and offered to surrender; Clifford continued:

"But the attack was already under way. The whole tremendous process had been put in motion. Wave after wave of Flying Fortresses [B-17s] were approaching the target. Fifty, eighty . . . and when their number got into three figures the men in the assault craft, rapidly approaching the island, stopped counting. They had never seen anything like that bombing. At last the planes flew away. The British cruisers were still firing, but the one brave Italian gun which had been replying was silent now. At noon, zero hour, the attackers disembarked. On one of the beaches there were a few bursts of machine-gun fire, but they were short and ineffectual. Not a shot was fired in the harbour. As the assault craft came skimming in, shabby, dusty Italian troops began popping out of ruined houses and hoisting white flags. They were waiting to surrender. Admiral Pavesi, apparently bewildered by the situation, fled into the hills. They did not find him until six o'clock. The commander sent an emissary with an interpreter to chase him, and finally he consented to walk down to the airfield. Pantelleria village, where 3,000 fisherfolk used to live and kept their boats, was a rubbish heap. There were big stretches of the countryside practically covered with bomb craters. The airfield was littered with bits and pieces of Italian fighters. But the superb underground hangar remained untouched beneath its artificial hill, and its great white-washed interior was crammed with an incredible collection of junk. A couple of hundred Italian prisoners squatting on the ground and chattering like magpies. Some 50 Germans standing aloof; they were Luftwaffe technicians. A dozen absurd little tanks. Two biplanes of astonishing antiquity. Then a couple of hundred two-decker beds littered with clothing, books and letters, cartridges and razors and bottles of ink. Upstairs in a tunnel-like gallery was the Luftwaffe mess and store-room. Great 7-lb tins of butter from Holland or Denmark, excellent tinned pears, 40-lb cheeses, brandy, wine and beer, crates of cigarettes, real coffee. The Luftwaffe, at any rate, is still eating luxuriously."

Pantelleria had long been a thorn in Malta's side. Neighbouring Italian-controlled islands of Lampedusa, Linosa and Lampione were soon to follow.

* * *

Spitbombers from Malta were active again on the afternoon of 11 June, eight from 152 Squadron attacking a factory at Pozzallo, scoring two direct hits on the factory, other bombs seen to explode near the railway line, on the main road between the target and the town, and in the town. There was only light, inaccurate flak and no fighter opposition was sighted by the escort drawn from 232 and 242 Squadrons and led by Grp Capt Hugo. Comiso aerodrome was the target for eight Spitbombers of 1435 Squadron led by Wg Cdr Duncan Smith but heavy cloud prevented an attack so Pozzallo was bombed instead. On this occasion four MC202s were seen by the escorting Spitfires from 126 and 1435 Squadrons but were not engaged. In an attempt to draw enemy fighters into the air, 14 Spitfires from 185 and 229 Squadrons carried out an offensive sweep over southern Sicily during the early evening but only served to attract the attention of heavy and accurate flak from the Comiso area. All returned safely.

Next day (12 June), the advance elements of 324 Spitfire Wing began flying in from Tunisia led by Grp Capt G.K. Gilroy DSO DFC. The remaining squadrons would arrive on the morrow led by the newly appointed Wing Leader, Wg Cdr H.S.L. Dundas DFC. All five squadrons were led by seasoned campaigners; 43 was commanded by Sqn Ldr M. Rook DFC and had only recently joined the Wing, 72 by Sqn Ldr S.W. Daniel DFC, 93 by Sqn Ldr W.M. Sizer DFC, 111 by Sqn Ldr G.U. Hill DFC RCAF, and 243 by Sqn Ldr E.D. Mackie DFC RNZAF. The new squadrons were based at Hal Far and retained their autonomy as 324 Wing, while 111 Squadron was transferred to Safi where it temporarily joined 126 and 1435 Squadrons of the Safi Wing.

In the meantime the offensive against Sicily continued unabated. The factory power station at Marzamemi was visited during the afternoon of 12 June by six Spitbombers of 1435 Squadron, the sections led by Wg Cdr Duncan Smith and Plt Off Atkinson. Bombs were seen to fall on the target. On the return flight a small military-type barge was seen just off the coast, which was duly strafed, but no enemy aircraft were encountered. An afternoon sweep by 19 Spitfires from 81 and 154 Squadrons attracted the attention of three FW190s south of Syracuse but no engagements occurred. Earlier in the day, a Swordfish of the ASR Flight successfully located a dinghy and its occupant, a German airman, was rescued by an ASR launch from Malta, but the Swordfish failed to return and searches were subsequently carried out for it by four Spitfires of 229 Squadron, a Wellington and a Beaufort, but all to no avail. However, news was later received that the missing aircraft had landed safely at Sousse on the Tunisian coast. On arrival the Swordfish pilot, Sgt Syd Cohen, had a remarkable story to tell:

"During the air-sea rescue mission, the plane got a fit of the Gremlins. I swept down on a landing field and saw a few burnt-out aircraft, but we were still not sure that it was Lampedusa. Then we saw white objects being waved by figures on the edge of the field. Two Italian officers came up to our aircraft, followed by civilians. We were vastly intrigued by the leader of the deputation. He was wearing a Tyrolean hat with a large plumed feather (headdress of the crack *Bersalieri*), a leather jacket, shorts and high boots, and he burst forth into voluble Italian. We gathered that the Italian was offering the island's surrender. In view of the accidental nature of my mission it was a bit of a shake-up, but I put on a bold heart, and asked to see the Commandant of the island. I was taken to the Commandant's villa and presented to a high ranking officer. We were joined there by a further contingent, including our Tyrolean friend. Our session was interrupted when everybody suddenly made a dash from the room. The reason was that an air raid was starting, but there was no sound of gunfire or bombs. I concluded that the nerves of my hosts were wearing a bit jagged. We followed them down a steep flight of steps into an operational room 75 feet below ground level. I tried to explain that I was not an Allied emissary; but they asked me to return to Malta and inform the authorities of the offer to surrender. They gave me a scrap of paper with a signature on it.

We decided to make for Tunis. We returned to our aircraft and were about to crank her up when four or five of our fighter-bombers zoomed over at zero feet. Two more fighters sheered off when they spotted the markings on our plane. Twelve single-engined bombers [US P-40s or A-36As] next began bombing the harbour. Our Tyrolean friend reappeared and advised us to leave at once, as the heavy bombers would probably be coming over very soon. He urged us to leave before the raid started, and we took off, reached Tunisia and landed, where I went to an American camp nearby and produced the Italian surrender chit. My crew now call me 'The King of Lampedusa.'" [12]

Naval vessels were despatched to Lampedusa to formally accept the surrender. Linosa followed the next day, its garrison of 140 Italians raising the white flag on the approach of a Royal Navy destroyer, and a third Italian island, Lampione, was occupied soon thereafter. With the Allies now in control of the islands, Wg Cdr J.D. Bisdee DFC – who had commanded 601 Squadron at Malta during the previous year – was appointed Garrison Commander and Military Governor of Lampedusa, Brigadier-General A.C. Strickland USAAF being appointed to similar offices at Pantelleria, where American Spitfires from the 31st FG and squadrons of P-40s soon took up residence.[13]

Two Spitfire Vs of 1435 Squadron fitted with long-range tanks were airborne at 0740 on the morning of 13 June for an offensive sweep over southern Sicily, but once again no enemy aircraft were encountered. A total of 36 Spitfires – a dozen IXs drawn equally from 126 and 185 Squadrons, plus 24 Vs from 229 and 249 Squadrons – were airborne just after 1100 to escort US Liberators briefed to bomb Gerbini and Catania aerodromes. On approaching the bombers at the rendezvous point, one of the Liberators fired at Flt Lt Ron Green's aircraft (EN479/MK-N) which sustained some damage. Other 126 Squadron pilots sighted four MC202s south of Cape Passero although these did not attempt to engage, while those from 229 Squadron observed four Bf109s and three MC202s attacking the bombers at 25,000 feet near Comiso. One Spitfire pilot fired at a Macchi without tangible results, the enemy fighters then breaking off their attacks on the bombers, but over Gerbini three FW190s and at least ten Bf109s and Macchis dived on the escort but were evaded without damage. As the coast was re-crossed on the homeward journey, more enemy fighters attacked and three Spitfires chased a FW190 at deck level, Flt Lt Les Gosling (JK428/X-A) claiming strikes on its tail and starboard wing. As 229 and 249 Squadrons withdrew from the target area three Bf109Gs of II/JG53 attacked and promptly shot down the Krendi Wing Leader, Wg Cdr John Ellis (JK533/JE), Sgt Jock Davidson (EF569/X-Z) of 229 Squadron, and Sgt B.W. Sheehan RNZAF (ER811/T-J) of 249 Squadron. In the ensuing series of combats strikes were scored on the cockpit of a Messerschmitt by newly commissioned Plt

---

[12] As related to *Reuter*'s Special Correspondent at Allied HQ in North Africa. Syd Cohen survived the war but, in May 1948, having volunteered to fly for the embryonic Israeli Air Force, he was killed when the Norseman utility aircraft in which he was flying crashed at Rome's Urbe Airport. Also killed in the crash was the legendary Canadian fighter pilot George Beurling, a veteran of Malta's 1942 air battles who had similarly offered his services to the Israelis. Sabotage was suspected.

[13] Spitfires of the 52nd Fighter Group remained responsible for the air defence of Tunis and Bizerta, and reported a further three victories against FW190s on 12 June (credited to 1/Lt Robert E. Armstrong Jr, 1/Lt James O. Tyler and 2/Lt Robert L. Burnett III of the 4th FS) against an attempted interception of Allied shipping; ten days later 1/Lt Albert C. Adams Jr of the 2nd FS claimed a FW190. One more victory would follow before the Group moved to Sicily in late July after the invasion, 1/Lt Armstong claiming his third victory, a Ju88, on 8 July.

Off Don Nicholson (JK879/T-B) of 249 Squadron, who recalled:

"The 109s were spotted coming down on us from the rear and we broke right to turn towards them. I had just straightened up when I saw in front of me a 109 coming towards me from my left. I just pushed the firing button and the 109 flew through my line of fire. I saw a couple of strikes near the cockpit and then it was gone – all very sudden and over in a few seconds. I did not see it go down but John Beatson confirmed seeing it dive vertically and also seeing an aircraft hit the ground. This may have been my victim. Anyway, the Intelligence Officer said 'probably destroyed' – who was I to argue!"

It is believed that Wg Cdr Ellis was shot down by Maj Michalski for his 58th victory. Apart from the Gruppenkommandeur's victory, two more Spitfires were claimed by Lt Karl Paashaus and Obfw Herbert Rollwage of 5/JG53; the latter's victim (his 40th) apparently crashed near the village of Mineo. Two more Spitfires from 249 Squadron crashed on landing, one of which – EF539/T-F flown by Flt Sgt Jack Hughes – had been damaged in the action, although neither pilot was injured; Hughes noted:

"Scrap over target with ME109s and FW190s. Wingco Ellis, Sgt Sheehan and Sgt Davidson missing. I got shot up. Port aileron and control broke, no air pressure and no ASI. Crossed Catania airfield at 2,000 feet and chased out to sea. Crash-landed at Luqa doing about 200 mph. Kite written off."

All three missing pilots were later reported to be prisoners and were entertained in JG53's mess at Comiso by Hptm Friedrich-Karl Müller, Kommandeur of I Gruppe, and his officers. Next day Wg Cdr Ellis was flown to Germany. Fw Reiter remembered meeting Sgt Jock Davidson, a Scot, although he apparently thought he was a New Zealander but had obviously confused him with another of the captured pilots, Sgt Bernie Sheehan:

". . . we had him as our guest for a day. In the evening there was a promised bout of heavy drinking, in which our colleague enthusiastically took part. By about midnight he was completely drunk and we set out for my tent, which he was to share with me. It was a clear, starry night as we walked to our tent quarters. On the way there he stopped. He stood, rather unsteadily, looking in the direction of Malta, and murmured over and over in a drunken, melancholy voice, 'There lies Malta, there lies Malta.'" [14]

Sgt Sheehan later recalled:

"Our altitude was 30,000 feet. I spotted and reported a gaggle of ME109s and Macchi 202s above, behind and attacking. We turned 180°. I fired, turned and was hit in the port wing. My attacker overshot. I fired and scored hits around the engine cowling but was forced to take evasive action. My Spitfire was losing power and overheating but I managed to get on the tail of a Macchi, fired and the e/a exploded. My aircraft was again hit, the instrument panel disintegrated, smoke and flames appeared and I decided to vacate. My parachute opened at about 15,000 and a 109 circled me several times, the pilot waving."

---

[14] see *Jagdgeschwader 53 Volume Two.*

He was plucked from the sea by an Axis rescue craft. It seems probable that he had been shot down by Italian Bf109Gs rather than MC202s, since in addition to the II/JG53 claims, Serg Magg Carlo Cavagliano of 153^Squadriglia reported the destruction of a Spitfire, which was chasing a German Bf109G, and this was seen to crash off the coast near Priolo after the pilot baled out. The Bf109G-equipped 3°Gruppo had only recently arrived at Comiso from San Pietro, where the Italian pilots had been training with their new mounts. Another Spitfire was lost during a late afternoon sweep, Sgt F.L. Jones of 242 Squadron being obliged to bale out of EE668 into the sea 25 miles north of Malta when his aircraft developed engine trouble. A dozen Spitfires from 229 and 249 Squadrons were airborne in relays between 1750 and 1930 to escort HSL107 despatched to rescue Jones who was picked up unhurt. One of the escorting Spitfires of 249 Squadron crashed on landing and was written off although the pilot was uninjured. Earlier in the day a PR Spitfire (EN421) of 682 Squadron flown by Sgt D. Penn, which had taken off from La Marsa in Tunisia for a reconnaissance to the Naples area, failed to return.

It was not only Malta that was receiving fighter reinforcements but Sicily also, Bf109Gs of Stab/JG77 landing at Trapani during the day following their flight from Germany, I and II/JG77 following a few days later. The Jagdgeschwader had just re-equipped following the end of the Tunisian Campaign, during which its pilots had claimed some 350 victories. Commanded by Maj Johannes Steinhoff, who had personally amassed 157 victories, of which 148 had been claimed in the East, JG77 had been the most successful of the Luftwaffe fighter units in Tunisia and could boast many aces within its ranks including the Kommandeur of I Gruppe, Oblt Heinz-Edgar Berres (44 victories, including seven in the East), and Hptm Siegfried Freytag (96 victories, of which 49 claimed in the East), Kommandeur of II Gruppe, both veterans of the bitter fighting over Malta in 1942. Others with substantial scores included Lt Ernst-Wilhelm Reinert (II Gruppe with 154 victories, including 100 in the East), Oblt Franz Hrdlicka (II Gruppe, 31 victories, of which 27 were gained in the East), Lt Armin Köhler (I Gruppe, 22 victories), Fw Otto Pohl (I Gruppe, 18 victories), and Oblt Ernst Laube (I Gruppe, 14 victories). Thus, a wealth of vastly combat-experienced pilots had arrived to strengthen and bolster the Sicilian fighter defences. Stab and II Gruppe were located at Trapani, I Gruppe at Sciacca. The Jagdgeschwader's III Gruppe was currently based in Sardinia. Also arriving at this time was a newly established FW190 fighter-bomber unit, IV/SKG10 commanded by Maj Heinz Schumann, which had been formed in France from the Jabo Staffeln of JG2 and JG26. IV/SKG10 located at Gerbini where II/SKG10 was based. Although the Luftwaffe was making an effort to increase its strength and defensive capability on Sicily, Mussolini was desperate for the Germans also to strengthen the mainland's weakened defences; during a meeting with his commanders on 14 June he stated:

"We have neither a powerful bombing force nor the fighters to protect it . . .
it is absolutely essential for Germany to supply our needs for AA defence in
our homeland, that is planes and guns."

But with the defeat of German forces in North Africa, the loss of military superiority on the Eastern Front, the ever-increasing aerial assault on Germany's industrial might by UK-based aircraft, and now the imminent threat of invasion of Sicily and southern Italy, there was little material assistance for Hitler to offer.

Meanwhile, on the evening of 14 June, a total of 38 Spitfires drawn from 81, 126, 154 and 232 Squadrons carried out a sweep of south-eastern Sicily, Wg Cdr

Gray leading in EN350/CG. An unidentified enemy aircraft was sighted by 154 Squadron and three Bf109s by 126 Squadron but no engagements ensued until 232 Squadron was attacked from astern by six to eight MC202s while pursuing seven Messerschmitts, at which Flt Lt W.A. Olmsted RCAF (JK274) and Flt Sgt A.V. Frewer RNZAF (JK235) fired but without observable results. Avoiding the assault, the Spitfires drew the Macchis southerly towards 81 Squadron which was flying at 26,000 feet in the Comiso-Noto area. The Wing Leader, at the head of the Spitfires, sighted 15 single-engined fighters – which were identified as Messerschmitts and Macchis – below and carried out a diving attack, personally shooting down one of the former while Flg Off P.G. Barber (EN181) and Flt Sgt G.S. Hulse (EN478) each claimed a Macchi damaged, although it would seem these were also Bf109s and that all three 6/JG53 machines were lost. Wg Cdr Gray later wrote:

> "I dived on a 109 and fired from 200 yards, observing cannon strikes on the fuselage. There was a large explosion behind the cockpit, petrol spewed out, and the plane finally caught fire." [15]

Fw Engelbert Hofmann was killed when his aircraft (WkNr15512) was shot down in flames near Donnafucata, south of Comiso (presumably Gray's victim). A second Bf109 (WkNr18286) was lost when Fw Hans Feyerlein baled out north-west of Scicli as the result of battle damage, while Uffz Reinhold Zimmermann belly-landed his crippled fighter (WkNr19921) at Comiso, having been wounded in the action. In return, Uffz Hermann Witt of 5 Staffel claimed a Spitfire although none was lost on this occasion.

Three more Spitfire squadrons flew to Malta from Tunisia during the day, 92 Squadron led by Sqn Ldr P.H. Humphreys, 1SAAF (Maj D.D. Moodie DFC SAAF), and 417RCAF led by the celebrated Sqn Ldr P.S. Turner DFC[16], who had dropped rank to take command of the Canadian Squadron, the three squadrons joining 244 Wing at Luqa. Both 92 and 1SAAF had seen much fighting in the Western Desert and Tunisia, 417RCAF being a relative newcomer to the Middle East although it had taken part in the closing stages of the Tunisian Campaign.

When 35 Spitfires from 324 Wing carried out their first offensive sweep over south-eastern Sicily at midday on 15 June, they met only heavy flak over Comiso, where six Spitbombers of 1435 Squadron escorted by eight IXs of 126 Squadron and six Vs from 1435 Squadron bombed the aerodrome. All bombs were reported to have fallen within the aerodrome perimeter, four exploding on the runway and six falling in the dispersal area. A large fire was seen in the dispersal area and heavy but inaccurate flak was experienced. The escorting fighters swept from north of Comiso to Scogletti and although several enemy fighters were seen near Comiso, they took evasive action and were not engaged. On returning to Malta two 324 Wing aircraft crashed on landing although neither pilot was injured. Two uneventful sweeps were carried out over south-eastern Sicily on 16 June, 35 Spitfires from 43, 72 and 243 Squadrons overflying Ragusa, Comiso and Gela during the late morning, followed by six IXs of 126 Squadron which orbited over Comiso, Biscari and Cape Scalambri at 20,000 during the late afternoon. No enemy aircraft were seen in the air but two were observed taking off from Comiso, using the grass and not the runways. Malta had two alerts during the day, at least

---

[15] see *Spitfire Patrol* by Wg Cdr Colin Gray DSO DFC.
[17] Sqn Ldr Stan Turner had fought in France in 1940, and in the Battle of Britain, before taking command of 249 Squadron at Malta in early 1942.

three enemy aircraft crossing the coast at 22,000 feet just before 1000, a further six approaching shortly before dusk. Spitfire patrols were airborne on both occasions but failed to intercept. A reconnaissance Ju88 of 2(F)/122 – F6+GK flown by Lt Josef Trager – despatched from Trapani to carry out a sortie over Malta, failed to return. Details of its exact fate are unknown although it apparently crashed into the sea with the loss of the crew, presumably due to engine problems.

Six Bf109s were sighted by Spitfires of 324 Wing near Ragusa while on a sweep of south-eastern Sicily shortly before midday on 17 June, but these avoided combat. The sweep by 37 Spitfires of 72, 93 and 111 Squadrons led by Wg Cdr Dundas was a prelude to the bombing of Comiso and Biscari by US Liberators, the bombing force itself covered by more than 70 Spitfires drawn from 322, Safi and Krendi Wings led by Grp Cpt Hugo, Wg Cdr Gray and Wg Cdr Billy Drake DSO DFC (the new Wing Commander Flying at Krendi). The escort made rendezvous with the bombers just north of Malta and provided cover as they withdrew. At least six enemy fighters were sighted by 185 and 229 Squadrons, though not engaged, while five Bf109s avoided action when approached by 81 Squadron but 232 Squadron, when halfway between Biscari and Syracuse, was attacked by three MC205Vs of 1°Stormo. Two fired wildly before diving away, the third being engaged by Wg Cdr Gray (EN534/EF-Y):

> "I got on the tail of one of them, and although my port cannon jammed I managed to hit him in the starboard wing and fuselage. This slowed him up a bit and enabled me to fire a burst in the cockpit from 150 yards. The aircraft flicked into a spin and began belching white smoke that finally turned black. He was last seen spinning 15,000 feet below, so I do not think he was going far." [17]

Wg Cdr Gray was credited with its destruction but the damaged Macchi nonetheless managed to reach its base at Catania but there it crashed on landing and was then destroyed; the pilot survived. US bombers also attacked San Pietro airfield where five Bf109Gs of 3°Gruppo were destroyed on the ground.

A dozen Spitfires of 72 Squadron flew top cover on a 324 Wing sweep led by Grp Capt Gilroy at midday on 18 June. Just after they crossed the coast enemy aircraft were reported over the R/T but not seen by the 72 Squadron pilots at this stage. At 1235, Flt Lt Dalton Prytherch reported that his engine had cut and that he would have to bale out. His aircraft (EN301) was seen losing height about ten miles south of Ragusa before a parachute appeared. Sgt K.E. Clarkson RAAF descended to fix the spot and initially observed his flight commander being dragged along in the sea by his parachute before losing sight of him. Wt Off Alan Gear joined Clarkson in the search but saw nothing. Meanwhile, the remainder of the Squadron flew inland as far as Ragusa, where at least a dozen enemy fighters were seen in the air but these were not engaged. However, Flg Off George Keith RCAF (JK429), a Canadian from Alberta with three victories to his credit from the Tunisian fighting, had become separated from the others and, as he was crossing the coast on the return flight, he saw a Bf109G approaching two Spitfires circling at 5,000 feet – presumably Clarkson and Gear. He at once attacked from above, the Messerschmitt breaking away at zero feet with Keith following. After about two minutes he had closed to within 300 yards and fired a two-second burst, observing strikes on the port wing root and glycol pouring from its radiators. He closed to 200

---

[17] see *Spitfire Patrol*.

yards and gave another two-second burst at which the Messerschmitt climbed to 800 feet. Its cockpit hood and some pieces flew off. In order to avoid colliding, Keith pulled away sharply to see a parachute descending and a puff of smoke as the aircraft apparently hit the ground. His victim was no other than Maj Michalski, Kommandeur of II/JG53, who managed to bale out of his damaged aircraft (WkNr16362) despite a wounded leg and broken ankle. He was soon picked up and taken to hospital at Ragusa.

Elsewhere, Messerschmitts engaged a patrol from 43 Squadron, Fw Reiter of 5/JG53 shooting down Flt Sgt M.K. Brown RNZAF who was similarly seen to bale out of his crippled aircraft (ES355/FT-S). Sqn Ldr Mackie of 243 Squadron observed one of the downed pilots, apparently Brown, climb into his dinghy about 15 miles south of Pozzallo. He orbited the dinghy and radioed Malta its position before returning to Hal Far.

A further 36 Spitfires took to the air before those of 324 Wing had returned, Wg Cdr Gray leading 322 Wing over south-eastern Sicily where five FW190s were seen at 23,000 feet north-west of Comiso, but these avoided combat. At the same time Wg Cdr Drake led a further 16 Spitfires of the Krendi Wing on a sweep west of Comiso, sighting a number of unidentified fighters which similarly avoided action. The remainder of the afternoon and early evening saw relays of Spitfires searching for the missing pilots in the Cape Passero-Pozzallo area, those from 243 Squadron again sighting the dinghy complete with pilot who waved as the Spitfires passed low overhead, but when Sqn Ldr Mackie and his section arrived over the position for the third time, the dinghy could not be re-located. Flt Sgt Brown was subsequently picked up by an Axis craft and thereby became a prisoner of war. Sqn Ldr Mackie later reflected:

> "With all the white horses, it was probably a fluke that I saw him at all. The dinghies were yellow, but they were only a pinpoint when you were looking for them from a few thousand feet. However, that's the fortunes of war." [19]

Offensive sweeps continued over the south-eastern corner of Sicily on the following two days, but no enemy aircraft were encountered by the Spitfires even when nine US Liberators attacked Reggio di Calabria and San Giovanni. Similarly, intruding German reconnaissance fighters over Malta skilfully avoided interception by Spitfire patrols, even though four IXs of 185 Squadron pursued two to within ten miles of Pozzallo. Malta's Spitfire pilots were beginning to become frustrated with the lack of combat, as epitomised by an entry in 81 Squadron's ORB:

> "Enemy aircraft are still very diffident about fighting and although the Squadron went over on a sweep and two scrambles, no interceptions resulted."

American bombers from North Africa continued to attack Castelvetrano, Milo and Borizzo aerodromes on the morning of 20 June, escorting P-38s being engaged by Bf109Gs of I and II/JG77 flying their first operational sorties from Sicily. Four were claimed shot down for the loss of three Messerschmitts. Italian Messerschmitts of 150°Gruppo also engaged the raiders, claiming a P-38 shot down for no losses. A diversionary sweep was carried out by 44 Spitfires of 322 Wing, but the only enemy fighter to make an appearance – a MC202 – wisely dived away northwards before it could be intercepted. This operation was closely followed by an offensive sweep

---

[19] see *Spitfire Leader* by Max Avery with Christopher Shores.

by Spitfires of 92 and 145 Squadrons led by Sqn Ldr Humphreys and Sqn Ldr Wade respectively, three Messerschmitts being sighted 20 miles south of Religione Point. The Wing Leader, Wg Cdr Olver (EN448/PO), chased these as far as Rosolini and closed to within 400 yards of one, firing with unobserved results. Spitfires of 601 and 417RCAF Squadrons also carried out their first operational sweep from Malta between 1500 and 1630. Two fighters were seen taking off from Comiso but these flew inland and were not engaged.

There was success and sadness for 72 Squadron when four Spitfires led by Wg Cdr Dundas were scrambled at about 1900, together with a quartet from 243 Squadron, on the approach of three unidentified fighters. Ten miles south of Pozzallo two Bf109Gs were sighted by Wt Off Alan Gear (EN144) at 26,000 feet and these were pursued towards Gela by him and Flg Off Gordon Sharp RAAF, while the Wing Leader and his No2 covered. As the two Spitfires closed the range, the Messerschmitts turned northwards and, when over Biscari, the leader – Oblt Leo Potjans, Staffelkapitän of 6 Staffel – did a slight turn to port and expertly shot down Sharp's aircraft (EN298), which crashed, killing its Australian pilot. Meanwhile, Gear attacked a Messerschmitt which he thought was the one that had shot down his colleague, but was in fact that flown by Fw Klaus Wagenknecht of 4/JG53, closing to about 50 yards and firing a three-second burst. He reported that the Messerschmitt (WkNr18080) flicked onto its back and went straight in. Wagenknecht was able to bale out and was picked up from the sea shortly afterwards. The missing pilot (Sharp) may have attacked Fw Otto Russ' aircraft (WkNr16619) – who had apparently joined the fight – before his own demise, since the wounded 4 Staffel pilot belly-landed his damaged machine at Comiso following this action.

Although the Spitfires carried out five offensive sweeps over south-eastern Sicily during 21 June – a total of 123 sorties being flown between late morning and early evening – only one solitary Messerschmitt was sighted, by pilots of 72 Squadron, and this avoided combat by diving away. The first sweep was in support of US Liberators again bombing Reggio di Calabria and San Giovanni in the morning, the Spitfires of 324 Wing crossed the coast at Punto Seccia and swept over Caltagirone and Palazzolo before returning via Pozzallo, while those of the Safi Wing strafed a column of M/T south-west of Vittoria. Despite the lack of opportunities for the patrolling Spitfires, there was much aerial activity over south-eastern Sicily during the day when eight MC202s of 91^Squadriglia (10°Gruppo) arrived at Catania from Ciampino, while more Macchis from 9°Gruppo flew in from Gerbini. The other two squadriglie of 10°Gruppo, 84^ and 92^, would also transfer to Catania within a few days.

Meanwhile, at Malta an alert was sounded shortly before 1830 when six enemy aircraft approached from the north although they did not cross the coast. Patrolling Spitfires from 1SAAF and 417RCAF Squadrons sighted only one aircraft, flying very fast at 37,000 feet, and were unable to engage. It was a similar story next day (22 June), 93 sorties being flown over south-eastern Sicily without even a hint of opposition apart from sporadic anti-aircraft fire. On the bright side, two Spitfires of 1435 Squadron flown by Plt Off W.E. Schrader RNZAF and Plt Off J. Filson successfully located a rowing boat with six men on board some 20 miles from Malta, to which a HSL was directed.

Two Bf109s were sighted by Spitfires of 324 Wing, sweeping ahead of 1435 Squadron's Spitbombers making for Pozzallo, during the afternoon of 23 June, although these were not engaged. Comiso had been the priority target for the fighter-bombers but heavy cloud obscured the possibility of accurate bombing and the alternative target was attacked instead, where bombs were seen to explode near the railway lines, sidings and crossroads to the east of the town. Four IXs of 185 Squadron led by Wg Cdr Drake patrolled over the Comiso area two hours later but failed to sight any enemy aircraft, although eight IXs of 81 Squadron which were airborne on a standing patrol were more successful. Control ordered one section to investigate two aircraft at 32,000 feet some 35 miles south of Pozzallo at 1905, two Bf109Gs being sighted although these turned away and dived to 2,000 feet in an attempt to escape. However, one Messerschmitt was intercepted by Plt Off W.I.H. Maguire (EN528/FL-S) and was claimed shot down into the sea five miles south of Pozzallo, the Rhodesian-born pilot's sixth victory.

Earlier in the day Malta's Command Engineering Officer, Grp Capt Reg Jordan, failed to return from a test flight in 126 Squadron's sole Spitfire VIII (JF352). He was not thought to have been shot down. Search aircraft sighted a dinghy about 40 miles to the north of Malta, which was assumed to contain the missing pilot, but sections of Spitfires despatched to search for it failed to make any further sightings. The 36-year-old Group Captain, who had twice been Mentioned in Despatches, was not rescued and was feared lost at sea. The latest Spitfire arrivals at Malta, 24 aircraft of 40SAAF Squadron, a tactical reconnaissance unit, landed at Luqa during the day and joined 244 Wing. Their arrival was marred by a landing accident when EP894 ran into ER227 on the runway, both aircraft sustaining damage. Not fighter-trained, the pilots of Lt Col J.D.P. Blaauw's squadron would come into their own once the landings on Sicily were underway.

A section of patrolling Spitfires from 111 Squadron were vectored onto a rare bird at 1100 on the morning of 24 June, one of the Luftwaffe's new Me410 twin-engined reconnaissance aircraft of 2(F)/122 from Trapani being sighted at sea level south of Cape Passero. Flt Sgt Frank Mellor (EN518) gave chase, the Messerschmitt gunner (Uffz Willi Weber) returning fire before his aircraft (F6+XE) dived into the sea taking him and his pilot, Oblt Ulrich Nauck, to their deaths. An afternoon sweep by 28 Spitfires drawn from 244 Wing proved uneventful, while a planned Spitbomber attack by 152 Squadron on a suspected ammunition dump at Vizzini was thwarted by heavy cloud, bombs being dropped on a factory at Pozzallo instead. Having earlier escorted a Liberator to Malta carrying Sir Archibald Sinclair, the Air Minister, Flg Off Hawkins of 1435 Squadron, accompanied by Flg Off B.B. Brooks, escorted a PR Spitfire to Cape Scalambri and along the coast to Gela, all three aircraft skimming the waves for the duration of the flight to avoid radar detection. No enemy aircraft were encountered.

The suspected ammunition dump at Vizzini was targeted again next day (25 June), a dozen Spitbombers from 152 Squadron attacking from 9,000 feet just before midday. The pilots reported that all bombs scored near misses on buildings within the target area. Sgt G.J. Whiteford RAAF, flying one of the escorting Spitfires of 81 Squadron, had a lucky escape when he blacked out following oxygen failure, his aircraft falling 10,000 feet before he regained consciousness and control. Comiso aerodrome was similarly raided four hours later, a dozen Spitbombers from 229 and 249 Squadrons carrying out the attack, but only three bombs were seen to burst on the east side of the aerodrome, the remainder falling outside the eastern perimeter. A large formation of B-17s from North Africa raided the Messina area during the morning, inflicting much damage, as recorded in the OKW War Diary:

> "Enemy air raid on Messina (200 aircraft). Heavy damage to private dwellings, public buildings, barracks and other military objectives. Fuel

store in flames, ammunition dump blown up. Rail link between Palermo and Catania cut. Casualties reported to date: 62 dead, 75 injured." [19]

MC202s and at least one D.520 of the 164^Squadriglia from Reggio di Calabria were amongst the defending fighters which engaged the raiders, the Italian pilots claiming seven bombers shot down for the loss of a MC205V and a MC202, the latter flown by the commander of 161°Gruppo, Magg Pietro Serini. US Marauders also attacked Trapani aerodrome where at least one Bf109G of 1/JG77 was destroyed and several ground personnel were killed or wounded. All serviceable Messerschmitts of II/JG53 were scrambled together with 23 aircraft of I/JG77, 31 from II/JG77, plus Maj Steinhoff in a Stab machine, the pilots ordered to intercept the B-17s on their return flight. In the event only two of the four-engined bombers were shot down, one falling to Steinhoff and the other to a pilot of II/JG77. A further eight were claimed damaged, and one Messerschmitt of 9/JG77 was shot down. The German fighters had been scrambled too late to be effective, as noted by Lt Köhler of I/JG77:

"We located the heavies 100 miles off Trapani. They were right down on the water, skimming the crests of the waves and heading for North Africa. By the time we had expended all our ammunition we found ourselves running low on fuel. This was something that alarmed old hands and new boys alike. Above us the sky was greyish blue. I could hear despairing cries." [20]

It was as a result of the unsuccessful interception that Reichmarschall Göring issued the first of his infamous directorates to Sicily's Jagdgeschwadern:

"During the defensive action against the bombing attack on the Straits of Messina the fighter element failed in its task. One pilot from each of the fighter wings taking part will be tried by court-martial for cowardice in the face of the enemy."

The threat was not acted upon since events would dictate otherwise but, following the attack on Trapani, Stab, I and II/JG77 were ordered to move to Gerbini from where the Geschwader was to concentrate its aircraft. The instruction emanated from GenMaj Adolf Galland, *General der Jagdflieger* (General of the Fighters), who had arrived to take charge of fighter operations. He summed up the position, as he saw it, to Maj Steinhoff:

"There's no doubt in my mind that the island's being softened up for a landing. Now that Pantelleria has surrendered without a shot being fired, they don't need aircraft carriers any more. Malta and Pantelleria are ideal springboards for their fighters – you might even say they're unsinkable aircraft carriers. The bombers are being flown from further away, from Tunis, Bizerta and Tripoli. We have got to employ the three fighter wings we have in a series of concentrated attacks. We can only make an impression on the enemy if we concentrate our strength. It's a very considerable risk since we haven't got enough airfields on the island. If we don't take the risk we'll merely keep on frittering away what little fighter strength we have at our disposal" [21]

But Galland's task was unenviable, and, in reality, impossible in the light of the aerial assault. He later wrote:

[19/20/21] see *The Straits of Messina*.

"Alternatively commanding from west and east Sicily, I instigated almost anything which was still justifiable. But we could really do nothing against the overwhelming Anglo-American superiority. Our pilots were exhausted to a terrifying degree. From North Africa and from Malta the American and British air fleets took us in a pincer move, and the grip became tighter every day. Our ports in Sicily, our bases, the supply and repair stations in the south of Italy – all were subjected to the Anglo-American hail of bombs. Bari, the assembly station for the aircraft replacements from home, was hit hard several times. Hundreds of new fighter aircraft were lost. The Luftwaffe was burning up in the southern theatre of the war." [22]

Spitfires from 249 Squadron were involved in escorting a communications aircraft to Pantelleria on this date (25 June), the pilots carrying out an unsuccessful search for the crew of a missing 23 Squadron Mosquito on the return journey. A further eight Spitfires from Luqa, together with a Walrus and an ASR Wellington, were despatched to search for a missing Spitfire (BS557/MK-C) of 126 Squadron which had been engaged on a practice flight. A pilot of 601 Squadron momentarily sighted the missing pilot, Flt Sgt J.A. Leckie RCAF, in the sea some seven miles south-east of Malta, but then lost sight of him again. Flt Lt Crockett, OC ASR Unit, conducted a sea search:

"I took HSL128 out to hunt for the pilot of a Spitfire who had ditched 16 miles south-south-west of Benghajsa Point. I left base at 1320 hours and searched with aircraft co-operation until darkness, but didn't see a thing. The sea was rough at the time, making the successful ditching of a Spitfire very unlikely."

Although the missing pilot was not located, hopes were briefy raised when an object was discerned floating in the sea by an accompaying Wellington, but when the launch arrived at the location the object turned out to be a dead dog. Meanwhile, two IXs of 126 Squadron escorted a PR Spitfire of 683 Squadron on a special task over Sicily, one of the escort strafing a gun position at Cape Scalambri on the return flight. Later, four IXs of 1SAAF led by Maj Moodie were scrambled at 1900 when two Bf109s were reported approaching the island, four Spitfires of 92 Squadron led by Flt Lt T.W. Savage being despatched to provide support. The South Africans sighted the Messerschmitts diving from 20,000 feet towards Sicily and Lts Doug Rogan DSO[23] and Arthur Higgo gave chase, but then lost them in the haze. One of the pursuing Spitfires, EN257 flown by Lt Andre deL. Rossouw apparently failed to pull out of its dive and crashed into the sea 15 miles south-west of Pozzallo; however, Uffz Hans Jürgens of 5/JG27 reported shooting down a Spitfire during the day and the 22-year-old South African pilot from Cape Province may have been his victim. Although a Beaufighter was sent out to search for the missing pilot no sighting was made. Later, wreckage and what appeared to be a khaki-clad figure were seen in the sea but the body was not recovered.

---

[22] see *The First and the Last*, by Adolf Galland.
[23] Lt Doug Rogan had previously served with 2SAAF in the Western Desert; credited with two victories (one shared), he was shot down in combat with Bf110s and severely wounded, subsequently having a foot amputated. Despite this handicap, and having been fitted with an artificial foot, he requested a return to operations, joining 1SAAF in early 1943. During the Tunisian fighting he claimed a further victory, plus two probables and a damaged, his courage and fighting spirit being recognised by the award of the DSO.

Three Spitfires from 1435 Squadron led by Flt Lt Bob Kleimeyer (JK950/V-M) were off at 0520 next morning (26 June) to continue the search for the missing pilot. About five miles off Cape Scalambri two Bf109Gs were seen circling a Red Cross-marked launch. Several rowing boats were also seen but there was no sign of a dinghy, although the area was searched thoroughly. Before returning to Malta, the pilots observed the rescue launch heading for the Sicilian coast. There was further action during the early morning, at about 0700, when four patrolling IXs of 185 Squadron were warned of six-plus unidentified aircraft approaching at 28,000 feet from the north. Messerschmitts were sighted and pursued to a position ten miles north-west of Scalambri where, after some manoeuvring, all four Spitfire pilots – Flt Sgts Sinclair (EN523/GL-K), Thorogood (EN403/GL-A), Mercer (EN401), and Sgt G. Harris (EN456/GL-P) – were in position to engage. All fired short bursts but observed no results. Greater success came the way of Wg Cdr Duncan Smith and Sqn Ldr Jackson who took off from Safi at 0800 in two IXs of 126 Squadron on a freelance patrol. South of Cape Scalambri they sighted ten Bf109Gs orbiting a large white Do24 flying boat of 6 SeenotStaffel. Of the ensuing few minutes, Wg Cdr Duncan Smith (flying JK611/MK-M on this occasion) recalled:

> "The 109s were dotted about round the flying boat in a very haphazard formation. Sweeping into the attack, I singled out a 109 flying rather wide, and, closing in, I opened fire giving him two bursts from slightly above dead astern. I saw strikes immediately round the cockpit and a piece broke off the port wing. The enemy winged over and dived towards the sea. I just had time to give another 109 a quick burst before I had to break and zoom climb away. Jackson in the meantime had fired at another 109, observing strikes and damage; but seeing me break, he followed in a corkscrew climb. I wheeled around quickly for another attack, and as I looked down I saw my first 109 hit the sea and explode, sending up a huge fountain of spray. The rest of the 109s were streaking for land, having left the old flying boat to fend for himself as best he could. To chase them was a waste of time, so I called Jackson, 'Lets tickle up the Dornier.' Overtaking the slow old flying boat, I throttled back and got into formation, after dropping the undercarriage to reduce speed. The Dornier pilot peered out and although I could not see his face too clearly, or observe his reactions, I reckon if he had had a whip he would have flogged his boat to death. I gave him a rude sign; then snapping up my wheels, turned for home. We didn't shoot down the Dornier because it was obviously on a search and rescue mission." [24]

It seems probable that Uffz Karl Hauer of 3/JG77 was Wg Cdr Duncan Smith's victim, his aircraft (WkNr18186) being reported down in the sea south-west of Sciacca, although the pilot survived having presumably baled out. 185 Squadron was in action again during a late afternoon patrol led by Flt Lt McKee which sighted three Bf109Gs 2,000 feet above, north of Gozo. The Squadron's South African member, Lt P.H. Bosch (EN404/GL-W) managed to close on one, as recorded in the Squadron diary:

> "In the chase that followed Lt Pete Bosch succeeded in closing with a 109 and claims damage. In this chase he dove his aircraft until he was off the clock and got a confirmed gun panel from his own kite."

---

[24] see *Spitfire into Battle*.

With black smoke pouring from its engine, the Messerschmitt was last seen diving towards the sea.

Offensive sweeps over south-eastern Sicily carried out by ten of 72 Squadron in the morning of 27 June, and by 26 Spitfires of 244 Wing in the afternoon, brought no reaction from Axis fighters and very little opposition from the AA defences. In Syracuse harbour about 20 barges were observed and a medium-size motor vessel was seen leaving harbour, but these were not attacked. On returning to Luqa, a Spitfire of 40SAAF piloted by Lt P.H. Donnelly ran into a second Spitfire on landing, writing off his own although he was uninjured. Gerbini aerodrome was the selected target for 16 Spitbombers drawn from 229 and 1435 Squadrons during the late afternoon, escort being provided by ten Vs from the same units, and top cover by 13 XIs from 126 and 185 Squadrons. All bombs were reported to have fallen within the perimeter, one scoring a direct hit on an occupied aircraft pen. Three MC202s attempted to interfere and one of these was claimed damaged by Sqn Ldr Jackson (JF419/MK-Z) of 126 Squadron. There was further excitement before the close of play when four IXs were scrambled by 185 Squadron at 1835 in pursuit of two unidentified aircraft reported approaching Malta from north of Grand Harbour. Sqn Ldr MacDougall led the chase to within five miles of the Sicilian coast before the two Bf109s were lost from sight.

Early on the morning of 28 June, an ASR Flight Wellington was despatched to search for the crew of a missing Wellington bomber which had crashed into the sea six miles off the Sicilian coast during the night. Escort was provided by 24 Spitfires from 324 Wing. At 0900, an empty dinghy, a dead body in flying clothes, and wreckage spread over a wide area was seen, but no survivors. Comiso was the target for a dozen Spitbombers (seven/229, five/249) in the afternoon, twelve Vs providing close escort while 15 IXs flew top cover. Bombs were seen to explode near the runway and along the north and east perimeters. An oil fire was started in the south-west dispersal area. A lone MC202 was engaged by a Spitbomber at 18,000 feet over Comiso but without observed results. Intense and accurate flak was experienced but none of the attackers was hit, although Plt Off P.M. McConnell of 126 Squadron crash-landed EN519/MK-S on returning to Safi. Apparently Bf109Gs of 5/JG53 were active, Fw Reiter claiming a Spitfire shot down at about 1800, his seventh victory, although its identity is unknown.

29 June was to prove a busy and hectic day for Malta's Spitfires, with a number of squadrons seeing heated action. Apart from the normal daylight standing patrols, the first operation was conducted by eight Spitbombers of 1435 Squadron led by Sqn Ldr O'Neill (ER498/V-E) which departed Safi shortly before midday to bomb Comiso aerodrome. Close escort was provided by seven Vs of 111 Squadron while ten Vs of 243 Squadron acted as medium cover, and six IXs (two/243, four/111) flew high above. The bombing commenced at 1235, two bombs falling north of the aerodrome, two exploding near the runway and the remainder on or near hangars, causing a large fire. As the Spitbombers withdrew, a small pall of smoke some two miles north-east of the aerodrome was observed, suggesting an aircraft had crashed and it was confirmed that AR560/DS (Wg Cdr Duncan Smith's personal aircraft) was missing. Its pilot on this occasion, Plt Off G.P. Bray RCAF of 1435 Squadron, was later reported to have been killed. During the attack three Bf109s were seen taking off from Comiso, but no engagements were reported and it would seem likely that Bray had fallen victim to ground fire which was reported to have been "terribly accurate". During this attack on Comiso, 5/JG53's rising star Fw Theo Reiter was severely wounded on the ground by a bomb splinter, resulting in the loss of his left arm. Italian Messerschmitts were also involved in this action,

Sottoten Giuseppe Ruzzin of 154^Squadriglia reporting an engagement with a Spitfire. He related that after exhausting his ammunition he flew alongside the Spitfire, which was apparently similarly without means of continuing the fight, and that friendly waves were exchanged before he headed back to Comiso.

A second strike at Comiso followed just after 1500 when 11 Spitbombers from 154 Squadron attacked, bombs seen falling among hangars and on or near the runway. A workshop was also strafed. Light and heavy flak was experienced, particularly from positions to the east and west of the aerodrome, two Spitbombers suffering damage although both reached Takali safely. On this occasion the enemy reacted strongly, at least 20 Bf109Gs – from Stab and II/JG53, plus 1/JG77 and 3°Gruppo – being reported by the escorting fighters of 322 Wing led by Grp Capt Hugo (EN534/EF-Y) and 232 Squadron became involved in a series of running fights during which a Messerschmitt was claimed shot down jointly by Sqn Ldr Arthur (JK656) and Flt Sgt J.W. Patterson (JK708), possibly White 6 (WkNr18370) of 1/JG77 in which Uffz Rolf Nolte-Ernsting failed to return, having been shot down over the sea. A second was claimed probably destroyed by Flt Lt Bill Olmstead (JK274) and a third damaged by Grp Capt Hugo[25], who was flying with 232 Squadron. A Spitfire (JK162) of 152 Squadron suffered flak damage during the attack on Comiso but Plt Off R.E.J. Macdonald was able to reach Malta safely, although it was believed by the Germans that several Spitfires had been shot down, as noted by Uffz Gerhard Waag of 6/JG53:

> "Fighter-bombers approaching our airfield; cockpit readiness then scramble. The bombs started falling shortly after take-off. Two Spitfires were shot down by flak, three by fighters. I myself lost my element leader and became involved with Spitfires. I saw two strikes on a Spitfire, but then I took six hits from machine-gun fire in my right wing. This was my first air combat, it was smashing." [26]

Spitfires were also claimed by Lt Karl Paashaus (his fifth victory) and Uffz Hermann Witt of 5 Staffel (his seventh), a third being credited to Fw Hans Feyerlein of 6 Staffel for his eighth victory, while Sottoten Ruzzin of 154^Squadriglia claimed one severely damaged. Despite having just achieved acedom, Lt Paashaus was not a happy man, as witnessed by a letter written to his parents:

> ". . . I assume that I will be able to come home from the middle to the end of July. I am already looking forward to it very much, for here it is the same every day, up at 4am, at readiness all day, bombs, air combat, heat, flies and to bed at 10 in the evening. It is tremendously wearing and one can't get used to it. I don't enjoy the southern theatre any more. You can imagine that this damned flying over the water is no fun, water and nothing but water, and if one goes down into it he drowns. Hero's death, lovely words, especially for the newspaper, but the subject is still death . . ." [27]

---

[25] Shortly after this flight Grp Capt Hugo, together with his Wing Leader, Wg Cdr Gray, was grounded, as the latter recalled: "I was unfortunately grounded because by some mischance I had seen the invasion plans, as had Piet Hugo, and it was feared that the Germans could get this information out of us if we happened to be shot down. We were not allowed to fly, which was unfortunate because we missed a bit of fun. But we were allowed to fly as soon as the invasion started."

[26/27] see *Jagdgeschwader 53 Volume Two*.

Comiso was targeted again that evening, a dozen Spitbombers drawn equally from 229 and 249 Squadrons tasked for the operation. However, at 1835, just before the start of the bombing run, an estimated 20-plus Bf109s and MC202s were seen near the aerodrome and the fighter-bombers were ordered to jettison their bombs, which apparently fell in the target area. The intercepting aircraft again included Italian Bf109Gs, seven aircraft of 3°Gruppo participating. Escorting Spitfire Vs and top cover IXs of the Krendi Wing led by Wg Cdr Drake were quick to come to the aid of the Spitbombers and a series of running fights then ensued, which ended ten miles south of Gela. Sqn Ldr MacDougall led the top cover IXs of 185 Squadron down to engage, Flt Sgt George Nadon (ES107) claiming a Macchi shot down before inflicting damage on a Messerschmitt, while his companion Sgt G.H. Meagher (EN523/GL-K) claimed another as probably destroyed. A third member of the same unit, Sgt K.R. Henderson (EN404/GL-W), reported strikes on the one he attacked, and two more were damaged by Flt Lt Les Gosling of 229 Squadron (EP838/X-W) and Flg Off John Beatson of 249 Squadron (EP928/T-S), with only the aircraft (JK122/X-B) flown by Flg Off Idema of 229 Squadron sustaining any damage in return; he was however able to land safely at Krendi on returning to Malta. Sottoten Ruzzin again claimed a Spitfire severely damaged but his companion, Ten Nicola Massaro, was shot down. Although no enemy aircraft were encountered, the pilots reported hearing over the R/T a pukka RAF-type voice enquiring: "I say, old boy, is that a 109 up my tail?" The reply came back, "If it is, old boy, you'll ruddy well know in a second or so!"

In between the second and third strikes against Comiso, Malta itself was subjected to intrusion by a small formation of Bf109Gs of 8/JG53 led by Lt Ulrich Seiffert to escort a reconnaissance Bf109G of 2(H)/14. These were reported approaching at 1615 at about 20,000 feet but four patrolling IXs of 185 Squadron were unable to intercept. One of the Messerschmitts (Yellow 13/WkNr18188) was flown by Uffz Hermann Harnisch, a 13-victory ace:

"We crossed over Malta from south-west to north-east, altitude between 6,000 and 7,000 meters [18,000-21,000 feet]. A large collection of ships lay on the roadstead at Valetta, evidence of the coming invasion of Sicily. Suddenly I was sitting in the dark. All the engine oil had flowed onto the canopy after a heavy jolt. I jettisoned the canopy and looked down, then descended to 2,000 meters [6,000 feet] in a steep spiral. Then the aircraft caught fire. I don't know what really happened. I assumed I had been hit by flak. After the fire broke out I baled out and soon afterward landed on the flat roof of a house in Zebbug [in Muxi Square]. I must have lost consciousness just before I landed and I didn't wake up until English soldiers placed me on a stretcher. Then I was transported to the 19th General Hospital."

The pilotless Messerschmitt meanwhile crashed in Grace Street at Zebbug. It missed the main buildings and came down in a yard, but its wingtip dislodged some roof tiles which fell into an adjoining room killing 17-year-old Catherine Vella, although nine members of the Bezzina family who were in same room were miraculously unhurt. A baby in a pram which was in the yard had been pulled inside the building a few minutes before the crash. Uffz Harnisch was to spend six weeks in hospital before he was sufficiently fit to be sent to a PoW compound. In the meantime Seiffert, the Staffelführer, wrote to Harnisch senior in Germany:

"It is with deep regret that I must inform you that your son did not report back from a flight on 29 June and to this day is still missing. He took off on that day as escort to a reconnaissance flight which was under my command and which was of a great height over Malta. He was under orders to complete the mission and then return with the flight back to base. [While] still over Malta, I noticed that your son put his machine in a curve to return, but continued in the same direction and out of sight. The other flight commanders also observed the same happening. At the time we believed your son was hit by flak. There was also the possibility that your son was air-sick. The possibility of a landing on the island or a parachute fall is naturally not discounted. Your son would in that case be a prisoner of war. We have still not given up hope."

Twenty-four Spitfires from 43 and 93 Squadrons were tasked to carry out an offensive sweep over southern Sicily during the late morning of 30 June, with four IXs of 111 Squadron providing top cover. Two aircraft of 93 Squadron collided on take-off although neither pilot was hurt. The remainder carried out the sweep, reporting no apparent activity on the aerodromes overflown although heavy flak was experienced over Comiso. In the afternoon 244 Wing despatched 20 Spitfires on a sweep of the Comiso area, but again no opposition was encountered.

Since early June a party of US Army Corps engineers from the 21st Engineer Aviation Regiment, with the aid of many locals, had amazingly constructed a landing ground on Gozo in just over two weeks in readiness to welcome the arrival from Pantelleria of the Spitfires of the US 31st Fighter Group. Of this tremendous feat, Maltese historian Philip Vella wrote:

"Since airfields and dispersal areas in Malta could not take the additional Spitfires required for [Operation Husky], it was decided to build an airfield on Gozo. A strip of cultivated land skirting the villages of Xewkija, Ghajnsielem, Nadur and Xaghra was chosen. Lord Gort [the Governor] requested Bishop Gonzi [Bishop of Gozo] to approach the farmers, who agreed to cede their fertile fields against adequate compensation. Construction was assigned to the Americans. The convoy carrying six officers and 196 men, and their equipment reached Marsalforn Bay on 6 June. Work on the east-west runway started two days later. Tractors, scrapers and mechanical shovels levelled the area; the historic Gourgion Tower, which stood in the way, had to be demolished. The American servicemen and Gozitan labourers worked in earnest with two shifts operating from 0500 to 2100 hours.

When Sir Keith Park [the AOC] visited the site some two days later, he ordered the construction of an additional runway as well as revetments or blast pens. Additional equipment and 70,000 sand bags were shipped from Malta; this required the setting up of three shifts working 24 hours a day. Work on the second runway started on 15 June with about 300 Gozitans constructing revetments of stone and sand bags. Both runways, each measuring 150 feet by 4,000 feet, were completed by 20 June, while work continued on the construction of taxiways, hardstandings and revetments. The new dispersal facilities provided accommodation for 78 aircraft. Work on the airfield was completed on 25 June." [28]

---

[28] see *Malta: Blitzed not Beaten.*

The three squadrons which comprised the 31st FG led by Lt Col Dean flew in on the morning of 30 June, but one pilot, 1/Lt George Stephens of the 308th FS, crashed into the sea while attempting a second landing. A second Spitfire from the same Squadron, ER165 flown by 1/Lt Edward Fardella, then ran into the wreck of a 309th FS Spitfire which had earlier crash-landed and was being removed from the runway by RAF personnel. LACs Ernie Nuttall and Jim Taylor of 3231 RAF Servicing Commando Unit were killed and two others seriously injured. Fardella was hurled from the cockpit as his aircraft disintegrated and was seriously injured. Meanwhile, four Spitfires from 229 Squadron were scrambled from Krendi to search for the missing American pilot, and an HSL was despatched from St Paul's Bay, but no trace of wreckage or dinghy was found. An hour later, however, a pilot of 126 Squadron sighted an oil patch one mile north-east of Gozo and directed the HSL to this point but nothing further was seen and Stephens was presumed lost with his aircraft.

With the invasion of Sicily imminent, and with the build up of USAAF forces in the area, the Americans decided to supplement the potentially overstretched RAF ASR services by providing a mini ASR force of their own and, to this end, three OA-10 flying boats (USAAF version of the USN PBY-5/RAF Catalina) arrived at Malta by the end of June. Originally five had set out from the United States but two had force-landed en route, one at Puerto Rico and the other at Rio de Oro in the Spanish Sahara where the crew had been interned. Due to lack of maintenance facilities at Kalafrana, the OA-10s were soon transferred to Bizerta (in late July), from where they would operate off Malta, Sicily and Sardinia until the end of the year, often with mixed American/RAF crews. Another unusual flying boat operating out of Kalafrana was an Italian Cant Z501 which had been captured during a Commando raid on Lemnos and flown to Malta by its Italian crew. Flt Sgt Ted Shute of the ASR unit recalled its first clandestine operation from Malta:

> " . . . [the Cant] was to be made ready for a special operations job that night, and I was in charge of the refuelling etc. One big problem arose over the type of lubricating oil required for the engine. The Italian flight engineer did not speak English. The best I could make out was that the engine required castor oil – I could not believe that, and thought he meant 'Castrol'. Fortunately, the CO of Kalafrana, Wg Cdr Mattingley, appeared on the quay and, as he was a pre-war Engineering Officer who had been called back for war service, he was familiar with older aircraft. He soon verified that the engine of the 1934-built flying boat did in fact require castor oil. Of course, that started another panic as it was by then already afternoon and the aircraft was required for use that night on the special operation. Phone calls were made to Naval, Army and RAF sick bays all over the Island, and soon motor-cycle couriers were arriving from all points bringing small bottles of castor oil until fortunately we had enough to top up the aircraft's engine."

Meanwhile, the Americans at Pantelleria received a surprise on the morning of 30 June when an Italian Bf109G of 150°Gruppo from Sciacca belly-landed on the aerodrome after its pilot, Serg Olindo Soligo, had run out of fuel following an encounter with US fighters. Soligo told his captors that six Messerschmitts of his Gruppo had taken off when Sciacca came under attack and that he had been intercepted near Pantelleria when at 13,000 feet, although his aircraft had escaped damage during the engagement.

While Malta was reaching a high state of readiness in preparation for its part in the impending invasion, the same could not be said of the preparedness of the British and American airborne troops being assembled in Tunisia.

Under the codename Operation *Buzzard*, Horsa gliders of the British 1st Glider Pilot Regiment were to be towed by RAF Halifaxes from Portreath in Cornwall to Salé airfield in Morocco, a minimum distance of some 1,300 miles, and from there to Kairouan on the Tunisian coast from where they were to operate in earnest against Sicily on the eve of D-Day. For the first part of the long and tortuous flight, Beaufighters would provide escort but once the Bay of Biscay was reached the Halifax-Horsa combinations were on their own. During the initial sortie by four combinations, one was forced to turn back due to adverse weather conditions and another broke its tow and the glider ditched in the sea; fortunately the three-man crew was rescued by a Norwegian corvette. The other two reached their destination safely, and soon others followed. Most made it although one combination fell victim to a Ju88 over the Bay of Biscay, and another was attacked by two FW190s in the same general area with the result that the glider was forced to ditch; the crew was eventually rescued by Spanish fishermen after eleven days in their dinghy, while another flight ended in disaster when, on reaching the Moroccan coast, two released Horsas sailed off into the desert and were not seen again. However, by 28 June, the first Horsas reached Kairouan, where they joined forces with the US 82nd Airborne Division, which had just taken delivery of some 350 Waco gliders that had been hastily assembled having arrived in North Africa by sea transport.

Since the gliders were to be towed into action by mainly slow and vulnerable, unarmed and unarmoured C-47s of the US 51st Air Transport Wing, it was therefore decided that they would have to be released two miles offshore to avoid flak. The Americans who were to fly the C-47s were in the main "pre-war civilian airline pilots who had not needed to know how to navigate because they had flown on fixed routes, being directed by radio beams from a tower" [29] while few had any combat or even night flying experience. There was little time for training for either pilots or paratroopers. A disaster was beckoning.

---

[29] see *Slaughter over Sicily* by Charles Whiting.

CHAPTER IV

THE BLITZ ON SICILY

1-9 July 1943

" . . . I am under no illusions as to the stern fight that lies ahead . . . they [the Axis fighters] are holding back and not fighting, obviously according to orders. We are going to embark on the land battle before we have won the air battle . . ." [1]

General Sir Bernard Montgomery on the eve of the invasion

Now assembled at Malta and on neighbouring Gozo in readiness for the impending invasion of Sicily were no fewer than 23 Spitfire fighter squadrons plus one Spitfire PR squadron and one Spitfire TacR squadron, comprising about 400 Vs, VIIIs, IXs, and a few PRIVs and PRXIs.

RAF Malta Order of Battle – Spitfire Squadrons

Luqa – 244	Wing Officer Commanding (designate):
	Grp Capt C.B.F. Kingcome DSO DFC
	Wing Commander Flying: Wg Cdr P. Olver DFC
92 Squadron	Sqn Ldr P.H. Humphreys
145 Squadron	Sqn Ldr L.C. Wade DFC
601 Squadron	Sqn Ldr J.S. Taylor DFC
417 Squadron RCAF	Sqn Ldr P.S. Turner DFC
1 Squadron SAAF	Maj D.D. Moodie DFC SAAF
683 Squadron (PR)	Wg Cdr A. Warburton DSO DFC
40 Squadron SAAF (TacR)	Lt Col J.D.P. Blaauw DFC SAAF

Takali – 322 Wing	Officer Commanding: Grp Capt P.H. Hugo DSO DFC
	Wing Commander Flying: Wg Cdr C.F. Gray DFC
81 Squadron	Sqn Ldr W.M. Whitamore DFC
152 Squadron	Sqn Ldr F.W. Lister
154 Squadron	Sqn Ldr A.C.G. Wenman
232 Squadron	Sqn Ldr C.I.R. Arthur
242 Squadron	Sqn Ldr M.C.B. Boddington DFM

Hal Far – 324 Wing	Officer Commanding: Grp Capt G.K. Gilroy DSO DFC
	Wing Commander Flying: Wg Cdr H.S.L. Dundas DFC
43 Squadron	Sqn Ldr M. Rook DFC
72 Squadron	Sqn Ldr S.W. Daniel DFC
93 Squadron	Sqn Ldr W.M. Sizer DFC
243 Squadron	Sqn Ldr E.F. Mackie DFC RNZAF

---

[1] see *Monty: Master of the Battlefield 1942-1944* by Nigel Hamilton.

Krendi (Wing)	Wing Commander Flying:	Wg Cdr B. Drake DSO DFC
185 Squadron		Sqn Ldr I.N. MacDougall DFC
229 Squadron		Sqn Ldr B.E.G. White
249 Squadron		Sqn Ldr J.J. Lynch DFC
Safi (Wing)	Wing Commander Flying:	Wg Cdr W.G.G. Duncan Smith DSO DFC
111 Squadron		Sqn Ldr G.U. Hill DFC RCAF
126 Squadron		Sqn Ldr H.S. Jackson
1435 Squadron		Sqn Ldr H.F. O'Neill DFC
Gozo – 31st Fighter Group USAAF		Lt Col Fred M. Dean USAAF
307th Fighter Squadron		Maj Mercer P. Davis USAAF
308th Fighter Squadron		Capt Thomas B. Fleming USAAF
309th Fighter Squadron		Maj Frank A. Hill USAAF

* * *

The first day of the new month (1 July) belied the intensive action that was about to erupt in the skies above and around Sicily. At 0950, two Spitfires of 232 Squadron were sent off to investigate shipping reported north-east of Malta, where the pilots – Flg Offs J.G. Woodill and J.L. Tayleur – eventually sighted a large patch of oil about seven miles north of St Paul's Bay. A few minutes later they saw three long, narrow craft, two very close together and the third half a mile in front and to the south, travelling eastwards, but these altered course to a southerly direction on being sighted. They dropped down to get a clearer view but were unable to find them again. Having orbited the area for a few minutes, they then flew within 20 miles of the south coast of Sicily before turning back for Malta.

At 1130, eight Spitbombers of 1435 Squadron with an escort provided by eight more from 72 Squadron and six IXs (four/72 Squadron, two/126 Squadron) flying as top cover, took off to bomb Biscari aerodrome, two returning early. A total of 14 250-lb bombs were released from 12,000 feet, ten of which were seen to fall outside the eastern perimeter while the other four exploded in the south-western dispersal area. Five miles north-west of Vittoria at least eight Bf109Gs of I/JG77 were seen at about 25,000 feet and engaged by the top cover, Sqn Ldr Daniel (EN309) of 72 Squadron claiming strikes on one during a three-second burst before it escaped in a steep dive, trailing white smoke from its radiator, while Sqn Ldr Jackson (EN402/MK-R) of 126 Squadron, accompanied by Wg Cdr Adrian Warburton (JK611/MK-M), also chased the Bf109s, Jackson firing at one with unobserved results. Evading the covering Spitfires, four of the Messerschmitts dived on the Spitbombers but without result, although Fw Otto Pohl of 3 Staffel claimed one shot down (his 19th victory) and Oblt Heinz-Edgar Berres of 1 Staffel probably a second. While 1435 Squadron was in the process of bombing Biscari, a further dozen Spitbombers – these from 185 and 249 Squadrons – began taking off from Krendi to carry out a repeat attack, escort being provided by seven Spitfires of 145 Squadron with four from 601 Squadron as top cover. Upon approaching the Sicilian coast the formation was warned of the presence of hostile fighters, the Spitbombers jettisoning their bombs although continuing towards the Biscari area. Two Bf109s were spotted at 15,000 feet near Ragusa by the top cover but were not engaged, and all returned safely to Malta.

During the day the PR Spitfires of 683 Squadron carried out six sorties, ranging far and wide, covering Rome, Naples and Taranto in addition to visiting a number of Sicilian and mainland airfields. Scrutiny of the subsequent photographs revealed:

> Catania: five Ju52s, one Z1007, three SM81s, three SM79s, five Ju88s, two Dorniers, four Bf110s, two medium and eight small aircraft; Comiso: six Ju88s, one Ca311-type, two medium and 45 small aircraft; Gela: two Z1007s and five small aircraft; Gerbini: eleven Ju88s, six Bf110s, eleven Ca310-type, nine medium and two small aircraft; Gerbini satellite No1: FW58, one large and 36 small aircraft; No3: three SM82s, one SM79, three small aircraft; No4 and No5: one Ju52, two medium and 40 small aircraft; No6: one Ju52, one Bf110 and 47 small aircraft; No8: 27 small aircraft; No9: six medium and 19 small aircraft.

The first sweep during the morning of 2 July by 30 Spitfires over south-east Sicily brought no reaction from Axis fighters, but a second, smaller force of 17 Spitfires drawn from 126 and 1435 Squadrons which set off just after midday caught a number of Bf109Gs of I/JG77 taking off from Biscari aerodrome. Flg Off Geoff White of 126 Squadron (JK672/MK-E) shot down Fw Herbert Zuck of 3 Staffel at low level after a long chase, seeing the pilot bale out before the Messerschmitt (Yellow 8/ WkNr15426) exploded on hitting the ground west of Comiso; Zuck was however reported to have been killed. Three other Messerschmitts were claimed damaged including one by Flg Off Stewart of 1435 Squadron. White recalled:

> "Once you got a 109 at ground level all they could do was to push the throttle full open and fly straight away from you. They didn't try to do any turning because they knew that we could out-turn them, so they were really in a very unhappy position."

As the Spitfires returned across the Malta Channel they were pursued by both FW190s and Bf109Gs, Plt Off Atkinson (JK282/V-U) and Flt Sgt S.H. Benjamin (JK139/V-X) of 1435 Squadron turning the tables on one of the FW190s which they claimed shot down into the sea. The same two pilots then each damaged a Messerschmitt. The next sweep, by 20 Spitfires from 185 (Sqn Ldr MacDougall) and 229 Squadrons (Sqn Ldr White), set out at 1400 and headed for the south-east corner where, over Scicli at 19,000 feet, two Bf109Gs were sighted 2,000 feet below. Both were attacked and claimed probably destroyed by Sqn Ldr White (JG838/X-W) of 229 Squadron and Flt Sgt George Mercer (EN403/GL-A) of 185 Squadron. One of these may have crash-landed at San Pietro. Sgt McKenzie (ER494/X-H) of 229 Squadron also fired at one but made no claim. Three more Messerschmitts were then sighted at about the same height, one of which Flt Lt H. Hopkinson (JK428/X-A) engaged and damaged, but Flt Sgt Jim Lowry RCAF (EN404/GL-W) of 185 Squadron was shot down and killed, probably the victim of Oblt Berres of 1/JG77 who claimed two Spitfires shot down (his 47th and 48th victories), while Fw Ryll of 2 Staffel claimed another (his third). In the forlorn hope of finding the missing pilot, eight Spitfires from 43 and 243 Squadrons were despatched to search the sea between Sicily and Malta but without success. A practice sweep was carried out during the late afternoon by a total of 42 Spitfires (ten/152, eleven/81, nine/154, twelve/242) to give the newcomers a taste of things to come without throwing them into the heat of battle. 152 and 81 Squadrons flew to Biscari where at least nine aircraft were seen on the western side of the aerodrome, and four others taking off, while 154 and 242 Squadrons overflew Comiso where eight aircraft were seen drawn up for immediate take-off. Neither aerodrome was attacked and all aircraft returned safely.

There was some respite for both Malta's pilots and those of the Sicilian-based units on the morning of 3 July, neither side flying any offensive sorties, but all was to change by mid-afternoon when Malta Command coincided its operations with those of US bombers attacking Sicilian airfields from the west. Sciacca was targeted by 11 A-20s of the 47th BG, escorted by P-40s of the 33rd and 324th FG. Bombs were seen to explode all over the airfield and a large fire was started. An estimated 12-15 Bf109Gs attacked the bombers and pursued them for some 20 miles out to sea. Other A-20s and a dozen Baltimores of 3SAAF Squadron attacked Trapani/Milo. As the raid approached the airfield a dozen Bf109Gs and FW190s intercepted and shot down two of the SAAF bombers, two others falling to accurate and heavy AA fire. An American bomber was also shot down. Bf109Gs from I/JG53, I and II/JG77 and 150°Gruppo, together with FW190s, engaged the raiders and claimed three bombers and seven fighters shot down, of which the Italian Messerschmitt pilots claimed one of each. For the loss of one P-40, three Bf109Gs and a FW190 were claimed by the escort, the latter being credited to 1/Lt Charles B. Hall of the 99th FS, the first all-Negro unit, who thereby became the first black American to be credited with an aerial victory. A FW190 and two Bf109Gs were lost including an Italian Messerschmitt flown by Ten Giovanni dell'Innocenti, one of the leading pilots with at least a dozen destroyed or damaged victories to his credit, who was killed.

While the A-20s raided Sciacca, six Spitbombers of 126 Squadron with close escort provided by 111 Squadron and top cover by three IXs led by Wg Cdr Dundas attacked Biscari aerodrome as a diversionary measure. The target was reached at 1615 and the fighter-bombers went into action. Bomb bursts were observed on the northern side of the aerodrome and a building was seen to receive a direct hit, while others fell in the dispersal area to the east and among buildings. As the Spitbombers pulled away they were intercepted by an estimated 20 Bf109s and MC202s. Half of these made a feint attack on the escort and then dived away, apparently hoping to draw them away from their charges, before they turned to attack the fighter-bombers. Meanwhile, the remainder of the Messerschmitts attacked the escort. In the ensuing series of dogfights, Sqn Ldr George Hill (EN303) of 111 Squadron shot down one of the Messerschmitts, apparently that flown by Uffz Walter Reinicke of 7/JG53 (White 9/WkNr18107), and Sgt H.R. Hall (EN252) claimed a second, while Flt Lt Ron Green (JF419/MK-Z) and Flt Sgt A. Bingham (EN481/MK-K) of 126 Squadron claimed two others damaged. With the skirmishing over, Wg Cdr Dundas, accompanied by Flt Sgt Frank Mellor of 111 Squadron, headed for the coast:

" . . . we were attacked and my companion's plane was damaged. Luckily we were by that time crossing over the coast and the enemy planes pulled away. I saw a thin trail of white smoke streaking out from the Spitfire beside me and called my No2 to tell him that his cooling system had been punctured. He replied that his engine temperature was already rising. We were still at about 16,000 feet, so I thought there was a good chance of him getting back to Malta. I throttled back, told him to follow close beside me and concentrated on steering the best possible course and on flying in such a way that we would cover the distance as quickly as possible.

When we were half-way home George Hill [111 Squadron's CO] came up on the radio to say that he was circling a dinghy with a man in it two or three miles south of Cape Passero. He asked for company. I asked George how much fuel he had. He replied about 25 gallons and added that some 109s had put in an appearance. By this time Malta was in sight, some 15 miles ahead. I called Control, passed on George's message about the dinghy and asked them to get the ASR boys to work. Then I told my No2 to carry on alone and ordered him to bale out if his temperature rose above 125 degrees.

Swinging round to the north again, I dived for Cape Passero, asking George for his exact position and altitude. He replied that he was under 500 feet and that six 109s were circling above, taking it in turns to make a pass at him. By good luck I saw them from a distance – a solitary Spitfire circling low over the water and a ring of Messerschmitts flying round a few hundred feet above. As I watched, one of the German planes detached itself and curved lazily down to attack. The Spitfire turned sharply to meet it and for a moment the two whirled round together, before the Messerschmitt zoomed up again to join the others. I opened my throttle wide, leant the nose down and charged in through the circle of Messerschmitts, taking a couple of snap shots as I went. Then I hauled up and round and came in for another whirl through. My hope was that by behaving in the most dramatic way possible I would confuse the enemy force into thinking there was more than one of me. To my relief and utter amazement the 109s flew northwards ..." [2]

Wg Cdr Dundas and Sqn Ldr Hill returned to Malta, both Spitfires landing practically dry. Sadly, Flt Sgt Mellor did not make it. He was lost with his aircraft (EN259) when it crashed into the sea en route. Uffz Jens Bahnsen of 8/JG53 claimed two Spitfires during the action as his 14th and 15th victories, while Uffz Revi Zielke of the same Staffel claimed another. While this attack was under way a further 35 Spitfires drawn from 81, 154 and 232 Squadrons took off to provide close escort and top cover to 36 B-25s of the 340th BG bombing Comiso. The rendezvous was made north of Malta and the bombers, stepped up from 11,000 to 17,000 feet, were escorted to and from the target area. No enemy aircraft were seen and the attack was considered a success. The only incident of note was the sighting of a dinghy 15 miles south of Scalambri. Even before the formations had returned, a further 24 Spitfires from 92, 145, 417RCAF and 601 Squadrons were airborne, searching for the missing Flt Sgt Mellor[3]. He was not found but Uffz Reinicke of 7/JG53 was. While HSL107 from Malta picked up the German pilot, four 92 Squadron Spitfires led by Flg Off B.D. Baker circled overhead, anticipating the rescue of the downed RAF pilot, the leader noting somewhat disappointedly:

"When the HSL arrived it was announced on the R/T that the occupant was a Hun."

Uffz Reinicke, the rescued pilot, later recalled:

"We were in the middle of a dogfight with a large number of Spitfires when my machine's engine failed, suddenly and without any action on the part of the enemy. I was at about 15,000 feet, and I tried to extract myself from the dogfight but that proved impossible. I reported my situation over the radio and then baled out. I made a good landing on the surface of the water and

---

[2] see *Flying Start* by Grp Capt H.S.L. Dundas DSO DFC.
[3] Flt Sgt Frank Mellor's body was later recovered from the sea off the coast of Sicily and buried at Catania; his commission was announced shortly thereafter.

got into my inflatable raft without difficulty; I attached my parachute to it as a sort of sea anchor. A short while later, after the air battle had broken up, I noticed three Spitfires, which began circling over me. Then they came down and headed straight for my raft – I was afraid that they were going to shoot at me and so every time a Spitfire approached I saved myself by jumping into the water. Then I realised that my English colleagues meant me no harm and instead they waggled their wings in a friendly way.

I spent several hours in the water, surrounded by the luminous patch of colour on the water's surface created by my dye packet. The Spitfires remained overhead in relays and saw to it that no 'Me' came too close. Then suddenly I heard English voices, although at first I couldn't see anything. A little later, however, an English rescue vessel appeared over the horizon and took me on board – I still remember well the eight life rings bearing swastikas which hung on the railing, each symbol of a German airman rescued by this boat. They gave me a pair of blue RAF trousers – much too big – and an equally large pair of canvas shoes.

And then I learned the reason for my special treatment from the Royal Air Force; the wingman of a British Squadron Leader [*sic*] had been shot down in the same air battle and had baled out. The whole time the British had hoped that I was their missing pilot and had therefore done everything in their power to keep me out of German hands. Using the English I had learned in school, I could only say, 'Sorry, I'm German.'" 4

During the night pressure was maintained upon the Axis defences, 15 Bostons of the RAF's 326 Wing and 22 B-25s of the 12th BG attacking Comiso, losing one of the former and two of the latter to flak. The tempo increased on 4 July as the Allied bombing attacks intensified, 601 and 1SAAF providing 16 Spitfires as close escort to 46 B-25s of the 12th and 47th BG raiding Comiso at about 1030, a further nine Spitfires from 154 Squadron flying top cover. On the return flight, four MC202s endeavoured to attack 601 Squadron and one pilot opened fire but saw no results. Meanwhile, 11 Spitfires of 242 Squadron flew a diversionary sweep in the Vizzini-Comiso area but saw no enemy aircraft. SAAF Baltimores raided Trapani/Milo, starting a large fire on the airfield where about 40 aircraft could be seen, while 36 A-36As (the USAAF's bomb-carrying version of the RAF's Mustang) of the 27th FBG strafed Milo, Sciacca and Castelvetrano airfields.

There was no lack of enemy opposition during the late morning raid on Catania by USAAF B-17s, a total of 42 Spitfire Vs and IXs (ten/72, ten/154, fourteen/232, eight/243) providing close escort while two IXs from 72 Squadron and two more from 243 Squadron flew top cover. Six of the escort were obliged to return early with various problems while the bombers droned eastwards to their target, flying at 22,000 feet. Bombs were seen to fall in the south-west corner of the aerodrome, and hits were also seen on hangars. South of the target area Bf109Gs and MC202s were encountered by 243 Squadron, two Messerschmitts being claimed destroyed by Sqn Ldr Mackie (JK715/SN-A) and Flg Off F.S. Banner (JK189/SN-L), the latter's victim falling in flames about five miles north-east of Catania. The last he saw of it was an oily mass on the water over which a floatplane and another Bf109 were orbiting. Meanwhile, Flg Off S.I. Dalrymple (JK614/SN-C) damaged a third Messerschmitt about ten miles north-east of Cape Passero, and Flt Lt K.F. MacDonald (EN148/SN-E) reported probably destroying a Macchi which was

---

4 see *Jagdgeschwader 53 Volume Two*.

attacking two Spitfires in the same area. Finally, a second Macchi was claimed damaged by Sgt D.J. Schmitz RCAF (JK666/SN-V), who found himself alone with four of the Italian fighters. He managed to get in a telling shot at one before making good his escape. One Spitfire sustained damage during the action though the pilot was unhurt and returned safely to Hal Far, possibly the victim of Messerschmitt pilot Ten Plinio Santini of 154^Squadriglia who claimed a Spitfire shot down. Sqn Ldr Mackie reported:

"As the Fortress bombers turned to starboard, I saw approximately six ME109s at 26,000 feet, which attacked myself and my No2. After evasive action I found myself in a suitable position to attack a 109 which was approaching from starboard. I fired three deflection bursts, the last from approximately 70 yards range. I saw cannon and MG strikes all over the cockpit and fuselage. The e/a immediately burst into flames. I last saw it at 25,000 feet going down vertically in flames with black smoke pouring from it."

Four of the big bombers were claimed shot down by pilots of II/JG77 which had scrambled 34 Messerschmitts on the approach of the raid, three Spitfires also being claimed, one each being credited to Gruppenkommandeur Hptm Freytag (his 95th victory), Uffz Gräff of 1 Staffel (his first) and Oblt Franz Hrdlicka, 5 Staffel's Kapitän (his 33rd). II Gruppe lost three Bf109Gs in the action, one pilot reportedly being shot down and killed by B-17 gunners while two others fell into the sea, one aircraft (WkNr15486) crashing south of Scicli, the other (WkNr19672) east of Syracuse, possibly victims of 243 Squadron; neither pilot was killed so presumably both baled out and were rescued. Messerschmitts of 5/JG53 also engaged the Spitfires, Obfw Rollwage (his 42nd victory) and Uffz Witt (his eighth) each claiming a victory. Nine MC205Vs and 26 MC202s of 4°Stormo also scrambled from Sigonella, San Salvatore and Finocchiata and reported meeting 60 bombers and 30 Spitfires, claiming one bomber shot down and a second shared with a German pilot, while Serg Corrado Patrizi of 84^Squadriglia claimed a Spitfire. Two more were claimed by Serg Magg Natale Molteni of 90^Squadriglia before his own aircraft, one of the MC205Vs, was hit in the engine by another and he was wounded; nonetheless, he managed to carry out a force-landing. A Spitfire was also claimed as probably destroyed by Serg Alfredo Bombardini of 97^Squadriglia, while a second Macchi from the same unit was shot down from which Ten Giovanni Barcaro baled out safely, possibly another victim of 243 Squadron.

The action in the region of Catania was only a start, though, as a further 31 Spitfires (9/185, 11/229, 11/249) set off from Malta shortly after 1100 to escort bombers raiding Gerbini, but rendezvous was not achieved. Control recalled the IXs and ordered the Vs to search for a bomber missing from the earlier raid which had been reported down in the sea about ten miles south of Sampieri. There was no sign of the crew or wreckage and all returned safely to Malta. The next bomber escort, by 20 Spitfires drawn from 92 and 145 Squadrons, made rendezvous as planned at about 1230, meeting a force of B-25s and B-26s north of Malta which had their own long-range escort comprising 20 P-38Gs. Gerbini was again the target where at least five big fires were started. Amongst the Axis fighters taking off to oppose this raid were six MC205Vs and 30 MC202s of 4°Stormo. On the return journey, when about five miles south of Comiso, a number of Macchis attacked a flight of P-38s, claiming five shot down. Top-cover Spitfires of 92 Squadron dived to assist, Flg Off Brendan Baker (ER470) being attacked head-on from close range but he was able to return fire and reported seeing strikes on the Macchi before it dived away. Four

IXs of 145 Squadron then spotted three formations of fighters identified as Re2001s flying at 16,000 feet and attempted to intercept, but the Italian fighters turned away and dived, followed by Flt Sgt Ted Daley RAAF (AB459), who failed to return. He was last seen flying straight and level at about 16,000 feet and was presumed to have been shot down and, indeed, Ten Mario Mecatti of 91^Squadriglia reported shooting down a Spitfire during this raid.

The Gerbini complex was the target for the next raid, B-26s bombing No4 and No5 Satellites shortly before 1400. On this occasion 21 Spitfires from 93 and 111 Squadron provided the escort, meeting about 15 Bf109s and MC202s in the target area. Macchis from 4°Stormo were joined by Bf109Gs of 150°Gruppo. The Italian pilots reported sighting 36 B-17s and 27 B-25s with a dozen escorting P-38Gs and about 30 Spitfires [sic]. Eight more Messerschmitts – from 2/JG53 – were scrambled from San Pietro to intercept the Spitfires, the German pilots reporting a series of fierce dogfights which extended as far as Lake Lentini. In this area Lt Herbert Brönnle, acting Staffelkapitän and an ace with 58 victories (of which 57 were gained on the Eastern Front), was seen to be shot down by a Spitfire, his aircraft (Black 8/WkNr18430) crashing north of the lake and exploding in a ball of fire. He was undoubtedly the victim of Wg Cdr Dundas (JL122/HD) and Flt Lt I.K. Crawford (JK643) of 111 Squadron, who shared in shooting down a Messerschmitt, while Sgt R.H. Trowbridge RAAF (JK307), also of 111 Squadron, reported damaging a Macchi. One Spitfire was slightly damaged in the action, JK924 flown by Plt Off R.K. Whitney, the pilot returning to Malta unhurt, where he made a successful landing. The returning pilots reported seeing a Marauder shot down into the sea. Pilots from II/JG53 claimed three B-26s during this raid, the Italians one B-25 plus two B-17s and probably two Spitfires – the latter claimed by Sottoten Luigi Giannella of 84^Squadriglia and Sottoten Sforza Libera of 90^Squadriglia, for the loss of one MC205V shot down in flames, from which Sottoten Leo Boselli baled out with leg wounds, and one MC202 which Libera force-landed at San Salvatore "full of holes"; others returned showing the scars of battle.

The last raid of the day again targeted Gerbini, and was escorted by 11 Spitfires of 126 Squadron including one VIII and five IXs, and a dozen from 43 Squadron. The bombers were not seen at rendezvous but were picked up by the IXs near Cape Passero on their way home. The Spitfires crossed the coast ten miles east of Religione Point at 12,000 feet and proceeded via Syracuse and Augusta towards Catania. At 1500, 126 Squadron engaged eight enemy fighters at 14,000 feet and in the ensuing dogfight Sgt J. Saphir RCAF (JK611/MK-M) became separated. Having climbed to 22,000 feet, he saw through a gap in the clouds two Bf109Gs flying west-south-west in line astern at 17,000 feet. He attacked and claimed both shot down; one of his victims may have been Uffz Alfred Ostermeyer of 4/JG53 who was wounded in action east of Catania, the other possibly Uffz Hans Jegg of 9 Staffel whose aircraft (WkNr15376) crashed north-west of Ragusa, although one of these was probably shot down by Flt Lt G.J. Cox (JK612/FT-V) of 43 Squadron who reported a successful combat between Gerbini and Catania. A third Messerschmitt, also from II Gruppe, belly-landed west of Ramacca. Two Spitfires also failed to return, 43 Squadron aircraft flown by Flt Lt Peter Reading (BR288/FT-F) and Flg Off Ron Barker (JK928/FT-A), the former crashing near Catania, the latter near Syracuse – "the two pilots had always flown as a section since first meeting at Algiers; off duty they had been close friends; now in death they were not divided"[5]. It would seem that the missing pilots had been intercepted

---

[5] see *43 Squadron* by J. Beedle.

by Bf109Gs of I/JG53, Obfw Bartusch of 1 Staffel claiming a Spitfire at 1515, Uffz Emil Wagner (1 Staffel) and Uffz Reinhold Gröber (3 Staffel) each claiming one ten minutes later. On the way home Flt Lt Cox and Wt Off P.J. Hedderwick RAAF of 43 Squadron attacked and damaged the locomotive of a goods train seen in Vizzini station, then strafed a blockhouse east of Cape Religione. Macchis were again involved in repelling this raid, 21 having been scrambled, Italian pilots claiming four P-38Gs shot down, while Sottoten Vittorino Daffara of 97^Squadriglia reported shooting down a Spitfire. On this occasion all Macchis returned safely. During the course of the raids on the Gerbini airfields, II/JG77 alone suffered the loss of seven of its aircraft, all damaged by blast or debris. That night the Allied bombers returned, 24 A-20s, six Baltimores and 23 B-25s bombing Sciacca. Enemy night fighters were seen but no contact was made.

Next day, 5 July, witnessed even more intensive combat as US bombers again pounded the airfields. The 24 Spitfires drawn equally from 229 and 249 Squadrons tasked to escort the first raid were not called into action when 36 B-25s of the 340th BG headed for Comiso in the morning, and instead were ordered to orbit Gozo until recalled half an hour later. As they landed a further 21 Spitfires (eight/145, four/152, nine/232) started taking off to escort the B-25s as they at last arrived to carry out the raid on Comiso. The close escort which flew at 9,000 feet saw bomb bursts on the eastern dispersal area and among workshops, and on the north-west dispersal area and hangars, where fires were started. Other bombs straddled the runway. Only a few aircraft could be discerned including one twin-engined machine. There was no aerial opposition and all aircraft returned safely. It was a different scenario when the next raid arrived and the force of B-17s heading for Gerbini was met near Ragusa by more than 100 Bf109Gs from all three Gruppen of JG53 and I and II/JG77, joined by 27 MC202s and MC205Vs of 4°Stormo, flying between 22,000 and 24,000 feet. Escorting Spitfires from 72 and 243 Squadrons endeavoured to hold the Axis fighters at bay, one Bf109G being claimed by Sqn Ldr Mackie (JK715/SN-A) of 243 Squadron who reported:

> "Whilst Fortresses bombed Gerbini, the Squadron covered the area, being intercepted by 30+ ME109s at 24,000 feet, which approached from the south-east as we neared Ragusa flying at 23,000 feet on a northerly course. The top layer of ME109s made diving attacks on the Squadron and a general mêlée resulted. Some time later I saw an ME109, line astern, and fired cannon from 100 yards range, breaking off to avoid a collision. Just before I broke away I saw cannon strikes on the fuselage and wings. The e/a rolled on its back, and went down streaming glycol. I saw it crash and burst into flames just north of Palazzolo. Flt Sgt Towgood, my No2, also saw the 109 crash."

Flg Off T.B. Hughes (EN358) of 72 Squadron claimed a second as damaged, but was apparently more successful than he imagined. These were evidently aircraft from I/JG53, which reported:

> "Oblt Klein and his wingman Hptm Eckert encountered enemy aircraft, 35 to 40 Spitfires, south of Catania. During the next 20 minutes the air battle drifted south to a point abeam Cape Passero. The two pilots became separated and continued to fight alone. After disengaging from combat the other aircraft flew to the spot when Oblt Klein and Hptm Eckert had last been seen. An air-sea search which was begun immediately found nothing." [6]

---

[6] see *Jagdgeschwader 53 Volume Two*.

Oblt Willi Klein (who had been flying White 7/WkNr18346), the Kapitän of 1 Staffel, had recently achieved his sixth victory, while Hptm Klaus Eckert of Stab (Black <1/WkNr15316), had a single victory to his credit from the Tunisian campaign. Other pilots from I Gruppe managed to reach the bombers, claiming two for the loss of one of its own pilots, III Gruppe reporting four victories. JG77 was equally successful, I Gruppe claiming two B-17s and one Mosquito (probably an aircraft of 60SAAF Squadron) while II Gruppe reported four victories against the bombers, plus five probables and a Mosquito probable. The inexperienced gunners aboard the B-17s claimed no fewer than 45 (!) enemy fighters shot down during this raid, for the loss of three of their own bombers. One Messerschmitt of II/JG77 suffered severe damage in an engagement south of Castelvetrano, while, according to the diary of Maj Johannes Steinhoff, Kommodore of JG77, his aircraft was also shot down by a Spitfire and he was obliged to force-land near Mount Etna:

> ". . . out of the corner of my eye, I saw the bombers below . . . But this was hardly the moment to dive on them. Each of us would very soon have had a Spitfire breathing down our necks, for the protective role of the enemy fighters demanded that they should swing round at once and attack us. At 28,000 feet the Spitfire could turn in an astonishingly narrow radius. There was no rational explanation for my decision to attack when I saw the two Spitfires flying below me . . . at all events I found myself suddenly in a steep dive with the speed building up enormously. Already the outlines of both my opponents had appeared in my sights. The No2, however, as if hearing a warning shout, suddenly turned his aircraft on its side and broke away to the left in a tight spiral. By now I had lost sight of his No1. Without hesitating – it was against all common sense – I decided to fight it out. Yard by yard I worked my way towards the Spitfire . . . One more full circle and then, perhaps, I would have him properly in my sights . . . There was a thud against the fuselage and I wrenched my head round. Looking past the armour-plate I saw a Spitfire in a steep turn a few yards behind. Smoke from his tracers groped towards me like fingers. My engine stuttered violently. Bullets shattered against the armour-plate behind my head with appalling cracks. Immediately the cockpit was filled with the smoke or cordite . . . I broke out of the circle, half-rolled and went into a vertical dive . . . At 6,000 feet it became apparent that no one was shooting at me . . ." [7]

Maj Steinhoff successfully crash-landed his stricken aircraft on a strip of cultivated land near the base of Etna, about 30 miles from Gerbini, the impact causing injury to the base of his spine. Soon afterwards, a Storch arrived, landed, and whisked the pained Kommodore to Trapani since Gerbini was still under attack. Despite the pain, he would be back in the air within a few days. Meanwhile, the Macchis also engaged the raiders, two B-24s being claimed shot down, one in conjuction with a German Bf109G, while Cap Franco Lucchini, commander of 10°Gruppo and the Regia Aeronautica's leading ace with over 20 victories, was reported to have shot down a Spitfire before he was himself shot down and killed. A second battle-damaged MC202 carried out an emergency landing at Gerbini, M.llo Gianni Bianchelli of 97^Squadriglia extricating himself shortly before his aircraft was destroyed by bombs.

The third major raid of the day occurred shortly after midday when 36 B-26s,

---

[7] see *The Straits of Messina*.

escorted by P-38s, again targeted Gerbini while 20 Spitfires from 92 and 1SAAF Squadrons, led by Sqn Ldr Humphreys and Lt Rogan respectively, provided top cover. Several fires were seen on the ground following the attack and other bombs were seen to fall on a road north-west of Catania. Although no enemy aircraft rose to challenge this raid, many were seen on the ground at Ragusa and Catania. US A-36As of the 27th FBG were again in action although the pilots were unable to locate Sciacca aerodrome, their primary target, owing to haze. A dozen bombed the harbour instead while the remainder bombed railway bridges, though no hits were claimed.

The action was now relentless as raid followed raid. More B-25s and B-26s attacked Gerbini and its satellites shortly after 1500, Spitfires from 81 and 242 Squadrons providing top cover. Bombs were seen to burst on the south-west corner of the main aerodrome, where fires were started. Four Bf109s were sighted at 20,000 feet over Gerbini but no engagement ensued. As the formation made its way back across the coast, three small naval vessels were observed off Bruccoli, two stationary and one steaming westwards, but were not attacked. Before the raiders and their escorts had reached their home bases, the next formation was on its way to attack Gerbini, 20 Spitfires from 126 and 1435 Squadrons providing top cover to the B-17s and their close-escort P-38s. The results of this latest attack could not be seen by the Spitfire pilots owing to heavy smoke over the target area, who anyway had their hands full when Bf109Gs and Macchis attempted to intercept over Gerbini. A Messerschmitt was claimed damaged by Flt Sgt F.K. Halcombe (JK368/V-J) of 1435 Squadron, Plt Off Chandler (JK139/V-X) similarly claimed a Macchi damaged, while Flg Off Geoff White (JK611/MK-M) of 126 Squadron shot down another:

" . . . a few Macchis made an attack on the edge of the formation. I attacked one of them, fired a burst at it and then followed it right down to the ground and eventually shot it down after a lot of aerobatic flying. The pilot baled out. There was quite a lot of AA once the pilot got out because he actually baled out right over his base. I looked around and saw a big aerodrome and thought it wasn't a very good place to be. I did a fairly fast climbing turn, and when I looked back there were about 30 AA bursts following me up. The first one was rather close because I heard a sharp crack."

His victim was possibly Serg Corrado Patrizi of 84^Squadriglia who baled out of his disabled MC205V near Gerbini. A second Macchi pilot, Sottoten Leonardo Ferrulli of 91^Squadriglia, who was seen by colleagues to shoot down a bomber from which three men baled out, and a P-38, was then himself shot down by a Spitfire. He managed to bale out but was too low, his aircraft crashing near Scordia.

The last bombing raid of the day was targeted against Biscari aerodrome, 24 B-25s of the 12th BG releasing their loads at about 1700 while Spitfires from 43 Squadron flew top cover and ten from 111 Squadron as freelance cover. A further 20 (eight/229, six/249, six/185) provided close escort. Bombs exploded all over the aerodrome, and particularly in the north-west dispersal areas and among the main buildings. No flak was experienced but an estimated 12 FW190s of III/SKG10 led by Hptm Fritz Schröter and a similar number of Bf109s were sighted by 229 Squadron at 5,000 feet, and bloody battle was joined. The Messerschmitts were probably from 3°Stormo, one Italian pilot claiming two Bostons shot down over Caltagirone at about 1730. Three FW190s were claimed destroyed, Flt Lt Les Gosling (LZ808/X-D) getting two and Flt Sgt R.H. De Tourret RNZAF (ER494/X-H) the third. Two of these were flown by Stab pilot Lt

Erhardt Wicht (WkNr1439) and Lt Günther Schlösser (WkNr0894) of 9 Staffel, both of whom were killed. Another was damaged by Flg Off Idema, while De Tourret reported also damaging a Bf109G, but the cost was high. Sqn Ldr Blair White[8] (JG838/X-W) was seen to be shot down by a FW190, and killed, as was Flt Sgt Rainald Salzman (EF520/X-O), possibly victims of Hptm Schröter and Lt Bruno Schäfer, who each claimed a Spitfire in this action[9]; the aircraft (JK124/X-G) flown by Plt Off G.W. Symons RNZAF was also hit and damaged, forcing the New Zealander to bale out into the sea, while fellow New Zealander Flt Sgt De Tourret crashed his damaged aircraft at Hal Far on landing; he survived but his aircraft did not and was written off. Yet one more 229 Squadron machine returned with battle damage although Flg Off Jack te Kloot RAAF (EP290/X-Y) was unhurt. The latter recalled:

"Jumped by FW190s, being on the outside of the turn after the Mitchells dropped their bombs and turned for home. Lost CO and a Flight Sergeant. I was shot up. Three cannon shells through starboard wing. My first introduction to the enemy in the air."

The action was not finished, however, as four miles south of Gela ten FW190s and Bf109s were seen and engaged by 43 and 111 Squadron, Flt Sgt W.J. Webster RNZAF (ES294/FT-P) of the former unit claiming damage to a FW190 "camouflaged dark blue". Owing to fuel shortage the Spitfires were not able to pursue their adversaries, which, in turn chased the Spitfires towards Malta, one 111 Squadron machine (EN291) having its controls badly damaged although the pilot, Flg Off W. Young, was able to reach Luqa where he force-landed, slightly wounded. Returning pilots reported seeing one enemy fighter burning on the beach south-east of Gela and one, possibly two, dinghies in the sea off Scalambri. With the return of the Spitfires to Malta, a further 39 drawn from 43, 92, 154, 232, 242, 243, 249, 1SAAF, and 417RCAF Squadrons were despatched in sections of four to search for the dinghies reported in the sea. One Canadian flying with the latter unit, Flg Off H.J. Everard RCAF[10], recalled:

"On arrival at the battle area, I peered unbelievingly at nine dinghies bobbing in the water – four of ours and five of theirs. In complete silence and in almost parade formation, we patrolled our sentinal line to the west whilst the enemy repeated our manoeuvre to the east. I concluded our cross-over turns and aircraft separations were much smoother and smarter than our opponents. This cat-and-mouse drama produced a river of sweat down my spine. This was my first opportunity to examine the enemy's principal fighter at relatively close range. After some time, a rescue boat from Sicily and another from Malta arrived and began to fish out their respective

---

8 Sqn Ldr Blair White had been shot down and wounded in France in 1940, and, having participated in the Battle of Britain, was shot down and wounded again a year later.
9 Available records suggest that all three of 229 Squadron's aircraft were shot down by FW190s, with at least one other, possibly two, damaged. III/SKG10 recorded only two claims, those by Hptm Schröter and Lt Schäfer, therefore it would seem probable that the two missing FW190 pilots, Lts Wicht and Schlösser, inflicted damage before their own demise.
10 Flg Off Hedley Everard, known as 'Snooks' to his friends, had flown Hurricanes with 17 Squadron in Burma the previous year, and had been credited with shooting down at least one Japanese fighter and an RAF Hurricane; fortunately, the pilot of the latter survived.

downed airmen. When the task was completed, we escorted our rescue craft back to Malta and I could see the 109s were providing the same cover to their boat." [11]

The 92 Squadron section led by Flt Lt Tom Savage located one dinghy which contained seven occupants, survivors of one of the American Mitchells lost during the day, and patrolled over it until relieved by a section from 1SAAF and three P-38s. An air-sea rescue launch from Malta, HSL107, duly arrived and took on board all seven American airmen. The second dinghy was sighted some 15 miles from Scalambri by the section from 243 Squadron, which tried unsuccessfully to direct the launch to the location. The section from 43 Squadron then arrived and dropped a Mae West containing distress signals, which was picked up by the occupant, Plt Off Symons of 229 Squadron, who later reported:

"On the way home from the target I was attacked by two FW190s, and my radiator, wings and fuselage were hit. I headed straight for home and about five miles south of Sicily, at 1,200 feet, I saw my engine temperature was rising very rapidly. I decided to bale out, and got out of my aircraft by undoing my straps, pulling the hood back, and pushing the stick violently forward. I cleared the aircraft successfully, pulled the rip-cord, and inflated my Mae West just before I struck the water. As soon as I touched the water, I released my parachute harness and had no trouble in inflating my dinghy. This was about 1700 hours. As soon as I looked around me, I saw two Spitfires circling me. They stayed near me for about 20 minutes.

Towards dusk I heard Spitfires approaching, so I fired my two star flares at the most favourable moments. The flares were seen and the Spitfires came nearer and circled me. Then three of the Spitfires went away to the south and the other remained over me, dropping his Mae West to me just at dusk. He circled two or three times then flew off. During the night I paddled on a course of approximately 180° and, as light broke, I could see the coast of Sicily behind me. I paddled on until the coast was out of sight. At approximately 1200 hours I saw a large number of bombers and fighters making for Sicily. I put out my fluorescine in the water. This was seen by a Spitfire from about 3,000 feet, and he circled me until two more Spitfires relieved him. At about 1435 hours I saw the ASR launch [Pinnace 1254 from Malta] approaching and was picked up at 1500 hours. I suffered no ill effects with the exception of slight blistering, and except during the midday period, felt no discomfort either from heat or cold. I ate three of the 'Horlick's Malted Milk' tablets and a small quantity of chocolate, and did not feel either hungry or thirsty."

Biscari and Trapani/Milo were the main targets for the night bombers, 21 B-25s and seven Bostons raiding the former, while a dozen Bostons and five Baltimores visited the latter. Several night fighters were seen but no engagements resulted and all aircraft returned safely.

American and SAAF bombers raided many aerodromes during the morning of 6 July, bombs falling on Gela, San Pietro, Trapani, Sciacca and Comiso. Four Bf109s intercepted the raid on Comiso but without result. The Italians reported that the raid on San Pietro damaged on the ground 13 Bf109Gs of 3°Gruppo, but four others from the same unit scrambled from Sciacca, as did six more of 150°Gruppo

---

[11] see *A Mouse in My Pocket*.

from Comiso, joining 15 MC202s and three MC205Vs of 4°Stormo. The Italian pilots claimed one bomber shot down with a second as probably destroyed, in addition to damaging two P-38s and two Spitfires. One Messerschmitt flown by Ten Virginio Pozzoli of 363^Squadriglia was severely damaged and, while attempting to land, it struck a wall and crashed, killing the pilot. Spitfires of 145, 232 and 601 Squadron provided escort, meeting Bf109Gs of I/JG77, Plt Off J.S. Ekbery (JK365/EF-D) of 232 Squadron claiming a Messerschmitt shot down which he reported crashed into the ground, probably that flown by Uffz Rolf Daum whose aircraft (WkNr18184) crashed at Sciacca although the pilot survived, while 601 Squadron lost Flg Off Wilf Seaman AFC (ER534), who did not and was evidently the victim of Lt Ludwig Licha of 3/JG77; a second aircraft from 601 Squadron was badly damaged but the pilot managed to get back to Malta, as did Lt H.E. Wells SAAF of 145 Squadron who reported being set upon by five aircraft identified as Re2001s and Messerschmitts. Despite damage to his aircraft (EE790) he gamely fought back but was unable to make any claims.

Ramacca landing ground was on the receiving end of two heavy raids in the morning, Bf109Gs of II/JG53 scrambling but not making contact. However, at about 1500, when the bombers returned, all three Gruppen were sent off, the German pilots reporting meeting between 30 to 80 B-17s and 20 escorting Spitfires including those of the 308th FS, one of the fighters being claimed by Obfw Günther Seeger of 7/JG53 for his 36th victory. Two of JG53's leading pilots also reported shooting down Spitfires in this action, Oblt Hans Röhrig, Kapitän of 9 Staffel, claiming his 71st victory, and Oblt Fritz Dinger, 4 Staffel's Kapitän, his 60th. Pilots of the American Spitfire Squadron reported being jumped by a dozen German fighters as they passed over Comiso and watched in horror as their new CO, Capt Thomas B. Fleming, was shot down in flames. 1/Lt Babcock, a new pilot, also failed to return and was presumed to have been similarly shot down.

While the action unfolded over the Sicilian coast, two Bf109Gs of 3°Gruppo flown by Sottoten Giuseppe Ruzzin and Serg Magg Carlo Cavagliano made a dash for Malta, where they were to reconnoitre the harbours for shipping. Thick haze prevented any sightings, and they only narrowly avoided being intercepted by a flight of five Spitfires by diving at full speed for the sea. Recovering with some difficulty, the two pilots nonetheless successfully escaped their pursuers and reached Comiso safely.

Newly arrived, newly promoted Grp Capt Brian Kingcome DSO DFC (who had just taken command of 244 Wing) led Spitfires of 126 Squadron as part of the escort to B-25s raiding Gerbini at about 1500, when two MC202s were seen attempting to attack the bombers but were driven off. During another bomber escort 81 Squadron sighted two Ju52/3ms flying at ground level and despatched a section of two to intercept, but they lost the transports in heavy haze. In the late afternoon USAAF bombers were back over Sicily and during a raid on Finocchiara landing ground two Macchis were destroyed, and a third seriously damaged, while one of the Macchi pilots suffered wounds. Bf109Gs from II/JG53 were again airborne to intercept 24 B-24s which were attacking Ramacca for the third time this day, but only one of the bombers was claimed damaged while Uffz Hermann Witt of 5 Staffel was seen to collide with another off Augusta, both aircraft going down. By 1750, 13 Spitfires including three IXs of 242 Squadron were airborne as cover to 50 B-24s bombing Catania and Gerbini aerodromes. The bombers released their deadly loads from between 22,000 and 24,000 feet. When leaving the Catania area, enemy fighters were seen climbing to intercept and 242 Squadron was ordered to engage, Sqn Ldr Boddington (JK260/LE-K) firing at a Bf109G from astern, seeing many machine-gun strikes before it rolled and dived vertically. During the roll a piece fell off the damaged aircraft. As he followed it down, a further six enemy fighters were seen and his No2, Sgt E.S. Doherty RNZAF (ER163/LE-J) attacked another Messerschmitt from astern, also observing strikes on its engine and cowling. Many pilots disliked flying over the sea, 21-year-old Eric Doherty from Gisborne, New Zealand, being one of these:

"I personally found it uncomfortable to fly over water every time one took-off – going to and coming back from operations. Especially coming back, if one was running short of fuel and perhaps being pursued. Worse still, short of fuel and out of ammunition – that was one of my lasting impressions of flying from an island."

During the day A-36As of the 27th FBG flew five separate missions against targets in the western part of the island, totalling 59 sorties, their main objectives being radar stations and sites. Bad weather that night restricted the bombers and only one small raid was made against Sciacca.

Italian records show no let-up for the defenders on 7 July when AA gunners reported shooting down a total of 14 bombers and fighters, while Axis fighters claimed five more including two P-40s by 4/JG53, an aircraft identified as a Martlet by Maj Steinhoff of Stab/JG77, and a P-38G by a Macchi pilot of 91^Squadrigia. The raids were logged by the Italians:

0939 – attack on Catania/Fontanarossa by 80 B-17s under escort of Spitfires;
1024 – attack on Trapani/Milo by 20 B-26s under escort of 23 P-40s;
1050 – attack on Gerbini by 80 bombers under escort of 12 Spitfires;
1123 – attack on Gela by unknown number of bombers;
1145 – attack on Gerbini by 70 bombers under escort of P-38s;
1200 – attack on Santo Pietro di Caltagirone by 23 B-26s;
1445 – attack on Catania/Fontanarossa by 30 B-24s under escort of Spitfires;
1656 – attack on Chinisia by 40 bombers under escort of 20 P-40s or Spitfires;
2155 – attack on Catania by 60 B-24s under escort of Spitfires.

During the morning attack on Trapani/Milo by Baltimores, 47 P-40s of the 324th and 325th FG reported meeting a dozen Bf109s and Macchis, a similar number of enemy fighters encountered by the 324th FG while escorting A-20s to bomb Chinisia/Borizzo airfield in the afternoon. The Americans claimed four for the loss of one of their own. A-36As continued their assault on radar stations in the west of the island, reporting a number of successful sorties.

Wg Cdr Billy Drake (JK228) led Spitfires of the Krendi Wing to rendezvous with B-17s tasked to bomb Gerbini at about 0930. The bombers were greeted by heavy and accurate flak over the target area, while four Macchis were sighted and engaged. In fact there were five Macchis of the 4°Stormo's 91^Squadriglia from Sigonella, the pilots reporting meeting many P-38s and Spitfires, one of the former being claimed shot down. Meanwhile, the others reported engagements with both bombers and fighters, claiming several damaged before Sottoten Simone Magri's aircraft was hit and the pilot wounded in the left leg, probably the victim of Wg Cdr Drake (his 25th, and last, victory), Flt Sgt De Tourett (JK368/X-C) of 229

Squadron claiming a second as damaged. 152 and 154 Squadrons of 322 Wing were also engaged in this operation but made no contact with enemy fighters. However, on the way home when about 15 miles north of Malta, Sgt T. Armstrong's aircraft (LZ163) collided with that flown by Plt Off Bob Macdonald (JK104), Armstrong's tail-less aircraft spinning down into the sea. The pilot baled out and was rescued two hours later by a HSL from Malta, while Macdonald belly-landed his damaged machine successfully at Takali.

Spitfires from 92, 601, 1SAAF and 417RCAF escorted 48 B-24s bombing Gerbini and its satellites at about 1430, and although they patrolled between Gerbini and Catania for 35 minutes no enemy aircraft were seen. In a second scramble by 4°Stormo Macchis, seven aircraft intercepted a formation of 60 B-26s escorted by P-38s and Spitfires near Vizzini. Three of the bombers were claimed damaged, including one by Ten Flavio Fratini of 97^Squadriglia who was then shot down and killed. An American Spitfire crashed on landing on returning from a sortie during the day, though the 308th FS pilot was not injured. Wellingtons of the Strategic Air Force bombed Comiso and Catania during the hours of darkness, while those of the Tactical Air Force targeted Comiso and Sciacca airfields. The Wellingtons of 205 Group, whose operations had been frustrated by bad weather over the past few days, were able to launch 90 aircraft to attack various airfields: the Gerbini complex, where results were generally unobserved, Catania, where crews were satisfied that the bombing was successful, and Comiso where only a third of the crews claimed any accuracy with their bombing.

The US bombers, escorted by 126 Squadron, raided Biscari at 0930 on the morning of 8 July, followed by an attack on Gerbini at 1130, escorting Spitfires not sighting enemy fighters although they were present on both occasions, but at 1230, during a further attack on Gerbini by B-26s and on Comiso by B-17s, Messerschmitts of both II/JG53 and II/JG77 were engaged by 72 Squadron. Plt Off R.J.H. Hussey DFM (ES281) saw a number of Bf109Gs circling to land at Comiso and dived on them from 14,000 feet, shooting down one which, he noted, had white wingtips. Sqn Ldr Daniel (JG793) destroyed a second. A third was seen to crash without apparently being attacked, although both Sgt C.M. Scott (JK372) and Flt Sgt K. Hermiston (JK771) claimed damage to two more. The airfield was then strafed and three aircraft claimed severely damaged, a Ju52/3m (credited to Hussey), a FW190, and an Hs129, while the administration building and wireless station were also attacked. II/JG77 reported the loss of one aircraft (WkNr16481) west of Comiso at about 1230, from which the pilot baled out safely, while an aircraft of JG53 belly-landed with battle damage. Eleven Spitfires from 242 Squadron accompanied those of 72 Squadron, Flg Off K.A. Edwards sighting a Bf109G at 1,000 feet below his height near Biscari. He carried out a diving attack, opening fire from 600 yards but failed to observe any results, and was followed by Sgt Doherty, who similarly failed to register any strikes as the Messerschmitt dived away. The B-17s, two of which were claimed shot down by II/JG53 and two more by II/JG77, were also under escort from 185 and 229 Squadrons, the latter unit now commanded by newly promoted Sqn Ldr Graham Cox formerly of 43 Squadron. 185 Squadron sighted seven Bf109Gs, one of which Sqn Ldr MacDougall (LZ809) claimed damaged. None of the Spitfire units suffered any losses or damage in this action.

An official report noted that 111 tons of bombs were dropped on Sciacca, Comiso and Biscari by a dozen Baltimores, a similar number of A-20s, and 70 B-25s from the 12th and 340th BG, with an escort provided by 36 P-40s. It was the turn of P-38s to attack the radar stations on the Pachino peninsula, one also being strafed south of Catania, the A-36As concentrating on railway junctions, road intersections and power plants. During afternoon raids by the heavy and medium bombers, when Gerbini, Catania, Comiso and Biscari were targeted, escorting Spitfires failed to engage any of the enemy fighters scrambled to intercept the bombers, although 81, 92, 601 Squadrons escorted a raid on Comiso by 24 B-25s when three Bf109Gs of Stab/JG53 were destroyed on the ground. A force of A-20s carried out a further raid on Sciacca when more than 35 Bf109s and FW190s attacked, escorting P-40s claiming seven destroyed or damaged for the loss of three of their own aircraft. Intelligence reported that three more satellite landing grounds were in use at Gerbini, and a new landing ground near Canicatti had been discovered. That night 67 Wellingtons of the Strategic Air Force raided Catania, Comiso and Gerbini airfields, while US bombers attacked Trapani/Milo and Sciacca. Two Wellingtons failed to return.

At Malta during the day a Spitfire from 92 Squadron, JK169, crashed on take-off, but Plt Off M.J. Fakhry RAAF, an Australian pilot of obvious Middle Eastern extraction, escaped with only slight injuries; another, from the 308th FS, crashed on take-off from Gozo in which the pilot, 1/Lt P. Dixon Van Ausdell, was also injured. Meanwhile, a detachment of Hurricane IIcs from 73 Squadron arrived at Luqa from La Sebala in Tunisia. The Squadron was in the process of re-equipping with Spitfires but retained a flight of Hurricanes for night flying duties. The detachment, under the command of Flt Lt J.P. Mills, was to operate night intruder/anti-searchlight patrols over the projected landing zones for the forthcoming invasion. Another Tunisian-based unit, 682 Squadron operating PR Spitfires from La Marsa, lost an aircraft from an afternoon sortie over Sicily and southern Italy when Flt Lt R.E. Walker DFM failed to return; he was killed when his Spitfire (EN659) crashed near Catania.

With the launch of the invasion just a few hours away, 9 July saw an intensification of bombing attacks, as recorded by the official US Naval historian:

"The penultimate contribution of the Air Forces was delivered on 9 July and the night before the landings. During daylight, 21 bombing and strafing missions – comprising 411 bombers escorted by 168 fighters, plus 78 fighters to strafe radar stations etc – struck airfields and other selected targets all the way from Sciacca to Taormina, sparing the beaches with the idea of concealing where the landings would take place. This seems to have had the contrary effect, as noted in the War Diary of the German Naval Command: 'In the course of the last few days the attacks on Sicilian airfields have skipped certain areas which are in the neighbourhood of harbours or landing areas. Enemy landing activities can be foreseen in these areas.' Luftwaffe headquarters at Taormina, as well as the nearby Church of San Domenico, were destroyed [where about 45 civilians were killed]. Between sunset and midnight, 63 British and 44 US bombers, in eight separate missions, bombed Syracuse, Catania, Caltagirone, Palazzolo and various airfields. The [US] Army Air Forces, as usual at this period of the war, were not always discriminating in target selection. The cities of Palermo and Catania were bombed without affording the Allies any military advantage. Churches were damaged or destroyed, many noble buildings gutted and civilians buried under the ruins of their dwellings. On the other hand, beach defences had neither been bombed, nor shelled, nor in any other way attacked before Zero hour, nor had the [enemy] mobile divisions of the interior been strafed." [12]

---

[12] see *Sicily-Salerno-Anzio* by Admiral Samuel Eliot Morison USN.

The attack on the Luftwaffe HQ at Taormina was carried out by A-36As of the 27th and 86th FBGs, when 186 500-lb bombs were released over the target area. Sciacca, Milo and Biscari airfields were again targeted, on this occasion by 32 A-20s of the 47th BG, while 54 B-26s raided Palazzolo, Piazza and Armbuni, and 23 P-38Gs bombed and strafed the Pozzallo area and the radar station at Cape Passero. The Americans claimed ten Bf109s and one FW190 destroyed plus a dozen Messerschmitts damaged for the loss of ten of their own – four A-20s, four P-40s and two A-36As. Among the Italian fighters that rose to challenge these raids were MC202s and presumably D.520s of 161°Gruppo from Reggio di Calabria. Two Spitfires were claimed by Macchi pilots from 10°Gruppo, Sottoten Vittorino Daffara and Sottoten Fabio Clauser, who reported meeting ten P-38s and 20 Spitfires east of Catania, although their opponents were probably P-40s rather than Spitfires.

Malta's Spitfires continued to escort the bombers throughout the day's operations, flying 164 sorties during the course of nine missions but meeting enemy fighters on only two of these. The day's only successes fell to 185 Squadron led by Flt Lt Wilmot during a Mitchell escort to Gerbini at 1725, when six FW190s and two MC202s were sighted and engaged, Flt Sgt Mercer (EN403/GL-A) claiming a MC202. His victim may have been an Italian Bf109G from 150°Gruppo, two of these having been sent out on a reconnaissance mission to search for signs of the approaching convoys. On the return flight the two Messerschmitts were intercepted by Spitfires and Ten Angelo Fornoncini (successful in at least ten combats) was shot down into the sea, his aircraft falling in flames. The pilot of the other Messerschmitt, Ten Cavatore, belly-landed his aircraft at Sciacca. Meanwhile, Sgt G.M. Buchanan RNZAF (EN349/GL-C) claimed a FW190 and Flt Lt McKee (EN533/GL-N) reported the probable destruction of a second FW190. The FW190s may have been from I/SchG2, Uffz Werner Minuth of 2 Staffel being reported missing although he later returned to his unit, presumably having baled out.

A further 339 Spitfire sorties were flown in protection of the invasion armada – approximately 2,000 ships and craft of all sizes – now approaching the Sicilian coast. The general plan was to employ two-thirds of all available fighter effort on close escort of the convoys when they came within 50 miles west of the south of Malta. These commitments required each squadron to fly two patrols during the day, thereby leaving the pilots and ground crews fresh for the assault on the following days. A few replacement pilots arrived from Tunisia aboard a Hudson during the day, including Flt Sgt Maurice Smith, a New Zealander with 43 Squadron:

> "We had a little bit of excitement when the port engine of the Hudson showed signs of packing up. All of us pilots on board had our parachutes in the middle of the floor and we grabbed them as fast as we could, but then decided we had better help this poor bugger [the Hudson pilot] if his engine was at risk. We were trimming the thing by rushing backwards and forwards, and all sorts of general activity, but it was getting lower and lower, and we only just managed to get across the cliffs at Malta and on to Hal Far. We just managed to stagger over the top of them."

None of the invasion convoys was attacked from the air during the hours of daylight, nor, according to Allied records, were they reconnoitred. Certainly the pilot of a MC205V of 4°Stormo who flew a reconnaissance sortie to Malta failed to make a sighting, although German records show that a convoy had been sighted south of Pantelleria as early as 0320 that morning, and the crew of another reconnaissance machine reported sighting five convoys south of Malta at about 1330, and another 30 miles north-west of Gozo at 1840 – but, of course, their ultimate destination was unknown. However, there could have been few amongst the Sicilian garrison who had not deduced for themselves that an invasion was imminent. The Kommodore of JG77, Maj Steinhoff, wrote:

> "During the past few days reconnaissance had revealed the presence of a powerful force of warships of all sizes in Valetta harbour and surrounding the island. That, combined with the violence of the bombardment and the enemy's non-stop reconnaissance flights, pointed to an imminent landing." [13]

Nonetheless, the German High Command retained doubts about the actual whereabouts of the intended landings until the eleventh hour. Greece – and specifically the Corfu-Arta-Pyrgos region on the west coast – was considered by the German Naval War Staff, even as late as 20 May 1943, to offer the greatest prospects of success for the Allies, although Sardinia – not Sicily – was also believed to be the only feasible alternative. Undoubtedly Operation *Mincemeat*[14] played its part in the Allied plan of deception.

To protect the convoys after dark, AI-equipped Mosquito and Beaufighter night fighters and intruders operated throughout the night over enemy airfields in Sicily and southern Italy. With nightfall came the Wellingtons, over 100 aircraft from 205 Group operating against targets in Sicily. Fifty-five bombed the Syracuse isthmus, and five attacked the seaplane base, while others raided Catania and attacked suspected enemy concentrations at Palazzolo, Caltanissetta, Canicatti and Caltagirone. Very little opposition was encountered and many fires were started.

As a result of this phase of operations, the Axis air force on Sicily was mainly confined to the use of Trapani/Milo and Sciacca airfields in the west, and the Gerbini complex in the east. Castelvetrano, Palermo, Chinisia/Borizzo, Biscari and Comiso were practically abandoned. It was believed that enemy air opposition was now largely neutralised by losses in the air and on the ground, and by the damage to Sicilian airfields, while the enemy's communication facilities for the supply and reinforcement of Sicily had been seriously impaired. But despite the battering Sicily's airfields had taken in recent days and the toll of aircraft destroyed in the air and on the ground, Fliegerkorps II (Süd) still posed a major threat to the invasion forces:

Fliegerkorps II (Süd) Jagdgruppen Order of Battle
Sicily, 9 July 1943

Comiso

Stab/JG53	6 Bf109G (2 serviceable)	Obstlt Günther von Maltzahn

Gerbini

II/JG53	23 Bf109G (18 serviceable)	Maj Karl-Heinz Schnell
4 Staffel		Oblt Fritz Dinger
5 Staffel		Oblt Martin Laube
6 Staffel		Oblt Leo Potjans

---

[13] see *The Straits of Messina*.
[14] *Mincemeat* was the codename given to a British secret operation in which a body dressed in the uniform of a Royal Marine officer was placed in the sea off the coast of Spain via a submarine. Attached to the body was a briefcase in which were documents purporting to confirm that the Allied landings were indeed to take place on the Greek west coast. The body was duly recovered from the sea and the documents were handed over to the German authorities as intended; see *The Man Who Never Was* by Ewen Montague.

II/JG77	39 Bf109G (18 serviceable)	Hptm Siegfried Freytag
4 Staffel		Oblt Heinz Dudeck
5 Staffel		Oblt Franz Hdrlicka
6 Staffel		Oblt Joachim Deicke
Stab/SchG2	1 FW190 (unserviceable)	Hptm Heinrich Brücker
II/SchG2	27 FW190 (16 serviceable)	Hptm Werner Dömbrack
Stab/SKG10	4 FW190 (2 serviceable)	Maj Günther Tonne
II/SKG10 }	8 FW190 (0 serviceable) 12 FW190 at Montecorvino	Hptm Hans-Jobst Hauenschild
IV/SKG10	25 FW190 (11 serviceable)	Maj Heinz Schumann

Catania

III/JG53	30 Bf109G (12 serviceable)	Hptm Franz Götz
7 Staffel		Lt Franz Barten
8 Staffel		Hptm Franz Schiess
9 Staffel		Oblt Hans Röhrig
2(H)/14	12 Bf109G (5 serviceable)	Oblt Ernst von Weyrauch

San Pietro

III/SKG10 }	7 FW190 (0 serviceable) 18 FW190 at Montecorvino	Hptm Fritz Schröter

Trapani/Milo

Stab/JG77	3 Bf109G (2 serviceable)	Maj Johannes Steinhoff

Sciacca

I/JG77	35 Bf109G (3 serviceable)	Maj Heinz Bär
1 Staffel		Oblt Heinz-Edgar Berres
2 Staffel		Lt Armin Köhler
3 Staffel		Oblt Ernst Laube

In addition, Hptm Werner Schroer's II/JG27 was at Vibo Valentia on the mainland with 22 Bf109Gs (14 serviceable), I/JG53 was also at Vibo Valentia with 35 Bf109Gs (15 serviceable) under the command of Maj Karl-Friedrich Müller, and IV/JG3 under Hptm Franz Beyer was at Lecce, also on the mainland, with 36 more Bf109Gs (28 serviceable). There were a further 50-plus Bf109Gs of III/JG77 (Maj Kurt Ubben) and II/JG51 (Maj Karl Rammelt) in Sardinia. All Bf110s and Me210s of Stab and III/ZG26 had been withdrawn to the mainland, together with the Bf110s of II/ZG1, where they joined the Ju88Cs of 10/ZG26. Only the Ju88C night fighters of 4 and 5/NJG2 under the command of Hptm Hueschens and Hptm Hissbach respectively, remained at Comiso, while the reconnaissance Ju88Ds, Me210s and Me410s of 2(F)/122 remained at Trapani, all Ju88 bombers having been withdrawn to the mainland. The bomber force available was nonetheless substantial: Stab, I and III/KG6 (63 Ju88s, 56 serviceable) were at Foggia, as were Stab, I, and III/KG76 (55 Ju88s, 29 serviceable), and I/KG1 (37 Ju88s, 18 serviceable). There were a further 24 Ju88s of III/KG30 at Viterbo, and 29 of III/KG54 at Grottaglie – a total of at least 200 Ju88s available at nearby mainland bases, plus 38 He111s of I/KG27 and Stab/KG100, 80 Do217Ks of II and III/KG100 and eight Ju88s of III/KG26 available at short notice in southern France. According to Italian records, Fliegerkorps II (Süd) currently had 932 aircraft in its inventory, but Feldmarschall Kesselring, C-in-C all German forces in Italy and Sicily was clearly not confident that any sustained Allied attack could be halted:

"The German air forces on the island, in so far as they were not withdrawn to Calabria and Apulia, were knocked out before the invasion even started – even on the Italian mainland they sustained considerable losses, and our fighters were too weak to redress the balance. Similarly, our flak was unable to protect the airfields, harbours and railway installations – it was just not powerful enough . . . With Ambrosio [Generale d'Armata Vittorio Ambrosio was the newly appointed Chief of the Comando Supremo, the Italian General Staff] in the saddle, our partnership was simply riding for a fall. There were often times when I reflected that it would be far easier to fight alone with inadequate forces than to have to accept so bewildering a responsibility for the Italian people's aversion to the war and our ally's lack of fighting qualities and dubious loyalty." [15]

Generale S.A. Adriano Monti, Commander of Aeronautica della Sicilia, had long pleaded with Rome to send reinforcements, and at last these started to arrive, some units flying to the few serviceable airfields on the island, others taking up station on the mainland in Calabria and Puglia. Despite this last-minute reinforcement, there remained under 200 combat aircraft on the strength of Aeronautica della Sicilia, of which just 79 were considered operational; for example, the Bf109G-equipped 3° and 150°Stormi reported only six of their Messerschmitts combat ready on the eve of the invasion. In Calabria there were a further 142 front-line aircraft, mainly new arrivals, of which 94 were ready for operations by the eve of the invasion:

Finocchiara/Fontanarossa/San Salvatore/Sigonella
4°Stormo CT	TenCol Armando Francois	
9°Gruppo CT	Cap Luigi Mariotti	18 MC202, 2 MC205V
73^Squadriglia	Cap Giulio Reiner	
96^Squadriglia	Cap Emanuele Annoni	
97^Squadriglia	Ten Giovanni Barcaro	
10°Gruppo CT	Cap Ranieri Piccolomini	20 MC202/MC205V
84^Squadriglia	Cap Luigi Gianella	
90^Squadriglia	Cap Ranieri Piccolomini	
91^Squadriglia	Ten Mario Mecatti	

Comiso
3°Gruppo Aut CT	TenCol Aldo Alessandrini	21 Bf109G (all unserviceable)
153^Squadriglia	Cap Olivio Monesi	
154^Squadriglia	Cap Giuseppe Tovazzi	
155^Squadriglia	Cap Bruno Alessandrini	

San Pietro di Caltagirone
150°Gruppo Aut CT	TenCol Antonio Vizzotto	21 Bf109G (15 unserviceable)
363^Squadriglia	Cap Mario Bellagambi	
364^Squadriglia	Cap Giuseppe Giannelli	
365^Squadriglia	Ten Fausto Filippi	

Chinisia
21°Gruppo Aut CT	Magg Ettore Foschini	33 MC202
356^Squadriglia	Cap Aldo Li Greci	
361^Squadriglia	Cap Francesco Leoncini	
386^Squadriglia	Cap Trento Carotti	

[15] see *The Memoirs of Field-Marshal Kesselring*.

Palermo
    377^Squadriglia CT   MC202/CR42
Castelvetrano
    16°Gruppo CT   22 MC202
      167^Squadriglia
      168^Squadriglia
      169^Squadriglia

The survivors of 151° and 153°Gruppi had been ordered to evacuate Sicily and make for Caselle, leaving just seven combat-worthy MC202s and their pilots at Palermo to operate under the control of 21°Gruppo based at Chinisia. As soon as it was obvious that the invasion was under way, 351^ and 360^Squadriglie of 155°Gruppo CT with 20 MC202s were ordered to fly to Chinisia from Monserrato, Sardinia, while 362^Squadriglia Aut CT with eight Re2005s under Cap Germano La Ferla arrived at Sigonella. On the mainland in Calabria and Puglia, ready to be called in to action in the defence of Sicily, were:

Reggio di Calabria
  161°Gruppo Aut CT   Cap Adriano Porcu   11 MC202, 7 D.520
    162^Squadriglia   Cap Genesio De Nicola
    164^Squadriglia   Cap Adriano Porcu
    371^Squadriglia   Cap Rodolfo Guza
  157°Gruppo CT   12 MC200
    163^Squadriglia   Cap Mario Burroni
    357^Squadriglia
    371^Squadriglia
Isola Capo Rizzuto/Crotone
  101°Gruppo Tuffatori   12 Re2002
  102°Gruppo Tuffatori   20 Re2002
  156°Gruppo Assalto (one flight only) 5 G.50bis
Gioia del Colle
  121°Gruppo Tuffatori   Magg Luciano Orlandini   13 Ju87D
    237^Squadriglia B.a'T 6   Ju87D
  98°Gruppo BT 11 SM84

Despite the last-minute reinforcements there remained a shortage of fighters.

* * *

By now the Allied task forces were nearing their designated stations in readiness for the dawn assault. Colonel Carlo D'Este neatly set the scene:

> "In early July the Allied convoys began forming in ports along the Tunisian and Moroccan coasts and in the Middle East. By 6 July the Western Mediterranean became one gigantic floating traffic jam as vessels joined to form the elements of the Western Task Force. They were joined temporarily by the RN's Force V carrying the Canadians on the final leg of their long journey from Scotland. As ships darted about, forming themselves into the intricate patterns that comprised a naval task force, LSTs, LCIs, minesweepers, attack transports, cargo ships, destroyers and cruisers dotted

the horizon as this mighty force sailed east along the Tunisian coast. To enemy eyes the fleet appeared to be en route to some unknown Mediterranean target. Once past Lampedusa the task forces slowly swung their helms to port and began moving towards Malta where they were joined on 9 July by the Eastern Task Force bearing the Eighth Army.

For Axis forces the first warning that Sicily was about to be invaded came at 1630. Three hours earlier reconnaissance aircraft on routine patrol in the Mediterranean Sea had spotted five convoys in the waters south of Malta. When word of this discovery finally reached [Generale d'Armata Alfredo] Guzzoni's headquarters at Enna, it was stated that the convoys were headed in the direction of Sicily and that each consisted of 150-180 landing craft and warships, escorted by at least two battleships. Shortly after 1800, another report revealed the approach of additional convoys and confirmed the presence of the two battleships, one aircraft carrier, four cruisers and considerable air power. Guzzoni was in no doubt that the long-anticipated Allied strike against a Mediterranean target was about to fall upon Sicily. At 1900 he ordered a preliminary alert and three hours later he placed all Axis garrisons on the island on full alert." [16]

There were in fact two aircraft carriers as part of the RN's Force H, *Formidable* and *Indomitable*, with 73 Seafire and Martlet fighters between them, plus 27 Albacores for anti-submarine and reconnaissance duties. Of this total, *Formidable* had 28 Martlet IVs but only five Seafire IICs of 885 Squadron commanded by Lt Cdr(A) R.H.P. Carver DSC, while *Indomitable* could boast 28 IICs of 880 and 899 Squadrons (Lt Cdr(A) W.H. Martyn DSC and Lt Cdr(A) R.B. Howarth, respectively), plus a dozen LIICs of 807 Squadron commanded by Lt Cdr(A) K. Firth. In support of the invasion, Force H was to operate in the Ionian Sea, between 60 and 120 miles east of Sicily.

Of this tense period, as the seaborne elements of the invasion force took up station, the official USN historian added:

"At nightfall on 9 July the water off Sicily seemed deserted. Yet despite the windy weather and rough sea, the coastal defenders were aware of the presence of a huge fleet of vessels somewhere in the darkness. Filled with American and British soldiers, the ships were moving toward the island. The Italian and German island defenders could do little except await the resumption of Allied air bombardments that would signal the start of the invasion." [17]

In fact the start of the invasion was to be heralded by British glider-borne troops of the 1st Airlanding Brigade of the 1st Airborne Division, tasked to attack and hold strategic positions south of Syracuse, although the operation went terribly and tragically wrong. The force comprised over 2,000 troops drawn from 2/The South Staffordshire Regiment and 1/The Border Regiment, aboard 136 Waco and eight Horsa gliders piloted by men of The Glider Pilot Regiment, 110 of which were towed by C-47s of the US 51st Troop Carrier Wing, the remainder by 27 RAF Albemarles and seven Halifaxes. The air armada departed from six airfields in the Kairouan area of Tunisia, although seven failed to cross the coast for various

---

[16] see *Bitter Victory* by Colonel Carlo D'Este.
[17] see *Sicily-Salerno-Anzio*.

reasons. 137 eventually set out for the long flight across the Mediterranean. All was not well, though:

"... the glider pilots had learned little of the very difficult art of judging distance across the water off a coastline, and the tow pilots had insufficient practice in night navigation. These shortcomings were to have grievous consequences." [18]

Near midnight Admiral Sir Andrew Cunningham, C-in-C Allied Naval Forces, along with many others, went to the cliffs at Malta to catch a glimpse of the gliders:

"They were flying at only three or four hundred feet in pairs of towing aircraft and gliders, sometimes in twos and threes, sometimes in larger groups, with their dim navigation lights just visible. In the pale half-light of the moon they looked like flights of great bats. Occasionally we could hear the drone of engines above the howling of the wind." [19]

Those peering into the night sky could not have imagined the tragic events about to overtake many of the glider crews. Aboard one of the Wacos was Colonel George Chatterton, commander of the newly formed Glider Pilot Regiment, who wrote later:

"... I wondered if German fighters were likely to intercept, and I remember experiencing a sense of astonishment when they did not come, and, as the darkness descended, a feeling of elation that we had got away with it, for we would have been sitting ducks if a force of fighters had come across us. And what a target we would have made!" [20]

Although there were no reports of tugs or their gliders being attacked by night fighters, at least one Ju88C of II/NJG2 was airborne and its crew radioed base with the news that they had "sighted five bombers apparently full of people." Winds of up to 35mph buffeted the glider train as it approached Sicily, and heavy AA fire forced many of the pilots to take evasive action, dispersing formations, some tug pilots releasing their gliders prematurely. To make matters worse, a gunner aboard an Allied merchant ship off Cape Passero opened fire on a C-47. Another ship followed suit. Soon, in the dark sky above, all was chaos and mayhem as disorientated tug pilots flew in all directions. Of the chaotic disaster, one historian has written:

"The first flight of tows released their gliders ... Behind them other flights jostled for positions to be next. The confusion was growing rapidly ... Suddenly all hell broke loose. The Italian defenders had finally woken up to the danger. Searchlights stabbed the night sky. Signal flares, red for danger, sailed upwards to explode in a burst of unreal light. Green and white tracer zipped into the darkness. Then the first flak batteries opened up ... The tracer and the generally threatening air of the shoreline confused, and in some cases panicked Colonel Dunn's pilots. Confusion set in. Some pilots released their gliders at 300 feet so that they passed through and not under

---

[18] see *The Mediterranean and Middle East, Volume V* by Brigadier C.J.C. Molony.
[19] see *A Sailor's Odyssey* by Admiral of the Fleet Lord Cunningham.
[20] see *The Wings of Pegasus* by George Chatterton.

the main body. This added to the chaos as other pilots were suddenly confronted by the silent planes heading straight at them on a collision course. Pilots weaved and turned their unwieldy planes in an attempt to avoid a crash. Some pilots decided they had had enough. They did not even try to unload their tows. Instead they turned about and headed for North Africa again. Others released their gliders miles away from the landing zone and fled for safety . . ." [21]

Of the 137 gliders that had finally crossed the Mediterranean, 68 Wacos and one Horsa ditched in the sea with the loss of 252 highly-trained troops. Not all those who came down in the sea were drowned, however. The twelve survivors of one glider were relieved when a cruiser suddenly appeared and dropped anchor. After swimming over to it they climbed up the anchor chain and startled a lone sailor who thought they were the enemy. He immediately called for help and the luckless paratroopers were almost beaten senseless before it was realised who they were. Among those rescued was the commander of the 1st Airborne Division, Maj General G.F. Hopkinson being plucked from the sea by HMS *Keren*. Another which came down just off the coast was the Waco commanded by Colonel Chatterton, forced to ditch when it came under heavy tracer fire from positions ashore. Both he and Brigadier P.H.W. Hicks, commander of the 1st Airlanding Brigade, were among the survivors who reached shore. On board another ditched glider one of the pilots was lost but the survivors started to swim for the shore. After about two hours in the water they were picked up by an Italian Navy motor launch and taken to Syracuse. As the launch entered the bay at dawn, many gliders could be discerned in the sea with men standing on the wings. The Italians were persuaded to go to their aid and went from glider to glider, eventually pulling into harbour with over 100 survivors on board.

Two gliders were reported shot down by ground fire, one of which, a Horsa, crash-landed into a wall south-west of Syracuse. Both pilots were killed as were many of the occupants. Of those gliders that safely reached the coast, 54 landed over a 25-mile area between Cape Passero and Cape Murro di Porco, thereby making it impossible for the troops to carry out any form of combined operation. Only a dozen of these came down in the assigned landing zones. Ten turned back towards Tunisia, bringing with them news of the disaster:

> "There was an immediate outcry among those Red Devils still in the camp. Brigadier Hackett, temporarily in charge of the 1st Airborne Division, ordered that the Division should be confined to their various camps. He feared that his men would take justice into their own hands and lynch the pilots of Colonel Dunn's Air Transport Command." [22]

One glider came down near the Mareth Line in Tunisia, the crew being under the impression they were actually in Sicily and emerged ready for action. Another landed in Sardinia, and one came down on Gozo, as recalled by Plt Off Frank Cockett, an RAF Medical Officer:

> "Before turning in, I am taking a quiet stroll by the edge of the strip when, to my amazement, I see a fairly large aircraft making for the strip in absolute silence. Suddenly, I realise it's a glider and it seems to be making for the

---

[21]/[22] see *Slaughter over Sicily*.

patch of land just to the right of the strip. I jump into an American jeep, which happens to be standing just there, and drive off in haste towards the obvious landing area. It comes down and glides very roughly and jerkily to a sudden jolting halt, and I am on the spot at once. It doesn't seem to be an enemy glider but, in fact, I can't see any markings in the dusk. So, perhaps rather foolishly, I dash up to the door of the glider and to my surprise it opens quite easily. I put my head inside and it is full of troops. They all seem unnaturally still, as if they were stunned, so I say 'Hello, everybody'. I wonder what on earth is wrong and then, suddenly, it hits me. The stench of concentrated vomit and sickness in that small crowded glider is unbelievable. I reel back to take a gulp of fresh air.

The pilot, who is draped over his seat, appears almost unconscious and says, 'Where are we?' I reply, 'Gozo'. He says, 'Where is that? Are we behind the lines?' No', I say, 'You're in Gozo, which is just near Malta and you are just near an RAF airstrip.' At this, there is a noticeable stirring amongst the prostrate bodies in the glider: something like a sigh of relief. But, everybody in that aircraft is absolutely and totally prostrate with air sickness. The first thing to do is somehow to get them out of that awful stench. The fresh air works it's miracle and within about five minutes they are all sitting up, relaxing, and congratulating themselves on being alive. Apparently, they had been towed by an American plane with the intention of coming down behind German lines in Sicily somewhere. However, the plane had lost its way completely and was running short of fuel when, suddenly, they saw land beneath them. The glider had been cast free without more ado and they came down, grateful to be on dry land. I cannot help feeling that it is just as well that they landed on friendly territory, as I could have taken the whole lot prisoner, single handed, when I opened the door of that glider as no one was capable of even moving, let alone putting up any resistance!" [23]

To coincide with the ill-fated 1st Airborne Division's assault on Syracuse, the Americans planned a similar action to the area east of Gela, but using paratroops. No fewer than 227 C-47s were to convey 3,405 men of the US 82nd Airborne Division, these also departing from airfields around Kairouan in Tunisia. The high winds and general lack of experience among the pilots resulted in 25 C-47s mistakenly joining the British force, the paratroopers aboard these aircraft being dropped in the Noto area. Other pilots became disorientated and, consequently, those paratroops destined for Gela found themselves spread along 50 miles of the coast. Eight C-47s failed to return from this operation and were presumed to have been shot down by the defences or Allied naval fire:

"The same sort of confusion which had plagued the British Airlanding Brigade now set in. Pilots, unable to spot the DZ, turned and flew out to sea once more to regroup and make another attempt. Others dropped their paratroopers blind and at too low a height. Some panicked and flew straight back to Africa, as the Italian flak turned its attention on the air fleet. The first plane was hit. Smoke streaming from its port engine, it raced to the ground, carrying its cargo of paratroopers to their deaths. Minutes later another C-47 was struck and disintegrated in mid-air. No parachutes fell from the ball of black smoke . . ." [24]

---

[23] see *The Maltese Penguin* by Frank Cockett.
[24] see *Slaughter over Sicily*.

An official report succinctly summarized the night's disastrous airborne operations:

> "Both these airborne operations were a comparative failure, but the few
> airborne troops and parachutists who landed in the right places at the right
> time contributed to the success of the landings."

Others were more damning. General Hopkinson, commander of the 1st Airborne
Division, pulled no punches and put the blame for the needless deaths of his men
"exclusively on the cowardice and incompetence of Colonel Dunn's pilots."[25]
General Montgomery's private thoughts undoubtedly concurred with those of his
men, but he was rather more conservative and objective when he wrote, on
reflection:

> "The big lesson is that we must not be dependent on American transport
> aircraft, with pilots that are inexperienced in operational flying; our airborne
> troops are too good and too scarce to be wasted. We must have our own
> aircraft, and our own RAF pilots; in fact it must be an all-British show, the
> air part being handled properly by the RAF and not by a different Army who
> do not know our ways" [26]

From Malta during the night, Mosquitos intruded against enemy bomber airfields
in Sicily and Italy to screen the approaching invasion forces, while half a dozen
Hurricanes operated against searchlights on south-eastern Sicily and Mosquitos
and Beaufighters flew convoy protection patrols off the Sicilian coast. The
Hurricanes were from the 73 Squadron detachment operating out of Luqa and two
failed to return, one of which (HW242) was flown by Flt Sgt Cyril Edwards:

> "[Flt Sgt] Frank Bramley and myself were the rearguard action. We were
> assigned to patrol parallel to the coast and at a distance to look out for and
> destroy any enemy night fighters that might attempt to join in the fun. Frank
> was on the left side of the action and I was to the right, covering Capes
> Passero and Murro di Porco – two eyeball Hurris against the Ju88s with all
> the radar imaginable, that used to operate from the Gerbini complex.
> Nothing happened for about an hour, apart from the flak being squirted
> seawards against all and sundry, then at the end of the patrol I dropped in for
> a little light strafing before turning for home. There was flak about but I am
> not sure if I got hit. I turned south and called Luqa for a vector only to find
> that my radio was dead. I set a course based on the briefing wind, not
> knowing that it had changed dramatically, and when Malta didn't appear I
> tried a square search to no avail, finally bailing out when the Merlin was
> running on fumes. I got down OK to find there was a 40 knot surface wind
> and a six-foot sea to welcome me." [27]

The second Hurricane, HM135 flown by Flt Sgt Bramley also failed to return, and
the pilot was posted missing. Meanwhile, Edwards had scrambled into his dinghy,
which would be his 'home' for the next four days until rescued by one of the

---

[25] see *Slaughter over Sicily*.
[26] see *Bitter Victory*.
[27] see *The History of 73 Squadron, Part 2* by Don Minterne.

American OA-10s of the 1st Emergency Rescue Squadron from Malta:

> "I had rationed myself to a teaspoon of water a day, all the while thinking
> longingly of the barrel of beer that sat on the bar counter [at Luqa] for all
> flying personnel to quaff. As a result of my boating trip I lost 30-lbs in
> weight, and almost most of my night vision, which had been rated as
> exceptional. I also acquired a tan which was so intense and lasted so long
> that on return to the UK in KD [khaki drill] I was mistaken for a member of
> the Indian Air Force. In the four days I spotted a couple of White Sharks,
> which I learned much later were fairly common in the Med at that time,
> attracted by the many bodies floating around." [28]

At the same time a dozen B-17s from North Africa, equipped with anti-radar
devices, maintained continuous patrols about eight miles off the coast between
Licata and Syracuse, and were joined in this task by six similarly-equipped
Wellingtons which patrolled further out. By these means it was hoped that enemy
radars would be rendered ineffective. At 0115 the heavy guns of the Royal Navy
began bombarding targets in Catania. Admiral Cunningham reflected:

> "The die was cast. There was nothing more we could do for the time being."

---

[28] see *The History of 73 Squadron, Part 2.*

CHAPTER V

D-DAY: INVASION

10 July 1943

"I was wrong. The Allied Air Forces had definitely won the air battle, and this was quite apparent from the first moment we stepped ashore in Sicily. The enemy air force was swept from the sky and was never allowed to inconvenience us . . ." [1]

General Montgomery, on reflection following the invasion

The Western Naval Task Force carrying the US Seventh Army was to make landings at three designated areas, codenamed CENT – from Marpina eastwards up the coast for some 20 miles, DIME – a short stretch of coast on either side of Gela, and JOSS – a longer stretch on either side of Licata. The first waves landed on the beaches at 0245 and encountered machine-gun and light artillery fire. Supporting warships fired rockets at the batteries and destroyers engaged enemy searchlights. Commencing at 0424 small formations of FW190s, Messerschmitts, Ju88s and Italian fighter-bombers began dropping flares and attacking the troops in the CENT area. Dive-bombers attacked the cruisers USS *Philadelphia* and *Jefferson*. A little later the air attack spread to the JOSS area where the beaches and landing craft were bombed and strafed by fighter-bombers and Ju88s. The US destroyer *Maddox* was sunk by Ju87s in the DIME area with the loss of eight officers and 203 hands; 74 survivors were later plucked from the sea. The minesweeper USS *Sentinel* was also severely damaged, with the loss of ten crew killed and 51 wounded, and sank five hours later. The US Navy also lost two LSTs and one merchant vessel, including LST313 reportedly attacked by a "Messerschmitt bomber", in which a score of soldiers and one sailor were killed, and many guns and vehicles destroyed; about 80 other men were rescued. Despite a fierce AA barrage put up by the warships, only the USS *Swanson* was able to claim a success when her gunners reported shooting down a Bf110.

The Americans called for air cover and 11 Spitfires, including four IXs, of 242 Squadron which had taken off at 0424, were ordered to assist. Flg Off W.S. Lindner returned at 0520 with his R/T unserviceable and reported having sighted a small vessel, probably a patrol boat, burnt out about six miles south of Gela. Meanwhile, the remaining ten Spitfires patrolled over the area from 0500 to 0530, being greeted by heavy AA fire from the gunners aboard the American vessels, who engaged all aircraft indiscriminately. A number of seemingly lone German bombers were encountered throughout the duration of the patrol. The first, identified as a He111, was sighted by Sqn Ldr Mike Boddington (JK260/LE-K), apparently about to attack shipping, and was promptly shot down in flames

---

[1] see *Monty; Master of the Battlefield 1942-1944.*

between Cape Scalambri and Gela, his eighth victory. The Heinkel was an aircraft of I/KG26 operating out of Salon in southern France, which was reported missing after a combat with the loss of Uffz Walter Rather and his crew. When the Spitfires eventually arrived over the American vessels they were greeted with heavy AA fire from the gunners. Flg Off W.R.M. Lindsay saw a Ju88 at a distance of 700 yards but was unable to attack. A second bomber was attacked and damaged by Plt Off W.N. Dutton five miles south of Gela, while Flt Lt Paddy Chambers DFC RNZAF (EN304/LE-D) and his section were south of Comiso when they sighted a Ju88 flying low with two Italian fighters, identified as MC200s, as escort. Chambers ordered Wt Off Peter Gatley to attack the bomber while he engaged one of the Macchis with a three-second burst, shooting it down in flames for his eighth victory. Gately could only claim damage to the Ju88 before it escaped. One other Spitfire was over the beaches about this time, a PR aircraft flown by Wg Cdr Warburton of 683 Squadron, who had been briefed to photograph the initial landings. One of his flight commanders, Flt Lt Phil Kelley, remembered:

" . . . almost as soon as he arrived over the beachhead, US Navy gunners from ships offshore promptly riddled his aircraft with good and accurate shooting. The Warburton luck held. The plane was severely damaged but Warby just managed to get back to Malta. One aileron was hanging in shreds and there was a hole in one wing which has been described as 'big enough to pass a bucket through.'" [2]

Meanwhile, in the area of the British landings further to the east, a German reconnaissance aircraft reported several large ships off the coast at 0440, and dropped flares. The Eastern Naval Task Force finally arrived off the Sicilian coast at about 0500 and landings began almost immediately at five designated points, codenamed ACID NORTH – from Cape Murro di Porco, ACID SOUTH – from a point south of Avola to a point halfway between Calabernado and Marzamemi, BARK EAST – a short stretch of coast northwards from Marzamemi, BARK MIDDLE – from Cape Passero to Cape Correnti, and BARK WEST – from Pozzallo eastwards to a point on the coast south of Pachino. Opposition to the Eighth Army was confined to elements of an Italian division which was soon overcome. One war correspondent landing with the Canadians wrote:

"I landed alongside the first wave of assault companies on the sandy beach of Costa del Ambra, four miles south-west of Pachino, at 0515, and the Canucks have been rushing ahead ever since. The Italian beach defences, which folded up like a concertina, were merely barbed wire and some machine-gun posts which fired a few bursts and then gave up. On our beach the enemy were evidently counting on the sand bar, 15 feet offshore, as a natural defence. But the Canadians surprised them completely by coming in, in the heavy surf, and battling ashore through rough water up to the waist . . ."

Reuters correspondent Desmond Tighe arrived with British assault forces aboard a landing craft:

"The assault craft slithered and bumped over the rocks. The forward gangway was swung down and the men, heavily loaded with kit and

---

[2] see *Warburton's War* by Tony Spooner DSO DFC.

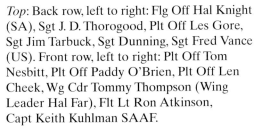

Top: Back row, left to right: Flg Off Hal Knight (SA), Sgt J. D. Thorogood, Plt Off Les Gore, Sgt Jim Tarbuck, Sgt Dunning, Sgt Fred Vance (US). Front row, left to right: Plt Off Tom Nesbitt, Plt Off Paddy O'Brien, Plt Off Len Cheek, Wg Cdr Tommy Thompson (Wing Leader Hal Far), Flt Lt Ron Atkinson, Capt Keith Kuhlman SAAF.

Middle left: Left to right: Sgt Ron Hind, Flt Sgt M. B. Zobell RCAF, Plt Off Matt Reid RCAF, Sgt Jim Tarbuck, Plt Off D. Sinclair RCAF, Flg Off Hal Knight (SA), Sgt George Nadon RCAF, Sgt Webster, Flg Off Gordon Lapp RCAF, Sgt J. D. Thorogood.

Bottom left: Plt Off Jerry Billing RCAF (left) and Plt Off Al Laing RCAF.

Bottom right: Sqn Ldr Malcolm MacLeod RCAF, CO of 249 Squadron, killed in action 11 March 1943.

Top left: Flt Lt John Long RCAF of 126 Squadron was killed in action 28 January 1943.

Top right: Flt Lt Ken Debenham of 249 Squadron and Wg Cdr Timber Woods DFC, former CO of 249 Squadron; both were later posted missing on the same sortie, probably as a result of an aerial collision.

Middle left: Rescue of Sgt Don Goodwin RCAF of 229 Squadron by HSL107 on 28 January 1943.

Middle right: Sqn Ldr Nip Heppell DFC commanded a flight in 1435 Squadron before taking command of 229 Squadron, being wounded in action shortly thereafter.

Bottom left: Flg Off Hap Kennedy DFC RCAF; credited with eight victories (six shared) flying from Malta during 1943.

Bottom right: Rescue of Plt Off Bob Taggart RCAF of 229 Squadron by HSL107 on 3 March 1943.

Top: Spitfire Vc JL316 of GCII/7.

Bottom left: Sous-Lt Constanin Feldzer claimed a Ju88 near Pantelleria.

Bottom right: Sgt-Chef Louis Kann claimed a shared FW190 during the invasion of Pantelleria.

PILOTS OF 229 SQUADRON

Top left: Sqn Ldr Tommy Smart DFC, CO of 229 Squadron, killed in action 12 April 1943.

Top right: One of the top-scoring pilots flying from Malta and Sicily in 1943, Flt Lt Les Gosling DFC RCAF was credited with ten victories (one shared) before his death on 19 July 1943.

Bottom: Sqn Ldr Blair White, CO of 229

Squadron (centre) was killed in action with FW190s of III/SKG10 on 5 July 1943; on his left is Sgt J. D. McKenzie; on extreme right is Sgt Fergus Davidson who was shot down and taken prisoner on 13 June 1943; extreme left front row is Flt Sgt Rainald Salzman who was killed in the same action as Sqn Ldr White.

Top: Sqn Ldr Lynch's Spitfire Vc, EP829 T-N, in which he claimed the 1,000th victory; note the additional small 'T' added to the code to make T-NT. Dynamite indeed!

Above: One of Sqn Ldr Lynch's victims on 10 May 1942 was an RS14 seaplane, which he misidentified as a similarly configured Z506B.

Left: Sqn Ldr John Lynch DFC, an American in the RAF and CO of 249 Squadron, recorded Malta's 1,000th victory on 28 April 1943. By the time he left Malta in July his score stood at 17 including 7 shared, 15 of which he had claimed while with 249 Squadron.

PILOTS OF 242 SQUADRON

PILOTS OF 92 SQUADRON

Top left: Group of 242 Squadron pilots at Malta: front row, centre is Sqn Ldr Mike Boddington DFM; on his right is Flt Lt George Silvester, and on his left is Flt Lt Paddy Chambers DFC RNZAF.

Top right: Flg Off Tony Snell of 242 Squadron was shot down on the first day of the invasion and was captured after many adventures.

Middle: 242 Squadron Spitfire Vcs in Sicily including LE-P (right) and LE-G (left).

Bottom left: Sqn Ldr Peter Humphreys, CO during the invasion period.

Bottom centre: Flg Off Gordon Wilson RCAF, the first Allied pilot to force-land in Sicily and walk back to safety.

Bottom right: Pilots at rest in the dispersal hut at Luqa, left to right: Lt Albie Sachs SAAF, Flg Off Brendan Baker, Flt Lt Tom Savage (killed in action on the first day of the invasion), Plt Off Rex Probert RCAF.

Top left: Relaxing at Malta. Sqn Ldr Graham Cox, CO of 229 Squadron during the invasion, shot down three Re2002s on 10 July 1943.

Top centre: Flt Lt Raoul Daddo-Langlois of 93 Squadron had flown with 249 Squadron during the 1942 Malta blitz; he was lost on the first day of the invasion.

Top right: Plt Off Jack Hussey DFM of 72 Squadron claimed several victories during the fighting of July 1943, and was later awarded a DFC.

Bottom left: Flg Off Norman Jones of 152 Squadron shot down three Re2002s on 19 July 1943, and two Bf109s six days later.

Bottom centre: Flt Lt Jim Gray of 93 Squadron, a former US Eagle Squadron pilot. Shot down over Italy at the beginning of 1945, he spent the last few months of the war as a PoW.

Bottom right: Flt Sgt Raymond Baxter, who flew with 93 Squadron during the invasion, later commanded a flight of 602 Squadron.

SOME OF THE AIR COMMANDERS

Top left: Wg Cdr Mike Stephens DSO DFC led the Takali Wing in early 1943.

Top centre: Wg Cdr Adrian Warburton DSO DFC, the legendary PR pilot.

Top right: Wg Cdr Peter Olver DFC, Wing Leader of 244 Wing, was shot down on the second day of the invasion, and spent the remainder of the war as a PoW.

Middle left: Wg Cdr Hugh Dundas DFC was Wing Leader of 324 Wing.

Middle right: Sqn Ldr Duke Arthur DFC, the Canadian CO of 232 Squadron.

Right: Sqn Ldr George Hill DFC, CO of 111 Squadron, another of the many Canadians operating over Sicily at this time.

SOME OF THE SUCCESSFUL NEW ZEALANDERS

Top left: Flg Off Geoff White DFC of 126 Squadron claimed four Bf109s and a MC202 during the bitter skirmishing of June and July 1943.

Top right: Flg Off Stan Browne DFC of 93 Squadron claimed two Ju88s and a Bf109 in July 1943.

Middle left: Plt Off Eric Shaw of 72 Squadron claimed a MC202 on 12 July 1943.

Middle right: Sgt Eric Doherty DFM of 242 Squadron claimed three Ju52s on 25 July 1943.

Left: Sgt Jim Robinson of 81 Squadron claimed two Bf109s on 28 August 1943.

FIGHTER LEADERS

Top: Senior pilots of 244 Wing, from left to right: Sqn Ldr Stan Turner DFC CO of 417RCAF Squadron, Sqn Ldr Peter Humphreys CO of 92 Squadron, Wg Cdr Wilf Duncan Smith DSO DFC Wing Leader, Grp Capt Brian Kingcome DSO DFC, OC 244 Wing, Sqn Ldr Lance Wade DFC CO of 145 Squadron.

Bottom: Some of the successful pilots of the Ju52 massacre of 25 July 1943 with Wg Cdr Colin Gray DSO DFC, 322 Wing Leader, in the centre, flanked by pilots of 152 Squadron.

op: Pilot and groundcrew of 209^Squadriglia eside one of the new Re2002 dive-bombers at 'rotone.

1iddle left: The high-performance MC205V was qual to the Spitfire Vc; shown here in the arkings of 351^Squadriglia.

1iddle right:A number of ex-Vichy Dewoitine 520s were supplied to the Regia Aeronautica, ying with 161ºGruppo based at Reggio di 'alabria. There is no record of any encounters ith RAF Spitfires.

ight: One of the first Bf109G-6s supplied to 53^Squadriglia at Comiso.

Top left: MC202 of 151°Gruppo CT showing the newly introduced Roman numeral code numbers on the fuselage.

Top right: Uffz Herman Harnisch, a 13-victory ace of 8/JG53, was shot down by AA fire over Malta while engaged escorting a reconnaissance mission on 29 June 1943. He baled out safely and was captured but his aircraft crashed on a house in Zebbug, killing an occupant.

Middle left: Oblt Günther Hannak, a 47-victory

ace of 7/JG27 carried out an emergency landing at Luqa on 5 May 1943; his aircraft, GP+12, was not seriously damaged, and is shown here propped up on oil drums.

Bottom: Uffz Walter Reinicke of 7/JG53, seen here, was shot down into the sea on 3 July 1943 while flying this highly-decorated aircraft White 9+1. He was rescued and taken to Malta.

A FEW OF THE LUFTWAFFE ACES...

Top left: II/JG53's Kommandeur Maj Gerhard Michalski had 58 victories when he was shot down and wounded in combat with 72 Squadron Spitfires on 18 June 1943.

Top right: Hptm Siegfried Freytag of II/JG77 had raised his tally to 98 victories before being shot down and wounded on 10 July 1943.

Middle left: Oblt Heinz-Edgar Berres of 1/JG77 was shot down and killed in action with Spitfires on 25 July 1943, having claimed 52 victories.

Middle right: Obfw Herbert Rollwage of 5/JG53 claimed four of Malta's Spitfires during May, June and early July before himself being wounded in action with his score at 47.

Left: Oblt Armin Köhler of 2/JG77 had 25 victories by the end of August 1943.

Clockwise from top left:

a. FW190 fighter-bomber, possibly of II/SKG10, pictured at Crotone on 13 July 1943.

b. Magg Pietro Serini (right) of 161° Gruppo and the Adjutant of II/SchG2 at Reggio di Calabria, with one of the Gruppe's FW190s in the background.

c. Spitfire Vc EP188 T-Y of 249 Squadron was hit and crash-landed near Marzameni, Sicily on 30 April 1943; Flt Sgt Don Cruse was taken prisoner.

d. Spitfire PRIV of 683 Squadron showing feint markings (LY) of previous ownership, 3 PRU.

e. Lt Colonel Fred M. Dean's Spitfire Vc FM-D at Gozo.

f. Flt Sgt Jack Hughes RCAF in the cockpit of h 249 Squadron Spitfire Vc T-B; note the symbols representing bombing sorties (26 recorded).

g. Bf110 3U+ET of III/ZG26 at Comiso.

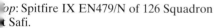

Top: Spitfire IX EN479/N of 126 Squadron at Safi.

Middle left: Spitfire IX GL-H (MH704) of 185 Squadron at Hal Far.

Middle right: Spitfire Vcs of 152 Squadron at Lentini East, LZ807 UM-V in the foreground.

Above left: Spitfire Vcs AN-V (BR470) with AN-W, AN-F and AN-O of 417RCAF Squadron.

Above right: Spitfire Vc JK322 FL-4 of 81 Squadron at Lentini, one of the casualties of the Luftwaffe attack on the night of 12/13 August 1943; note the name "Joy" beneath the cockpit.

Right: Spitfire Vc AN-Q of 417RCAF Squadron.

Top: Spitfire Vc JK642 SN-P of 243 Squadron scrambles from Comiso on 20 July 1943.

Middle left: Abandoned Bf109G White 14 of JG53 at Comiso.

Middle right: Spitfire Vc ES352 FT-Y of 43 Squadron at Comiso.

Bottom left: Flg Off Milt Jowsey and Plt Off Rex Probert at Lentini with the captured Arado 66C in which they almost crashed.

Above right: Spitfire Vc at Comiso with abandoned Bf109G Yellow 14+- of 6/JG53 in background.

Right: Abandoned MC202 of 4°Stormo with remains of Fieseler Storch in foreground.

weapons, plunged into the surging sea and stumbled ashore. Suddenly the silence was broken by the sharp crack of rifle and machine-gun fire. Bullets sang over our heads and twanged into the metal sides of the assault craft. A dull, tawny light was creeping over the sky and revealing an amazing sight. As far as the eye could see were craft of every imaginable type, riding proudly barely two miles from the shore; tank-landing craft chugged towards the beaches while British cruisers and destroyers covering them slammed shells into the enemy positions. Suddenly [we] spotted the grey-green wreckage of a floating aircraft. We altered course and pulled aboard nine nearly exhausted paratroops [sic]. They had been in the water since 11 o'clock the previous night, when they landed just short of the shore . . ."

Among the many thousands of soldiers scrambling from the landing craft onto the beaches was Royal Signals Cpl Jack Lee, attached to the Royal Engineers of the 50th Northumbrian Division:

"I remember seeing wrecked gliders showing dark against the night sea. We found later that these had carried some of the South Staffs airborne troops released too early. We transferred into landing craft for the actual landing, each of us having to carry some 50-lbs of sappers' stores – explosives etc – against the arrival of our transport. A very clear memory I have, as we waded ashore on what turned out to be a virtually unopposed arrival in the Golfo di Noto, was the sight of my pipe floating out of my shorts' pocket, fast moving out of reach.

We had fighter cover from first light – Spitfires if I remember correctly – but there were very soon Lightnings [P-38s]. Our instructions were that all twin-engined aircraft were enemy, so the Lightnings were greeted with spirited AA fire, especially from the Oerlikons of the merchant ships beginning to gather in the area. As usual, on such occasions, I saw no harm done . . ."

The Luftwaffe was slow to react, but at 0535, the crew of a reconnaissance Ju88 sent out to investigate the reports of landings around the Pachino isthmus, suddenly broadcast a warning of the presence of Spitfires. This was probably the aircraft engaged by Plt Off J.M. Staniforth (JK986) of 93 Squadron who claimed damage to a single Ju88 south of Syracuse at this time while patrolling at 6,000 feet with a dozen other Spitfires led by OC 324 Wing, Grp Capt Gilroy. One of the Spitfires was flown by Flt Sgt Raymond Baxter[3]:

"We took off in the dark to give top cover to the beaches, climbing to a considerable height. Before it got light I saw far below what I took to be the lights of a train which then appeared to disappear into a tunnel. I thought we had really taken them by surprise. Then I thought again – there is no railway there! It was a stream of tracer that I had seen. We patrolled for an hour and a half before returning to Malta. On arrival we said to our Intelligence Officer, 'You might have told us about the amphibious gliders'. He responded 'What amphibious gliders?' 'We said, Oh Christ!' We had seen the gliders dropped short by the Americans, which had fallen into the sea."

---

[3] Raymond Baxter was later commissioned and commanded a flight in 602 Squadron during the closing stages of the war in Europe; he became famous postwar as a journalist-cum-BBC radio and TV broadcaster.

The next patrol was led by Wg Cdr Dundas:

> "The Wing had been allotted a particular stretch of beach to protect, south
> of Syracuse. It was our job to maintain a patrol over this area throughout the
> day, in squadron strength. 'Sheep' Gilroy had decided to lead the first patrol,
> taking off at first light. I was taking Micky [Sqn Ldr Rook] and his squadron
> [43] to relieve him. Each squadron was due to spend 35 minutes on patrol
> and I had given strict orders that formation leaders were to start for home as
> soon as their time was up, provided that their relief had arrived and they
> were not engaged by the enemy." [4]

Fighter operations were being controlled by three GCI stations mounted on Tank
Landing Ships off the beaches at CENT, BARK and ACID, which were used as
forward links for GCI Malta. In addition there were seven Headquarters Ships
located off each beach which acted as Forward Fighter Controls. These Headquarters Ships directed fighters mainly by the informative method – passing information from radar or visual observations, supplemented by Y Service information. The
Fighter Controllers were linked to Malta and other Headquarters Ships by R/T.

Grp Capt Gilroy and Sqn Ldr Mackie jointly led a dozen Spitfires of 243
Squadron to patrol over ACID beaches shortly after dawn, but delayed their return
to the extent that the Spitfires started to exhaust their fuel beyond the safety level,
resulting in the loss of Flg Off Leslie Connors RAAF (JL375/SL-Z). He was heard
to call over the R/T: "I'm at 5,000 feet and will have to make a force-landing."
Shortly thereafter his aircraft was seen to go into the sea about a quarter of a mile
off the coast near Hal Far. Another pilot reported seeing him swimming strongly
towards the coast, but by the time a HSL had arrived he could not be found, and
was assumed to have drowned. Three other Spitfires were obliged to make
emergency landings at Safi due to fuel shortages.

43 Squadron subsequently carried out its first patrol over the beaches at about
the same time and, at 0620, two FW190s were reported below. Two Spitfires were
ordered to engage and dived down on them, Flt Sgt Webster (ES294) opening fire
on one with a two-second burst from 300 yards astern. Hits were scored on the
cockpit and the engine, at which the FW190 burst into flames, rolled over and
dived into the sea ten miles south of Syracuse, and was possibly the aircraft of
3/SchG2 (Yellow G/WkNr1420) in which Uffz Hans Schragow was killed,
although German records report his loss to AA fire. Of the fighter-bomber attacks
on the ships, the *Daily Telegraph*'s correspondent wrote:

> "The enemy's favourite trick seems to be for the fighter-bombers to sweep
> down from behind the hills and drop bombs on the shipping, then machine-
> gun along the line and make off before our fighters can reach them."

Spitfires from 322 Wing were also airborne at 0530, Wg Cdr Gray leading 154
Squadron to patrol over CENT beach but meeting no enemy aircraft. The Wing
Commander noted:

> "The invasion was an amazing sight with ships of all sizes nosing up on the
> beach. However, not a single enemy aircraft appeared." [5]

---

[4] see *Flying Start* by Grp Capt Hugh Dundas DSO DFC.
[5] see *Spitfire Patrol*.

A dozen Spitfires of 242 Squadron led by Sqn Ldr Boddington were over the CENT area between 0845 and 1000, including two flown by Lt Col Laurie Wilmot and Maj Charles Laubscher of the SAAF, both of whom were acting in the supernumerary role. A fire was observed burning about five miles south of Licata and a medium-size vessel was on fire offshore, before two Bf109Gs and a Macchi appeared at about 0950, but owing to an adverse direction an attack was not possible. The Macchi may have been a photo-reconnaissance MC205V (351-00) of 351^Squadriglia flown by its commander, Cap Giovanni Franchini, who had been briefed to fly low and fast over the beaches to take pictures of the landings. A jubilant Franchini returned safely to Chinisia where he reported having successfully carried out his mission without attracting ground fire, having apparently taken the beach defences by surprise, only to find that someone had forgotten to load film into the aircraft's camera.

On the patrol between 0830-0915, 12 Spitfires of 145 including four IXs led by Sqn Ldr Lance Wade met eight Bf109Gs in the Cape Passero area. The CO and his No2 chased three of the Messerschmitts, which dived away, Wade (EN186) following one down, firing and gaining strikes on the fuselage and starboard wing, at which it went into a vertical dive. Wade continued following but when he fired again, one cannon jammed causing his aircraft to go out of control. After an inverted loop he managed to right it but by this time the Messerschmitt had disappeared. This was probably an encounter with Bf109Gs of II/JG53, whose pilots reported a combat with four Spitfires at about this time although no claims were made. Messerschmitts of III/JG53 were also active before midday, escorting Bf110s of ZG1 to the Syracuse area but there were no reports of contact with patrolling Spitfires.

A dozen Spitfires of 93 Squadron led by Flt Lt J.A. Gray and newly arrived Flt Lt N.W. Lee DFC set off at 0900 for the unit's second patrol of the morning. The formation was bounced by six MC202s south of Syracuse and a number of dogfights ensued. One Macchi, following an attack by former US Eagle Squadron pilot Jim Gray (JL323), was last seen diving at 10,000 feet with flames and glycol issuing from its engine and was claimed probably destroyed. Seven MC202s and three MC205Vs of 9°Gruppo led by Ten Antonio Canfora had scrambled from Catania when 25 B-25s escorted by 20 Spitfires were reported approaching from the direction of Cape Passero; two Spitfires were claimed shot down by Ten Canfora and M.llo Gianni Bianchelli of 97^Squadriglia. A few minutes later another flight of seven MC202s from 73^Squadriglia led by Ten Vittorio Squarcia took off from Finocchiara and reported meeting 40 Spitfires, of which two were claimed by the combined fire of Ten Squarcia, Sottoten Dal Molin and Serg Teresio Martinoli. Three Macchis sustained damage in the combat, one possibly the victim of Flt Lt Gray. At about the same time two TacR Spitfires of 40SAAF Squadron on reconnaissance east of Syracuse were reported to have been attacked by another Spitfire[6] – but more probably by one of the Macchis – and Capt G.C. le Roux DFC (EP690) was shot down into the sea two miles offshore after his attacker had closed to about 50 yards. Le Roux had no time to bale out and his No2, Lt E.C. Webb (ER706), orbited the spot for a short while but saw no sign of a parachute or dinghy. On leaving the scene Webb initially flew the wrong course for Malta and ran out of fuel, so baled out over a convoy some eight miles south of the island, and was picked up from his dinghy by a destroyer at 1030 after 20 minutes in the sea.

---

[6] Despite enquiries and research, no documentation has been found to confirm that another Spitfire shot down Capt le Roux's aircraft. It seems probable that he was victim of a MC202 from 4°Stormo.

The Spitfire patrols were not around at 1015 when six Bf109Gs of II/JG53 appeared over the beachhead near Gela, but patrols of P-38s and P40s were, and these were bounced by the Messerschmitt pilots who claimed five P-38s, one P-40 and a USN floatplane shot down, the latter apparently an OS2U Kingfisher spotter biplane from one of the American cruisers. US Navy historian Admiral Morison later wrote:

> " . . . four SOCs, catapulted from *Boise* and *Savannah* in the early light, hovered over the Gela plain without fighter protection. Within a few minutes several fast-climbing Messerschmitts flew over from Gerbini airdrome [*sic*] and beat them back. *Savannah*'s senior aviator was killed in flight; his radioman skilfully landed the riddled plane in the sea, only to have it sink immediately. He was rescued. *Savannah*'s second plane also splashed and sank . . . the ship's commanding officer sent his two remaining planes in the air. One was shot down by German fighters and the other driven off. Lt C.G. Lewis USNR, in one of *Boise*'s planes, radioed, 'Two Messerschmitts on my tail, stand by to pick me up.' And, a few moments later, 'Belay that, they've gone back for reinforcements!'" [7]

Wg Cdr Gray (EN350/CG) led another patrol of 154 Squadron aircraft to the CENT area just before midday:

> "At lunchtime I again took off with 154 Squadron for another patrol over CENT beach, and this time towards the end of our patrol we were bounced by eight Messerschmitt 109s. We saw them coming and turned in to them, whereupon two of the aircraft broke to the west and started to dive, hotly pursued by Sgt Rathwell and myself. I fired at the first one from 400 yards closing to 300, hitting him in the starboard wing and fuselage. There was a large explosion, many pieces fell off, and the plane burst into flames. I then pulled to one side and urged my No2 to have a go at the second aircraft, but he was too slow and the 109 left the scene at high speed before Rathwell could get anywhere near." [8]

Other Spitfires from the Squadron were also engaged between Gela and Cape Scalambri, Plt Off H.D. Costain (EN520) claiming a Messerschmitt damaged while Wt Off S.F. Cooper's aircraft was badly shot up by another and crashed on landing; the pilot survived, shaken but otherwise unhurt. A Bf109 (WkNr16348) of 8/JG53 was lost although the pilot was able to bale out, probably the victim of Wg Cdr Gray. Meanwhile, other Bf109s from II/JG53 on free chase between 1230-1313 reported combat with 15-20 Spitfires but made no claims, although another of the USN Kingfisher spotters, an aircraft from the cruiser USS *Boise*, was shot down by a Messerschmitt.

1435 Squadron flew the next patrol, Wg Cdr Innes Westmacott, Safi's Station Commander, flying one of their aircraft (JK139/V-X) but no enemy aircraft were sighted; he noted:

> "Covering invasion of Sicily – patrol 9,000 feet over ACID beaches and shipping south of Syracuse. Saw a few explosions inland otherwise nothing but masses of our own ships. Flew with 1435 Squadron."

---

[7] see *Sicily-Salerno-Anzio*.
[8] see *Spitfire Patrol*.

601 Squadron sighted a FW190 during an early afternoon patrol but this climbed away "too quickly" for interception. For the US 31st Fighter Group at Gozo, the 307th FS flew an early afternoon mission over the beaches but 1/Lt John E. Johnson was shot down by American ships' gunfire and crashed a short way inland. He survived and was rescued by American troops. An official report records that at about 1415 a Spitfire coming in to make a forced-landing in the CENT area was accidentally shot down in flames by an LST, and this presumably refers to Johnson's aircraft. A second US Spitfire was shot down over the convoy, 1/Lt John K. Conley being obliged to bale out and later plucked from the sea. The 309th FS flew five separate missions from Gozo during the day, all of them uneventful. The Group's other squadron, the 308th, suffered a crash-landing on Gozo by one of its Spitfires although the pilot was unhurt.

There was no further aerial opposition to the Spitfire patrols until mid-afternoon when a dozen Bf109Gs were encountered about six miles south-west of Cape Murro di Porca at about 1600 by a dozen Spitfires of 92 Squadron. Flt Sgt Michael Askey, a Canadian ace with five victories from the Tunisian fighting, fired at one of the Messerschmitts although he made no claim. Meanwhile, another section sighted two MC202s at their own height to starboard, one of which was attacked by Sgt K. Warren as it manoeuvred to engage his No1, but the Macchi pulled away before results could be observed. Almost immediately AA bursts were seen three miles out to sea off Avola, where six Ju88s of I/LG1 were attacking shipping. One of the bombers was seen to be shot down by Flt Lt Tom Savage (JL182) but he was then believed to have been hit by gunfire from one of the warships; apparently unable to bale out, he was lost with his aircraft and his body was later recovered from the sea. Flg Off Milt Jowsey RCAF, who was flying close by, recalled:

> "Over the landing craft we found six Ju88s, numerous MC202s, 109s and Ju87s. We, and me in particular, came in too fast and overshot the 87s. I saw Flt Lt Savage shoot down one Ju88 and while in pursuit of another, at about 10,000 feet, he was shot down by RN flak. We were very loath to pursue e/a near RN ships as they only seemed to get close to us."

Another Ju88 was claimed damaged by 2/Lt Johnny Gasson SAAF (ER470) but a second Spitfire was also shot down, Rhodesian-born Flt Lt Eric Dicks-Sherwood baling out of EP440 into the sea, from where he was picked up by a trawler, none the worse for wear, and taken to Malta. Although it was believed that both missing Spitfire pilots had been shot down by AA fire, the Messerschmitt pilots from II/JG27 claimed two Spitfires shot down, Lt Willy Kientisch of 6 Staffel claiming the first, his 37th victory, east of Syracuse. Two minutes later Hptm Ernst Börngen, 5 Staffel commander, claimed another (his 26th), south-east of Syracuse.

At about the same time, east of Avola, 12 Spitfires of 93 Squadron encountered the same formation of Ju88s, reporting nine bombers escorted by one Bf110 and two FW190s, which were attacking Allied shipping. Flg Off Stan Browne RNZAF (LZ840) promptly shot down one of the bombers into the sea. A second Ju88 was claimed damaged by the combined fire of Sqn Ldr Sizer (JL220/HN-C) and his No2, Flt Sgt Raymond Baxter (JK868/HN-H), who recalled:

> ". . . we saw 20-plus bombers coming in to bomb the fleet. We turned to attack them, when someone called '109s up sun!', but we were pretty well ready for them. Wilfie, our CO, to whom I was flying as No2, called 'Break!'. Suddenly there were no Spitfires! Wilf climbed sharply into the

sun, effectively inverted. To keep up with him I went through the gate – one of the rare occasions on which I did this. I saw a 109 go by in the opposite direction, pretty close. We kept on climbing – and I thought if I drop out of this due to lack of speed I'd be a dead duck. Wilf just hung on and on, then brought us down right in the position to attack the 88s. We both got hits on one, but were going too fast to press the attack further, and could only claim a damaged. Nothing we could do about it really. There were 109s and 88s all over the place, then suddenly, as it happens, the sky was empty.

We got ourselves sorted out, and Wilfie called the boys to reform. We were still pretty high up, and he asked how I was for fuel. I checked the gauges and told him I was not well placed – I realised that I didn't have enough to get back to Malta. Wilfie said 'Stay with me', and sent the rest of the boys on ahead. He got into a controlled descent, and we cleared the Sicilian coast, still looking out for hostiles. We could then see Malta and Gozo, and by the time we got down to 3,000 feet, we were only about ten miles out, still at bale-out height. I checked the fuel gauges again – there was nothing showing on the starboard and just a flicker on the port. 'It'll be all right', said Wilfie, 'I'll clear you for an emergency landing at Gozo'. There was an emergency strip there, covered with Somerfeld tracking. I went straight in with a steep, closed throttle approach and landed with just four gallons left. Wilfie flew on, telling me to fly back to base as soon as the aircraft had been tanked up. I had a cup of tea while refuelling took place, took off 15 minutes later, and rejoined the boys on Malta."

Two bombers were lost by 2/LG1 in this action – L1+PK of 2 Staffel flown by Fw Paul-Heinz Müller, from which there were no survivors, and L1+QK flown by Uffz Gerhard Heuser which went down eight miles east of Augusta. There was one survivor from L1+QK, air gunner Uffz Gustav Mayer, a 22-year-old Austrian on his 57th operation, who told his captors:

"We climbed to 13,000 feet [from a landing ground south-west of Foggia] led by Lt Friedrichs and made rendezvous with other bombers from bases near Naples as well as some from the direction of Bari – probably 40 aircraft all told. We were in the rear starboard position. Over the target area the aircraft was put into a steep dive from 9,000 feet but we had no time to observe the result of our attack for immediately on flattening out at about 3,000 feet, I spotted two Spitfires, one above the other and directly astern. The first attack wounded the W/Op [Uffz Kurt Hoffmann] and in the second the aircraft caught fire and the pilot ordered us to bale out. I saw only one other member of the crew [the observer] bale out successfully. I was rescued by a destroyer and landed at Malta."

A further nine Spitfires of 93 Squadron led by Wg Cdr Duncan Smith were back over the beaches by 1630, when the pilots sighted at least six Ju88s bombing shipping. MC202s put in an appearance and were chased away but without any claims being made. As the Spitfires swept down over ACID beach, the gunners put up a heavy and accurate barrage, hitting two of them. Wg Cdr Duncan Smith managed to nurse his damaged aircraft back to Malta but Flt Lt Raoul Daddo-Langlois crash-landed EN466 on the beach, suffering a severe skull fracture in the process. He was gently removed from his aircraft and placed aboard a lighter to be taken to a hospital ship, but another bombing raid developed and the lighter was sunk, Daddo-Langlois, a veteran of the 1942 Malta air battles, being lost with it. His Spitfire may have in fact been the victim of a Messerschmitt as Lt Karl-Heinz Kapp of 4/JG27 reported shooting down one south of Avola at about this time, his third victory.

243 Squadron fared no better on its second ACID beach patrol than it had during its earlier one, losing another Spitfire and its pilot. Again led by Grp Capt Gilroy, the ten Spitfires encountered two MC202s near Cape Murro di Porca, Gilroy chasing one at which he opened fire but without tangible results. Half a dozen Ju88s were then sighted in the distance, dive-bombing ships off Cape Murro di Porca, but no interception was possible before the bombers disappeared inland. Heavy AA fire was experienced in the area and the aircraft (EN148/SN-E) flown by Flg Off Geoff Blunn was seen losing height and did not return. It was assumed that he had fallen victim to flak but at least two Bf109Gs of I/JG53 were in the area at this time, Uffz Hermann Holstein of 2 Staffel claiming a Spitfire shot down at 1610, Lt Wilhelm Esser of Stab claiming a second four minutes later.

Twelve Spitfires of 242 Squadron had set off at 1530 to patrol the CENT beaches led by Sqn Ldr Boddington and again including Lt Col Wilmot, but one aircraft got off late and was not able to catch up. The remaining aircraft reached the patrol area at 1545 and were greeted by heavy AA, mainly from the ships. In the centre of CENT area about eight enemy aircraft were observed at deck level, apparently about to attack the ships. Sqn Ldr Boddington (JK260/LE-K) and his No2, Flg Off C.W. Coulthard, engaged a Bf109G flying at 2,000 feet, the CO scoring hits and seeing one wing starting to break off as he pulled away. By the time Coulthard attacked the Messerschmitt was already doomed, with smoke pouring from its engine, although he was credited with a share in its destruction. This was probably an aircraft (WkNr18369) of 5/JG53 which was reported lost near Sciacca, although the pilot survived, presumably having baled out safely. Two minutes later Flg Off A.N. Snell was heard to call over the radio: "Exhausted ammunition and being attacked by two 109s, heading for beach". Snell belly-landed his aircraft (ER856/LE-S) near a lake three miles south of Gela, undoubtedly the victim of Lt Alfred Hammer of 4/JG53 (flying White 14/WkNr18398) who claimed a Spitfire at 1642, his sixth victory:

> "My *Schwarm* and I were flying high cover over the *Stabsschwarm*. Sometime during the mission I spotted four Spitfires about to attack us from behind and above. I immediately radioed my Kommandeur, Maj Schnell: 'Four Spitfires at five o'clock.' The Kommandeur acknowledged my report but dismissed them as our own aircraft. The Spitfires came nearer and again I called: 'Four Spitfires behind us.' The result was the same, the Kommandeur insisted they were ours. But then with one of the Spitfires almost in firing position behind me, I took advantage of my superior height and led my machines in a dive in front of my Kommandeur, so that he ended up with the four Spitfires behind him. Suddenly aware of the true situation, he shouted excitedly over the radio, 'Spitfires behind me, Spitfires behind me!' I turned towards the Spitfires to relieve him of his burden. I opened fire on the first Spitfire while in a right turn and let it fly through my bullets. I immediately saw that I had hit the Spitfire, which began leaving a trail of white smoke. The other three Spitfires immediately took to their heels, while the one I had hit made a belly-landing in a ploughed field, after which its pilot immediately ran away . . ." [9]

---

[9] see *Jagdgeschwader 53 Volume Two*.

His victim, Flg Off Tony Snell, later recalled:

> ". . . I saw four Messerschmitt 109s slice out of some clouds down towards
> the beaches. We wheeled after them. I got a quick squirt at one and saw him
> start to smoke. Then, without warning, I had the horrible sensation of feeling
> several pneumatic drills hammering abruptly into the armour plate behind
> me. During the next five minutes I was continually dodging out of the way
> of one of the 109s, only to find another diving on me. My engine was
> smoking . . . there were tongues of flame streaking past my cockpit. I was
> 200 feet over rocky ground, saw a little green field, snapped down my flaps,
> cut switches, and then put her down, grinding her belly on the field . . ."

Having safely extricated himself from his burning aircraft, Flg Off Snell was to
experience some amazing adventures. He hid until darkness, but then stumbled onto
a group of Italian soldiers, to whom he presented himself as a Vichy French officer
serving with the Italian forces, and managed to escape although wounded by
grenades thrown at him as he ran away. He then found himself on an airfield and
encountered a group of Germans, who accused him of being a spy and summarily
'executed' him. He was left for dead, having somehow survived two bullet wounds
to his right shoulder, two through the left arm, one through his right hand, one that
grazed his left hip, and one near the spine. As dawn broke he managed to stagger to
his feet and was again confronted by German soldiers and this time was able to
convince them that he was a pilot not a spy. Following treatment locally for his
wounds, he was transferred to a hospital on the mainland.[10]

When pilots of 43 Squadron were returning from a second patrol from over the
beaches at about 1800, during which Flg Off Paddy Turkington (EF594) had
chased a FW190 for three minutes, firing two bursts but to no avail, three crashed
aircraft identified as FW190s were seen on the beach about five miles south of
Syracuse. The fate of the pilots is not known although during the day Maj Gerhard
von Kaldenburg, Kommandeur of 14/SKG10, was reported to have been shot
down and killed by AA fire, but apparently in the vicinity of Gela.

Wg Cdr Duncan Smith (JK650/DS) led a further sweep during the evening,
comprising a dozen Spitfires of 1435 Squadron, one of which was flown by Wg Cdr
Warburton who had persuaded the CO, Sqn Ldr Hugh O'Neill, to let him accompany
their next sweep over the beaches, as recalled by Flt Lt Kelley of 683 Squadron:

> "Warby was so hopping mad [about being shot up by the American gunners
> earlier in the day] that straightaway he went off to Takali [sic] and persuaded
> some of his old friends there to organise a fighter sweep over Sicily to lure
> the ME109s up so that he could let off steam by having a go at someone . . .
> they arranged a sweep with no less than three flight or squadron commanders
> flying in the same formation. Warby flew as No2. There was later one hell of
> a row about it because it was a serious breach of orders for three flight
> commanders to fly together in the same formation – in this case it was three
> plus Warby . . ." [11]

---

[10] see *Escape – or die* by Paul Brickhill. Having made a partial recovery from his wounds,
Flg Off Snell was then put on a train bound for Germany. En route, while still in Italy, he
and an army officer managed to escape by jumping out of a carriage window. They found
refuge with a friendly Italian farmer who contacted the Italian Resistance and with their help
eventually reached Switzerland. He received the DSO for his courage and resolution.
[11] see *Warburton's War*.

At 1930, when over the Syracuse area at 15,000 feet, six Bf109Gs were sighted at 13,500 feet and attacked. Six FW190s attacking shipping were also engaged, and before long a further six Bf109Gs joined the fight. Wg Cdr Duncan Smith later recalled:

> "Leading 1435 Squadron on patrol, I ran into a mixed formation of Macchi 202s and FW190s attempting to bomb the ships. We broke up the enemy formation and I latched on to an FW190, hurtling after him in a steep dive. I gave him a short burst without seeing any result, except that he immediately jettisoned his bomb. I tried desperately to get into a better position but had to break off as the FW190 flew straight into a wall of AA fire pouring toward us from the ships. As I zoomed away, I glanced behind and was surprised to find two ME109s on my tail, both firing hard, but luckily missing me with yards to spare. Two pilots belonging to 'Peggy' O'Neill's flight, acting as top cover, damaged one of the 109s and destroyed [*sic*] the other." [12]

The Wing Leader's No2, Plt Off T.G. Anderson (JK803/V-T), managed to damage one of the FW190s, while Wg Cdr Warburton (EN290/V-G) flying with the top cover claimed a Bf109G probable and a second damaged, a third Messerschmitt being damaged by Plt Off Atkinson (EP286/V-K), but at a cost, two Spitfires failing to return. Flt Lt Monty Rowland RNZAF (EN295/V-B), a New Zealander from Wellington, was killed in this action, although Flg Off Stewart (JL361/V-N) was luckily plucked from the sea, shaken but unhurt. It seems probable that both II and III/JG53 were involved, although their claims appear excessive. III Gruppe was flying a free chase when Spitfires were engaged shortly after 1930, Obfw Günther Seeger of 7 Staffel alone claiming a hat-trick (at 1932, 1935 and 1942), while Oblt Hans Röhrig, Kapitän of 9 Staffel claimed another at 1935. At about the same time II Gruppe was escorting Bf110s of II/ZG1 to attack the landing zones when Spitfires were also encountered, two being claimed by Uffz Hans Ewald of 4 Staffel at 1940 and one by Oblt Martin Laube of 5 Staffel at 1948.

The day's air fighting ended in spectacular fashion for a patrol of 229 Squadron Spitfires and tragically for 5°Stormo's 239^Squadriglia, which entered action for the first time with its newly delivered Re2002 fighter-bombers, attacking and sinking the illuminated hospital ship *Talambra* in Augusta harbour. The Spitfires led by Sqn Ldr Graham Cox (LZ820/X-U) were patrolling over shipping in the Syracuse-Cape Passero area when they were directed to go to the stricken vessel's aid shortly after 1900, sighting eight radial-engined aircraft which they identified as MC200s. In rapid succession, Sqn Ldr Cox shot down three – probably including MM7337 flown by TenCol Guido Nobili, commander of 5°Stormo, whose aircraft apparently hit the steel cable of a barrage balloon as it fell – Ten Renato Beverina (MM7353) and M.llo Zaccaria Perozzi (MM7361), all of whom were killed. A fourth fighter-bomber was pursued by Flg Off O.C.H. Stanford-Smith (JK220/X-M), Flg Off R.H. Small (JK536/X-K) and Flt Sgt Taylor (LZ808/X-D), which they jointly claimed probably destroyed. This was probably the seriously damaged machine flown by Serg Luigi Banfi which crash-landed at Reggio di Calabria.

These final successes raised the Malta Spitfires' claims for the day to nine destroyed, three probables and 11 damaged for the loss of 13 Spitfires, one of

---

[12] see *Spitfire into Battle*.

which had crash-landed at Takali; six pilots had been killed and one taken prisoner. A costly start for the Spitfire squadrons.

Without an adequate warning system, and with the airfields already battered by constant bombing, the Jagdgeschwadern could do little to stem the Allied assault, although 39 Bf109Gs of II/JG51 were hurriedly flown to Trapani from Sardinia to assist II/JG27 and II/JG77. Throughout the daylight hours US bombers and fighter-bombers from North Africa continued to pound the airfields and defences, the Gerbini complex being attacked by a total of 79 B-17s and the western airfields at Sciacca and Trapani by more than 70 B-25s; at the latter base one Bf109G of II/JG77 was totally destroyed and at least five others damaged. A further 36 B-25s raided Palazzolo Acreide, while 24 B-17s and 28 B-24s bombed the marshalling yards at Catania. Vibo Valentia airfield on the mainland was also visited, 21 B-24s being responsible for the raid, P-38s escorting. Two groups of P-38 fighter-bombers of the 1st and 14th FBGs were despatched in formations of a dozen aircraft throughout the daylight hours at 30-minute intervals to thwart any enemy counter-attack in the eastern sector of Sicily, while A-36As of the 27th and 86th FBGs maintained a similar programme over the western and central areas. The A-36As flew a total of 169 sorties attacking communications and positions in the Agrigento, Barrafranca, Caltanissetta, Grammichele and Vallelunga areas, for the loss of two aircraft believed to have been the victims of flak. In addition, three B-25s were lost during the day's raids and at least 18 other bombers sustained damage, while a total of 17 Axis fighters were claimed shot down by the escort and bombers' gunners. II/JG77 at Trapani scrambled a dozen Bf109Gs at 0840 when bombers approached Sciacca, but escorting P-40s kept them occupied, two of which they claimed shot down. The P-40s from Pantelleria similarly claimed two Messerschmitts shot down for no losses. It was a similar story when II Gruppe was again scrambled at 1750, its 12 Bf109Gs being joined by one from StabStaffel and six from II/JG53. On this occasion the bombers were engaged but only one was claimed shot down by II/JG77, plus two of the escorting P-40s. The Italian D.520s of 161°Gruppo at Reggio di Calabria were also scrambled to intercept B-24s over the Messina Straits, claiming two shot down. Some reinforcements had reached southern mainland bases during the day, Magg Silvio De Francesco leading 35 Fiat G.50bis fighter-bombers of 159°Gruppo Assalto to Crotone, 14 of these being flown by pilots from 158°Gruppo.

By the evening of D-Day, a GCI station had been disembarked and came into operation that night. This station and the others still operating from LSTs proved to be of great assistance in forward fighter control, effectively extending the range of Malta's controllers. They played a similar role after darkness when controlling the night fighters, which were active and successful that night, Beaufighters shooting down two Ju88s and possibly a third, plus a Z1007bis, in the Augusta and Syracuse areas, while another Ju88 was claimed probably destroyed by a Mosquito crew south-east of Castelvetrano. With the onset of darkness, further raids were carried out by almost 150 bombers against Trapani/Milo, Sciacca and Gerbini, the latter by 14 Wellingtons of 205 Group.

CHAPTER VI

THE AIR FIGHTING INTENSIFIES

11-13 July 1943

". . . I look upon the fighters in the south with contempt. I demand an immediate improvement and expect every fighter pilot to display more fighting spirit. If this improvement is not forthcoming, aircrew – from Kommodore down – must expect to be demoted to the rank of Flieger and sent to the Eastern Front as infantry."

Reichmarschall Göring to his fighter pilots in Sicily, 11 July 1943

With bridgeheads firmly established, Allied land forces made further advances in the coastal area on D-Day+1 (11 July). Among the early arrivals to come ashore near Pachino were General Montgomery and Vice-Admiral Lord Louis Mountbatten. They and their staffs had been conveyed from Malta aboard the destroyer HMS *Antwerp*. Borrowing a DUKW (an amphibious landing vehicle) they motored to Syracuse in the afternoon, narrowly avoiding a disaster en route, as recalled by Lord Mountbatten:

"We came to a long, narrow village which had a main road running through the centre, where it forked. Monty was sitting beside the driver; his ADC, I and my staff officer were sitting in the back. Suddenly there was a rat-tat-tat of machine guns and we saw a Messerschmitt flying down the main street gunning all the vehicles. All of us in the back immediately flung ourselves down, but not so Monty who sat bolt upright and didn't even turn his head to look at the Messerschmitt. As luck would have it we reached the fork just before the aircraft reached us; we went down the right-hand fork and the aircraft went down the left-hand fork and so we were missed. But Monty never turned a hair and didn't seem to be afraid." [1]

Elsewhere, progress was made northwards and westwards from Syracuse along the roads leading to Catania and Caltagirone, respectively, while to the south Avola and Noto fell and the escarpment to the west was occupied. Further south Rosolini, Spaccaforno and Pozzallo were captured and an advance was begun towards Modica and Ragusa. To the west of this area American troops of II Corps advanced to within two miles of Vittoria, effected some penetration in the Gela area, and occupied the high ground east, north and west of Licata. The resistance offered to all these advances was still feeble, although at 0800 both German and Italian units counter-attacked. Twenty German Mark IV tanks attacked towards the south on the Ponte Olivo-Gela road, breaking through the infantry and approaching to within

---

[1] see *Mountbatten* by Philip Ziegler.

1,000 yards of Gela before being stopped by artillery fire. Another force of about 40 tanks was stopped by the combined fire of rocket guns, tanks, anti-tank guns and artillery, and a lighter attack by ten Italian tanks and infantry was repulsed with little difficulty. These attacks lasted until about 1630.

For Malta's Spitfires air fighting began at 0505 when a dozen Spitfire Vs of 43 Squadron patrolled over the beaches south of Syracuse. Wt Offs Hedderwick (JG724/FT-H) and R.W. Leeming RAAF (ES292) sighted what they identified as a Me210 flying north at 5,000 feet. They chased it for 50 miles and finally shot it down near Cape Armi, the aircraft crashing into the sea with one engine on fire. Their victim was probably a reconnaissance Ju88D of 2(F)/122, possibly F6+GK piloted by Fw Willi Möller which was reported shot down by Spitfires south-east of Sicily; there were no survivors[2]. Fourteen Spitfires of 72 Squadron led jointly by Grp Capt Gilroy (JK143) and Sqn Ldr Daniel (JK173) were in the same general area but failed to meet any enemy aircraft. As 43 Squadron returned from its patrol, eight more Spitfires – four Vs, three IXs and one VIII of the 309th FS led by Capt Payne – commenced a covering patrol in the Gela area when a mixed collection of ten-plus twin-engined aircraft believed to have been Do217s, one aircraft identified as a He177 (*sic*), and a Ju88 were seen attacking shipping, as were two FW190s. One of the twin-engined aircraft was claimed probably destroyed by 1/Lt Wright, and a second was damaged by Capt Payne, but the ships' gunners fired at friend and foe alike and two of the Spitfires were damaged by AA fire although both were able to return to Gozo safely. The 'Do217s' were in fact Bf110s of II/ZG1 which reported being attacked by Spitfires, one aircraft of 4 Staffel (S9+DM) being shot down south-east of Mazzarino and its pilot, Stfw Paul Rapp, wounded. Despite the attention of the American Spitfires, the fighter-bombers succeeded in hitting an ammunition carrier, which blew up violently, throwing debris high into the air. The American pilots made no mention of sighting any Bf109Gs, although the records show that aircraft from III/JG53 provided escort for 20 Bf110s of II/ZG1 operating in the Gela area at this time, while Ju88s from I/KG76 were also active in the area.

South-east of Gela at about the same time (0640) eight patrolling Spitfires of 242 Squadron sighted a lone Ju88 which approached the shipping from out of the sun from about 8,000 feet. Two sections led by Sqn Ldr Boddington (JK260/LE-K) attacked the aircraft, the CO engaging from quarter astern, closing to 100 yards. The bomber's port engine caught fire and the pieces were seen to break away. Sgt Eric Doherty then attacked and saw strikes before Flg Off J.A. Stock delivered the *coup de grâce*, the burning aircraft crashing into a valley four miles east of Biscari; this was possibly another reconnaissance Ju88D from 2(F)/122, F6+NK flown by Uffz Oskar Klammer which was reported to have been shot down by Spitfires[3]. Eight more Ju88s were sighted by 229 Squadron, flying towards Gela at 22,000 feet but on sighting the Spitfires they turned inland and avoided combat. A lone Ju88 was observed bombing shipping by a patrol from 417RCAF Squadron but on sighting the Spitfires it dived northwards and was not seen again. Wg Cdr Duncan Smith led a patrol of 126 Squadron south of Syracuse but the only excitement occurred when an escaped barrage balloon was sighted and shot down by the Wing Leader.

The Americans were back over the Gela beaches between 0800-0845, six Vs and two IXs of the 307th FS led by Capt John M. Winkler sighting four FW190s

---

[2] Killed with Fw Möllers were Lt Karl Sartory, Uffz Georg Bosch and Uffz Peter Salgert.
[3] Uffz Klammer and his observer, Lt Jürgen Prellwitz, were both wounded, but Uffz Georg Homeier, the W/Op, was killed, while the gunner survived unhurt.

which were approaching the shipping. Capt Winkler claimed one of the fighter-bombers, possibly that flown by Oblt Helmut Berger of IV/SKG10, who was shot down and wounded (although German records suggest he was the victim of flak), but intense AA fire from the ships prevented the others from attacking the remaining three. On the return flight 1/Lt August Goldenberg's aircraft developed engine trouble. He failed to arrive at Gozo and was feared lost at sea. The 309th FS was back at 0925, ten Spitfires (six Vs, three IXs and one VIII) led by Maj Frank Hill meeting a lone Ju88 15 miles north-east of Gela. Maj Hill and Capt Chandler engaged this and shot it down but not before the rear gunner had put some shots in one of the Spitfires. Their victim may have been an aircraft of 1/KG76 which was shot down into the sea off the south coast; there were no survivors of Lt Harry Frey's crew of F1+HH.

Between 1015 and 1115, the Kittyhawks of 239 Wing from Safi led by the legendary Grp Capt Johnny Darwen DFC went into action to provide close-support for the ground forces. The three squadrons (112, 250 and 3RAAF) put up 31 aircraft although three had to return early, and were escorted by Spitfires of 243 Squadron. Enemy vehicles on the Catania-Lentini road were attacked. Fifteen stationary M/T were sighted six miles south of Catania but only a number of near misses could be claimed. Near Carlentini a further four M/T were attacked and two received direct hits, although three more seen between Catania and Licata escaped being hit. All aircraft returned safely, a total of 58 250-lb bombs having been dropped with very little result.

Taking off at 1055, a dozen Spitfires of 72 Squadron led by Sqn Ldr Daniel were tasked to patrol over the beaches south of Syracuse and encountered a formation of radial-engined Italian fighter-bombers believed to have been MC200s, but which were in fact ten G.50bis of 159°Gruppo led by Cap Filippo Greco. The Italian pilots had been promised an escort of German Bf109s but these failed to rendezvous. Sqn Ldr Daniel (JK173) and Flt Lt M.V. Christopherson (JG793) shared in destroying one, while Sgt Hermiston (JK275) probably destroyed another and damaged a third, one more being damaged jointly by Plt Off Jack Hussey (EN358) and Sgt R.C. Pearson (EN258/RN-B). As the Squadron reformed prior to returning to Malta, Flg Off George Keith (JK637) became detached and failed to turn up. It was thought that he had run out of fuel and crash-landed "somewhere in Sicily". In fact, he landed at Pachino airfield where he was greeted by members of 3201 RAF Servicing Commando, who had arrived the previous day with stocks of petrol, oil and ammunition, ready to assist any Spitfire in need of their service. Flg Off Keith, who had managed to reach the airstrip on his last few drops of fuel, was their first customer. A refuelling party inspected and serviced the Spitfire and within the hour the Canadian pilot was able to take off from a nearby road and was soon back at Malta, where he reported that he, too, had shot down a 'MC200', and had then engaged a Ju88 which he also claimed destroyed, possibly an aircraft from III/KG54.

Three of the G.50bis were shot down in this encounter with 72 Squadron, all three pilots being posted missing including Ten Aldo della Corte and Serg Magg Keller. As the remaining seven Italian fighter-bombers landed at Reggio di Calabria, the airfield was subjected to a heavy raid by B-24s and five were destroyed or severely damaged, although none of the pilots was injured. The Alarm Flight comprising seven MC202s of 161°Gruppo was scrambled to intercept the bombers, returning pilots claiming two shot down. While the G.50bis of 159°Gruppo were being savaged by the Spitfires, more Italian fighter-bombers from Crotone attacked British ground forces south of Syracuse, eight newly arrived

Re2002s of the 5°Stormo led by Magg Giuseppe Cenni, a former ace Ju87 pilot, successfully carrying out their mission without interference from the Spitfires.

Another victory came the way of the 307th FS shortly before midday, eight Vs and four IXs in the Gela area sighting two FW190s as they approached shipping. The Spitfires attacked, forcing both fighter-bombers to jettison their bombs, one – possibly the aircraft flown by Obfw Alexander Abendroth of 7/SKG10 – then being claimed shot down by Capt Collinsworth and the other damaged by 1/Lt Wootten. The next success for the Spitfires came shortly after midday, a dozen of 93 Squadron (eight Vs and four IXs) led by Sqn Ldr Sizer meeting a number of Ju88s escorted by two Bf109Gs south of Syracuse. US P-38Gs of the 14th FS were also in the area and one of these joined Flg Off Lloyd Hunt RCAF (JL219/HN-X) in shooting down one of the Messerschmitts, while other Spitfires engaged the bombers, one of which was claimed by Plt Off G.S. Richardson (EN140). A second was attacked over the cruiser HMS *Warspite* by Flg Off Stan Browne (LZ840) and his No2, fellow New Zealander Plt Off Roy Fisher RNZAF (BS553), and shot down into the sea. Browne was heard to yell over the R/T that he had been hit by AA fire and was trying to land at Pachino. He got down safely and his aircraft, LZ840, was only slightly damaged. A patrol of 145 Squadron Spitfires happened upon the scene but just too late to become involved, the pilots reporting that the Ju88s spread out fanwise on their approach, although the crew of one was seen to bale out while under attack by another Spitfire, obviously one of 93 Squadron's victims; the Ju88s were probably from II/KG77, 3Z+JN piloted by Uffz Helmut Untermark of 5 Staffel being shot down with the loss of one member of the crew, the other three being captured, while 6 Staffel lost 3Z+HP from which there were no survivors of Lt Walter Hötzender's crew.

In the early afternoon four Ju87Ds of 207^Squadriglia were escorted to Licata by seven MC205Vs of 351^ and 360^Squadriglie. The dive-bombers attacked their targets and escaped serious damage from ground fire, while the Macchis reported an engagement with Spitfires, probably a patrol of 229 Squadron led by Flt Lt Les Gosling (LZ808/X-D) who added another victory to his growing tally when he attacked a single MC202 at 13,000 feet over Comiso. Gosling fired a short burst from astern at 200 yards range and the Macchi caught alight and fell away, possibly an aircraft of 386^Squadriglia flown by Sottoten Germano Gennari. There followed a break in aerial encounters for Malta's Spitfires until 1550, when seven of 92 Squadron – three IXs and four Vs – led by Wg Cdr Peter Olver (EN448/PO), patrolled between Cape Scalambri and Gela. AA bursts were seen about three miles away to the south and upon investigation a dozen Ju88s – probably aircraft of I/KG6 and/or III/KG54, both units being in the area – were sighted at 10,000 feet over Priolo, and 30 unidentified fighters could be seen stepped up to 15,000 feet. Wg Cdr Olver led the Spitfires in to attack the bombers, as he later recalled:

"The Americans were unable to maintain air cover over the landings, so I was asked if 244 Wing could cover their landing as well as our own. The Germans were putting their major effort into the Americans, so I led the first patrol over the American beach and we saw a few German fighters that didn't like us much. Then we saw a formation of about a dozen Ju88s coming towards the Americans. They did too steep a turn to port when they saw our Spitfires, which threw their formation into disarray before they reached the target. I took the last 88 and it went down below the remainder, which were scrambling back into a bunch and retiring up north. The other Spits took on other 88s. My Ju crashed and the crew baled out. My aircraft must have got a stray bullet in the fuel tank. When I discovered that my legs were getting burnt I undid the straps, got my feet onto the seat, opened up the throttle fully – the engine was still running perfectly – then turned and headed for the sea. Salt water being good for burns, I knew that I would be picked up quickly with all the invasion shipping there. Because I was so low I decided to jettison the canopy, which was possibly a mistake because the flames came up over my face, but got out although I broke my arm and dislocated my shoulder on landing.

The Germans had pushed the Americans back considerably so I fell on enemy territory. Apart from the kitchen lads who first captured me, I was quite well treated and certainly by two senior NCOs of the Hermann Göring Parachute Division who sorted out the kitchen boys and took me in the sidecar of their motor cycle to a doctor. I was in Sicily for about ten days amongst a lot of German wounded, and some American wounded. The German pilot whose Ju88 I had shot down was brought up in a car to meet me where I was being held near Caltagirone. I think he was a Warrant Officer or some such, he looked deadly pale with a great bandage round his head. He could speak some English and kept asking me why I had gone on firing at them after they had started to bale out. I didn't think the obvious answer would give him much satisfaction – that I wanted to make a proper job of it. I did see a couple of white dots shoot over my aircraft which would have been parachutes before they opened. It was after this that their aircraft hit the ground." [4]

Meanwhile, the remaining six Spitfires of 92 Squadron pursued the Ju88s northwards, four being claimed shot down, one by Flt Lt R.W. Richardson (ER470), who also damaged a second; one by Flg Off Milt Jowsey (EN188/QJ-6); another by Lt Albie Sachs SAAF (ER871); and a fourth by Wt Off S.R. Fry (EN152), with one more being claimed probably destroyed by 2/Lt Johnny Gasson SAAF (ES148/QJ-E). Flg Off Jowsey, on his return to Malta, said that he saw a Spitfire crash on land. He was flying at deck level and as he turned and climbed he saw a parachute 3,000 feet above. He circled it and thought that the airman dangling below its shrouds waved to him, which led him to believe that it may have been Wg Cdr Olver which, presumably, it was. Of his victory, Jowsey reported:

"Flying No3 Black Section [at 11,000 feet], reported enemy aircraft at 5 o'clock. Turned about towards them and dived to 6,000 feet when I saw 12 Ju88s in a slight dive. I picked on one Ju88 [and] made starboard quarter to full astern attack closing to 150 yards. Broke off and came down port quarter to full astern attack closing to 100 yards. White smoke started to pour out of starboard engine, all return fire I could see stopped. Ju88 up to now had been doing gentle turns while diving. I made a third attack from starboard quarter to full astern closing to 150 yards. The Ju88 which was now less than 1,000 feet went in 45 degrees angle dive and crashed into the ground. A shower of dust came up. Crashed eight miles north of Niscemi."

---

[4] When the Germans withdrew from Sicily, Wg Cdr Olver was taken across the Straits of Messina in a landing craft to a German hospital in Reggio before being moved northwards to Naples where he was sent to a hospital in an American POW camp near Capua, north of Naples, for some weeks. A transfer to Poland eventually followed, Olver ending up in Stalag Luft III at Diepholz.

I/KG6 reported the loss of two Ju88s, one of these crashing near Militello in which Lt Rudolf Haschke and his crew of 3E+GH were lost, while three crew members of Uffz Helmut Becker's 3E+LL of 3 Staffel were able to bale out; this was possibly the aircraft shot down by Wg Cdr Olver. Meanwhile, III/KG54 reported the loss of three of its aircraft including B3+FR of 8 Staffel flown by Lt Helmut Kissel, who reported that his aircraft had also been shot down by Spitfires and therefore may also have been a victim of 92 Squadron. Lt von Brunn's crew of B3+KR, also of 8 Staffel, were able to bale out, apparently the victim of AA fire, while Hptm Kurt Lehmann of 9 Staffel carried out a crash-landing at Grottaglie in B3+FT following fighter attack. However, it should be noted that at about the same time as 92 Squadron was in action, or perhaps a little earlier, US P-40s from Pantelleria also reported a combat with Ju88s escorted by Bf109s, the American pilots similarly claiming four bombers plus a Messerschmitt probably destroyed, for one loss.

Next on the scene were a dozen Spitfires of 72 Squadron including one flown by Wg Cdr Prosser Hanks, Hal Far Station Commander. These patrolled the Noto beaches but no enemy aircraft were encountered. The 309th FS put up four Vs, two VIIIs and two IXs for its next patrol over the Gela beaches between 1600 and 1630, meeting a single Bf109G which Capt Payne reported to have shot down over Pozzallo. This was possibly Lt Karl-Heinz Messer of 2/JG53 (WkNr18407) who failed to return from a combat south-west of Navo, and was presumed killed. Other Allied fighters and fighter-bombers were around, Lt Hans-Joachim Kögler of 1/JG53 claiming a Spitfire at 1615, while Uffz Holstein of 2 Staffel reported shooting down a P-40 at the same time. As the 309th patrol withdrew, its place on the patrol line was taken by seven more Spitfires (three Vs, four IXs) from the 308th FS led by Capt Paulk. Six twin-engined aircraft again identified as Do217s were encountered and attacked as they prepared to dive-bomb shipping. The majority were seen to jettison their bombs and three were claimed shot down by Capt Paulk, 1/Lt Callander and 1/Lt Wilfred L. Waltner, while 1/Lt Woodrich damaged another. One Spitfire was damaged by return fire. The Americans had again encountered Bf110s of II/ZG1, this unit reporting a further three of its aircraft shot down: S9+BN of 5 Staffel crashed about three miles east of Gela in which pilot, Fw Hermann Gerdes, was wounded; Oblt Wilhelm Dreher's aircraft was also shot down east of Gela, he and his gunner surviving unhurt, while both Uffz Franz Hillmann and his gunner were wounded when they were shot down in the same area. A fourth aircraft (S9+KN) of 5 Staffel returned with minor damage though the air gunner, Uffz Richard Blind, was wounded.

239 Wing's Kittyhawks were airborne at 1810 to attack Gerbini airfield, escort again being provided by 243 Squadron. North of Vizzini two MC202s were seen flying at 9,000 feet and one of these was attacked by Sqn Ldr Mackie (JK666/SN-V):

"On the way to base after Kittyhawks had bombed Gerbini, we were flying south at 12,000 feet when two MC202s were sighted north of Vizzini at 9,000 feet travelling south to south-east. We dived on them. I attacked one from astern, firing cannons and machine-guns from 150 yards range. I myself saw no results from the attack."

However, Sqn Ldr Mackie's No2 saw a cloud of white smoke issue from the Macchi, which turned sharply and dived away, while Flt Sgt Dave Towgood reported seeing a red flash under its fuselage. It was credited to the CO as damaged. More fighters were engaged by ten Spitfires of 126 Squadron in the Noto area between 1825 and 2015, when 20-plus enemy fighters identified as FW190s,

Bf109s and MC202s were seen approaching shipping at 14,500 feet. Wg Cdr Duncan Smith (JK650/D-S) led the attack, shooting down a Macchi before engaging a FW190 which he claimed damaged:

> "Soon after getting on patrol I spotted four Macchi 202s immediately below and realised they had not seen us. I went down on them with my number two, and was about to open fire on the lead Macchi when they saw us and broke into our attack, still keeping immaculate formation. Thereafter a hectic dogfight took place. This Italian pilot really knew what he was doing: apart from giving a splendid aerobatic display, I found that each time he stayed and turned he gained on me in the turn. I looked frantically for help but there was no sign of my number two. Knowing my Spitfire's capabilities so well, I pulled her up sharply into corkscrew turns into the sun as steeply as I could. I expected to hear and feel unwelcome bangs of exploding shells in my fuselage but nothing happened until suddenly I felt my Spitfire shake violently and next moment we were spinning – I caught her after a couple of turns and getting control again looked for the Macchi. Sure enough there he was, slightly to one side and below me asking to be shot down. My first burst caught him in the cockpit area and wing root and he went up in flames, shedding bits as he winged over and dived into high ground overlooking Noto. He must have thought he had got me when he saw me spin." [5]

The combat was probably with MC205Vs of 96^Squadriglia, five aircraft of this unit led by Cap Emanuele Annoni taking off to strafe Allied troops on the beaches around Syracuse. The Macchi pilots reported meeting Spitfires and USAAF P-40s, five of which were attacked and one being claimed by Sottoten Fabio Clauser for the loss of Ten Otello Gensini who baled out and was rescued; he reported that he had been shot down by a Spitfire. A formation of five Re2005s of 362^Squadriglia was also in the area, escorting G.50bis of 158°Gruppo which were attacking shipping off Syracuse. Spitfires were engaged by the Reggiane pilots and three claimed shot down, one apiece by Cap La Ferla, Ten Edoardo Vaghi and M.llo Tullio Arduini, but Ten Luigi Nitoglia failed to return from his first operational flight while another aircraft returned with damage to its tail and starboard wing and Ten Enrico Salvi was forced to carry out an emergency landing at Sigonella. An Italian fighter identified as a MC202 was claimed shot down by Flg Off Geoff White (JK950/MK-H) and another was probably destroyed by Flg Off B.W. Clarke (JK972/MK-L), the former also reporting strikes on two Bf109Gs he then attacked; two further Messerschmitts were claimed damaged by Sgt J.S. Davidson (JK522/MK-O), and another by Flt Sgt Bingham (EN493/MK-Y).

At about the same time, ten Spitfires of 111 Squadron were patrolling the beaches between Syracuse and Cape Passero when they saw the air fight, sighting a further eight enemy fighters high above. Sqn Ldr Hill (EN518) led six of his pilots to assist 243 Squadron while the other four engaged the high cover identified as Re2001s (*sic*) and MC202s, two of the former being claimed destroyed by Sgt Hughie Eccleston RAAF (JK728), and one of the latter by Flg Off Fred Mellors (JK217). Their victims may have been the two Re2005s of 362^Squadriglia; Ten Giulio Torresi of the same unit claimed a Spitfire shot down. Another Reggiane was damaged by Sgt K.R. Allen (EN252). Meanwhile, Sqn Ldr Hill claimed a radial-engined aircraft which he thought was a FW190 or a MC200, and Sgt R.F.G.

---

[5] see *Spitfire into Battle*.

Wilson (JK221) damaged a second. These were in fact Re2002 fighter-bombers of 102°Gruppo from Crotone led by Magg Cenni on their second mission of the day. They had just released their bombs when Spitfires attacked and three were promptly shot down: Ten Lorenzo Lorenzi (MM7344) and M.llo Guido Buffarini (MM7354) of 209^Squadriglia were killed, as was Sottoten Salvatore D'Arrigo (MM7346) of 239^Squadriglia. Serg Magg Bruno Melotti[6] was able to fire at one of the Spitfires, which he claimed probably destroyed. His victim was probably Sqn Ldr Hill whose aircraft was hit during the action. With his Spitfire streaming glycol, he attempted a landing at Pachino, where his aircraft struck a tree. The damage was not serious, however, and Hill was not hurt. Sgt Ken Allen also landed at Pachino but only to refuel and rearm. Shortly after the latest arrivals, and while Allen's aircraft was being refuelled, the airfield was strafed by six Bf109s, causing one RAF Commando and several army casualties, also "putting a couple of bullets through the Engineer Officer's cap", and a few more through one of the Spitfires.

While the Spitfire patrols endeavoured to keep the skies clear of enemy aircraft over the beaches, 24 Kittyhawks were searching for targets in the Lentini-Vizzini area, but ground visibility was bad owing to dust and haze and no suitable targets were located. With a dozen Spitfires of 1435 Squadron providing the escort, the formation returned to Malta with bombs intact. One of the last patrols of the day was flown by 11 Spitfires of 43 Squadron between 1930 and 2110. No enemy aircraft were sighted but Flg Off Harry Lea's aircraft (JK616) developed a glycol leak and Lea was obliged to force-land on an uncleared and almost certainly mine-strewn beach near Pachino, fortunately without detonating any. Carefully making his way across the beach, he located a fox-hole in which he hid for a day and a night whilst the battle raged all around, eventually hitching a lift back to the landing area from where he was returned to Malta on board an LST.

It had proved to be a costly evening for the Italian fighters and fighter-bombers in action against the Spitfires, losing one MC205V, one Re2005, and three Re2002s, plus another Re2005 seriously damaged, in addition to three G.50bis and two MC202s in the morning. By the end of the day the Spitfire pilots from Malta, together with the P-40s of the 33rd FG from Pantelleria, had claimed 28 enemy aircraft shot down, plus five probables and 17 damaged, of which the Spitfires were initially credited with $23^1/_2$-4-16, for just three losses, two Spitfires and one P-40, in the course of 872 sorties. The credits were raised to $25^1/_2$ when Flg Off Keith of 72 Squadron returned to claim two more[7]. On the battlefield the body of a German pilot was recovered which led the authorities to believe, incorrectly and for reasons now unclear, that it was that of Oblt Ernst von Weyrauch, commander of 2(H)/14. The real identity of the unfortunate pilot is not known but it was not von Weyrauch. The German fighter pilots had done their best to counter the continuous attacks, I/JG53 alone losing three pilots killed or missing, and III/JG53 the services of three of its aircraft, one of which had been shot down and another badly damaged in a crash-landing following battle damage. Their morale was given a further severe blow that evening when another damning rebuke – as quoted at the beginning of this chapter – arrived from Reichmarschall Göring.

During the day the Bf109Gs of Hptm Franz Beyer's IV/JG3 arrived at Ramacca from Lecce, where the ground staff of JG53 took on the technical maintenance of

---

[6] Postwar, Bruno Melotti became a personal friend of Nicola Malizia but sadly died several years ago.
[7] In addition, the missing Wg Cdr Olver had shot down a Ju88 but this fact was not known at the time since the Wing Commander had been taken prisoner.

the Messerschmitts. Elsewhere on this day the NWAAF heavy bomber effort, carried out by 83 B-17s, was again directed against the marshalling yards at Catania. Explosions and huge fires were caused, the smoke from which could be seen for 140 miles on the return journey, and many hits were registered on the warehouses, repair buildings and oil storage installations; a merchant vessel was sunk in the harbour. The attacks on the Gerbini landing ground were continued by 47 US Marauders and the western airfields at Milo and Sciacca were bombed by 27 Marauders and 36 Mitchells, respectively. An estimated 22 fighters opposed the raids, of which four were claimed shot down by the escorting P-40s and bombers' gunners. Almost 100 P-38s were despatched on offensive sweeps and to bomb targets of opportunity in central Sicily, and an even greater number of A-36As attacked transport columns, trains and airfields, destroying or damaging 248 vehicles, two locomotives and several grounded aircraft, particularly in the region of San Caterina, Caltanissetta and Porto Empedocle. Fighter escort for the bomber and fighter-bomber formations was provided by a total of 117 aircraft from NWAAF, and 22 Spitfire sorties from Malta acted as escort to bombers attacking Gerbini. The US Ninth Air Force Liberator attacks were again concentrated against the air bases in the toe of Italy. Sixty-eight effective sorties were flown against the airfields at Vibo Valentia and Reggio di Calabria and widespread damage to airfield facilities and grounded aircraft was reported. Considerable air opposition was encountered and two enemy aircraft were destroyed without loss to the Liberators.

That night, the main attacks on Sicily were delivered against air and supply bases in the west of the island. Forty-eight Mitchells effectively bombed Bo Rizzo airfield and 30 Wellingtons attacked targets at Trapani, Marsala, and Mazzara de Vallo, causing fires and explosions. The Wellington attacks preceded a naval bombardment scheduled to commence at 0100 hours and great care had to be taken to be off the target before this began and to keep clear of the Navy's formidable AA fire. A further Wellington force of 26 aircraft bombed and machine-gunned hangars and ground aircraft at Porto Corvino Ravello airfield near Salerno on the mainland, where German bombers were based. From Cyrenaica pressure was maintained during the night against the enemy's air bases across the Messina Straits, a dozen Liberators and Halifaxes successfully attacking Reggio di Calabria airfield. Malta-based Mosquitos continued their intruder patrols over the enemy's air bases in northern Sicily and southern Italy, shooting down an unidentified aircraft over Crotone. RAF night fighters were also active, shooting down two Ju88s and a He111 which were operating against Allied shipping off the landing beaches.

Allied land forces were also on the move during the night; in particular, US Seventh Army troops occupied the important airfield at Comiso, where repairs were begun immediately by moonlight. Meanwhile, the US Troop Carrier Command launched its second paratroop assault, aimed at dropping men of the 82nd Airborne Division in front of the Allied advance in the Gela area, the operation codenamed *Husky II*. It was even less successful than the earlier attack and out of the 144 C-47s (carrying 2,300 men) which were despatched, 23 failed to return, and a further 37 were severely damaged. Hurricane intruders from the 73 Squadron detachment were airborne and one pilot, Sgt Wilf Mygind RNZAF, observed what he thought were barrage balloons falling in flames, describing them as "22 balls of fire", before he turned for home, unaware until later that he had witnessed such a tragedy. Some troopers managed to bale out before their aircraft crashed but 60 pilots and crewmen were killed, and 97 troopers were killed or were posted missing, including the Assistant Division Commander. It was unfortunate that the arrival of the transports coincided with an attack on naval ships offshore by Axis aircraft, and ships' gunners fired at anything that came within range. There were also reports of some transports being attacked by enemy aircraft. It seems probable that at least one C-47 was shot down by a Ju88C night fighter of I/NJG2, Oblt Riedelberger claiming such a victory, his first. Firing from the ships started spasmodically but had soon became general. It was difficult to blame the ships for engaging low flying aircraft in the circumstances, and the rules for engagement had been frequently debated: it had been agreed that ships were free to open fire at night at aircraft whose approach indicated "hostile intent", and that friendly aircraft which were obliged to fly over the Allied convoys and ships offshore should do so at heights above 6,000 feet. The naval commanders had attempted to ensure that all units were notified of the time and route of the aerial convoy, but clearly not all had received the instructions. All three airborne operations were criticised by both British and American commanders alike, and echoed by the official US Navy historian, who wrote of the latest débâcle:

> "It seemed incredible that the Air Force would lay on so hazardous a flight at low level – over an assault area heavily committed in combat, where enemy raids had been frequent for two days – and for no sound purpose . . . And what if an enemy air raid were taking place when the transport planes arrived? Nobody seemed to have thought of that." [8]

Such was the utter shock and dejection felt by the Allied commanders over the abject failure of the airborne operations, and the wastage of highly-trained troops, that most eradicated thoughts of ever again employing airborne troops. General Eisenhower blamed General Patton and called a halt to further airborne operations until a formal enquiry had been conducted; the US Air Force also blamed the Army, as did the RAF, Air Marshal Sir Arthur Coningham (AOC NWATAF) calling it "a soldier's air operation". Despite these setbacks and recriminations, the war went on. To the ordinary front-line soldier, sailor and airmen that meant fighting another battle and hoping to survive another day.

By D-Day+2 (12 July) the Allies had established operational bases along the whole southern area from the central invasion beachhead at Licata to the port of Augusta. Advanced units had reached and were holding Ragusa and Palazzolo, and elements of the US Seventh Army and the British Eighth Army had made contact in that area. Comiso had been occupied during the night by troops of the US 45th Division, and Ponte Olivo and Biscari were taken on the 12th. There was some excitement at newly captured Comiso airfield during the day, as noted by Colonel D'Este:

> "Unaware of its capture, the pilot of a Ju88 was fired upon by US anti-aircraft artillery as it landed at Comiso. The enraged pilot taxied to a halt and emerged from the cockpit shaking his fist at what he thought were his own inept gunners. Several Spitfires were also fired upon . . ." [9]

Units of the Royal Navy entered Augusta harbour, which had been subjected to bombardment from the sea, and the town itself was occupied in the early hours of the following morning; port installations were found to be almost intact.

Heavy air attacks were made during the day on the Messina communications in order to hinder the enemy's reinforcement plan. B-17s of the NWAAF carried out

---

[8] see *Sicily-Salerno-Anzio*.
[9] see *Bitter Victory*.

79 sorties against the Messina railway bridges, and 72 Liberators attacked the ferry slipways and railway yards at San Giovanni and Reggio di Calabria. Gerbini airfield and its satellites were on the receiving end of further attacks by 36 Mitchells, and Agrigento and Canicatti were bombed by Marauders. In addition, nearly 1,000 sorties were flown by US P-38s, P-40s and A-36As on sweeps and strafing missions against the enemy's rear lines of communications in southern and central Sicily, American fighter pilots claiming four Messerschmitts and two MC202s during the course of the day's activities. One of these victories was gained over a Bf109G of 3/JG77 flown by Uffz Franz Schmidt, who was on a reconnaissance sortie in the region of La Galite, an island off the Tunisian coast, when he was shot down by US Spitfires of the 5th FS of the 52nd Fighter Group based at Korba in Tunisia; two Messerschmitts were claimed 15 miles east of Bizerte by 2/Lt Irwin Gottlieb and Flt Off Louis M. Weynandt, but Schmidt was the only one lost and he baled out into the sea[10]. Next day, during the afternoon, he was rescued from his dinghy by a Walrus of 283 Squadron crewed by Sgts W.S. Lambert and K.R. Pugh.

The main air effort from Malta was still directed to the provision of fighter cover for the landing beaches and shipping in the occupied harbours. First into action, during a patrol over the landing beaches south of Syracuse, were ten Spitfires of 243 Squadron led by Sqn Ldr Mackie. Near Palazzolo two Bf109Gs were sighted by the Canadian Sgt Schmitz (EN357/SA-N), who attacked one at 200 yards range. Flashes were seen on the starboard side of the Messerschmitt, which was last observed in a steep dive at 3,000 feet, but no claim was made as Schmitz was uncertain whether the flashes seen were cannon strikes or reflected sunshine. Near the end of their patrol, a number of pilots saw two aircraft go down in flames, one to the south of Calabernato, and one to the east, and were probably victims of 72 Squadron which recorded meeting at least half a dozen Bf109Gs of 7/JG53 led by Lt Franz Barten, and a few MC202s, in the Augusta area. Flt Lt A.H.Jupp (JG746) claimed a Messerschmitt probably destroyed while Sgt Keith Clarkson (EN309) reported shooting down a second which apparently dived into the sea, probably the aircraft (Yellow 6/WkNr15522) flown by Uffz Heinz-August Barth of 7/JG53 who was killed in this action. Flg Off Keith (JK429) continued his good run and reported shooting down a MC202, but one Spitfire (JG771) failed to return although Sgt J.B. Morris was able to carry out an emergency landing near Pachino[11]. Patrols from 43 Squadron and the 307th were also active at this time, the American Spitfires meeting a lone FW190 of Stab/SKG10 flown by Fw Hermann Heiss over the landing beaches near Ponte Olivo, which Capt Harry L. Barr shot down in a diving attack; Heiss was killed. Meanwhile, Flg Off Paddy Turkington (EF594) of 43 Squadron pursued a single Bf109G which he had sighted flying at 3,000 feet near Augusta harbour. After firing a few bursts, Turkington closed to within 200 yards to deliver the *coup de grâce* only to have his cannons jam. One fortunate German pilot lived to fight another day.

When 242 Squadron landed at Takali shortly after 0700 following its early morning patrol over the CENT area, one Spitfire was found to be missing. It was

---

[10] At the end of the month Spitfires of the 5th FS claimed two FW190s shot down off the Tunisian coast (by 1/Lts Franklin A. Everett and Everett K. Jenkins Jr), these victories taking the 52nd Fighter Group's total past the 100 mark, its first having been claimed during the *Torch* landings in French North-West Africa at the end of the previous November.

[11] Since his aircraft required major surgery, Sgt Morris was returned to Malta aboard a departing LST, arriving on the 14th.

the aircraft flown by Sgt K. Campbell, who was last seen at about 0645 travelling south of Cape Scalambri. Later in the day news reached the Squadron that Campbell was safe with the Navy, and that an attempt was being made to salvage his aircraft. On arriving back at Takali two days later, he recalled:

> "Towards the end of the CENT area patrol my windscreen became oiled up and I lost No1. When No1 did a turn through the sun and set off for base, I called for homing on all buttons with no response. Continued south to southeast but, owing to the oil on the windscreen and hazy visibility, I was unable to find Malta. Then set course for Sicily and, after finding the coast, turned a right circuit near Pachino. I could not find Pachino aerodrome but then saw another Spitfire about to land, and followed him, landing in a flattish field between the aerodrome and the town. The propeller was damaged as the aircraft came to rest in a small ditch."

Shortly thereafter, ten Spitfires of 126 Squadron including three IXs sighted about four Bf109Gs making a low-level attack on road traffic west of Syracuse. A section led by Flg Off Geoff White (JK672/MK-E) was ordered to carry out a diving attack, White shooting down one before damaging a second. A further six Messerschmitts were seen flying south at about 7,000 feet south of Syracuse but these turned away and avoided combat. White's victim was possibly an aircraft of IV/JG3, Uffz Kurt Schmidt of 11 Staffel being reported shot down and killed in the Syracuse area. Both 1435 Squadron and 1SAAF shared the Syracuse patrol line between 0720 and 0855, the former unit meeting about 30 Bf109Gs – including aircraft of IV/JG3 – to the west of their position and at the same height. Many dogfights ensued, the Spitfires coming off best on this occasion, two Messerschmitts being claimed shot down by Flt Sgt Norman Harrison RNZAF (JK929/V-P), who also badly damaged a third, while a probable was credited to Plt Off R. Morris (EP286/V-K); three more were damaged by Flg Off Hawkins (EN290/V-G), Plt Off J.R. Spiers (JG920/V-C) and Flt Sgt S. Butler (BS357/V-L). The Spitfires sustained no damage but IV/JG3 suffered further losses. 1SAAF meanwhile dived on four other Messerschmitts, and were in turn attacked by six others, but the ensuing combats were indecisive with only Lt Schalk van der Merwe getting in a burst at long range without tangible result. Lt Otto Wessling and Uffz Hans Schäfer of 10 Staffel each claimed a Spitfire. Further to the west, at 10,000 feet over beaches near Cape Scalambri, a section of three Spitfires of an 81 Squadron patrol were attacked from astern by a similar number of Messerschmitts, but these dived away as the Spitfires turned to meet the attack. The Spitfires followed and all three opened fire but no claims were made. Another pilot spotted enemy M/T moving along the whole length of the Palagonia-Caltagirone road and, dropping down to 1,000 feet, attacked a convoy of between six and eight vehicles including several towing artillery guns. Hits were observed and troops were seen to disembark and scatter.

While these actions were taking place, 31 Kittyhawks escorted by a dozen Spitfires of 601 Squadron bombed gun positions which were holding up the Eighth Army's advance towards Priolo. Bombing was carried out from heights between 3,000 and 1,500 feet, but haze and dust made observation of results difficult. Nonetheless, a direct hit was scored on a building, while two M/T were destroyed by strafing. Light AA fire was experienced from the target area but none of the attacking aircraft was hit. However, the operation was marred when two

Kittyhawks of 250 Squadron collided and crashed into the sea. One pilot was rescued but the other was lost. Shortly thereafter, at 0920, a dozen Spitfires of 229 Squadron on patrol over the beaches north-west of Cape Scalambri at 17,000 feet sighted at least 20 fighters below, at 10,000 feet, flying south. The formation evidently comprised Bf109Gs from I/JG53 and IV/JG3, FW190s, MC202s and Bf110s, which were attacked in a dive, two Bf109Gs being shot down by Flt Lt Gosling (LZ808/X-D) and Flt Sgt F.R.M. Cook (ER533/X-R) while Flt Sgt D. Andrew (JK811/X-F) accounted for a Bf110 – possibly an aircraft of II/ZG1 – two more of which were engaged and damaged by Flt Sgt W.G. Bromhead (EF638/X-N) and Sgt W.G. Downing (BR299/X-S). One of the Spitfires (JK233/X-X) was shot down into the sea and Plt Off Tony Williams was killed.

Eight Spitfires of 152 Squadron patrolling east of Gela were directed to the scene of the battle near Comiso, Sqn Ldr Freddie Lister (ES112/UM-U) shooting down a Bf109G near Ragusa from which the pilot was seen to bale out, almost certainly another aircraft of IV/JG3. But the Messerschmitts hit back, shooting down two Spitfires flown by Sgt N.E.C. Dear (JK305), who survived[12], and Sgt Bob Quine RAAF (JK511), a 20-year-old from Queensland who was killed; a third (JG751) force-landed behind enemy lines although the pilot, Flg Off J.A. Tooth, reported over the radio of his downed machine that he was uninjured; he made good his escape and reached Allied lines. On his return to the Squadron three days later, Tooth reported that after firing all his ammunition at a Bf110, without tangible result, he was forced to crash-land near Gela due to a glycol leak. On scrambling out of his aircraft he hid in a ditch until dark, then made his way to the coast where he contacted an army unit. It seems probable that the Bf109Gs were from I/JG53 and IV/JG3, Fw Kurt Braasch of 3/JG53 claiming a Spitfire at 0924 for his eighth victory, and Uffz Emil Wagner of 1 Staffel getting a second (his third) three minutes later, but lost Uffz Ernst Mrwik of 1 Staffel (WkNr18519/SN+RC) who was taken prisoner; he may have accounted for the third Spitfire lost before being shot down himself. Meanwhile, six-victory ace Uffz Holstein of 2 Staffel (WkNr15313) force-landed north of Comiso, and was injured, while a second pilot from this Staffel ditched his aircraft (WkNr18494) east of Lake Lentini, and was rescued unhurt. IV/JG3 also suffered a number of casualties.

There occurred another major clash shortly before midday, when a dozen Spitfires of 72 Squadron (including four IXs) led by Sqn Ldr Daniel encountered a large mixed force identified as 30-plus Bf109Gs (of IV/JG3), MC202s (six), MC205Vs (four) and radial-engined fighter-bombers believed to have been MC200s, escorting a single Ju52/3m transport in the Augusta area; in fact, the fighter-bombers were G.50bis of 159°Gruppo from Gela led by Magg De Francesco, the same unit 72 Squadron had fought with the previous day. The Ju52, presumably an aircraft of I/TG1, was promptly shot down by Plt Off B.J. Ingalls RCAF (EN358), who also damaged a Bf109G, one of the latter being claimed shot

---

[12] When Sgt Dear returned to the Squadron on 27 August he reported that he had followed Flg Off Tooth into the attack and had seen his leader come under fire from astern. He then attacked what he assumed was a Do217 (obviously a Bf110) which he believed he shot down before his own aircraft was hit. He baled out at 3,500 feet and on landing was fired at by a person or persons unseen and wounded in one heel; having hidden until dark, he was eventually found by a US patrol and taken to hospital. His victory had apparently been witnessed by the Americans, and on his return to the Squadron he brought with him a note signed by a US Army colonel to this effect.

down by Sqn Ldr Daniel (JK429), his twelfth victory (one shared)[13]. Another Messerschmitt was damaged by Flg Off W.J. Cameron, who also claimed a FW190 damaged, although this was probably a G.50bis. Meanwhile, five of the fighter-bombers were claimed shot down, plus one more probably so, and three others damaged, the victories being awarded to Flg Off Tom Hughes (JK746), Flg Off John King (JK468), Sgt A.M. Griffiths (EN309) two plus a damaged, and Flg Off R.D. Scrase (JK275), who also claimed a damaged; a probable was claimed jointly by Flt Lt M. Johnston RCAF (JK990) and Sgt Scott (JK372), the latter also claiming one damaged, and another damaged was credited to Wt Off T.R. Caldwell (JK637) to give a final total of 7:1:7 for no losses. 159°Gruppo's losses were four shot down: two pilots baled out, one of whom, Serg Gianfranco Bussola of 388^Squadriglia, was captured; the other, M.llo Vittorio Giordano of 391^Squadriglia, was killed; two others crash-landed including one flown by M.llo Silvio Ferrigolo, also of 391^Squadriglia, who was wounded in the back. He attempted to carry out an emergency landing on a salt lake at Magnisi near Syracuse, but the aircraft (MM6061/391-10) sank into the salt and he failed to survive[14]. The leader of the Italian fighters, Cap Francisco Leoncini, claimed a Spitfire shot down, while Serg Magg Carlo D'Alanno, one of the G.50 pilots, claimed another, with the Messerschmitt pilots claiming four more, two by 11 Staffelkapitän Oblt Gustav Frielinghaus and one apiece by Lt Wessling (his second of the morning) of 10 Staffel and 12 Staffel's Lt Herbert Kutscha, for the loss of Lt Fritz Voss of 11 Staffel who was reported shot down and killed near Augusta. The Messerschmitts may have also become involved with P-40s of the 58th FS from Pantelleria at about the same time, the Americans reporting meeting at least seven Bf109s over the Licata area and claiming two shot down. One P-40 failed to return and a second was damaged.

At 1155, seven Ju87Ds of 237^Squadriglia took off from Isola Capo Rizzuto/Crotone led by Magg Orlandini, commander of the newly formed 121°Gruppo Tuff, to attack Allied shipping. They were due to be escorted by MC202s of 4°Stormo near Mount Etna, but the fighters failed to rendezvous, so they continued alone to Augusta where the 7,200-ton merchant vessel *Ocean Peace* was claimed sunk by Serg Magg Oberdan Naccari. At that point Spitfires of 601 Squadron arrived on the scene and two *Picchiatello*[15] were shot down into the sea, and a third force-landed at Fontanarossa while the remaining four landed at Catania, two bearing the scars of battle although neither Ten Vincenzo Marcocci and Serg Ruggero Cracco[16], nor their gunners, were injured. Of the missing crews, Sottoten Poggioli and his gunner were killed, while Naccari's aircraft was forced to ditch, the Stuka turning over onto its back. Nonetheless, Naccari and his gunner, Av Vittorio Rimoldi, were rescued from the sea later that afternoon by a German

[13] Sqn Ldr Steve Daniel went on to claim a further five victories before the war ended, raising his score to 16^1/$_2$. Post war he remained in the RAF and in 1951 was posted to Korea to fly F-86s with the USAF, when he damaged a MiG-15 jet fighter (see *With the Yanks in Korea Volume I* by Brian Cull and Dennis Newton).
[14] M.llo Ferrigolo's body was not recovered until May 1950; it had been preserved in the salt.
[15] The Ju87 was named *Picchiatello* in Italian service, which literally translates as "crazy dive-bomber".
[16] Three of the four Ju87s returned to Crotone once refuelled and rearmed but Serg Cracco's aircraft had to remain at Catania for further repairs; next day however it was destroyed during an attack on the airfield, leaving Cracco and his gunner to make their own way back to the mainland and safety.

lighter, Rimoldi reporting that he had shot down the Spitfire that had attacked them. This would appear to have been the aircraft (EP966) flown by Sqn Ldr John Taylor which was severely damaged and subsequently crashed while attempting to land on a beach near Syracuse; 23-year-old Taylor, the son of the Vicar of St Olaves in Suffolk, with 15 victories to his credit (two shared), was killed. Two other Stukas were claimed probably destroyed by Flg Off Percy Sewell (ER566) RCAF, who had flown with 601 Squadron from Malta during the 1942 battles, and 2/Lt M.A. Hagico[17] (ER181), although both their victims subsequently crashed; and three others were damaged including one by Flg Off Alex Blumer RAAF, and possibly another by Flt Lt Maurice Hards DFM (EN268), a ten-victory ace from the desert fighting.

During the afternoon two Spitfires touched down at Pachino, out of which climbed Air Vice-Marshal Harry Broadhurst DSO DFC AFC, AOC Western Desert Air Force, and Wg Cdr John Loudon DFC, the Kittyhawk Wing Leader. Following a brief inspection of available facilities, the AOC decided that the three squadrons of 244 Wing could move in next day, as noted by Wg Cdr Duncan Smith:

> "Thus 244 [Wing] earned the distinction of being the first RAF formation to operate again from Continental soil since the fall of France in 1940." [18]

Shortly before 1530, two A-36A Mustangs of the RAF's 1437 Flight[19], which had just arrived at Luqa, flew the unit's first strategical-reconnaissance mission over Sicily. As Sqn Ldr S.G. Welshman DFM, the CO in HK947/A, and Flg Off J.L. Griffith DFC (HK945/B) approached Giardini Bay at Taormina, two barges and a landing craft were sighted and all three vessels were strafed by cannon and machine-gun fire. The next Spitfire patrols found it was all quiet on the southern front until a mid-afternoon patrol of 243 Squadron led by Sqn Ldr Mackie (JK715/SN-A) encountered three MC202s north of Lentini, one of which the CO claimed probably destroyed:

> "I attacked one of these MC202s from astern and saw cannon strikes on the fuselage from 200 yards range. The e/a half-rolled and dived, and I followed, still firing. I last saw the Macchi in a vertical dive at 5,000 feet, white smoke pouring from it. One mile from the coast and east of Mass Reitano, I saw on the ground a fire and white smoke, which was not observed before the attack."

An hour later, at about 1700, 72 Squadron again found itself in the thick of the action, when a dozen aircraft led by Flt Lt Arthur Jupp engaged "a large number" of Messerschmitts and Macchis north-east of Carlentini at between 9,000 and 12,000 feet. The Macchis, both MC202s and MC205Vs, were from 4°Stormo, and were joined in battle by a dozen Re2002s of 5°Stormo which had been attacking

---

17 Born in Smyrna, Greece, Marcel Hagico lived in the Belgian Congo pre-war and became a Belgian citizen. He was later killed in Italy.

18 see *Spitfire into Battle*.

19 1437 Strategical Reconnaissance Flight had recently been formed from the A-36A Mustang Flight of 14 Squadron, an RAF Marauder anti-shipping unit which had acquired, on loan from the USAAF's XII Air Support Command, six A-36As which were allotted RAF serial numbers HK944-947, HK955 and HK956. While flying escort duties as part of 14 Squadron, the Mustangs had shot down a Ju52/3m and two Fiat RS14 seaplanes off the Sardinian coast.

tanks and motor transports advancing over the Catania plain. The Spitfires tore into the enemy fighters and two Bf109Gs were claimed shot down by Plt Off Jack Hussey (EN258/RN-B) and Sgt Scott (JK372), while Plt Off Eric Shaw RNZAF (JK450) reported shooting down a Macchi. His victim may have been the MC202 flown by Sottoten Gino Lionello of 361^Squadriglia, which failed to return from a sortie during the day. An Re2002 flown by Ten Renalto Moglia of 102°Gruppo was also hit during the action and force-landed between Acireale and Riposto. Meanwhile, Flt Lt Jupp (JG746) claimed the probable destruction of a Messerschmitt, as did Flg Off George Keith (JK637), and three more were damaged by Sgt Clarkson (EN358), Sgt Pearson (JK275) and Flg Off John King (JK468). One Spitfire, JK429 flown by Sgt J.B. King, failed to return; King was later reported to be a prisoner of war. Sgt Bert Griffiths returned to Malta with his aircraft (EN309) badly damaged, and Plt Off Hussey landed safely despite damage to his aircraft's tail unit. It would seem that their opponents were again from IV/JG3, Lt Otto Wessling of 10 Staffel claiming his third Spitfire of the day, and a second being credited to Fw Herbert Chucholowius of 11 Staffel, which reported the loss of Uffz Adolf Jakubik near Lentini. 12 Staffel also lost a pilot, Lt Rudolf Tenner being shot down and killed, possibly during this action, while Uffz Hans Schäfer of 10 Staffel belly-landed after being hit by a Spitfire. He survived unscathed and was able to make his way back to Ramacca. For its successes achieved during the day, AOC Malta sent a signal of congratulations to Sqn Ldr Daniel and his pilots of 72 Squadron.

During an evening reconnaissance of the Lentini and Pozallo areas by two TacR Spitfires of 40SAAF Squadron, Lts K. Robinson and B.V. Clarence were jumped by three Re2005s of 362^Squadriglia over Catania and Robinson's aircraft was shot down by Ten Giulio Torresi. Although Lt Clarence's Spitfire also sustained damage, he was able to reach Malta where he landed safely. Ten Enrico Salvi, who witnessed the action, reported a slightly different version of events. He recalled that while Ten Edoardo Vaghi was approaching to land he was attacked by a Spitfire, although his aircraft was not hit. It was then that Ten Torresi appeared and shot down Robinson's aircraft. The South African managed to bale out and was immediately captured by German troops inspite of spirited opposition of nearby Italian airmen, who claimed he was their prize since he was shot down by their fighters. This was a sorely needed victory for the Italians whose last remaining airworthy Bf109Gs of 150°Gruppo at Sciacca were flown to Palermo by Cap Mario Bellagambi, Ten Carillo and Ten Giovanni Chiale.

All was quiet for the next hour or so, patrolling Spitfires not meeting any enemy aircraft until about 1900, when engagements with Bf109Gs and MC202s were reported by 1435, 229 and 93 Squadrons. A dozen Spitfires of 93 Squadron including two IXs were in the Syracuse area when six Bf109Gs were seen below at about 2,000 feet, and were immediately attacked by Sqn Ldr Sizer (JL220/HN-C) and Flt Lt Norm Lee (LZ837), each of whom reported damaging their quarry before it escaped. On returning to Malta, Sizer was obliged to make a belly-landing at Hal Far as his aircraft had burst a tyre on take-off; the aircraft was only slightly damaged. Meanwhile, a dozen Spitfires of 229 Squadron were patrolling at 16,000 feet between Syracuse and Augusta when they were attacked from out of the sun by ten Bf109Gs. None of the Spitfires was damaged and Flt Lt Les Gosling (LZ808/X-D) was able to turn the tables on one, shooting it down for his second victory of the day and his ninth overall. Possibly the same formation of Messerschmitts was engaged by a dozen more Spitfires of 1435 Squadron in the same area, although the pilots reported also meeting 15 MC202s. In a fierce action

Wg Cdr Duncan Smith (JK650/DS) claimed a MC202 destroyed, although his own aircraft sustained damage, while Flt Sgt Sydney Benjamin (EN287/V-F) was shot down and killed, and the aircraft (EN290/V-G) flown by Flt Sgt A.W. Smith was slightly damaged. Bf109Gs from both III/JG53 and II/JG27[20] were active during this period, aircraft from the former Gruppe escorting Ju52/3ms which dropped paratroops south of Catania; although the unit's history records "inconclusive combat with three Spitfires", 7 Staffel's Kapitän, Lt Franz Barten, reported shooting down a Spitfire at 1828, while Fw Heinrich Steis of 4/JG27 claimed another about ten miles west-south-west of Augusta at 1930. Wg Cdr Duncan Smith, who was fortunate to have survived the action, later wrote:

" . . . my attention was drawn to three Macchis that dived across in front of us, then pulled up in a perfect formation loop. The next moment we were jumped by some fifteen Macchis and about ten ME109s . . . I pounced on a Macchi, and from slightly astern pumped a couple of bursts into him. Immediately smoke poured out and big pieces broke away from the cockpit area with bits of canopy showering and glinting in the bright sun, like drops of rain. The Macchi winged over quite slowly and dived away steeply, out of control. It was obvious the pilot was dead ..." [21]

The Wing Leader's aircraft was then attacked from astern by a Messerschmitt:

"There were two enormous bangs behind my back and the Spitfire seemed to double up with pain as the stick was wrenched out of my hand. I heard a high-pitch whine in my ear-phones and my radio went dead. The Spitfire then pitched in a steep nose-up attitude and next thing I remember was that I was spinning. Collecting my wits, I struggled with the controls, and using brute force got the Spitfire out of the spin and level again . . . I had lost a lot of height and was down to 3,000 feet . . . I set course for Malta praying for my Spitfire to hold together, for if I had to bale out over the sea, I would not be able to send a Mayday call . . . It seemed ages before I picked out the dark smudge ahead that was Malta and dragged myself in on my engine for an adventurous landing at Safi . . . My Spitfire was in a mess. Cannon-shells had blasted a couple of large holes in the side. One had burst against the radio and armour behind my seat. Another, having made a hole the size of a football, had torn the control wires to shreds. The elevator was hanging on by one thread of frayed wire . . . Another cannon-shell had torn big pieces out of the elevator and rudder surfaces ..." [22]

Despite the damage, the Spitfire was not written off. Wg Cdr Duncan Smith's claim for a Macchi destroyed was reduced to a probable by the IO since it was not seen to have crashed; this final claim gave Malta's Spitfires a total of 23 destroyed for the day, including 11 Bf109s, plus nine probables and 21 damaged, achieved during the course of 897 sorties and for the loss of eight Spitfires, with four pilots killed and two taken prisoner. In addition, the 33rd FG claimed one Bf109 for the

---

[20] Elements of II/JG27 were attached to JG53 during the day and were dispersed to the airfields at Catania, San Pietro and Ramacca, where they were serviced and maintained by ground staff of JG53.
[21]/[22] see *Spitfire into Battle*.

loss of one P-40. The newly arrived Messerschmitt unit, IV/JG3, had been hardest hit, losing nine of its aircraft during the day's actions, with four pilots killed, against claims for eight Spitfires shot down. I/JG53 lost three aircraft (one pilot PoW, one injured), III/JG53 lost one (pilot killed), II/JG77 lost one (Hptm Freytag, the Gruppenkommandeur, who had recently scored his 98th victory, was shot down by P-38s; he baled out, wounded), and III/JG77 lost one to North African-based US Spitfires (pilot POW).

The Ju52/3ms which III/JG53 had been protecting during the afternoon were engaged in dropping the paratroops of the 3rd Regiment (FJR3) of the 1st Parachute Division, an operation which continued until evening. Although the transports had flown from southern France unescorted, on reaching Sicily they were provided with fighter protection, one of the Messerschmitts flown by Fw Arno Fischer of JG53's 1 Staffel, who recalled:

> "We were flying straight across the Straits of Messina when below us we spotted a seemingly endless stream of Ju52s flying very low over the sea. We later learned that the aircraft were supposed to drop parachute troops near Catania; given the large number of Ju52s one could only call it tremendous luck that there were no Spitfires in the air, for they could have inflicted a slaughter upon the defenceless transports." [23]

FJR3 had been airlifted from its base near Avignon in southern France. The vulnerable unprotected Heinkel transports had been attacked by up to 20 P-38s over the Straits of Messina, and it is believed that several were shot down or damaged. Colonel D'Este wrote " . . . a disaster was averted only when low fuel forced the US planes back to their North African bases." [24] The commanding officer of FJR3, Obslt Ludwig Heilmann, had flown to Sicily earlier in the day to reconnoitre personally the landing zone, an area between the Gornalunga and Simeto rivers on the plain of Catania:

> " . . . Heilmann departed from Avignon for the non-stop flight to Sicily. As his aircraft approached Catania, Heilmann could see the city was under Allied air attack. Thick black clouds rose into the morning air from the city. Heilmann's pilot was forced to seek cover by flying at low altitude in the foothills surrounding Mount Etna. As Heilmann later recalled, the pilot acted like an infantryman as he wove into Catania whose airport still had fresh, smoking craters from the recent air attack. High above the airfield RAF Spitfires circled as the pilot landed . . ." [25]

At 1815 the first paratroops landed, 1,400 men of FJR3 successfully coming down in the dropping zone. The 2nd Battalion was sent forward to Francoforte to assist German troops defending Vizzini, while the remainder took up defensive positions between Carlentini and the sea. Feldmarschall Kesselring had also flown to Sicily during the morning, having first ordered the 1st Parachute Division into battle:

> "My flight to Sicily yielded nothing but a headache . . . Accompanied by von Senger [General Fridolin von Senger und Etterlin, commander of the XIV Panzer Korps in Italy], I visited all the front-line positions . . . One

---

[23] see *Jagdgeschwader 53 Volume Two*.
[24]/[25] see *Bitter Victory*.

disappointment followed another. The Italian coastal divisions were an utter failure, not one of their counter-attack divisions reaching the enemy in time or even at all – the Napoli Division in the south-west corner of the island had melted into thin air. The commandant of the fortress of Augusta meanwhile surrendered without even waiting to be attacked. Cowardice or treachery? Whether or not the court-martial promised me by Mussolini was ever held I never discovered. The west of Sicily had no further tactical value and had to be abandoned. But even so the east of the island, or an extended bridgehead round Etna, could only be held for a short time. The two German divisions which were bearing the brunt of the battle alone were no longer sufficient – a third was urgently needed if the Etna Line were to be consolidated speedily. However, I no longer had to reckon with a landing in Calabria, a move I had been specially afraid of ..." [26]

The Allies were also airlifting more paratroops to the battle zone, a small detachment of the British 1st Airborne Division being flown in two RAF Albemarles of 296 Squadron from Tunisia to north-west Sicily for a special operation; they were to attack and harass the enemy lines of communication and rear areas, but the operation was not a success and one Albemarle was lost.[27]

During the night of 12/13 July the Allied air forces kept up their round-the-clock bombing programme. Forty-six US Mitchells attacked Termini docks while 45 Wellingtons bombed enemy concentrations at Caltanissetta and Enna; other Wellingtons went for the Gerbini airfield complex, at the same time US light bombers were attacking Sciacca and targets south-east of Palermo, and RAF heavy bombers from Cyrenaica were raiding air bases at Crotone, Reggio di Calabria and Vibo Valentia. Amongst the many aircraft destroyed or damaged on the ground were the surviving G.50bis of 159°Gruppo, a dozen at Crotone and 16 at Reggio, while two pilots and two mechanics from the Gruppo were wounded during these attacks. RAF night fighters and intruder Mosquitos from Malta roamed far and wide, and in the clear moonlight conditions accounted for five Ju88s, three He111s, two Z1007bis, and one Do217, all achieved without loss to themselves. These bombers were part of a force of 115 German and Italian aircraft including torpedo-bombers that had set out to attack Allied shipping in the Syracuse area. The successes of both torpedo and bomber aircraft were few and their losses extremely high; captured aircrew complained that they had been forced to fly very low because of their fear of the night fighters, with the result that they had presented an easy target for the defending ships' AA guns.

Grp Capt Kingcome, Officer Commanding 244 Wing, arrived at Pachino at first light on the morning of 13 July, accompanied by Sqn Ldr Wade of 145 Squadron; they were followed soon afterwards by the Spitfires of the Wing as each squadron completed its first patrols of the day. The aircraft were serviced by the RAF Commandos of 3230 SCU and advanced parties of ground crews. At the same time ground personnel of the 309th FS started preparing Ponte Olivo landing ground for use by the air echelons of the 31st Fighter Group. Enemy air activity over the beachhead at Gela was very slight and only four attempts were made to reach the beach landing area of the Advanced HQ of the US XII Air Support Command, and

---

[26] see *Memoirs of Field-Marshal Kesselring*.
[27] The pilot of this aircraft, Wg Cdr Peter May AFC DFC(US) Gold Medal (China), who was killed, had previously served with the Chinese Air Force. At the time of his death he was commanding the RAF's 38 Group.

three of these attempts were turned back and one enemy aircraft shot down. One Bf109, however, managed to penetrate the fighter screen and attacked the beaches at Gela. More RAF Commandos had by now reached Comiso airfield where, following an inspection, a total of 45 Bf109s, several MC202s, a Ju52, two Ju87s, two Ju88s and a Fi156 Storch were found abandoned, some of which were considered to be serviceable. The RAF Commando (3201 SCU) were in for a surprise, for early that morning two Ju87s touched down:

"... two Luftwaffe [*sic*] pilots absent-mindedly landed their Stuka dive-bombers at Comiso, realised their mistake and tried to take-off – quickly. They may have been misled by the presence of the Messerschmitts and the lack of Allied aircraft, but 13 July was not their lucky day and they were both shot down. Three of the four occupants were killed in the ensuing crashes, but one pilot survived to be taken prisoner." [28]

A little later, when Spitfires from 43 Squadron arrived at Comiso, remains of the incident were still gruesomely evident, as witnessed by Flg Off Ron Rayner:

"I remember it well as I parked my aircraft in a dispersal area adjacent to a runway, which was an established airfield – my Spitfire was dispersed next to a Stuka with Italian markings which had tipped over on its back with the two dead crew members still hanging in their straps, right next to my aircraft!" [29]

The 13th also proved to be the last day on which the enemy put up any effective aerial resistance over Sicily. Vital coastal radar posts had been lost to the invasion forces and other key installations inland were constantly attacked by US fighter-bombers, as were the established airfields and landing grounds in the eastern half of the island. Targets attacked by bombers of the NWAAF during the day included Catania and Milo/Trapani airfields, which were visited by a total of 76 B-17s, while 23 US Marauders raided Carcitelia landing ground and more than 100 Mitchells bombed targets at Enna. US fighter- bombers meanwhile strafed targets of opportunity in the Castelvetrano, Termini, Corleone, Caltanissetta and San Caterina areas, where a total of 118 transports were claimed as destroyed, as were six locomotives and 45 railway carriages and trucks.

First action for Malta's fighters occurred at 0500 when a dozen Spitfires, including three IXs, of 111 Squadron carried out a dawn patrol over the landing beaches between Noto and Augusta. At first light six Ju88s – part of a larger formation of ten aircraft of II/KG1 led by Oblt Müller that had taken off from San Pancrazio to attack shipping off Augusta – were observed silhouetted against the horizon and intercepted by the Spitfires about five miles south of Syracuse. The bombers had just attacked three or four merchant vessels east of Augusta when the Spitfires struck. Two were promptly shot down by Sqn Ldr Hill (JK389) and Flt Lt Laurie McIntosh RAAF (JK307/JU-U), and five members of the two crews were seen to escape by parachute. Hill's aircraft was damaged by return fire although he was able to reach Pachino and land safely despite being fired upon by the airfield's AA defences. He reported seeing three crewmen bale out of his victim before it hit the ground. This was probably Lt Alexander Polowiec's V4+HM of 4 Staffel. The

[28] see *A History of the RAF Servicing Commandos* by J.P. Kellett & J. Davies.
[29] see *A Few of the Many* by Dilip Sarkar.

other Ju88, V4+ZP of 6 Staffel flown by Uffz Martin Adolph, crashed on land about ten miles south-west of Augusta, in which the pilot and two other members of the crew were killed, only the W/T operator Uffz Kurt Lenk surviving. He later told his captors that both engines of his aircraft were put out of action following the attack by a single Spitfire, which also killed the gunner, Gfr Günther Holzenburg. Only with great difficulty was Lenk able to bale out, at 3,000 feet, and came down in the sea from where he was picked up by a rescue craft.

Having taken off at 0650, a dozen Spitfires including four IXs of 243 Squadron patrolled over the Gerbini area when eight Ju87s – Italian-flown dive-bombers of 216^Squadriglia led by Cap Piero Pergoli which had arrived at Crotone the previous evening – were seen flying northwards at 10,000 feet in line abreast. There appeared to be no fighter escort, and Sqn Ldr Mackie (JK715/SN-A) led the charge, ordering Flg Off Frank Banner to provide top cover with his quartet of IXs. Mackie later reported:

> "We attacked from astern having come out of the sun. I made attacks on three e/a. (1) I attacked one Ju87 from astern firing from 100 yards range, and giving it another short burst from 60 yards distance. Its bomb was jettisoned. The 87 disintegrated in mid-air. (2) I attacked another from astern at 50 yards range. This a/c burst into flames. (3) Using machine-guns only I attacked a third e/a from 60 yards range. This e/a started to stream glycol."

Four more were claimed destroyed, two by Flt Sgt H.C. Payne[30] (JK614/SN-C) and one apiece by Plt Off E.A. Lawrence (JK113/SN-B) and Sgt Roland Jaques (JK666/SN-V); Lawrence, a Jamaican known as Ned, also damaged one, as did Plt Off L.E. Gregory (JK642/SN-P), Flg Off Stuart Dalrymple. (JK946/SN-G), Plt Off M.D. Einhorn (JK370/SN-S) and Wt Off I.N. McLaren (EF549/SN-R). Seven of the eight Ju87s failed to return, one of which probably fell to 93 Squadron (see below). There were not many survivors amongst the inexperienced crews, all of whom with the exception of Cap Pergoli were flying their first sorties of the war – and for many it was their last. Cap Pergoli and his gunner survived when their aircraft crash-landed about three miles from Syracuse, although Pergoli was injured; they were taken prisoner, as was wounded air gunner Av/Sc Enrico D'onta. He told his captors that following an attack by Spitfires his fuel tank burst into flames and the aircraft crashed and burnt out; his pilot was missing, presumed killed. The seven missing crews were:[31]

> Ju87D/3 Cap Piero Pergoli (pilot) and Av/Sc Chiarello (gunner) PoWs
> Ju87D/3 Sottoten Arrigo Calzoni (pilot) and Av/Sc Calvi (gunner) missing
> Ju87D/3 Sottoten Reale (pilot) and Av/Sc Tarantini (gunner) missing

---

[30] Although he claimed two Ju87s, Flt Sgt 'Micky' Payne was credited with only one, plus one damaged; he commented "That miserable old devil Spy [the Intelligence Officer] reduced that to one destroyed and one damaged, and I had to tell him that next time I would bring back the German pilot's number, rank and name!" (see *Spitfire Leader*).

[31] Owing to the confusion of the time, there are understandably gaps in Italian records and therefore there may be some inaccuracies regarding the participants of those lost on this operation. It would appear that Sottoten Calzoni, Av/Sc Storti and Av/Sc Tani were killed, although that latter's unit is officially recorded as 256^Squadriglia rather than 216^Squadriglia (presumably a clerical error); while Serg Borrelli's date of death was recorded as 17 July, which would imply that he succumbed to injuries sustained on 13 July.

Ju87D/3 Serg Cori (pilot) and Av/Sc Cosconati (gunner) missing
Ju87D/3 Serg Carlini (pilot) missing and Av/Sc Enrico D'onta (gunner) PoW
Ju87D/3 Serg Onofrio Borrelli (pilot) and Av/Sc Renato Storti (gunner) missing
Ju87D/3 Serg Mancini (pilot) and Av/Sc Vinicio Tani (gunner) missing

On hearing the action over the R/T, Flg Off Banner (EN148/SN-E) led the four IXs towards Catania where four Bf109Gs were seen in line-astern in the circuit, Banner attacking two of these and claiming one probably destroyed and the other damaged. A twin-engine aircraft identified as a Do217 was then seen preparing to land, and was attacked and severely damaged by Banner, his No2, Sgt Pat Davoren RAAF (EN313/SN-D) applying the *coup de grâce*, the bomber – probably a He111 from either I/LLG2 or KGrzbV.25 – crashing into the sea half a mile offshore. One Spitfire was slightly damaged by return fire.

At about the same time as 243 Squadron was decimating the Ju87s of 216^Squadriglia, ten Spitfires of 93 Squadron were patrolling the Augusta area, led by Grp Capt Gilroy. Several enemy aircraft – mainly more He111s of I/LLG2 and KGrzbV.25 – were seen landing at Catania and Gilroy led four aircraft to attack these, as recalled by Flt Lt Jim Gray:

> "We attacked an He111 just touching down; pulled up and then went after a Ju88 just north of Catania. I observed the Ju88 in flames as I departed the scene and proceeded south. As I withdrew I was attacked by four 109s; one of them succeeded in poking holes in my fuselage. Luckily, Sgt Andrew had climbed into the sun and attacked the rearmost 109, leaving it in flames. This manoeuvre certainly discouraged the remaining 109s that were on my tail. Sgt Bridger was shot down near the aerodrome, as I recall, but escaped capture."

In addition to shooting down the Messerschmitt, Sgt Jim Andrew (JK603) was also credited with shooting down the Heinkel, which he believed to be carrying troops, while Flt Lt Gray (JL232) shared the Ju88 with Grp Capt Gilroy (flying GKG, his personal aircraft). The Ju88 was probably V4+AM of 4/KG1, flown by Lt Hans Mackmüller, reported to have been shot down by fighters south of Catania, from which one crewman was able to reach German lines after baling out. Two more He111s were claimed damaged by Sgt J.L. Liggett (JK606), apparently as they were just about to land, both of which evidently crashed. A MC202 and a Ju87 were damaged on the ground by Plt Off Roy Fisher (JK306), while Sgt F.W. Bridger (ES282) reported damaging a Bf109G on the ground before he was shot down by another[32]. His victor was probably Oblt Erhard Niese of 7/JG77 who claimed a Spitfire at 0735. Meanwhile, the other Spitfires engaged three Bf109Gs, Flg Offs Stan Browne (JK720) and Pat Rivett RAAF (JK362) jointly claiming one destroyed – without firing their guns – as Browne recalled:

> "Rivett and I attacked a Messerschmitt over Sicily and drove it down. It got into a valley and it was unable to make the turns – we were getting closer to it but the pilot was so busy evading us that he hit the side, tumbling over. Neither of us had fired a shot."

---

[32] Sgt Frank Bridger, who was captured, managed to escape that night but after two days without food he gave himself up; however, he was able to escape again and eventually reached Allied lines and was back with the Squadron by 24 July. He was later commissioned and was awarded a DFC.

Their victim was probably Lt Josef Dritthuber of 3/JG77, who was killed. A final victory was claimed for 93 Squadron by Flg Off Cyril Bamberger[33] (JL219/HN-X) who came across a lone Ju87 south of Catania – undoubtedly a survivor of 216^Squadriglia's disastrous encounter with 243 Squadron – and shot it down into the sea. The Heinkels attacked had certainly been carrying paratroops, the last elements of FJR3 from Pogliano on their way to join their comrades. On board one was Lt Martin Pöppel, who later wrote of his arrival at Catania:

"Two of our planes are ablaze on the airfield. Has there been a raid just before we got here? If so, our tired old crate [which had lagged behind the rest of the formation] brought us luck after all. We haven't even stopped rolling when a lorry shoots out and orders us to be quick. British fighters have attacked two of our planes during landing and set them on fire. In addition, two aircraft are still missing. Appalling casualties before the bloody operation has even begun."[34]

The two He111 transport groups involved in the paratrooping operation, I/LLG2 and KGrzbV.25, reported heavy losses from fighter attack, six Heinkels being totally destroyed and four others seriously damaged, presumably by P-38s during the passage from southern France, and Spitfires of 324 Wing:

I/LLG2
He111H RE+DM (7027) 100% Fw Wilde KiA
He111H GG+SJ (7400) 100% Fw Öser WiA
He111H KN+YE (8251) 60%
He111H CC+ST (4853) 50%
He111H CC+SV (4855) 50%

KGrzbV.25
He111H NB+UX (8083) 100% Uffz Missbach KiA
He111H NI+JD (8172) 100%
He111H DN+DC (8275) 100% Ofw Zinser WiA
He111H (5486) 100% Uffz Wurzer WiA
He111H (3778) 30% Fw Hilbert WiA

Other aircraft destroyed on the ground at Catania during this or subsequent attacks included two six-engine Me323 Gigant transports, while a number of anti-tank weapons were also lost together with key personnel amongst the paratroops. While 243 and 93 Squadron were thus heavily engaged, a further eight Spitfires (four Vs, four IXs) of 242 Squadron were patrolling north-west of Augusta at 0715 when ten Bf110s were sighted by the IXs led by Flt Lt George Silvester. Not realising at first they were enemy aircraft, since they fired four red recognition signals on sighting the Spitfires, Silvester took his two sections into a stern attack. He attacked one from slightly before with a burst of cannon and machine-gun fire, following which it erupted in flames and crashed near a lake north-west of Augusta. One crewman

---

[33] This was Flg Off Bamberger's 4th victory and his third Ju87; he had served in the Battle of Britain and later at Malta.
[34] see *Heaven and Hell* by Martin Pöppel.

was seen to bale out. Flt Sgt Evan Morgan attacked another with three four-second bursts and both engines caught fire. It was last seen losing height at 1,000 feet. He then saw a Spitfire attacking another Bf110 and also engaged, observing strikes on its tail. This was possibly the machine attacked by Flt Sgt J.J. Ronay, who reported that its port engine exploded after he attacked with cannon fire, the doomed aircraft seen to dive into Augusta harbour, having first jettisoned its bombs. Ronay then attacked another Messerschmitt, seeing strikes on its port wing and starboard engine before it escaped. Yet another Bf110 came under attack from Flt Sgt L. Courtney, at which it jettisoned its bombs before its starboard engine burst into flames. This aircraft was also seen to hit the ground.

Meanwhile, the four Spitfire Vs led by Sqn Ldr Boddington (JK260/LE-K) arrived on the scene, the CO immediately getting on the tail of one Bf110, closing to 50 yards. He reported that its port engine burst into flames and then the aircraft "blew up", the wreck falling near to a crashed FW190. Flg Off Stock attacked two more of the Messerschmitts, seeing strikes on the starboard wing and engine of one, and strikes on the fuselage of the other. As against claims for five Bf110s destroyed and three damaged, III/ZG26 reported the total loss of three aircraft and their crews:

> 3U+LS Obfw Heinz Sielaff and Obfw Walter Kobele killed
> 3U+RS Uffz Helmut Skrizipczyk and Gfr Georg Janusch killed
> 3U+BT Fw Josef Ruth and Fw Helmut Schimhof killed

111 Squadron took off at 0800 for its second patrol of the morning, again led by Sqn Ldr Hill (JG937). When flying over the beaches between Augusta and Noto at 10,000 feet, several FW190s were sighted, one of which was claimed destroyed by the CO, Sgt Arthur Adams (JK728) claiming a second as damaged. 111 Squadron was relieved over the patrol line by ten Spitfires of 72 Squadron, these also meeting a number of fighters identified as Bf109s and MC200s (the latter were in fact Re2002s of 101° and 102°Gruppi) just after 1000. Plt Off Jack Hussey (EN258/RN-B) reported shooting down a 'Macchi' before he joined Sgt Bert Griffiths (EN144) in destroying a Bf109G between Novo and Augusta. It would seem they shot down Hptm Hans Röhrig, the Staffelkapitän of 9/JG53 with 75 victories to his credit, who was killed when his Messerschmitt Yellow 4 (WkNr15063) crashed in the Syracuse/Catania area. Fw Martin von Vacano later wrote to Röhrig's father:

> "We were to protect a group of our Ju52s which were supposed to drop paratroopers onto the plains of Catania. After about 30 minutes flying time we became involved with Spitfires, which attacked from above. We became split up, and on landing at our base we discovered that Oblt Röhrig was missing. No aircraft was seen to crash during the air battle, which took place about 15 kilometres west of Augusta. We were unable to investigate what happened, as the area above which the air battle was played out was already occupied by the enemy . . ." [35]

I/JG53 was fortunate not to lose a number of its pilots during the day when the Gruppe was ordered to transfer its remaining serviceable aircraft from Vibo

---

[35] see *Jagdgeschwader 53 Volume Two*.

Valentia to Lecce near Taranto, as Fw Arno Fischer of 1 Staffel recalled:

"Since there were more aircraft than airworthy pilots, eight or ten of us were loaded into Galland's personal He111 and flown back to Vibo Valentia to collect the remaining Bf109s. Just as we made our approach to land about a dozen Fortresses began dropping their bombs on the airfield and surrounding area. The He111 driver – who was probably overtired and nervous (both of which are dangerous in flying) – misjudged his height, meaning he came in too high to put the bird down on the ground in time. Instead of being flat, the airfield at Vibo was convex like a crystal watch – and quite small as well. Anyone who touched down too late did not have enough room to brake to a stop before reaching the end of the landing field. The blockhead first put the wheels down in the centre of the airfield and even then didn't realise that he could have avoided killing or seriously injuring people by immediately retracting the undercarriage. But instead the He111 roared through 2 Staffel's big armourers' tent at considerable speed – ordnance sergeant killed, several others seriously injured. The terrain then fell away steeply about 30 to 40 metres to the coast of the Tyrrhenian Sea. Luckily for us the He111 came to a stop on the small slope and did not catch fire. Since everyone but me was strapped in, most got away with minor bruises and abrasions; some required hospitalisation, however, and were taken away immediately." [36]

Fw Fischer was pulled unconscious from the wreck, regaining consciousness four days later, and two other pilots, Oblt Theodor Flink and Fw Herbert Franke of 3 Staffel, were also taken to hospital.

MC202s of 4°Stormo were airborne over the Augusta area during the late morning, a patrol from 93 Squadron intercepting a formation of seven Macchis at 1115, one of which Sqn Ldr Sizer (JL219/HN-X) claimed shot down. Another was engaged by Flt Lt Norm Lee (JK306) and Flt Sgt Raymond Baxter (JK868/HN-H), who believed they probably destroyed it, and four others were damaged by Lee (two), Plt Off Richardson (EN140) and Sgt W.F. Hockey (LZ840). The Spitfires suffered no losses. 243 Squadron was back in the thick of the action at midday, meeting about a dozen radial-engined Italian fighter-bombers which they took to be MC200s, but which were in fact part of the same Re2002 formation encountered earlier by 72 Squadron. The Reggianes were seen to be dive-bombing two cruisers off the coast in the Augusta area, Wg Cdr Dundas (JL122/HD) and Sqn Ldr Mackie (JK715/SN-A) each claiming one shot down; another was damaged by Sgt G.T. Melville (JK790/SN-Y). A MC202 which attempted to interfere was engaged and damaged by Flt Lt G.E. Gruwys (JK666/SN-V). One Spitfire sustained slight damage during the action. 101°Gruppo reported that both Sottoten Arduino Vidulis and Sottoten Dante Bartolucchi of 208^Squadriglia failed to return, one of whom (Vidulis) was seen to crash into the sea near Augusta, and a third carried out an emergency landing at Crotone seriously damaged. At noon, off Avola, the Liberty ship *Timothy Pickering* received two direct hits and may have been a victim of the Reggianes; on board the troop transport about 100 British soldiers and 30 members of its American crew were killed. Following his third victory for the day, Sqn Ldr Mackie's score now stood at 14 including two shared; of his latest victory, he reported:

---

[36] see *Jagdgeschwader 53 Volume Two.*

"After manoeuvring I got behind one e/a, now identified as MC200s [*sic*] and closed to 100 yards, firing cannon and machine-guns. Pieces broke off e/a which began to emit clouds of black and white smoke. The starboard wing was almost shot away. I saw the e/a crash into the sea from a height of 1,000 feet. Flt Sgt Towgood saw two e/a crash into the sea, one of which was a MC200 shot down by Wg Cdr Dundas."

This latest victory took Wg Cdr Dundas' score to nine of which five had been shared. During the early afternoon, when 92 Squadron was flying its second patrol of the day, Flg Off Gordon Wilson RCAF (EN152/QJ-3) ran out of fuel:

"We did our early morning patrol and landed at Pachino. I was typically dressed: hadn't shaved for two days, and had my pyjama top under my tunic and scarf – in fact, quite rough! Later that day we took off for a second patrol. Returning to base in formation, I noticed I was completely out of fuel. Calling up the leader to explain my predicament brought me no response. I made the decision I must force land. The field I picked looked fair, although it had irrigation ditches on two sides and a ploughed field at the end. It looked good enough. My confidence soared, so I put the wheels down and dropped to a perfect landing over the irrigation ditch and let it roll, and roll, and roll. Just before it came to a stop, I hit the ploughed field – just enough to put the Spitfire on its nose – only a damaged prop. However, there I was hanging in my safety harness and cockpit, about seven feet in the air, and waiting for the tail to drop. Finally I climbed out, down the side, and to my horror saw about 30 people running towards me. I had landed a short distance from a Sicilian villa."

Fortunately for Flg Off Wilson the natives were friendly, and he was able to return to his unit the following day, the first Allied pilot to force-land in Sicily and walk back (see Appendix II).

There was a reduction in aerial activity in the afternoon, only small groups of Axis fighters and fighter-bombers appearing. One 72 Squadron patrol was led by Wg Cdr John Louden but no enemy aircraft were seen, but three Messerschmitts were sighted by a patrol from 81 Squadron north-west of Cape Scalambri at 1350. Initially engaging the fighters head-on, the Spitfires manoeuvred into position for stern attacks, Sqn Ldr Whitamore (JK285) and Sgt W.J. Robinson RNZAF (FL-3) each claiming one damaged before they were able to escape. The next engagement did not occur until almost two hours later, on this occasion two Bf109Gs bouncing a dozen Spitfires of 93 Squadron at 7,000 feet east of Canicatti, two Spitfires sustaining damage which necessitated them carrying out landings at Pachino for repairs; Flg Off Rivett was unhurt but Plt Off Richardson (EN140) was slightly wounded. It was believed the attackers were MC202s but Messerschmitt pilots of II/JG27 reported action with Spitfires at this time, 1535-1540, Hptm Ernst Börngen of 5 Staffel and Lt Willy Kientsch of 6 Staffel each claiming one shot down.

During an evening patrol over the Syracuse area by a dozen Spitfires of 1SAAF led by Maj Moodie, about seven FW190s and Bf109s were seen some 2,500 feet below. The South Africans dived on them but only Lt Colin Halliday, half rolling on to two Messerschmitts, was able to get in a telling burst at one, seeing pieces fly off before it evaded and dived away. 249 Squadron at last got into the action when, at 1900 while escorting a dozen 112 Squadron Kittyhawks over Lentini, they reported seeing five FW190s flying due east in line astern. Sqn Ldr Lynch (JK465/X) and his No2 dived to attack one of the fighter-bombers, which went into a steep dive to port. Lynch closed and fired two short bursts at 300 yards range, observing hits on the port wing root. He reported that the aircraft then turned sharply to port, burst into flames and fell into Catania harbour. Meanwhile, two MC205Vs of 91^Squadriglia flown by Ten Mario Mecatti and Ten Giorgio Bertolaso sighted two Kittyhawks near Caltanissetta and jointly claimed one shot down. It would seem that their victim was either the Squadron CO, Sqn Ldr G.H. Norton (FR793) or the American Wt Off Fred Vance (FR502), formerly of 185 Squadron, both of whom failed to return from this mission, and both were later confirmed to have been killed. Spitfires from 229 Squadron also carried out two Kittyhawk escorts during the day, on both occasions Lentini being targeted by the dive-bombers, the Squadron's final patrol of the day being led by Wg Cdr Drake and included Wg Cdr Tyson, Krendi Station Commander. No enemy aircraft were sighted. The last action of the day occurred at 1930 when 1435 Squadron recorded meeting eight Bf109s east of Gela while patrolling at 15,000 feet, but were unable to close range sufficiently to engage although one or two pilots fired at extreme range with unobserved results. However, Wt Off P.J.N. Hoare (EP573/V-A) then reported an encounter with a Re2001 which he claimed damaged.

So ended another successful day for Malta's Spitfires, a total of 732 sorties being flown during which 24 enemy aircraft were claimed shot down, plus three probables and 25 damaged, achieved for the loss of one Spitfire. On the downside, the Americans reported that Spitfires had erroneously shot down a P-40 of the 33rd FG and damaged a second, while their fighters claimed three Bf109s and a MC202 during the day. In return, Messerschmitt pilots claimed two P-38s one of which was credited to Oblt Frielinghaus of IV/JG3, his 69th victory, the other to Obfw Johann Pichler of 7/JG77, his 36th. IV/JG3 recorded that two of its aircraft had been hit in combat with Spitfires during the day, Lt Kutscha carrying out a skilful one-wheel landing at Ramacca without inflicting much additional damage to his machine, while Lt Hans Iffland returned with a shattered cockpit canopy. He reported that his aircraft had been hit from above and head-on, splinters having grazed his head and shoulders. With Ramacca temporarily supporting aircraft from IV/JG3, II/JG27 and JG53, fuel and ammunition reserves rapidly decreased, with very little opportunity for restocking. The landing ground was devoid of hangars and with only basic technical facilities available for the hard-working groundcrews. It was clear to all that the Axis air forces in Sicily were beaten in the air; overwhelmed and exhausted, surviving German and Italian pilots and aircrew were withdrawn to the mainland, leaving behind many unserviceable aircraft, IV/JG3 recording that three unflyable aircraft were blown up when the survivors withdrew to Lecce. At the same time Spitfire units had begun moving into Sicily, with 244 Wing now firmly established at Pachino.

During the night more British paratroops were dropped over the plain of Catania in order to secure the key bridge at Primosole over the River Gornalunga. A total of 105 C-47s, seven Halifaxes and 23 Albacores were employed, with 19 gliders in tow, some of which carried jeeps and six-pounder guns, but again it was a costly venture: ten C-47s, three Albacores and one Halifax were lost, but the paratroopers did succeed in seizing the bridge and were able to remove the demolition charges placed there by the enemy. While they were able to hold the position until 0900 the following morning, the survivors had to withdraw owing to lack of ammunition. Beaufighters and Mosquitos were again active although not as successful as the previous night, their bag totalling five enemy bombers. US Mitchells and light-bombers continued their assault against positions and concentrations at Enna, while Wellingtons raided the marshalling yards at Messina and Palermo.

CHAPTER VII

THE AIR BATTLE IS WON

14-31 July 1943

". . . I saw three Junkers in formation just ahead of me and a shot at the leader caused him to burst into flames and dive into the sea. I then turned to his number two, and the same thing happened. From the spectacular results it looked as if they must have been carrying petrol. It was all over in a few seconds. I could not see a single Junkers still in the air, and every time I saw a German fighter he had a Spitfire on his tail." [1]

Wg Cdr Colin Gray, Wing Leader 322 Wing, 25 July 1943

By the morning of 14 July, British Eighth Army patrols were in contact with enemy rearguards in the Chiaramonte-Monterosso area, while a German counter-attack against the seaplane base at Augusta was quickly repulsed. Air reconnaissance revealed that German troops who had originally been in western Sicily had now retreated eastwards and were concentrated in the north-eastern part of the island. Meanwhile, American forces captured Biscari airfield, Mazzarino and Canicatti. The ground fighting was going the way of the Allies, as was the contest to control the air.

During the day Malta-based Spitfires continued to cover the beaches, but only a total of 40 enemy aircraft were reported airborne throughout the daylight hours and, of these, four were shot down by Spitfires. Among the early risers, 126 Squadron flew a dawn patrol over south-east Sicily, sighting two Bf109Gs east of Augusta at 12,000 feet but these dived away before contact could be made. At about the same time Flt Lt Les Gosling led an uneventful patrol of eight Spitfires of 229 Squadron over the DIME beaches at 10,000 feet. Better luck came the way of nine patrolling Spitfire Vs and two IXs of 72 Squadron in the Augusta area at 0745 when they sighted a number of Bf109Gs of I/JG77 below and engaged in a diving attack. Three of the Messerschmitts were claimed shot down, one each by Flg Off George Keith (JK637) and Flg Off Ken Smith (EN258/RN-B), Keith sharing a second with Plt Off Jack Hussey (JK372), while Plt Off Eric Shaw claimed a probable and Sgt Bert Griffiths a damaged. One Spitfire was damaged in return, although two were claimed destroyed by Obfw Kurt Niederhagen and Fw Hans-Dieter Vogel of 1 Staffel. Despite the claims by 72 Squadron, I Gruppe reported no losses.

Mid-morning saw ten Spitfires of 229 Squadron, led by Sqn Ldr Cox, escorting US Mitchells to again attack Enna, where bombs were seen to fall north and north-west of the target, but no enemy aircraft were encountered. None were sighted either by 126 Squadron when it escorted Kittyhawks to bomb Caltagirone, nor were any encountered until early afternoon when, between 1430 and 1520, ten

---

[1] see *Spitfire Patrol*.

Spitfires of 81 Squadron led by Sqn Ldr Whitamore, including five IXs, intercepted six Bf109Gs over Lentini at 8,000 feet, one section engaging, the CO (EN492/FL-E) claiming one probably destroyed when it was last seen at 1,000 feet with glycol and smoke pouring from its engine. He was unable to finish it off owing to his cannons jamming. This was almost certainly the aircraft (White 3, WkNr18151) flown by Obfw Johann Pichler of 7/JG77, who baled out, wounded, north-west of Lentini. Pichler had scored his 36th victory only the previous day when he shot down a P-38G. The other section meanwhile encountered five MC202s south of Gerbini flying at 9,000 feet, one of these being claimed shot down by Flg Off W.J. Goby (EN478) who chased it down to ground level. 4°Stormo admitted the loss of a MC202 during the day. Two of the Spitfires landed at Comiso to refuel before returning to Malta.

92 Squadron, now operating out of Pachino, also met enemy aircraft when patrolling north of Augusta and gave chase to three FW190s. These could not be caught but the six MC202s – possibly aircraft from 351^ and 360^Squadriglie – bounced the patrol from out of the sun, badly damaging Sgt T.E. Brister's aircraft (ER636) although he was able to reach base. Flg Off Milt Jowsey (EN333/QJ-7) and Plt Off Rex Probert RCAF (EN416), flying together but separate from the Squadron, engaged Macchis, as Jowsey reported:

> "Flying Black 1 of section of two [with Plt Off Probert], separate from rest of Squadron, approximately five to ten miles south of Mount Etna saw three MC202s flying west, 5,000 feet below. Half-rolled, and as we closed they dropped bombs. There were nine more flying on the starboard. I attacked the third MC202 in formation, opening fire with intermittent bursts. The MC202 climbed and I had to throttle back as I was in his slipstream in a nearly vertical climb, at 50 yards range. Pieces fell off and, as cannons finished, the starboard wing fell off and he rolled to the right and went down vertically. I was then engaged by eight-plus MC202s, unable to out-turn them but out-climbed them easily. They had white wingtips, [but] not white spinners."

Meanwhile, Probert attacked the other two and reported that one crashed south of Mount Etna while the other escaped in a damaged condition. Patrols were maintained over Syracuse and Augusta throughout the day by 244 Wing but no further encounters occurred. With more of the southern coast now secure, the advance element of 417RCAF Squadron rejoined the other squadrons of 244 Wing now moving into Sicily, but one aircraft (ER134) was severely damaged when it hit a tree on landing, as noted by Flg Off Everard who led the first section to Pachino:

> "It was a short, narrow air strip gouged out of an olive grove . . . My first precautionary landing was almost a crash and I relayed the hazards by radio to my three companions as they landed in turn. Two of them made it, but the third ended up unhurt in the trees at the end of the strip." [2]

The unfortunate South Africans suffered another case of mis-identification during the day when Lt M.E. Robinson's 1SAAF Squadron Spitfire (EN300) was shot down in error by US P-38 off Catania. Robinson was able to bale out and was rescued from the sea by a Greek destroyer, which then conveyed him to Syracuse. 40SAAF was fortunate not to lose another pilot during an evening tactical

---

[2] see *A Mouse in My Pocket.*

reconnaissance patrol, when four Bf110s bounced the Spitfires flown by Lt Clarence and Lt Johannes Kruger; the latter's aircraft was holed but not seriously damaged, and he was able to return to base. Neither pilot had seen the Messerschmitts until they were making their attacks. Kittyhawks of 239 Wing were again active, flying 34 escorted sorties against targets in the Caltagirone and Lentini areas, while 24 US P-40 fighter-bombers made their first appearance in the Sicilian campaign, when they bombed enemy M/T near Lentini. US B-17s, Mitchells and Marauders of the NWAAF flew a total of 173 daylight sorties, chiefly concentrated on Messina, and were joined in these attacks by 73 Liberators of the US Ninth Air Force. Enna was again targeted by 60 US medium bombers, while US fighter-bombers attacked Milazzo docks and barges at Scaletta.

Despite the intensity of the air fighting following the invasion, the two Royal Navy carriers *Formidable* and *Indomitable*, providing air protection for the vast seaborne armada east of Sicily, had not been involved in any significant action, as confirmed by Sub Lt Gordon Reece RNZNVR of 885 Squadron:

> "We took part in the invasion to some degree. We were just covering the
> landings although we may have flown one or two strafing attacks in support
> of the army, but there was nothing spectacular there."

Although Ju88 shadowers had made brief appearances, none had ventured sufficiently closely to have been intercepted by the Seafire and Martlet patrols until 14 July, when a patrol of Seafire LIICs from 807 Squadron were vectored onto a Ju88. Led by a Free French pilot, Lt de Vaisseau R.L.A. Claude[3], the Seafires closed in as the reconnaissance aircraft attempted to make good its escape, but accurate shooting by the German rear gunner hit Claude's aircraft, which fell in flames with the loss of the pilot. The remaining Seafires gave up the pursuit and searched in vain for signs of their leader.

During the hours of darkness 15 Ju88s of II/KG76 attacked shipping off Syracuse; six failed to return including F1+EF of 6 Staffel which was shot down by ships' AA and crashed into the sea. Lt Bregtschneider and two of his crew were reported missing, only the W/Op being rescued from the sea and became a POW. F1+MP flown by Fw Peter Mint was also shot down, two of his crew surviving as prisoners. These were just two of at least a dozen bombers which fell to the defences that night, which included the Ju88 flown by the commander of 2/KG6, Hptm Dörn. Malta-based Mosquitos and Beaufighters were again extremely successful, the crews claiming nine Ju88s and three Italian bombers. US Bostons and Baltimores were also out, attacking transport on the road south of Villarosa to Enna, in addition to bombing Lercara, while Mitchells bombed the base at Palermo and Wellingtons attacked Messina, others raiding Naples.

On 15 July, the Allied land forces re-captured the important Primosole bridge and by the evening held a line which extended from Primosole via Scordia-Grammichele-Mazzarino-Riese-Canicatti-Favara to Palma. The whole of the

---

[3] Lt de Vaisseau Claude had flown Loire-Nieuport LN-40 dive-bombers with the Aéronavale during 1940 before escaping to England, via Gibraltar to continue the fight. He had 'stolen' a Glenn Martin from Senia airbase near Oran immediately following a ceremony during which he had been awarded a Croix de Guerre, and had reached Gibraltar safely with his mechanic; the latter had accompanied him under protest, however, and was sent back to North Africa. Claude joined the RAF, was trained on the Spitfire and was eventually posted to 118 Squadron in 1942, but later requested a transfer to the Fleet Air Arm, joining 807 Squadron with two other Free French pilots.

Hyblean plateau was now in Allied hands and the Eighth Army was beginning to spread on to the plain of Catania, but it turned out to be a relatively quiet day for the Spitfire units despite continuous patrols entailing 171 sorties being flown throughout the day. Between 1110 and 1200, eight Spitfies of 1435 Squadron escorted Kittyhawks to the Biancavilla area where two Italian Bf109Gs were sighted. These attempted to attack the Kittyhawks but were driven off. Later, near Augusta, a single Messerschmitt made an unsuccessful attack before it, too, was forced to flee. At about the same time, four Spitfires of 92 Squadron were jumped by six MC202s in the Syracuse-Augusta area, Flg Off Milt Jowsey (ES148/QJ-E) and Flt Sgt Mike Askey each claiming one damaged, the latter chasing his quarry along a ravine west of Syracuse at nought feet. As it climbed, Askey closed to 100 yards and fired, seeing pieces fall off including the hood whilst black smoke poured from its engine. Meanwhile, after expending all his ammunition, Jowsey continued to trail his victim for five minutes just in case the Macchi pilot found it possible to reverse the situation, as he reported:

> "Flying Red 3. Fifteen miles west of Syracuse I saw four MC202s diving towards Syracuse on port side. I dived on one and, as I was closing, another attacked me. I broke to the left and then turned onto his tail, closed to 250 yards. I fired at him with intermittent bursts and saw some pieces come off the fuselage. I saw a number of strikes on the fuselage and behind the cockpit. I ran out of ammunition but stayed on his tail for about five minutes so he would not get on mine."

It would seem that 92 Squadron had again encountered Macchis of 351^Squadriglia, the unit's Serg Alessandro Masetti claiming a Spitfire shot down (although this may relate to the previous day's action with 92 Squadron). 1SAAF Squadron's diarist reported a bizarre incident which occurred at Pachino during the day:

> "This morning an audacious Jerry flew a black-crossed aircraft, which resembled a Stinson, right across our aerodrome at 500 feet. Fighters, who were up, thought it must simply be a captured aircraft flown by a British pilot. And so Jerry got away with it!"

Presumably the aircraft involved was a Fi156 Storch, a few having been based on the island with *Verbindungsstaffel Sizilien*, a communications flight. Elsewhere on this otherwise relatively quiet day, Oblt Wolf Ettel, the highly successful Staffelkapitän of 8/JG27 flew his first patrol from Brindisi since arriving from Greece with the remainder of III/JG27 the previous day. He reported shooting down a Spitfire south-east of Noto. His victim, however, may have been an A-36A of the US 111th TacR Squadron which reported a loss in this area. The Germans suffered a severe loss during the day when the celebrated Maj Günther Tonne, Kommodore of SKG10, was killed in a take-off accident at Vibo Valentia. The survivors of IV/JG3 were again in action during the day, now operating from Lecce, and were involved in intercepting B-24s. On this occasion the unit lost 10 Staffelkapitän Oblt Franz Daspelgruber, a 46-victory ace.

More Malta squadrons were moving across to Sicily, 111 Squadron arriving at Comiso during the afternoon, where it joined amongst others 43 and 93 Squadrons; 111 Squadron's diarist noted:

> "Our pilots at once took advantage and were soon in possession of two Fiat

cars, one Mercedes-Benz and various other playthings. The general state of
the airfield and buildings paid tribute to the efficiency of our bombing. The
hangars and buildings are wrecked, and the place is littered with damaged
aircraft, most of which are ME109s."

Throughout the day US fighter-bombers continued their attacks on M/T and enemy
positions across central Sicily and around Mount Etna, while US Mitchells again
targeted Palermo and A-36As bombed Termini railway station to hinder enemy
reinforcements reaching the north-western sector of the island. US B-17s and
Liberators meanwhile carried out daylight raids against mainland targets, both
Naples and the important air base at Foggia coming under heavy attack. The bombers
were back under cover of darkness, Wellingtons flying 62 sorties against the docks
and marshalling yards at Reggio di Calabria and San Giovanni, and the airfields at
Reggio, Vibo Valentia and Crotone, and 46 US Mitchells raiding Randazzo among
other targets. That same night Feldmarschall Kesselring flew to Milazzo in northern
Sicily in a flying boat, as it was now impossible for aircraft to make a safe landing
on land, particularly in the dark. He visited the front-line commanders:

> "[I] gave General Hube, the commander of XIV Panzer Korps, detailed
> instructions on the spot. His mission was to dig in on a solid line even at the
> cost of initially giving ground. In defiance of the axioms of the Luftwaffe
> hierarchy I placed the heavy flak under Hube's command. Hube could hardly
> count on any air support in the daytime, so to compensate I was anxious to
> leave no stone unturned to accelerate the arrival of the 29th Panzer
> Grenadiers. I also told him that I was reckoning with the evacuation of Sicily,
> which it was his job to postpone as long as possible. The defence preparations
> on both sides of the Straits of Messina were proceeding apace and were now
> under his direction. The next day was again devoted to visiting the front and
> to a conference with [Generale d'Armata Alfredo] Guzzoni [commander of
> the Italian Sixth Army] – I left him with the feeling that our chances of
> holding the British Eighth Army were not entirely hopeless. On the whole I
> was satisfied. Hube was the right man in the right place . . ." [4]

The two RN carriers operating off eastern Sicily, 50 miles off Cape Passero,
continued to maintain fighter and anti-submarine and anti-surface vessel patrols
without further incident until just after midnight on 15th/16th, when an enemy
torpedo-bomber – apparently an SM79 of 130°Gruppo AS from Littoria –
succeeded in putting a torpedo into the side of *Indomitable*, inflicting severe
damage. The intruder had been mistaken for an Albacore returning early from a
nocturnal sortie. When the torpedo struck, six Albacores were out on night patrols
and on returning to the carrier individually these were signalled to fly directly to
Malta. All arrived safely despite the crews' fears that patrolling Beaufighter night
fighters might mistake them for the enemy, although one landed at Hal Far with a
large hole in its fuselage having been fired on by an Allied destroyer which it had
overflown. *Formidable* covered the damaged *Indomitable*'s return to Malta, which
effectively ended the FAA's involvement in Operation *Husky*.

On 16 July elements of the Eighth Army began to infiltrate across the
Gornalunga and threatened the Gerbini landing grounds, while further west the
Canadians took Caltagirone with support being provided by US Mitchells. German

---

[4] see *The Memoirs of Field-Marshal Kesselring*.

counter-attacks were unsuccessful. Spitfires of 1SAAF were patrolling over shipping off Syracuse during the early morning when radar picked up a plot of enemy aircraft approaching. Two Spitfires flown by Lt Schalk van der Merwe and Lt Bernie Trotter were scrambled from Pachino to investigate, meeting a dozen twin-engined aircraft which they identified as Do217s, but were in fact Bf110Gs of III/ZG26, escorted by Bf109Gs and MC202s. They immediately attacked and van der Merwe succeeded in damaging one of the 'bombers', observing black smoke coming from one engine, before the escort was able to intervene. Both were able to evade and returned to base safely. The damaged Messerschmitt also returned to its base. Shortly thereafter, Grp Capt Kingcome landed at Pachino from where he then conducted an aerial reconnaissance of the landing ground at Cassibile, to assess its suitability for operations.

During a sweep by 81 Squadron in the morning, a dozen Bf109Gs of II and III/JG27 were seen flying west at 11,500 feet over Lentini and were engaged. Flg Off Bill Maguire (EN492/FL-E) reported shooting down one Bf109G in flames, Flt Sgt Graham Hulse[5] (flying loan aircraft J) claiming a probable, and Plt Off Alan Peart RNZAF (FL-4) one damaged. At about the same time, nine Spitfires of 72 Squadron led by Flt Lt Arthur Jupp patrolled north of Augusta to north of Catania at 10,000 feet. At 0730 ten unidentified aircraft were observed bombing Augusta harbour, but then the Spitfires engaged 15 Bf109Gs about three miles west of Augusta. Sgt Bert Griffiths (EN309) was seen to shoot down a Messerschmitt but his aircraft was struck by fragments from his victim, fell out of control and crashed. A parachute was seen to open but it was not possible to say whether this was Sgt Griffiths or the German pilot. The action occurred within Allied lines and it was hoped that Griffiths had survived, but his body was later recovered from the wreckage of his aircraft. Sgt John Connolly RAAF (JK826) also reported shooting down a Messerschmitt. In these actions against 81 and 72 Squadrons it seems probable that II/JG27 lost three pilots: Hptm Ernst Börngen, Kapitän of 5 Staffel was shot down and wounded after having just scored his 28th victory, a B-24, while Uffz Hermann Wulff and Uffz Dagobert Stangelmeier, both of 4 Staffel, were killed.

There was no further air action until late in the evening when 232 Squadron carried out offensive patrol over the Catania area at 13,000 feet. At 1840, 16 to 20 Bf109Gs, again from II and II/JG27, were seen flying at 15,000-16,000 feet north of Catania. The Spitfires climbed to engage, the three IXs attacking from 21,000 feet. Two of the Messerschmitts were claimed shot down by Plt Off Joe Ekbery (EN365/EF-C) and Plt Off Howard McMinniman RCAF (EN464), and two others damaged by Flt Lt Cal Peppler RCAF (JK758) and a third by Flt Sgt E.A. McCann (JK807). There were no Spitfire losses even though Fw Alfred Müller of 4/JG27 claimed one at 1835 and Oblt Wolf Ettel of 8/JG27 claimed a second five minutes later, but III Gruppe suffered two losses and both Uffz Horst Scherber of 7 Staffel and Uffz Gerhard Hache of 8 Staffel were shot down and killed south of Catania. Eight Spitfires from 92 Squadron covered a large number of warships off Syracuse in the afternoon, including *Rodney* and *Nelson* which bombarded Catania at dusk.

During the day there was a devastating raid on Vibo Valentia by a total of 117 US Mitchells and Marauders which effectively wiped out Jagdgruppe Vibo: JG77,

---

[5] Flt Sgt Graham Hulse was later commissioned and awarded a DFC. He remained in the RAF post-war and in 1952 was posted to Korea to fly F-86s with the USAF. After shooting down three MiG-15s (two shared) he was himself shot down on 13 March 1953 (see the forthcoming Volume Two of *With the Yanks in Korea* by Brian Cull and Dennis Newton).

I/JG53 (which alone lost 20 of its aircraft) and much of II/JG27 (II/JG53 and IV/JG3 had transferred to Lecce to replenish). The survivors of II and III/JG27 remained the only German fighter units in southern Italy still operational. US Mitchells were active again after dark, 30 bombers raiding enemy positions west of Catania. Of the attack on Vibo Valentia, Lt Köhler of I/JG77 wrote:

> "Toward noon 105 [*sic*] bombers came and destroyed the Jagdgruppe Vibo Valentia, which had about 80 aircraft. Not a machine was left intact, not even the Ju which had just landed. Fuel trucks, hangars, aircraft, autos, everything was burning. The German fighters in Italy have been wiped out." [6]

The Eighth Army extended its Primosole bridgehead north of the river on 17 July, and continued to push armoured units across the Gornalunga; to the west the Canadians continued their successful push and captured Ramacca and its airfield, and Piazza Armerina, while the Americans took Pietraperzia, Serra di Falco, Agrigento and Porto Empodocle. 154 Squadron gained the first success of the day for the Spitfires during an offensive patrol over the Gerbini-Catania area, when six Bf109Gs of II/JG27 escorting two MC202s and a single MC200 were intercepted at 0900, 19,000 feet south of Catania. The enemy turned away and dived towards Catania and out to sea, followed by the Spitfires. Flt Lt Alan Aikman (JK649) reported shooting down a MC202 before he damaged a second, the MC200 being claimed probably destroyed by Flg Off G.M. Haase (EN520). Meanwhile, Flt Sgt Edward Artus (EN199/HT-U[7]) engaged one of the Messerschmitts, which he claimed destroyed, and then damaged a second, while another was damaged by Flt Lt Ron Thomson (MA414). One Spitfire, BR635 flown by Flg Off M. Davies, was damaged in the action and crash-landed at Takali on return, apparently the 19th victim of Obfw Franz Stigler of 6/JG27 who claimed a Spitfire north-west of Augusta at 0925. II Gruppe reported losing an aircraft south-east of Catania from which the pilot baled out safely and unharmed.

Eleven Spitfires of 232 Squadron patrolled over the Catania area between midday and 1400, a Gotha glider being observed on the aerodrome. This was strafed from 100 feet and damaged. While flying towards Augusta at 20,000 feet seven Bf109Gs were intercepted and followed down to sea level, whence they swung round to race over the aerodrome at Catania. One Messerschmitt was claimed destroyed by Flt Sgt Patterson (JG792) and a second damaged by Sqn Ldr Arthur (JK656), but Sgt Alan Frewer (JL125) was shot down near Comiso. He later returned. A second Spitfire was lost when the engine of Plt Off Vernon St John's aircraft (JK807) seized, obliging him to bale out. He, too, returned safely. Their opponents appear to have been four Bf109Gs of 10/JG3, as suggested by Uffz Hans Schäfer's account:

> "We were supposed to fly to Sicily with a flight, taking a refuelling stop in Reggio di Calabria, in order to find out in which area the Hermann Göring Division was still fighting. Our flight consisted of Fw Krais, Uffz Stretz, Lt Iffland and myself. In the sea area before the tip of the boot of Italy, we came up against a flight of Spitfires. We immediately turned and attacked. We scored two shootings-down, one by Uwe Krais and the other probably came from we three others. After that, we got to Reggio. The place had been

---

[6] see *Jagdgeschwader 53 Volume Two*.
[7] see Appendix III regarding the fate and fortune of Spitfire EN199.

bombed, and the craters had been filled so that it seemed beautifully smooth. While coasting to a stop, Lt Iffland slipped into one of these filled craters and sank in so deeply that the tips of the propeller were cracked and twisted. After this, the machine could be flown, but it was no longer operational. I assume this is what saved us, because after reporting to our Gruppe by telephone, we were ordered back. Uffz Stretz' machine still wasn't in working order, so he wasn't able to set out on the return flight with us." [8]

During another sortie Oblt Wolf Ettel, the highly successful Staffelkapitän of 8/JG27 with 124 victories to his credit failed to return and was reported to have been shot down by ground fire while strafing British positions south-east of Lentini. A Spitfire was also lost to ground fire during the course of a patrol by four Spitfires of 1SAAF. A dozen small aircraft were spotted in pens at Gerbini but before Lt Doug Rogan could lead his sections down to strafe, Lt G.T. van der Veen reported over the R/T that he had to carry out a force-landing, presumably having been hit by ground fire. He was seen to make a successful wheels-up landing about one mile west of Priolo. Meanwhile, Lts Rogan and Jan van Nus swooped over the landing ground to carry out a strafing run, Rogan putting a long burst of cannon-fire into the grounded aircraft, which included four bombers. Van der Veen made good his escape from enemy territory and later returned to his unit.

During the day the Italians lost another of their ASR Red-Cross marked Z506Cs when the civilian aircraft, I-DOMP flown by Cap Federico Mondo, became entangled with returning US B-24s between Sicily and the Tunisian coast. Apparently the bomber closed in on the unarmed seaplane and its gunners casually shot it down into the sea. The pilot was lost but the other three members of the crew were rescued by another ASR Cant, I-DIVO commanded by Cap Annibale Pecoroni.

By the end of the day all five squadrons of 244 Wing had moved forward to the landing ground at Cassibile, the AOC, Air Vice-Marshal Park, paying them a visit in his personal Spitfire. With the squadrons busily settling in to the new bases, the odd inevitable accident occurred. The most serious and tragic concerned 111 Squadron's EN502 which hit a roller on taking off from Comiso, the crash killing Sgt Ken Allen, a 20-year-old from Manchester. 72 Squadron was also at Comiso, as were 43, 93 and 243 Squadrons; the American Spitfires of the 307th FS were now at Licata, while the 308th and 309th FS had moved to Ponte Olivo. Still operating from Malta, 229 Squadron was involved in escorting naval vessels north of Malta during the day, other aircraft from this unit escorting Dakotas to Pachino. The vital part played by Malta's Spitfires in the invasion was recognised when the AOC Malta received a message of congratulation from General Eisenhower:

"It is obvious to every individual in the Allied Command that except for the Malta Air Force and the constructive accomplishments of the whole Malta Command during the past year, the current attack could scarcely have been classed as a feasible one. In spite of the fact that these things cannot now be published I should like the officers and men of your Command to know of my profound obligation to them and to be assured that as soon as considerations of security permit, there will be recorded public as well as official credit for their outstanding services. Please tell them in my name that during my recent hasty visit to your Command I was impressed by their universal evidence of exemplary efficiency, enthusiasm, and fighting spirit. With cordial regards."

[8] see *Jagdgeschwader 3* by Jochen Prien.

The AOC added his own thanks to the officers and men of his Command.

1435 Squadron saw some action during an early morning offensive patrol on 18 July, meeting four Bf110s with an escort of Bf109Gs over the Catania plain. Flt Sgt Norman Harrison (JK929/V-P) claimed two probably destroyed, plus a third as damaged before his own aircraft was hit by return fire. He was able to return to base safely. Meanwhile, Flt Sgt A.W. Miller (JK803/V-T) damaged one of the escort. It seems that these aircraft were part of a formation of at least eight III/ZG26 aircraft engaged in bombing Catania harbour, and were also encountered by a patrol from 72 Squadron, as Sgt Cliff Piper RNZAF (JK786) recalled:

> "We had been out on a trip and had just turned round and started to come back when I sighted some Messerschmitt 110s, and called to the CO. I didn't recognise the type at first, but I could see the swastikas. Sqn Ldr Daniel said they were 110s and he had a poop at one and reckoned he hit the rear gunner, because the fire stopped. Then I went in and had a poop and the next minute the plane crashed onto the ground. One of the other boys, Jack Hussey [ES107], came in and had a poop at it on the ground and set it alight. When we got back he asked me if I would give him half, which I did, but actually I shot the thing down. The CO didn't claim anything."

One Bf110G – 3U+FT of 9/ZG26 – crash-landed north of Mount Etna, in which both Obfw Willi Bründl and his gunner Fw Hans Wolfsteiner were wounded. It would seem they were the victim of 72 Squadron rather than 1435 Squadron, but they may have been attacked by both. Bf109Gs were also met by a patrol from 229 Squadron shortly before 0800 in the Catania area, two from 4/JG53 attacking one section of Spitfires, Sgt Don Ripper's aircraft (JK394/X-Z) was singled out by Oblt Fritz Dinger[9] and was hit in the propeller by a cannon shell, which snapped off a blade. Ripper, an Australian from Victoria, crash-landed about two miles behind friendly lines, and was uninjured. Uffz Robert Gugelberger, Dinger's No2, wrote in his diary:

> "My first combat. Flew as the chief's wingman. Suddenly my chief jettisoned his auxiliary tank and began to turn. I got rid of my tank and stayed with the chief. All of a sudden to my left, about 1,000 meters lower, I saw 18 to 20 Spitfires flying in the direction of Etna. They were climbing peacefully and apparently hadn't seen us. Then two Spitfires separated from the others and approached us from 11 o'clock. My chief turned toward them and attacked. I held my position on his left. He fired at the left Spitfire and there was black smoke. Then the others were there. It all happened so quickly and then we had to break away." [10]

Flg Off Bill Maguire (EN492/FL-E) of 81 Squadron added another victory to his growing tally during an early afternoon sortie, claiming a FW190 shot down; this was his eighth kill. Shortly after the return of his patrol, his squadron and the others of 322 Wing moved to Lentini East. There was further action in the evening when eight aircraft of 43 Squadron, flying a patrol over the Syracuse-Lentini-Augusta

---

[9] This was Oblt Fritz Dinger's 65th victory; after raising his score to 67 he was killed by a bomb splinter during a raid on Scalea airfield by US bombers nine days later, on 27 July 1943.

[10] see *Jagdgeschwader 53 Volume Two*.

area, sighted an estimated ten Bf109Gs at 1820, north-west of Catania at 15,000 feet. The Spitfires engaged and Messerschmitts broke formation, Flg Off Paddy Turkington (EF594) attacking one from 600 yards down to 150 yards before his cannons jammed; he claimed it damaged. Meanwhile, Wt Off Leeming's aircraft (ES292) was attacked by another and received many hits, one bullet grazing his thigh. Despite the damage he was able to land at base although the aircraft was written off. It seems probable that the Messerschmitts were from II/JG27, since during a mission over the Bay of Catania pilots from this Gruppe reported meeting Spitfires which were escorting an RN convoy. Fw Anton Wöffen claimed a Spitfire (probably Leeming's aircraft) but lost his No2, Lt Peter Lux, who was seen by his colleagues to have been shot down into the sea about 15 miles east of Cape Molino by another Spitfire (presumably Turkington); Lux was posted missing.

Throughout the daylight hours, day after day, photographic-reconnaissance Spitfires ranged far and wide, over Sicily and southern Italy, and one of these (EN153) flown by Flt Sgt 'Mick' Tardiff of 683 Squadron failed to return from a sortie to Foggia; he survived to be taken prisoner. Two days earlier, the Squadron's Plt Off Keith Durbidge DFM (EN420) was jumped by four Bf109s over Messina but was able to evade and escape. Meanwhile, US and RAF fighter-bombers were very active throughout the day, flying a total of 244 sorties, the biggest effort being made by A-36As which concentrated on Adrano across the Simeto river, on the road leading south-east to Catania, and in support of the US Seventh Army advance. US P-40s added their weight, bombing railway yards at Alcamo and Castelvetrano in addition to warehouses, trains and fuel dumps, while after darkness Mitchells targeted the enemy's positions at Catania. The Germans attempted to hit back after dark, six torpedo-armed He111s of 3/KG26 taking-off at midnight to attack ships east of eastern Sicily and south of the Gulf of Taranto, after which they were to land at Grottaglie. One of these, 1H+CK flown by Lt Heinz Bickel, overflew a small Allied naval unit and was shot down into the sea; a successful ditching was carried out and the crew was rescued and taken to Malta.

Shortly before 0730 on the morning of 19 July, Flt Lt Les Gosling was leading a section of 229 Squadron whilst carrying out a sweep of the east coast when four Bf110s of II/ZG1 were sighted at 11,000 feet, and immediately attacked. In the ensuing combat Gosling's aircraft (LZ808/X-D) was hit when he was about ten miles off the coast adjacent to Mount Etna. As he turned in the direction of land black smoke could be seen pouring from his aircraft, and it was reported that he baled out over the sea, but it seems likely that this was actually his No2, Sgt Bill Downing. It seems probable that Gosling had been attacking one of the two Messerschmitts only to be shot down by its gunner. His aircraft is believed to have crashed in the vicinity of Gallodoro, taking him to his death; his body was later recovered and buried in Catania Cemetery (see Appendix IV). Meanwhile, Sgt Downing reported over the R/T that he had shot down two of the Messerschmitts, but he was then shot down himself, presumably by Oblt Willi Hartmann, the Staffelkapitän, who claimed a Spitfire in this action. Two of the Messerschmitts were indeed shot down, Uffz Franz Hillmann's S9+EH crashing north-east of Riposto with the loss of both crew members, and Fw Bernhard Grundt's S9+CN falling about 15 miles north of Taormina; the pilot survived but his gunner was killed. Downing's aircraft (EP444/X-L) crashed in the sea off Riposto, and he was last seen by other members of the Squadron standing in his dinghy about eight miles off the coast. He was later rescued by the Germans and taken into captivity. Flt Lt Richardson led four 92 Squadron Spitfires to search for the missing pilots, a dinghy being sighted five to ten miles east of Catania, but it was empty. A few days later Sqn Ldr Cox wrote to Flt Lt Gosling's mother:

> "Goose, as we all knew him, had been on a show over enemy territory. He chased a formation of enemy aircraft and presumably his aircraft was hit by return fire, and as he turned in the direction of land was seen to bale out. The whole Squadron carried out an intensive search, but could find no trace of him.
>
> I can well understand the weight of your anxiety and all the members of the Squadron and myself send our sincerest wishes to you during this difficult period. Goose was awarded a Bar to his DFC the day before he was shot down and there was never a better-earned one. I am enclosing his brevet which I thought you might like to have . . . If I get any more news I will let you know immediately."

A more successful action was fought in the morning by a quartet of Spitfires from 152 Squadron on convoy patrol five miles north-west of Augusta when 15 Re2002s of 5°Stormo approached and attempted to attack the ships – three troopships escorted by three destroyers. One Reggiane, flown by Serg Bragè, had been forced to return due to engine problems. As the others approached the convoy they were greeted by intense AA fire and it was believed that one was immediately shot down. Despite an escort provided by six MC202s from 21°Gruppo and 14 Bf109Gs of JG53, six of the fighter-bombers were shot down by the Spitfires, three by Flg Off Norman Jones (JK829/UM-E), and one apiece by Flg Off Roy Kingsford (JK327) and Sgt Len Smith (ES308), who jointly shared the sixth. The fourth Spitfire was seen to be attacked and apparently damaged by Cap Gino Priolo and was forced out of the fight, but Priolo was among those who failed to return, together with Cap Mario Sodi, Cap Mario Parodi, Ten Gino Tarini, M.llo Antonio Lucifora, and Serg Magg Federico De Rosa; Priolo and Tarini of 208^Squadriglia were killed, as was Lucifora of 238^Squadriglia. Parodi baled out over the Messina Straits and was in the sea for two days before he reached shore, eventually returning to his unit at the end of the month; Sodi and De Rosa had returned earlier. A seventh Reggiane had belly-landed at Botricello, seriously damaged, as a result of this action.

Shortly thereafter, eight Spitfires of 1SAAF led by Capt Hannes Faure were vectored on to enemy aircraft over Augusta, where three FW190s were spotted almost at sea level. Capt W.M. Langerman and Lt van der Merwe were first to attack, but Langerman's aircraft developed engine trouble and he pulled away. Van der Merwe got in an effective attack before his cannons jammed but by then Capt Faure had arrived and he applied the *coup de grâce*. The fighter-bomber's tail hit the sea, causing the aircraft to rocket about 500 feet into the air whence the pilot, Oblt Fritz Holzapfel of 13/SKG10, was seen to bale out before it crashed into the water, although Holzapfel failed to survive. An Allied destroyer in the harbour reported shooting down a second FW190, the third escaping. Apparently only one was lost. 72 Squadron failed to find any enemy aircraft during its morning patrol in the Catania area, but a large convoy was located and attacked, two sizeable diesel lorries being strafed and destroyed by Flt Lt Arthur Jupp and Flg Off John King. Kittyhawks were summoned to the area and these destroyed at least a further six M/T.

In the afternoon Grp Capt Kingcome led eight Spitfires of 1SAAF as escort to Kittyhawks of 239 Wing north of Mount Etna. When over Randazzo, in poor visibility, Lt Colin Halliday suddenly reported the presence of three Bf109Gs and a FW190 in the immediate vicinity, but his aircraft (EE785) was promptly shot down by Hptm Franz Beyer of IV/JG3, the Spitfire shedding its wings before it hit the ground and burst into flames. Revenge was swift and Lt Warwick Wikner closed on the Messerschmitt flown by Obgfr Reinhard Hagedorn of 11 Staffel, who was also killed, while Lt G.W. Hillary claimed another as damaged.

Pilots and ground personnel of 244 Wing at Cassibile had a surprise visit shortly before lunch, when a damaged B-24 of the 329th Bombardment Squadron touched down at the landing ground. On board was a dangerously wounded crew member who, despite immediate treatment, subsequently died. During the hours of darkness more than 25 Ju88s and He111s operating from the Viterbo/Pratica di Mare area carried out a raid on Malta, specifically aimed at shipping in Grand Harbour when, in addition to dropping bombs, mines were laid. Eight civilians were killed and 14 severely injured, the main casualties occurring at Qormi, Sliema and Valetta. On the ground the British Eighth Army was running into stiff opposition and south of Catania fierce fighting continued against forces of the Hermann Göring Division, which was about to be reinforced and supported by the 15th Panzer Grenadier Division approaching from the east. Even heavier fighting flared to the west of Catania where the Canadians of the 1st Infantry Brigade held their ground while elements of the Eighth Army confronted elements of the Panzer Grenadiers. The Germans were fighting determinedly in order to keep open the road running eastwards and in the hope of reinforcing the north-eastern stronghold with Italian forces.

Allied troops were continually supported by Kittyhawks and US fighter-bombers with little interference from Axis fighters. Spitfires experienced no air engagements during the next two days, even though a 601 Squadron patrol pursued three FW190s in the Gerbini-Catania area on 20 July, and two Bf109s the next day. On this latter occasion Flg Off Percy Sewell (ER855) gave chase and was able to get in an attack but the Messerschmitt dived away before results could be observed. Only one encounter was reported on 22 July, when Wg Cdr Duncan Smith and Flt Sgt Greenwood were escorting a PR Spitfire – EN425 flown by Wg Cdr Warburton – off the east coast of Italy during the morning. Four Messerschmitts were sighted and evaded. Next day it was the turn of Flt Sgt Bill Gabbutt to avoid becoming a victim of the Messerschmitts when three attempted to intercept his PR Spitfire (MB773) over Foggia. On one sweep over the Catania-Gerbini area by 185 Squadron, Flt Lt Wilmot's aircraft was turned upside down when flak burst just below him. Next day Sgt Robbie Roberts (EN482/GL-E) was a member of a section of 185 Squadron Spitfire IXs scrambled from Krendi after a high-flying Ju88 reconnaissance aircraft, but in spite of reaching 33,000 feet they were unable to make a sighting. Four Bf109s were seen when off Cape Stilo and the mission was abandoned. On occasion, Spitfires joined the fighter-bombers in strafing convoys and other suitable targets. 601 Squadron, led by its new CO, the celebrated Polish pilot Sqn Ldr Stanislaw Skalski DFC and Bar with about 20 victories to his credit, again sighted FW190s on 23 July but were unable to engage, while 145 Squadron twice scrambled Spitfires in vain attempts to intercept the high-flying 'shufti kites', the German reconnaissance aircraft which daily overflew the main occupied airfields. The pilots of two Mustangs of 1437 Flight reported sighting a dinghy which contained one occupant, about 13 miles south of the tip of Italy, following which a search of the area was conducted.

By this time every German aircraft that could be flown had left Sicily, while the Italians retained just 28 fighters, mainly MC202s, of which only four were serviceable. Nonetheless, a patrol of eight Bf109Gs of I/JG77 operating from Crotone spotted 15 Kittyhawks escorted by an equal number of Spitfires on the morning of the 23rd, but there were no engagements. However, Uffz Hans

Zimmermann of 2 Staffel was shot down and killed by Italian flak near Milazzo during the offensive sweep. Following mainly uneventful fighter sweeps and fighter-bomber escorts on 24 July, the Spitfires enjoyed a red letter day on 25 July, as noted by 244 Wing's diarist:

> "After 92 Squadron [led by Sqn Ldr Humphreys] had escorted Kittyhawks who bombed the road between Adrano and Biancoville, everyone was buoyed up when it was learned [via an Ultra intercept] that convoys of transport aircraft were ferrying into Sicily. To intercept them 145, 417 and 601 Squadrons swept eastwards from Cape Milazzo, but nothing was seen but the scenery. 322 Wing had beaten us to it. They were the first patrol and intercepted some 25/30 [sic] Ju52s escorted by 20-plus fighters. They bagged 21 of the Ju52s, four [sic] ME109s and one MC202, with the addition of one probable ME109."

The Ju52/3ms were from I/TG1 but there were only ten machines in the aerial convoy, well spread out, with escort provided by a dozen Bf109Gs from I/JG77 and II/JG27, plus a small formation of MC202s from 161°Gruppo. Wg Cdr Colin Gray (flying ES112/UM-U of 152 Squadron) led the Spitfires from 322 Wing; he later wrote:

> "A fierce argument developed between Piet Hugo [OC 322 Wing] and me as to who was going to lead the Wing. I said it was clearly my job as I was the Wing Commander Flying, but Piet finally pulled rank. Fortunately the matter was resolved because at that moment the AOC rang and told Piet he wanted him to remain on the ground in case something further developed. There was no time to assemble the pilots for briefing, so I did the best I could by phone with the commanding officers of 81 and 242 Squadrons, and then leaped into the air with most of 152 Squadron behind me. There should have been 36 aircraft altogether, but only 33 staggered off the two runways and set course for Milazzo in strict radio silence.
>
> We crossed the front-line, but were past before they could fire at us, and we arrived at the Gulf of Milazzo at sea level to see a great gaggle of Ju52s circling prior to landing on the beach. A quick look around showed an escort of Messerschmitt 109s and Macchi 202s about 3,000 feet above them. There looked to be about 20 or more Ju52s and a dozen or more fighters, but there was not time to see precisely how many before we were on them. I ordered 81 Squadron with their Spitfire IXs to tackle the fighters, and the rest of us dived straight into the transports before the escort knew what was happening. I saw three Junkers in formation just ahead of me and a shot at the leader caused him to burst into flames and dive into the sea. I then turned to his number two, and the same thing happened. From the spectacular results it looked as if they must have been carrying petrol. It was all over in a few seconds, and I pulled up to see if there were any more and what had happened to the escorting fighters. It was quite a mêlée as there was more than 30 of us milling around. I could not see a single Junkers still in the air, and every time I saw a German fighter he had a Spitfire on his tail." [11]

Wg Cdr Gray then spotted a lone Messerschmitt and pursued it for some minutes

---

[11] see *Spitfire Patrol*.

but could not get within range, so broke away and returned to Lentini, where he learned that 152 Squadron had claimed eight Ju52/3ms and two Bf109Gs, 242 Squadron claimed seven Ju52/3ms, a Bf109G and a MC202, while 81 Squadron claimed four Ju52/3ms and three Bf109Gs, making a total of 28 destroyed including the two claimed by the Wing Leader for the loss of one Spitfire, in which Flg Off Reg Marshall RNZAF of 152 Squadron was killed in JL245. Individual claims for Ju52/3ms by 152 Squadron pilots were: Flg Off Roy Kingsford (JK327) two; Sgt S.L. Bradbury (JG871) two; Flt Lt Geoff Baynham (JL240) one; Sgt Len Smith (LZ807/UM-V) one; Sgt R.O. Patterson (ER645) one; another was shared by Flg Off E.R. Burrows and Plt Off Bob Macdonald, and yet one more by Flt Lt Baynham and Flg Off Norman Jones (JK829) shared with two pilots of 242 Squadron, Plt Off N.L. Myers and Plt Off Edwards. For 242 Squadron Sgt Eric Doherty (LE-A) alone claimed three, Wt Off Peter Gatley one, and Flg Off John Maxwell one, while 81 Squadron's four claimants were Flg Off Goby (EN565), Sgt W.E. Caldecott (JK322/FL-4), Sgt D.W. Rathwell RCAF (EN247), and the Australian Sgt Whiteford (ER565). Flt Lt Baynham of 152 Squadron reported that he was so close to his victim when it blew up that his cockpit was filled with smoke, and on landing he found a length of parachute cord lodged in his radiator. There were not many survivors from the transports; however, the pilot of 1Z+AB, Lt Labert Mäder, was rescued in a wounded condition although his five crewmen were reported missing. The body of another Ju52/3m pilot, Lt Walter-Karl Kampmann, was recovered from the sea by a British vessel and taken to Malta for burial. A German R-boat was later seen north of the Messina Straits, apparently searching for survivors, and this was attacked and sunk by Allied aircraft.

Flt Sgt Larry Cronin RAAF (JL188) of 81 Squadron claimed two of the Messerchmitts shot down, one near Cannitello and the other over northern Sicily, while his CO, Sqn Ldr Whitamore (EN492/FL-E) claimed another, and Flg Off Goby damaged one. Flg Off Norman Jones of 152 Squadron also claimed two Messerschmitts, and reported that the pilot of the second was seen to bale out at low level over the sea before he opened fire. Flg Off Roy Kingsford claimed a probable after his own aircraft was hit in one wing; he pursued his attacker across the Straits of Messina where it was last seen flying in a narrow gully, smoking badly. This was possibly the aircraft flown by Oblt Gerhard Strasen of Stab/JG77, who crash-landed WkNr18640 after he had been wounded, but not before he had claimed a Spitfire, his fifth victory. Another Bf109G was claimed by Sgt H.R. Kelly of 242 Squadron, two others being damaged by Flg Off John Maxwell and Flt Lt George Silvester, the latter also shooting down a Macchi of 161°Gruppo. One of the missing pilots was the celebrated 52-victory ace Oblt Heinz-Edgar Berres, Staffelkapitän of 1/JG77 who was lost in a newly delivered aircraft, BF+QU (WkNr18101); another missing pilot was Uffz Madaun of 1 Staffel, but he survived after being shot down in WkNr18683. A fourth Messerschmitt was lost by JG77 when WkNr18329 was shot down, the Stab pilot also surviving. Two pilots of II/JG27 were also shot down and killed, Uffz Albert Salzer of 4 Staffel, who crashed near Cefalu, and Obfw Fritz Meikstat of 5 Staffel, who went missing north-west of Messina; a second machine of 4 Staffel belly-landed near Cape Orlando, while in return Fw Heini Steis reported shooting down a Spitfire for his 20th victory, presumably Flg Off Marshall of 152 Squadron.

During the evening, Sqn Ldr Wenman was leading a patrol of ten 154 Squadron Spitfires which were returning to base, when the two rear aircraft were bounced by an unidentified aircraft about two miles east of Catania. Flg Off Eric Rippon's aircraft (JK461) was shot down and the pilot baled out into the sea, and was seen to clamber into his dinghy. He was later rescued by the Germans and became a prisoner for the duration. Meanwhile, Flg Off Peter Furniss (ER967) was also attacked by the same aircraft, and was slightly wounded in the left shoulder, but was able to return to Lentini East and land safely. The identity of their assailant is unknown, although a pilot of 232 Squadron, which was accompanying 154 Squadron, reported that a lone Bf109 joined behind the top cover and shot down the Spitfire. By the end of the day the squadrons of 244 Wing had also moved forward, landing at Lentini West. Next day saw a patrol of 145 Squadron Spitfires searching for enemy movement off the coast at Milazzo, Sqn Ldr Wade (MA336) strafing two MTBs with cannons and machine-guns and observing strikes on both.

German bombers returned to Malta shortly after midnight on 26 July, where they were greeted by a barrage of AA fire from the ground batteries and naval units in Grand Harbour; six raiders were claimed shot down, three by the gunners and three by the night fighters. One victim of the latter was Lt Gerhard Knepler's Ju88 of 3/KG6 which was shot down about 30 miles east of Syracuse from which only the observer, Gfr Erwin Neu, was rescued to become a PoW. There was one casualty on the ground as a result of the raids, Vincent Attard of Zabbar, the last Maltese civilian to lose his life through bombing.

Flt Lt Hards led six Spitfires of 92 Squadron to escort Bostons attacking Agira and Cape Milazzo during the morning of 27 July, meeting no opposition in the air. At 1245, six Spitfires of 43 Squadron set out to escort Kittyhawks to Messina, but the latter failed to rendezvous so the Spitfires carried out an offensive patrol instead. When over the aerodrome at Reggio di Calabria one section dived down to 12,000 feet to carry out an inspection and spotted a Bf109G at 1,000 feet, which had apparently just taken off. The Squadron's newly arrived flight commander Flt Lt Eugeniusz Horbaczewski DFC (MA345), a Polish ace with eight victories, attacked first but, surprisingly, missed. However, his No2 and No3 – Plt Off Wilmer Reid RCAF (JK782) and Flt Sgt Tom Johnson (LZ293) – were on target and the Messerschmitt, an aircraft (WkNr15682) of 2(H)/14, crashed in flames one mile south of the aerodrome, its pilot, Oblt Gerhard Weinert, surviving with injuries.

During the day the 307th FS was ordered to move to Palermo from Agrigento, to where it had only recently arrived. The 309th FS, which remained at Agrigento, lost an aircraft when WZ-Z developed engine trouble, although 1/Lt Mehroff was able to bale out safely. On the other side, II/SKG10 also lost an aircraft due to an accident when Obfhr Helmut Wenk of 6 Staffel, blinded by dust from the aircraft taking off ahead, struck a tree to one side of the airstrip at Crotone. The Fw190 skidded away and shed both wings, drop tanks, undercarriage and its bomb, which fortunately did not explode; Wenk was shaken but otherwise unhurt. While the Allies could easily afford to lose aircraft at this stage of the war, the Germans could not. The British came close to losing three of their top commanders when General Montgomery's personal B-17 almost overshot whilst landing at Palermo. On board the aircraft, apart from the General himself, was his CoS Major-General Francis de Guingand, Air Vice-Marshal Harry Broadhurst, AOC Western Desert Air Force, and his ADC Capt John Henderson, who later wrote:

> "We went down this runway and it absolutely ate it up. The hangars were at
> the end and it wasn't long enough. I remember sitting in the glass dome in
> which I always sat, and I saw the hangar coming up – the pilot did the most
> amazing job. He swung the whole thing round and we landed on our side. I
> mean he put all the brakes on one side and revved one engine and swung the
> whole thing round – which wrote it off. That was the end of it. It collapsed

on one side. We got out pretty shaken." [12]

But according to Air Vice-Marshal Broadhurst, General Montgomery took it all in his stride:

"It was hilarious to me: Monty was sitting there reading, quite unafraid of anything. We should never have gone there in that aeroplane . . . He should never have had it but he adored it." [13]

To enable him to continue his aerial inspections, the Americans generously gave General Montgomery a USAAF C-47 to replace the damaged B-17.

While aerial combat was becoming rarer as each day passed, Flg Off Dicks-Sherwood (JL388) and 2/Lt Johnny Gasson (ER871) of 92 Squadron were in luck when, during a patrol on the morning of 28 July, they bounced a low-flying Bf109G over Augusta, which Dicks-Sherwood shot down for his seventh victory (two shared). The pilot baled out and the Messerschmitt crashed into the sea. It seems that Uffz Karl-Eugen Hettler of 1/JG77 was the unlucky pilot, although he survived to be taken prisoner. He had been flying White 5 (WkNr18119) on a reconnaissance sortie. Not so fortunate was Plt Off Howard McMinniman of 232 Squadron who, with his No2 Sgt L.J. Bowring (JK831), was on harbour patrol during the early afternoon when seven Bf110s of 9/ZG26 were sighted, four in line astern, then 500 yards behind tailed three more, also in line astern. McMinniman (JK274) was seen to attack the last machine in the first section, which he then pursued northwards after it had jettisoned its bombs, but he did not return and evidently fell victim to the Messerschmitt flown by Fw Josef Scherbaum. Meanwhile, Bowring attacked the last Bf110 of the second section and saw strikes along its fuselage before it got away. The 31st Fighter Group also lost a pilot and Spitfire during the day when 1/Lt Robert Heil of the 309th FS was shot down by flak in the vicinity of San Fratello; his aircraft was seen to hit the ground and burn. The only excitement for the Spitfires next day occurred when 92 Squadron escorted Baltimores to Cape Milazzo during the morning. Wg Cdr Duncan Smith, who was leading, sighted two fighters over Nicosia but they turned out to be A-36As. Two more American Spitfire squadrons arrived in Sicily on the 30 July when the 2nd and 4th FS of the 52nd Fighter Group, now under the command of Lt Col J.S. Coward, flew to Boccadifalco airfield, the Group's 5th FS remaining at Korba in Tunisia although it would follow two weeks later. Meanwhile, two pilots from the 309th FS reported an action during the day when 2/Lts Fred Trafton and Mutchler met two Bf109Gs off Randazzo. The Messerschmitts bounced the American pair but failed to register hits as they sped past. Trafton and Mutchler followed them in their dives and reported that both crashed straight into the sea without a shot being fired. Apparently neither were awarded as confirmed victories.

The last day of the month saw the loss of a Mustang pilot of 1437 Flight, the unit's first casualty, when Flt Sgt K.C.B. Stanley (HK945/B) was shot down by AA fire near Agata in northern Sicily during a reconnaissance in the Milazzo-Messina area. The section leader, Flg Off R.M.C. Jones, saw Stanley's aircraft on fire and then his own aircraft (HK944/C) was hit in the tail and starboard wing, causing a fire. Nonetheless, Jones was able to reach Pachino where he landed safely. Further to the west, USN cruisers *Philadelphia* and *Savannah* and six destroyers carried out a

[12] see *Monty: Master of the Battlefield, 1942-1944* by John Henderson.
[13] see *Bitter Victory*.

bombardment of shore batteries at San Stefano di Camastra near Palermo, and were targeted in the afternoon by FW190s. Initially two of the fighter-bombers attempted to dive-bomb but were chased away by patrolling Spitfires, before a dozen more arrived and attacked the *Philadelphia* although the cruiser escaped damage.

With the end of the month came Grp Capt Kingcome's general report on the activities of 244 Wing, and his personal assessment of the campaign to date:

> "So far, the Sicilian campaign has been the reverse of our anticipations. We expected the Hun to come out of his lair in droves, but though when we were in Malta there were enticing stories of formations of 40-plus lurking at a judicious distance from the operations we covered and the sweeps we did, in the main he just refused to play. The conclusion is that for us the campaign was more or less over before we started. So excellently timed and so devastating were the attacks we carried out on his landing grounds that any enemy aircraft on Sicily which were not grounded for the duration at the time the invasion started, were obliged to scuttle off to safer retreats on the mainland, which for the most part put them out of range.
>
> Since we became operational at Malta we have flown a total of 3,052 sorties, the peak days coming around the invasion period. Out of 131 enemy aircraft intercepted, 11 were destroyed, [with] three probables and 12 damaged. Where enemy formations were not taken by surprise, the greatest ingenuity and tenacity had to be employed in bringing them to combat."

The general reports pertaining to 322 and 324 Wings would undoubtedly have mirrored the findings expressed in Grp Capt Kingcome's report.

* * *

As a result of a meeting of the Fascist Grand Council on the evening of 24 July, a motion of no confidence was passed on Il Duce, Benito Mussolini, Italy's Fascist Dictator for the past 21 years. King Victor Emmanuel formally dismissed him next day, after which he was arrested and taken off to Podgora Barracks to await his fate. Marshal Pietro Badoglio was appointed to form a new government, without one Fascist member, and contact was immediately secretly made with the Allies with the aim of negotiating a surrender. The Italians basically wanted to change sides but the Allies were not happy to fight side-by-side with such recent enemies. Of the downfall of Mussolini, Feldmarschall Kesselring wrote:

> "When the news reached me on 25 July that Mussolini was under arrest I at once asked for an audience with the King. Before going to see the King I had an interview with Badoglio, who in answer to my questions merely informed me of what I already knew from the royal proclamation. My audience at the palace lasted almost an hour and was conducted with striking affability. His Majesty assured me that there would be no change as to the prosecution of the war; on the contrary it would be intensified. My impression . . . was that a mask of exaggerated friendliness concealed the reserve and insincerity of this interview.
>
> Mussolini's downfall and arrest poisoned the relations of the highest German and Italian state departments. Hitler saw in this sudden turn of events no ordinary government crisis but a complete reversal of Italy's policy with the object of ending the war as quickly as possible on favourable terms, even if it meant sacrificing her ally. The first step, in Hitler's opinion,

was to 'mop up' the royal family and Badoglio – there would be no particular difficulty in clearing them out. Happily, he discarded this idea conceived in the first paroxysm of excitement. It was subordinated to Hitler's wish to rescue Mussolini so that they could reshape a common policy together, a feeling of solidarity which prompted him to order its execution by any means available." [14]

Hitler initially asked the new Italian government to hand over the deposed Mussolini, whom he intended to restore to power, but the request was refused. Having been moved half a dozen times to foil would-be rescuers, Mussolini was eventually snatched by Luftwaffe paratroopers in a daring operation and taken to Hitler's headquarters at Rastenburg in East Prussia.

In the event, it would not be until 3 September that the Italians finally agreed to unconditional surrender, and 8 September before the surrender was announced – much fighting with many lives lost would be the bitter price to pay for the delay – while Sicily still had to be cleared of Axis troops and her skies swept of Axis aircraft to enable the Allied springboard to be stocked and provisioned for the invasion of the Italian mainland.

---

[14] see *Memoirs of Field-Marshal Kesselring*.

CHAPTER VIII

THE END IN SICILY: THE GERMAN DUNKIRK

August 1943

"No enemy aircraft were seen during that patrol nor later in the day when we patrolled between Randazzo and Troina. What has happened to the Luftwaffe?"

92 Squadron diarist, 3 August 1943

As if to prove the Luftwaffe had not shot its bolt, in the early hours of 1 August a total of 25 Ju88s of KG26 and Do217s from III/KG100 flying from bases in southern France raided Palermo and caused considerable damage to the main dock, destroyed ration and petrol supplies, blew up an ammunition train, sank the British coaster *Uskide* and damaged two USN minesweepers, *Strive* and *Skill*. Two of the Dorniers were intercepted by US Spitfire VIIIs of the 2nd FS flying from Boccadifalco airfield, one being shot down by 2/Lt Norman E. English at 0600 about 60 miles north of Salina Island, and the other by Capt Norman L. McDonald five minutes later, 15 miles north-east of Stromboli Island, his eighth victory (one shared). Two Do217s were indeed lost, only one man surviving from Lt Werner Bürckle's crew to be taken prisoner, while all four members of Lt Silvio Schenk's crew were posted missing. McDonald gained the rare distinction be being awarded a DFC by the grateful British authorities for this and his earlier victories. German bombers raided Palermo again three nights later when two USN destroyers (*Shubrick* and *Mayrant*) were damaged.

One of the other US Spitfire squadrons, the 307th FS, now transferred from Palermo to Termini East where it joined its sister 308th FS. This latter unit – on its first operational mission from this airfield – was jumped by six Bf109s when over the west coast of Italy, near Paetti, and during a brief skirmish 1/Lt Charles R. Ramsey claimed one of the assailants as probably destroyed. It would seem that his victim was Oblt Franz Hrdlicka of 5/JG77, who crash-landed his aircraft (WkNr18747) south of Cittanova following a combat with Spitfires in the morning; the 35-victory ace was unhurt. It was not all one-way traffic, though, since eight FW190s of 6/SKG10 from Crotone carried out a surprise attack on a munitions dump at Nicosia, east of Mount Etna. They dive-bombed the dump, setting it on fire, and on their return flew along the Nicosia-Taormina road and strafed Allied vehicles, but here two of the fighter-bombers were shot down by AA fire, Fw Arno Achter over the Messina Straits, the other flown by Obfw Rudi Riepelsiep crashing near Cittanova; both pilots were killed. A third aircraft, piloted by Obfhr Helmut Wenk, suffered three hits from a mobile anti-aircraft gun but nonetheless managed to land safely at Crotone.

1SAAF Squadron started the day by escorting a Dakota carrying General Alexander from Cassibile to Malta. Later, when escorting a dozen Baltimores attacking Randazzo, a single Bf109 was seen north of Adrano by the South Africans but it quickly made off. Few of the other RAF units saw enemy aircraft during the day and there were no engagements. The CO of 152 Squadron, Sqn Ldr Freddie Lister (ES112/UM-U), had a lucky escape when strafing west of Cesaro. Having completed his strafing run, he found himself heading straight for a hillside. He pulled as hard as he could on the stick, which caused him to black-out. When he recovered he fortunately found himself clear of the hill and was able to return to Lentini and land safely. On inspection of his aircraft it was found that the Spitfire's radiator had been damaged by a tree or similar object. A pair of Mustangs of 1437 Flight carried out an afternoon reconnaissance of the east coast, Flg Off Griffith and Wt Off H.M. Leggo strafing a staff car and rolling stock while thus engaged. Near Cape Spartivento a radar station was discovered and strafed, this becoming a target for subsequent bomber attacks until it was nullified.

It was a similar pattern next day (2 August), the squadrons maintaining continuous patrols over Syracuse and Augusta without incident. General Alexander continued his series of visits and inspections, 601 Squadron escorting his Dakota to Palermo. Despite the lack of action for the fighters, Kittyhawks and US fighter-bombers were out and about, searching for likely targets, and shortly after midday one formation was intercepted near Mistretta by ten Bf109s of I/JG77 led by Lt Armin Köhler of 2 Staffel who claimed one shot down for his 25th victory, a second being claimed by Lt Ludwig Licha of 3 Staffel, but Uffz Sauer's Messerschmitt (WkNr18687) of 2 Staffel was shot down although the pilot survived unhurt. The German pilots apparently initially believed their opponents to have been Spitfires and claimed accordingly but these were probably American A-36As of the 27th FBG.

A patrol of 243 Squadron Spitfires, which were escorting Kittyhawks of 250 Squadron on a fighter-bomber mission, encountered eight Bf109s of I/JG77 engaged on a *Freie Jagd* shortly after midday on 3 August, and during the brief skirmish Flg Off Frankie Banner (JL139/SN-J) claimed one shot down west of Bronte for his fifth victory, and a second damaged, while newly arrived Flt Lt M.R.B. Ingram DFC (JK991) – an RNZAF ace pilot with six victories – damaged another near Mount Etna. The German pilots reported sighting two Spitfires and nine Kittyhawks, two of the latter being claimed by StFw Karl Kühdorf and Fw Ryll for their seventh and fifth victories respectively, for the loss of the aircraft (WkNr20257) flown by Lt Behrendt Luftkampf who belly-landed his damaged machine at Taormina, the pilot suffering injuries and the aircraft a write-off. 1SAAF Squadron, while escorting another formation of Kittyhawks, was attacked by half a dozen Bf109s in the Milazzo area but these dived away when the Spitfires turned into them. A patrol from 601 Squadron also came under attack during the day – by an overzealous American A-36A pilot. One of the offended pilots commented: "[I] took a dim view of this, giving it a one-and-a-half second burst."

Three sections each of two aircraft from 92 Squadron escorted a Walrus which attempted to rescue one of the downed Kittyhawk pilots in the sea off Riposto, but only wreckage was seen. Later, 92 Squadron escorted Kittyhawks strafing the road between Fuimfreddo and Barcellona, the diarist noting: "No enemy aircraft were seen during that patrol nor later in the day when we patrolled between Randazzo and Troina. What has happened to the Luftwaffe?" On the ground the battle for Troina was favouring the Allies but one of the main problems Allied troops experienced was that of coming under fire from their own aircraft. The American fighter-bomber pilots in particular were very inexperienced:

"During the battle for Troina, Canadian troops in Regalbuto were bombed several times by US fighter-bombers . . . A-36s strafed the [US] 1st Division CP for the third time in a single day. On another occasion when American aircraft disregarded prearranged yellow recognition signals and repeatedly strafed a [US] 2nd Armoured Division column, the frustrated troops finally fired back in self defence, despite orders not to fire on friendly aircraft. A P-38 was shot down and the pilot was able to bale out safely, but the Air Corps got the message. Later, when the statistics were compiled it was found that the 2nd Armoured lost more men and equipment (fourteen vehicles and 75 men killed or wounded) to 'friendly' air attacks than to the Luftwaffe." [1]

Mustangs of 1437 Flight were again active, two flown by Lt P.D.L. McLaren SAAF (HK946/F) and Flt Sgt H.H. Proud (HK947/A) being despatched to carry out a reconnaissance in the Cape Orlando area, where McLaren's aircraft was hit by flak. The dive-brake on the port side was damaged, making the aircraft difficult to control but, nonetheless, the pair continued their low-level mission, overflying Reggio and the Messina Straits, before heading back to Francesco landing ground, where Proud landed safely. McLaren, however, was unable to reach the airfield and belly-landed his damaged aircraft at Lentini East instead, suffering head injuries in so doing.

72 Squadron lost one of its more successful pilots on 4 August, when Flg Off George Keith's aircraft (JK637) was hit by flak while ground strafing in the Catania area. The Canadian baled out over the sea but hit one leg on the tailplane as he did so. He was located in the sea and was picked up by an ASR Walrus, X9506 of 284 Squadron flown by Sgt D.J. Lunn with crew of Wt Off N. Pickles and Flt Sgt J. Bradley, about three miles east of Catania. Sgt Lunn realised that he could not take off in the area so taxied to position near Augusta and then took off. Within ten minutes of landing back at Cassibile, where the seriously injured Flg Off Keith was carefully unloaded and rushed to hospital, there to succumb to his injuries next day, Lunn took off again in another Walrus and a fresh crew to rescue a Beaufighter crew down in the sea off Catania. Spitfires from 152 Squadron provided escort to the Walrus. On a later mission, two of that unit's aircraft, MA261 and ES308, sustained damage from AA fire but both pilots were able to return to base safely. 145 Squadron similarly suffered damage to two of its aircraft, Flg Off J.F. Carswell RCAF being obliged to carry out an emergency landing in JF874 at Gerbini.

A German prisoner who fell into British hands at this time claimed that he was Uffz Erich Scholl, a pilot of 2/JG53, and told his RAF interrogators that he had been shot down in combat with Spitfires near Messina shortly after 1215 on 4 August. He claimed to have accounted for two Spitfires before falling to a third. He also claimed that he had earlier served on the Eastern Front with JG22 [sic] where he had shot down 12 Russian aircraft before being transferred to Tunisia, where he claimed two P-38s and a Spitfire. Four more Spitfires and a P-38 were allegedly added to his tally over Sicily before he was shot down. His story was apparently a complete fabrication and his true identity remains unknown; he may not have even been a pilot.

Fighter-bomber escorts continued next day (5 August), 92 Squadron providing protection for Warhawks of the US 57th FG on an armed reconnaissance to the Messina area, where the formation was targeted by flak from both sides of the

---

[1] see *Bitter Victory*.

Straits. Sqn Ldr Humphreys' aircraft (EN333) suffered a large hole in its wingtip although he was able to fly it back to Lentini without too much trouble. Next day the VIIIs of 92 Squadron provided close escort to Mitchells bombing Randazzo. After the attack, as the bombers winged their way back, nine MC202s (in fact, MC205Vs of 9°Gruppo led by Cap Mariotti) dived on the Spitfires from 18,000 feet. They climbed away after the initial attack, having not succeeded in inflicting any damage, and were pursued by Flg Off Jowsey and Flt Sgt Askey who both fired but saw no results. Although none of the Spitfires was damaged in this skirmish, one was nonetheless claimed probably destroyed by Ten Necatti, and a second jointly so by Serg Magg Ceoletta and Serg Magg Gaspari.

Catania fell on 5 August, and with it its valuable airfield complex. During the first few days of August, Catania had showed signs of becoming untenable and the Hermann Göring Division had began pulling out. When British forces entered the town at dawn on the 5th, they did so without meeting any enemy opposition. Following this success, HQ 15th Army Group sent a signal to the AOC Mediterranean Air Command:

> "Indications suggest that Germans are making preparations for withdrawal to the mainland when this becomes necessary. It is quite possible he may start pulling out before front collapses. We must be in a position to take immediate advantage of such a situation by using full weight of the naval and air power. You have no doubt co-ordinated plans to meet this contingency and I for my part will watch situation most carefully so as to let you know the right moment to strike and this may come upon us sooner than we expect."

At the same time, Air Vice-Marshal Harry Broadhurst, AOC Western Desert Air Force, wrote to the AOC the Tactical Air Force, Air Marshal Coningham:

> "I suggest that it will need a combined air and naval plan to deal with it, something on the lines of the Tunisian affair but, of course, applied to the particular situation here. I quite realise that we can do a lot with the air forces immediately available, but the exceptional flak on both sides of the Straits of Messina will need, I think, the use of Fortresses if we are to maintain continuous air action to defeat an attempt at evacuation. Presumably the Navy will be able to prevent sea movement at night, but here again they may need some help from us."

It was estimated that the enemy would have available about 100 fighters and fighter-bombers which could provide cover for the evacuation, plus about 15 night fighters in the Naples area and approximately 100 long-range bombers. A plan was put into immediate operation whereby Wellingtons of the Strategic Air Force would commence night attacks on Messina and the barge anchorages north of the town, while B-17s would also carry out occasional daylight attacks on the town and medium bombers would attack landing grounds in the Crotone and Scalea areas, with long-range P-38Gs tasked to attack targets of opportunity in southern Italy.

Meanwhile, with the capture of Catania, many off-duty pilots visited the airfield looking for suitable trophies of war, Sqn Ldr Whitamore and Flg Off Maguire of 81 Squadron acquiring a MC202 which, with some help, they got in serviceable condition and it was flown to Lentini East by Maguire next day. Sgt Bill Robinson was among the Squadron pilots who had an opportunity to fly the Macchi. A few days later the same pilot recorded in his logbook a flight in a Breda 39 trainer, when he was able to give an airman a joyride. Another Macchi was located by pilots of 417RCAF Squadron, checked over and flown to Lentini West with Flg Off Snooks Everard at the controls:

> "Without benefit of air speed or other vital engine information, I was airborne in short order and headed to our airfield at tree top level. Fortunately there were no Spitfires aloft and the ack-ack defences were obviously unfamiliar with the Macchi 202 silhouette. By feel and control responses, I was able to extend the landing flaps and land without incident, although touch-down was faster than expected. I was imagining the furore in the control tower as I taxied back to the operations tent escorted by four jeep-loads of men with pistols and rifles at the ready. After shutting down and removing my tight-fitting souvenir leather helmet I was confronted by a gaping Wing Commander who could only repeat: Everard – you bastard!'. The Bull [Sqn Ldr Turner] was at the Wingco's elbow, and could hardly suppress his laughter, thank God." [2]

Not to be outdone, Sqn Ldr Turner and Flt Lt Bert Houle drove over to Gerbini to find their own aircraft, but en route their jeep drove over a land mine. Houle suffered perforated ear drums in addition to cuts and lacerations after being blown out of the vehicle, while the CO was trapped inside with injuries which kept him grounded for ten days. Meanwhile, pilots from 92 Squadron liberated a FW190 but this was pranged on landing at Lentini. Other interested parties picked over the spoils of war, and the South Africans located an undamaged Bf109G which Capt John Seccombe flew to Lentini West, followed by a captured FW190 in the hands of Capt Langermann, where they joined the SAAF Squadron's recently acquired MC202. However, the private air force was attacked by infiltrators who set fire to two haystacks between which the Macchi was parked, although the other two machines escaped damage. Flg Off Everard of 417RCAF continued:

> "In the evening that followed, I was intensely pleased to dogfight my Macchi against Spitfires. The South African squadron had picked up a ME109 following my successful sortie to the front. It too was used in simulated combat." [3]

Not to be outdone, 72 Squadron found a flyable Bf109G which one of its pilots managed to get airborne, only to find himself the target for the many gunners on and around the aerodrome, they having not been warned previously and unable to distinguish the British markings. An exciting few minutes followed, ground personnel running for cover believing they were about to be strafed. With the Messerschmitt taking evasive action, a Spitfire was scrambled from the airfield, circled and waggled its wings, signalling AA to cease fire. Finally the Messerschmitt came in making an excellent one-wheel landing; luckily the pilot escaped unscathed. Another Bf109G was also made airworthy by 72 Squadron and Flg Off Tom Hughes volunteered to fly this until it developed a glycol leak, at which he baled out and landed in a vineyard not far from Pachino. A few days earlier Hughes had flown a Caproni Saiman 200 biplane trainer found abandoned

---

[2/3] see *A Mouse in My Pocket*.

in a field near Pachino. Wg Cdr Gray also took the opportunity to fly a MC202:

> "It was manoeuvrable, very manoeuvrable, but certainly inferior in
> performance to the Spitfire IX. It was probably better than the Spitfire Vs
> that we still had in Sicily, but I would have thought it was certainly much
> slower and had a lesser rate of climb than the Spit IX."

While all this excitement focused on Catania, further to the west the air war
continued and a US Spitfire of the 4th FS flown by 1/Lt Leonard V. Helton engaged
a Bf109 about 40 miles north-east of Palermo which was claimed destroyed. When
escorting US Warhawks during a morning mission on 7 August to the Messina
area, a twin-engine aircraft was seen off the Italian coast flying at sea level by Flt
Lt Leighton Montgomerie (EN478) of 81 Squadron. Followed by his No2 and No3
– Sgts Caldecott (JK399) and Carlisle (JK367) – Montgomerie pursued the aircraft,
which was believed to have been a Ca309 Ghibli communications/reconnaissance
machine, and promptly shot it down into the sea aided by his companions. In the
course of another Kittyhawk escort to the Messina area by 601 Squadron, AA fire
damaged the Spitfire (ER556) flown by Flt Sgt M.R. Cooper RNZAF who,
nonetheless, was able to reach base and make a safe landing, but 154 Squadron lost
a Spitfire during the day when Flt Lt Ron Thomson baled out of ER163 just south
of Catania with engine trouble while escorting Kittyhawks bombing and strafing
barges. He landed safely and was soon located by Military Police and returned to
Lentini none the worse for his experience. Elsewhere, other squadrons were
similarly engaged on escort duties, 92 Squadron ensuring that a dozen US
Mitchells came to no harm while bombing to Randazzo, then later escorting
Warhawks of the 64th FS on an armed reconnaissance south of Messina. No enemy
aircraft were sighted during these missions. During one operation on this day,
however, Bf109s from II/JG77 did succeed in evading the escorts, Lt Ernst-
Wilhelm Reinert of 4 Staffel claiming two P-40s shot down and thus taking his
score to an amazing 156 victories, Uffz Philipp of 6 Staffel accounting for an
escorting P-38.

After much bitter fighting, Troina finally fell to the Americans on 7 August, the
official RAF report of the campaign noting:

> "The capture of Troina was one of the most significant events of the
> campaign. After this defeat the Germans never again sacrificed large
> numbers of troops to hold any position and their whole effort was bent on
> making a successful withdrawal of as many men as possible from Sicily."

After the battle of Troina, the US Third Division in conjunction with the Naval
Task Force made the first of three amphibious landings two miles east of
Sant'Agata with the object of outflanking the German positions at San Fratello; a
second landing was made at Brolo, the third north-west of Barcellona. The
outlying island of Ustica and the Lipari Islands were also captured.

The Luftwaffe continued to be concerned about what was happening at Malta,
frequent reconnaissance flights being undertaken by Ju88s of 1(F)/123 operating
out of Frosinone. One of these was intercepted by Spitfires of 185 Squadron on 7
August as it approached the island but escaped with only slight damage after its
gunner had shot down one of the intercepting Spitfires, EN403 flown by Plt Off
A.A. Wyndham, whose section leader, Flt Lt C.G. Chappell (EN533), claimed the
intruder damaged. Wyndham later reported:

"After an engagement with a Ju88 at 32,000 feet, I saw flames coming from my engine and as these became worse, I gave Ground Control my position and baled out. The time was 0750. I rolled the aircraft over onto its back and fell free of it. I made sure I was clear of the aircraft and then pulled my rip-cord and the parachute opened at once. As I was nearing the water I inflated my Mae West and turned the release unit. As my feet touched the water I pressed the unit and freed the harness. I inflated the dinghy and got into it without difficulty. The time was now 0800 approximately. At 0840 I saw the ASR Walrus a few miles away, headed directly towards me and I fired one signal flare. The Walrus landed alongside me five minutes later and I was taken on board."

American Spitfires had a highly successful encounter next day (8 August) with a formation of 20 FW190 and Bf109 fighter-bombers which attempted to attack shipping off Cape Orlando in the afternoon. Led by Capt John Paulk, the Spitfires of the 308th FS claimed three FW190s shot down, one by Paulk with the other two credited to 1/Lt Ramsey and 2/Lt Richard F. Hurd, while Capt Baker damaged another. One Spitfire was hit in the cockpit and Capt Williams, a new pilot, was wounded in head and back, but despite his wounds and great loss of blood, he was able to land back at base. The FW190s were from II/SKG10 which recorded the loss of three aircraft to Spitfires near Cape Orlando, in which Uffz Franz Gettinger and Uffz Friedrich Stöhr were both killed, while Uffz Helmut Ostermann baled out having been wounded.

During the course of this relatively action-filled day, pairs of Spitfires from 92 Squadron escorted an ASR Walrus to ten miles east of Taormina where another downed pilot, probably an American, was successfully picked up. The South African TacR unit, 40SAAF Squadron, lost a Spitfire during the day when Lt Waugh's aircraft was badly damaged by a near burst of AA over the Randazzo area while flying at 1,500 feet, although the pilot managed to reach base at Gerbini but then baled out due to the damage. The RAF's TacR 1437 Flight was fortunate not to lose an aircraft in similar fashion when Flg Off Griffith and Wt Off Leggo carried out a low-level reconnaissance mission. The two Mustangs came under intense light AA fire, Leggo's aircraft (HK955/D) sustaining damage although he was able to reach Francesco safely. The far-ranging PR Spitfires from both 682 and 683 Squadrons meanwhile continued their daily dangerous sorties over the Italian mainland, but only occasionally encountering aerial opposition: Flt Lt Phil Kelley of 683 Squadron in EN412 successfully evaded four FW190s near Crotone, while the unit's Flt Sgt Gabbutt was chased by a number of Bf109s near Crotone and again by more near Manduria, but evaded on both occasions.

Inevitably, there occurred a number of landing and take-off accidents among the various Spitfire units being deployed to the new airfields and landing grounds, many of which were pitted with bomb craters. The more serious incidents included that of the pilot of EP812 of 1435 Squadron who hit a parked Spitfire (ER645) of 152 Squadron when landing at Lentini, writing off both aircraft. A few days later 2/Lt J.P. du Plessis of 40SAAF Squadron overshot when landing at Gerbini and ran into a Bombay Red Cross aircraft (L5827). Both aircraft were badly damaged but fortunately du Plessis was not hurt and did not require the services of the aircraft he had inadvertently damaged. Then Flg Off H.G. Garwood of 417RCAF Squadron crashed when the engine of ES365 cut on take-off from Lentini West; he too survived with only slight injuries.

The unlucky II/SKG10 lost another aircraft and pilot on 10 August when a number of FW190s attempted to attack shipping assembled at Augusta. Four Spitfires of 1SAAF Squadron led by Capt Seccombe were scrambled at 1735 on the approach of raiders and were ordered to patrol the harbour, where two low-flying FW190s were soon spotted going north-east. Seccombe and his No2, Lt S.J. Richards, dived after these, the leader easily catching the fighter-bomber flown by Uffz August Woltering which crashed into the sea in a great splash. Meanwhile, Richards engaged and damaged the second FW190 which was last seen flying slowly to the north-east with one oleo leg dangling, its hood partly up and trailing grey smoke. Richards was unable to apply the *coup de grâce* owing to intense fire emanating from the harbour defences.

Seventeen Bf109Gs of II and III/JG77 on a *Freie Jagd* reported meeting 20 Spitfires near Mount Etna during the early morning of 11 August, Uffz Rolf Daum of II Gruppe failing to return. There appears to be no corresponding RAF action, so possibly Daum fell victim to American fighters or ground fire. American Spitfire pilots of the 31st FG were in luck later, however, the 307th FS meeting four enemy fighters which were attacking ships off Cape Orlando, these being identified as FW190s and MC202s, 2/Lt Robert B. Chaddock claiming a Macchi shot down while 1/Lt Carroll A. Pryblo and 2/Lt Delton G. Graham shared FW190. The 308th FS then encountered a separate formation of FW190s, Capt Baker shooting down one of these at 1640. One of the Spitfires, flown by 2/Lt Hurd, developed a glycol leak and crash-landed at San Stefano, the aircraft being written off although the pilot was unhurt. A second Spitfire, flown by Capt Williams, just returned from hospital, was hit by flak and Williams was again wounded, although he managed to land back at base from where he was rushed to hospital. The FW190s were from the luckless II/SKG10, both Uffz Hans Rademacher and Lt Klaus Jost falling victim to the American Spitfires, while Fw Günther Scheid was shot down by ships' gunfire; all three German pilots were killed.

During an attack by B-24s on targets near Rome during the day, one of the bombers was shot down by a captured P-38G flown by Colonello Angelo Tondi, a test pilot from the Test and Research Centre at Guidonia. The American fighter had landed in error at Cagliari in Sardinia on 12 June, and had been tested and evaluated before Colonello Tondi requested permission to fly it on operations. This was apparently the only successful sortie.

The Luftwaffe made one final fling on the night of 11/12 August, when an estimated 30 Ju88s from KG54 carried out surprise raids on the two Lentini airfields, and against Agnone where the Kittyhawks of 239 Wing were based, as well as the ports of Augusta and Syracuse – with some measure of success. Flt Sgt Harry Moore RNZAF, a pilot with 242 Squadron, recalled:

"Two German planes had made a very quick run over our airfield [Lentini East] during the day – the only time they came near it in daylight. That particular night I was put on guard duty in charge of the guard, and I was in the guard tent when I noticed it was bright outside – there was a flare coming down – I could have read a newspaper, it was so bright. Then more flares came down and as they got near the ground my main concern was, as it was summertime in Sicily and the grass around was tinder dry, this would be set on fire and spread to our Spitfires. So, at this stage, I very hopefully thought that I was going to beat out one of these flares as it came to the ground, and I grabbed a Mae West and headed out, but by this time the Germans started their attack. They would attack one plane at a time. Diving, they would drop two high explosive bombs followed by a canister of antipersonnel bombs. These bombs were exploding all around me and planes were being set on fire. It was a very frightening experience. I dived for the nearest ditch, which was a few yards from the runway, and a very shallow one at that.

After some time I just felt I had to get away from there, and dived through a very thick grove of bamboo and into an open area which had just been cleared by a bomb. In this area I met a local Sicilian and he was just as frightened as I was, and we were very pleased to see each other and we supported each other. After things had cleared, I brought him back to the aerodrome. In that raid which was directed at several airfields on the plain of Catania, I heard that there were 81 Spitfires destroyed or damaged, and 200 people killed. There were a very small number of Spitfires that were serviceable next day."

Grp Capt Kingcome, OC 244 Wing, added:

". . . we were bombed and strafed from low level. The attack seemed to last the entire night, but it can only have gone on for about 20 to 30 minutes. We lost far too many men and machines, even though our practice of dispersing as widely as possible saved worse casualties. It was a deeply disquieting experience that brought home to me the astonishing fortitude of the civilian population, always at the receiving end and always helpless to strike back. It was too easy to become detached and complacent when you were sitting in the comparative safety of the cockpit of a single-seat fighter and watching it all happen on the ground far below." [4]

417RCAF Squadron's Flg Off Snooks Everard remembered that the "ack-ack defences [at Augusta] sent up a cone of fire that resembled the flashing lights of a Christmas tree"[5], and that the airfield gunners initially remained silent so that the exact location of the landing grounds would hopefully be unnoticed, but:

"Suddenly the complete plain was illuminated by dozens of flares dropped from German pathfinder planes . . . Wave after wave of bombers kept arriving and strings of assorted bombs stitched across the plain. From my position at the mouth of the culvert I could see and hear multiple flashes just as if our grove was alive with fire crackers. The shrill whistle of flying shrapnel grew nearer. The trembling earth from the continuous explosions shook our bodies so that shivers of fear and shock continued some minutes after the last explosions . . . Two of our Spits had been demolished and five more were badly damaged . . . Upended aircraft, including my Macchi 202, were memorials to the success of the German raid." [6]

In a more light-hearted vein, 92 Squadron's diarist wrote:

"We entertained a nursing sister in the Mess this evening. She was an old friend of Doc Holt's but then Flt Lt Tony Bruce came on the scene. He it was who took the visitor out to have a look at one of our kites but during this very pleasant interlude, the Hun decided to bomb our airfield [Lentini West]. It

---

[4] see *A Willingness to Die* by Grp Capt C.B.F. Kingcome DSO DFC.
[5/6] see *A Mouse in My Pocket*.

was the same gallant Tony who threw himself over the body of the nursing sister to protect her from the blast. Three Spitfires were badly damaged and three more slightly damaged, but no casualties to personnel. There were three unexploded bombs on the taxying strip on the north side of the runway . .. "

92 Squadron's Flg Off Gordon Wilson recalled:

"It was the first time a nurse had visited 92 Squadron. She was the guest of the MO. We were finishing supper when the bombers hit the airfield. I found myself wrapped around a stone block. Realising the stone block could have been wrapped around me, I took off and with some three others found shelter in a stone house and under a heavy table. Flt Lt Carpenter – having enough to drink at supper – made three attempts to get to the aircraft but each time came a new load of bombs, and he retreated to under the table. Finally all of us did our best to rescue the Spitfires, many of them damaged and on fire. We had no casualties on 92 Squadron, but the other squadrons lost personnel."

During the course of the raids, some 26 Spitfires[7] and Kittyhawks were rendered unserviceable of which a number were complete write-offs including five of 322 Wing's aircraft at Lentini East, while upwards of 50 more sustained minor debris and blast damage. It is recorded that 27 military personnel were killed of whom at least nine were airmen of 244 Wing including two pilots of 232 Squadron, Plt Off Vernon St John and Sgt Wilf Atkinson RAAF; in addition, amongst the many wounded, was another 232 Squadron pilot, Flt Sgt P.E. King. 40SAAF Squadron's Capt R.H. Rogers suffered burns in leading fire-fighting on a blazing fuel dump. Members of the Royal Artillery defending the airfields suffered 31 casualties. At least one Ju88 failed to return from the operation, an aircraft of 8/KG54 crashing near Augusta shortly before midnight, and claims were made for the destruction of another four.

Taking off at 1400 on 12 August, Sqn Ldr Wenman of 154 Squadron led three others as Kittyhawk escort to Gioia Gulf where two sea craft were attacked but no hits seen. At this stage the engine of Sqn Ldr Wenman's aircraft (EN520) failed and he was obliged to bale out into the sea at about 1500, two of his pilots orbiting his dinghy to gain a fix. One of the faithful old Walrus amphibians from 283 Squadron was soon on its way, escorted by two of 81 Squadron and Wenman was picked up at 1630 about ten miles south-east of Vulcano Island by Sgt Divers and Flt Sgt Morabito[8]. Although there was no mention of Wenman's aircraft being attacked, nine Bf109s of I and II/JG77 were active in the area at this time and reported meeting four Spitfires and 25 Kittyhawks near Palmi, Lt Ernst-Wilhelm Reinert claiming a Spitfire shot down for his 157th victory. A dozen Bf109s of IV/JG3 were also in the area, claiming two Kittyhawks shot down for the loss of two of its own, one of whom (Uffz Oswald Hoffmann) was believed shot down by AA fire, while Fw Hans Mittenhuber baled out, wounded. As this drama unfolded, a further

---

[7] Spitfires destroyed during the raids on Lentini West included EN370, and JK510, JK541 and JK934 of 601 Squadron. 417RCAF Squadron also lost two Spitfires in addition to its captured MC202, which had one of its wings blown off, while amongst 81 Squadron's casualties at Lentini East was JK322/FL-4.
[8] A few days earlier Sgt Divers and Flt Sgt Morabito had rescued from the sea eight miles north of Milazzo, the pilot of a Do217 of III/KG100, Lt Joachim Zantropp, the victim of Beaufighter night fighter.

four Spitfires, these from 232 Squadron, carried another Kittyhawk escort during which six FW190s were seen north of Milazzo. Two were attacked and one claimed destroyed by newly promoted Wt Off Patterson (JK708) for his third victory (one shared). Two FW190s of II/SKG10 in fact crash-landed at Crotone including CL+PP (WkNr181698) flown by Obgfr Werner Cozclack, who was wounded. Patterson believed his victim had crashed into the sea:

> "I was flying Red 3 on escort to 12 Kittyhawks north of Messina. When we were passing Messina, the Kitties were subjected to heavy flak, and split us, making our task almost impossible, so we patrolled over the area. We were flying east at 12,000 feet when we saw six aircraft 3,000 feet above flying south. These were thought to be friendly but they must have been 190s. We climbed to about 16,000 feet, trying to keep them in sight, and saw them jettison what seemed to be long-range tanks. Evidently they had seen us because they kept above us, and suddenly three 190s dived down out of the sun, leaving four more above, and bounced us good and proper. I yelled and broke violently right and found myself almost on the tail of a 190 who seemed to be breaking away from the attack. He must have seen me coming round, for he went into a vertical dive. I followed him and opened fire with a short burst from about 400 yards with both cannon and machine-gun. I saw one cannon shell burst on its tailplane but it didn't seem effective as he continued his vertical dive. Although I could not close the range, I still followed, firing in short bursts. The dive continued from 16,000 feet right down until I thought it time to pull out, leaving the 190 still diving vertically. I levelled out at 1,000 feet to 500 feet and, looking round, saw a terrific splash just where I hoped to see one. I glanced at my ASI and it was still reading 450mph. I think that either the Hun could not pull out in time or else the strike I observed jammed or otherwise damaged the elevator controls."

On the morning of 13 August four Spitfire Vs of 417RCAF were sent off to search for a dinghy reported to be floating in the Straits of Messina, but as they approached at low level they were attacked by two MC202s. One Spitfire, EF593 flown by Plt Off Terry Field RCAF, who had only been with the Squadron five days, was shot down, and a second, LZ946 flown by Plt Off J.H.G. Leguerrier RCAF, received a cannon shell in the cockpit although the pilot escaped injury and was able to return to Lentini safely. The missing pilot, Field, was able to bale out and was taken prisoner. During a later sortie, Lt O.L. Dugmore of 40SAAF was hit by AA fire when carrying out a reconnaissance flight over Francoville. He managed to bale out but was too low and the 21-year-old from Cape Province was killed when his parachute failed to open properly – just one of the many dangers the low-flying reconnaissance pilots had to face.

Next day (14 August) at 1500, Sqn Ldr Arthur took off with three others from 232 Squadron to escort Kittyhawks to the Milazzo area where an estimated 25 Macchis appeared. These were in fact 16 MC205Vs of 4°Stormo led by Cap Luigi Mariotti, in two flights of eight, escorting Re2002s which were attacking M/T on the road leading to Randazzo near Catania. The Italian pilots reported meeting 20 (*sic*) Spitfires at about 14,000 feet which were engaged by one formation of Macchis. Five Spitfires were claimed shot down by Cap Mariotti, Ten Paolo Voltan, Ten Ferrazzani, Sottoten Renalto Baroni, and Serg Magg Giulio Fornalé, and three others were believed to have been probably destroyed by Sottoten Enrico Dallari, Serg Magg Fornalé and Serg Magg Massimo Salvatore. Ten Voltan returned with his aircraft damaged, presumably as a result of combat with Sqn Ldr Duke Arthur (MA295) and his No2, Sgt S.J. Davison (JK656), who jointly claimed a Macchi damaged when cannon strikes were observed on its fuselage and wing root. Another Macchi came back with its wings having suffered severe distortion during its dive to escape the attention of the Spitfire. Two of the 3RAAF Kittyhawk pilots also reported successes against the Macchis, Flt Lt Ron Susans claiming one destroyed, and Sqn Ldr Brian Eaton two damaged. Sqn Ldr Arthur reported a frustrating combat:

"I was leading four Spits on escort duty to Kittyhawks on an anti-shipping mission. Just north-west of Milazzo I saw about eight aircraft coming from the east on and above our level. I couldn't recognise them until they had passed in front, then I saw they were Macchi 202s. I watched these as they went into the sun when, suddenly, about six came down in front of us in a vertical dive, at the Kitties. I went after three but about eight more came in from the east and above. From then on we were attacked continually from above by groups of four-plus. I managed to get on the tail of a Macchi and chased him around the sky for a good two minutes, firing half-second bursts at him but only saw cannon hits on the tail unit. I fired eight one-second full deflection shots at him. When I had full throttle on, the Macchi was turning inside of me. When I throttled back I could get inside him but he immediately pulled out of range, and when I opened my throttle to catch him up, he turned inside me again."

The Italian fighter pilots again made a substantial number of claims against Spitfires next day (15 August), when Cap Annoni led ten MC205Vs from 4°Stormo to patrol over the Messina Straits. A mixed force identified as Spitfires, 'P-46s' and P-38s were sighted in company with two Beaufighters, and of these four Spitfires were claimed by Ten Vittorio Squarcia, Sottoten Arnando Dal Molin, Serg Alfredo Bombardini, and Serg Magg Teresio Martinoli; a fifth was claimed jointly by Cap Annoni and Sottoten Ferdinando Cima, and a sixth by Sottoten Piero Gobbato, whose aircraft was damaged in the action and crash-landed near San Ferdinando. Three of the 'P-46s' were claimed as probably destroyed, two being credited to Cap Annoni and the other to Ten Squarcia. Despite the number of claims for Spitfires, this action was apparently fought with US P-40s.

A pair of 1437 Flight Mustangs were out early in the morning over Messina, and as they dived down over the target area Flg Off Jones' aircraft (HK955/D) was holed in four places by light AA fire, but no serious damage was inflicted and he was able to continue the reconnaissance and return safely to Francesco landing ground. The odd engagement with enemy aircraft continued. Two Spitfire VIIIs of 145 Squadron were scrambled during the late morning, flown by Canadians Flt Lt W.J. Whitside (JF488) and Flg Off John Carswell (JF482), these being ordered to climb to 20,000 feet and warned of the presence of bandits in the vicinity. When ten miles north-east of Augusta, they were advised of enemy aircraft in the area and soon after four FW190s were seen at 500 feet, flying north-east. The Spitfires dived and the FW190s split into two sections, one heading north and the other eastwards. Flt Lt Whitside closed on the two going north, firing at one from 600 yards, closing to 200 yards. As he did so the other FW190 flew through his line of fire "shuddering violently before breaking away". The pilot of the first was then seen preparing to bale out, which he did but his parachute failed to open. This was evidently Obfw Ernst Rehwoldt (flying WkNr181686), who was killed.

Meanwhile, Flg Off Carswell was heard to call over the R/T that he was baling out. Later, a German pilot, Obfw Martin Claus (WkNr18093), was picked up from the sea by a rescue launch, who confirmed that he, too, had been shot down by a Spitfire, either the second victim of Whitside, or possibly Carswell's victim before he was himself presumably shot down by another. A Walrus was sent out to search for the missing pilot, the crew having been informed that he was in his dinghy off the coast, but this proved to have been the German pilot rescued by the launch.

Sqn Ldr Paul Rabone DFC RNZAF, a flight commander in 23 Squadron, who had paid a visit to Boccadifalco airfield to check its suitability for Mosquito intruder operations, having borrowed a Spitfire for the occasion, took off on the return flight to Malta at 1330, and ten minutes later encountered a twin-engine aircraft he took to be a Ju88 flying at deck level ten miles off Cape San Vito. He immediately gave chase and on closing in gave it a burst of cannon and machine-gun fire at which its port engine began to pour smoke. The fleeing aircraft weaved violently, and another burst brought return fire from top gun position. Two further short bursts caused the aircraft to stall and crash into the sea, where it sank immediately. No survivors were seen, Rabone continuing his flight to Malta where he landed at 1440[9].

There was further action next day (16 August), when four Spitfires of 92 Squadron led by Flg Off Brendan Baker (EN449) set off at 1750 as escort to US Warhawks of the 65th FS on an armed reconnaissance north of Messina; two of the Spitfires returned early, one escorting the other which had developed engine problems. Flg Off Baker and his Canadian companion Flg Off Gordon Wilson (JF354) remained with the Warhawks and, five miles south-west of Palmi, sighted five MC202s or MC205Vs which attempted to attack the American fighter-bombers. Wilson diced with three for several minutes until they dived away and were lost in the haze. Meanwhile, Baker was fighting for his life:

"Almost immediately I saw a 205 dive to attack a Warhawk. I closed on this enemy aircraft and after a chase got in bursts which sent it into a spiral dive. It crashed about two miles inland near Rosarno. Three MC205s then made a determined attack on me, one staying 500 feet above me all the time, so that I was prevented from climbing, whilst the other two made individual attacks from astern and full beam simultaneously. In one head-on attack my Spitfire was hit, whilst I was wounded in the right leg. I flicked onto the tail of a Macchi and gave it my remaining ammunition. The enemy aircraft burst into flames and disintegrated. During all this time the other two Macchis had clung to my tail, shooting away pieces from behind the cockpit and wings. The engine then threw out glycol and explosions started in the cockpit. I could do nothing but bale out. I was down to 1,000 feet and though my parachute did not open till I was at 300 feet, I landed safely in the sea, two miles off Gioia Tauro . . ." [10]

Italian records reveal that a dozen MC205Vs of 4°Stormo from Castrovillari led by Cap Mario Mecatti were involved in this action, the pilots reporting meeting 15 Spitfires – obviously mistaking the Warhawks for Spitfires – strafing targets over

---

[9] This was Sqn Ldr Rabone's fourth victory, the other three having been gained whilst flying Hurricanes in 1940; flying Mosquito intruders over Italy and later Northern Europe, he would gain a further five victories before being lost in July 1944.

[10] see Appendix V for Flg Off Baker's account of his capture and eventual release.

the Gioia Tauro plain. Four Spitfires were claimed shot down by Cap Luigi Mariotti, Sottoten Renalto Baroni, Ten Vittorino Daffara and Sottoten Fabio Clauser, the latter two also claiming probables; on returning to base, the nose of Clauser's aircraft was found to be covered in oil from his victim, which he reported crashed near the Stromboli volcano. No Macchi losses were recorded. Four Spitfires of 152 Squadron led by the new CO, newly promoted Sqn Ldr Bruce Ingram from 243 Squadron, also reported meeting enemy fighters during the day while escorting Kittyhawks to the Taormina area, where two Bf109s were attacking naval vessels. These were chased for some 35 miles before being lost in haze. While on a reconnaissance over the toe of Italy, Sqn Ldr Welshman and Flg Off R.M. McCall of 1437 Flight sighted an enemy fighter although it made no attempt to attack the Mustangs.

The German Dunkirk
Kittyhawks and US Warhawks continued fighter-bomber attacks on shipping in the Messina Straits, claiming direct hits on two Siebel ferries, one barge and one E-boat, all in the north end of the Straits. An increased number of enemy fighters, mostly MC202s, was sighted but no combats resulted. Despite the relentless assault, the vast majority of Axis ground forces were able to evacuate safely to the mainland, the last German troops embarking on the night of 16th/17th, abandoning their Italian allies and a great quantity of undestroyed material and supplies; of the 122,204 Axis troops taken prisoner, about 118,700 were Italian, while approximately 5,000 Germans had been killed (plus some 19,000 wounded, most of whom were evacuated; about 2,000 Italians (excluding civilians) had also been killed and an estimated further 5,000 wounded . The German evacuation had been accomplished in four different phases, the first having begun almost immediately after the invasion had commenced, with the removal of all non-essential units and their equipment; the second commenced soon after the American offensive in the Palermo area, when valuable radar apparatus was successfully removed to the mainland; the third began at the beginning of August when over 3,000 vehicles and almost 6,000 tons of equipment, ammunition and fuel, in addition to 13,000 troops, of whom a third were casualties, were carried across the Straits, while, during the period 11-16 August, almost 26,000 troops (plus 1,240 casualties), over 5,000 vehicles and 48 tanks got away. There would be recriminations on the Allied side when the success of the German evacuation was fully realised. General blamed general, the air force blamed the navy, the navy blamed the air force, the Americans blamed the British, and the British blamed the Americans – which left General Bogislaw von Bonin, XIV Panzer Korps' Chief-of-Staff, to comment:

> "In the following days we could hardly understand that the operation had been
> such a complete success. There had been so many chances against us." [11]

General Heinrich von Vietinghoff, commander of the German 15th Army, added:

> "From the German standpoint it is incomprehensible that the Allies did not
> seize the Straits of Messina, either at the same time as the landing [on 10
> July] or in the course of the initial actions, just as soon as the German troops
> were contained. On both sides of the Straits this would have been possible

---

[11] British losses including Canadians, RN and RAF and Commonwealth Air Forces personnel were approximately 5,500 killed and missing, with a further 7,500 wounded; American losses were almost 3,400 killed or captured including those of the USAAF and USN, plus about 6,500 wounded.

without any special difficulty." [12]

To General Montgomery it was obvious where the blame for the fiasco rested; he had earlier noted:

> "There has been heavy traffic all day across the Straits of Messina, and the enemy is without doubt starting to get his stuff away. I have tried to find out what the combined Navy-Air plan is in order to stop him getting away; I have been unable to find out. I fear the truth of the matter is that there is no plan. I cannot stop it myself. The trouble is there is no high-up grip on this campaign. Cunningham is in Malta; Tedder in Tunis; Alexander is at Syracuse. It beats me how anyone thinks you can run a campaign in that way, with the three Commanders of the three Services about 600 miles from each other. The enemy should never be allowed to get all his equipment out of Sicily, and we should round up the bulk of his fighting troops. It would clearly be impossible to stop him getting his key personnel away. But the rest we should stop . . ." [13]

With the fall of Messina and the effective end of fighting in Sicily, attention was turned to the Italian mainland, and specifically the other side of the Messina Straits. Canadian war correspondent Lionel Shapiro wrote:

> "American troops streamed into Messina from the west, followed closely by British troops pushing up from the south. The conquest of the island was complete. In the sleepy upper town of Taormina, an aged native trudged into the main square, carefully selected two sheets from a roll of paper under his arm, and slapped these on the town's official notice board. One was a picture of President Roosevelt, the other of Prime Minister Churchill."

An afternoon reconnaissance of the mountain roads in the toe of Italy was undertaken by a pair of 1437 Flight Mustangs flown by Flg Off Griffith (HK947/A) and Flg Off W.H. Gilliland (HK956/E) on 17 August, and after reconnoitring some of the roads the pilots found themselves over the east coast where they sighted what they took to be half a dozen Bf109s flying below the altitude. Diving on the leading aircraft, Griffith opened fire and shot it down into the sea. Continuing along the coast, Griffith and his companion carried out a low-level strafe of M/T but his aircraft was hit by 20mm flak. With flames coming from his engine, Griffith was just able to climb to 800 feet over the sea and bale out about 100 yards offshore from Cape Bruzzano. Having observed his leader climb into his dinghy, Gilliland radioed his position and within 30 minutes a Walrus – X9506 of 284 Squadron flown by Wt Off K.G. Hall and Flt Sgt J.R. Berry RNZAF – had alighted nearby and plucked Griffith from the sea. Also on board the Walrus was the pilot of the 'Messerschmitt' Griffith had shot down – Flt Lt Norm Lee of 43 Squadron! Lee had been leading a flight of Spitfires escorting the Walrus searching for another downed airman five miles north-east of Cape Spartivento, when the Mustangs attacked. With the engine of his aircraft (BR290) disabled, Lee had no choice but to bale out, the Walrus quickly coming to his aid. There is no record of the two rescued pilots' initial greeting – but presumably Griffith bought

---

[12] see *Bitter Victory*.
[13] see *Monty: Master of the Battlefield 1942-1944*.

Lee at least a couple of pints of beer on their return to Cassibile. While most of the fighter-bomber and bomber escorts failed to sight enemy fighters during this period, on the occasions when the Messerschmitts did put in an appearance, specially when in the hands of the Luftwaffe's few remaining *Experten*, it often proved a costly experience for the unwary, as B Flight of 243 Squadron found when escorting Kittyhawks east of Palmi on 18 August. The escort leader, Flt Lt Eddie Gruwys, later recalled:

"After the first attack, my section had broken and I became separated from it but not before I had seen a Spitfire going down in flames [this was JK642 flown by Sgt Roland Jaques, who was killed] at about 12,000 feet, and two other Spitfires still breaking. [I was then] attacked from below and astern, which severely damaged my aircraft [JK189]. Most of the controls were shot away, the tail unit damaged, the port and starboard mainplanes holed, parts of the elevator were missing, the port flap hanging in pieces, the radio was dead, and only the engine appeared untouched. The machine was almost beyond control. At first I decided to try a forced-landing to save the engine. When I realised the futility of this, I undid my straps and prepared to bale out. The hood refused to jettison, and I found it impossible to re-fasten my straps. After climbing from 3,000 feet to 5,000 feet and making for Lentini, I eventually forced off the hood after several attempts, whilst holding the stick between my knees. The hood struck the tail unit, rolling the aircraft on its back and my feet caught under the instrument panel. I hung suspended for a time until managing to kick myself free. I felt for the rip-cord [but] the parachute had slipped round my body. I dropped about 1,500 feet before I could pull the cord, when the parachute opened immediately. I now found it necessary to control the chute to avoid high-tension cables and eventually landed in a cactus grove, luckily in an open space. During the descent I saw my own aircraft crash in a vineyard and burst into flames."

Having survived his ordeal, Flt Lt Gruwys was taken to the nearest airfield and was flown back to Pachino aboard a Whitley transport two days later. He believed his assailant had been a FW190 but, although FW190s may well have been in the area, it seems probable that he and Sgt Jaques were shot down by a Messerschmitt flown by Lt Ernst-Wilhelm Reinert of 4/JG77, thereby raising his tally to 162; Reinert's recognition was also at fault since he believed his victims were P-40s, as did his companion, Lt Roth of Stab, who claimed a P-40 probably destroyed in this action.

Following an inspection of airfields in Sicily, it was established that at least 280 Bf109s, 70 FW190s, 80 Ju88s, 29 Me210s, 14 Bf110s, and one HS129 had been abandoned by the Luftwaffe, and 100 MC202s, 85 MC200s, 44 SM79s and eight Ju87s by the Regia Aeronautica – over 600 aircraft denied to the Axis, in addition to the estimated 740 believed to have been shot down by Allied fighters and AA fire between 1 July and 17 August. Approximately half this number of Allied aircraft had been lost during the same period. With a reduction in air combat patrols, many of the pilots were able to relax and explore their surroundings, as recalled by Flg Off Lloyd Hunt of 93 Squadron:

". . . an old Lancia diesel truck [had been] liberated at Pachino. It was a vehicle of perpetual motion because there were several barrels of diesel fuel in the back. It had a Harvard-type inertia starting mechanism which was wound up with a crank. A lever engaged the engine and it would roar into life. It had hard rubber tyres, and the passengers in the back were in for a very rough ride. Mayors in the towns and villages of Sicily had forced the citizens to deposit all their firearms in the town squares, and these were hastily picked up by the truck load of well-oiled pilots in their noisy chariot. I can remember recoiling in terror as someone drunkenly clambered aboard the truck by climbing over the side railings, a gun in his hand on the top rail pointed directly at my stomach!" [14]

Among aircraft captured at Lentini East was an intact Klemm 35 (5M-U) which a number of pilots enjoyed flying, including those of 242 Squadron, Flg Offs Coulthard and Lowther having undertaken the initial 'test flight'. At about the same time, Flg Off Milt Jowsey and Plt Off Rex Probert, two of 92 Squadron's Canadians, having been through the Tunisian campaign, were now informed that they were amongst those tour-expired and would shortly be returning to Cairo for posting; Probert recalled:

"Upon receiving this news, we decided to take a flip in our recently captured Italian biplane [in fact this was an Arado 66C] over the battlefield in the hopes of getting a few pictures. Everything was 100 per cent for some time until we decided to get our pictures from lower level. In the manoeuvring we got crossed up in our communications, which were visual and barely audible as we had no radio. Our aircraft went into a shallow, slow, turning dive, at which we both thought the other chap was flying it, and it wasn't until the last moment, just as the lower wing touched the dirt, that Milt gave a quick jerk on the control column and pulled the aircraft up, with only minor damage to the lower wing. Had he not done so, in all probability, we both would have been killed. That did it – there were no more plane trips, only parties until we got back to the sanctity of Cairo." [15]

He also had an amusing story to tell about his flight commander, Flt Lt Tony Bruce:

"Tony loved all animals, large or small, and it did not matter to him whether they crawled or walked. One day, in Sicily, where the Squadron was camped in a cotton field, we found that friend Tony was the proud owner of three very large snakes; all, I am told, were poisonous. It wasn't unusual for Tony to arrive in the Mess tent with at least one of these snakes draped around his neck as he presented himself for an evening beer or two. Naturally, this was much to the chagrin of the other Mess members, who, as a rule and, of course, under protest, quickly evacuated the Mess. On investigation, we discovered that these snakes, when not being carried around by Tony, were kept in a cardboard box, and not too big a box, at that. One afternoon Tony arrived in the Mess in a rage, demanding to know who had let his snakes out. Of course, no one knew, as everyone stayed as far away from the snake-box as possible. Now, there were three big snakes on the loose in the area, and nobody knew where they were. I can assure you that when we went to bed at night we all checked our sleeping bags with a flash-light before retiring – drunk or sober!

About two days later, while on a sweep, one of the Spitfires in the formation began to act strangely. It was dipsy-doodling all over the sky;

nipping in and out of formation, while at the same time neglecting to answer our calls. We thought, at first, he was being attacked by someone we couldn't see, but after some time, he returned to the formation and we all completed the sweep. Naturally, when we landed, we all went over to Jocko, an Aussie, and quizzed him about his strange behaviour. It was then that we discovered where one of Tony's snakes was – in Jocko's cockpit, stabbed through the head. It had emerged from under the instrument panel when Jocko had gone through 10,000 feet during the climb. Apparently, the snake was beginning to suffer from lack of oxygen. Unhappily, someone on the ground had left the coop-top open during the night and, I suppose, the snake crept into the cockpit to get warm. When it emerged there was a fight between Jocko and the snake. Fortunately, Jocko won; had it been some other pilot on the Squadron, the Allies might have lost a Spitfire. Many of us, under those circumstances, would have baled out, preferring to take our chances with the Italians. Such was life with Tony Bruce on the Squadron." [16]

Shortly thereafter, Flt Lt Bruce were posted to 417RCAF Squadron as a flight commander, where he joined a recently arrived ex-Malta veteran Plt Off Garth Horricks DFM, a Canadian on his second tour of operations who had flown Hurricanes from Malta in 1942 and had been credited with seven victories (two shared). Another new Canadian arrival in Sicily was Flg Off Hap Kennedy DFC, who joined 111 Squadron at Lentini having completed his tour with 249 Squadron at Malta; he remembered:

"The Sicilians were genuinely friendly, gave us wine and sold us large, brown fresh eggs. We [he and a fellow Canadian] hadn't seen fresh eggs since leaving Canada, and on our first opportunity bought a dozen each. The kind lady cooked them for us at once in a heavy iron frying pan. Four of us each ate a dozen eggs, absolutely the best eggs I have ever tasted." [17]

On 20 August it was the turn of one of Malta's resident Spitfire squadrons to see some action when Sqn Ldr MacDougall (JK333) led three others from 185 Squadron on an offensive sweep during the afternoon, the Spitfires having first refuelled in Sicily. Airborne again at 1535, they encountered a Z506B an hour later, flying at 1,000 feet some 20 miles south-west of Capri flying at 1,000 feet, and jointly shot it down into the sea, MacDougall sharing the unfortunate seaplane with Flt Lt Wilmot (JK521), Flg Off S.V. Baxter RAAF (EE865), and Plt Off W.E. Dunsmore RCAF (LZ809). No survivors were seen as the seaplane sank out of sight. The Squadron diarist noted:

"Four of A Flight went on an offensive stooge north of Sicily and managed to shoot down a Cant 506 off Capri. Some fun and very encouraging after this long period of practice."

With the stepping up of bomber and fighter-bomber operations over south-western Italy, the Spitfire units found themselves ever-more preoccupied with providing protection against enemy fighters which were being encountered in ever-increasing numbers, although fighter versus fighter engagements were infrequent at this time.

---

[16] see *We Happy Few* .
[17] see *Black Crosses off my Wingtip*.

On 21 August, eight Spitfires Vs of 92 Squadron flew as close escort to a Kittybomber formation, while six VIIIs of 145 Squadron flew as top cover, these being led by Wg Cdrs Duncan Smith and Warburton, the latter as keen as ever to get into combat. However, on this occasion, no enemy aircraft were encountered. Later, 417RCAF Squadron, with four VIIIs from 1SAAF as top cover, escorted another Kittyhawk formation which bombed targets at Paetti on the toe of the mainland. One Kittyhawk was shot down by AA fire and a Spitfire flown by Flg Off L.A. Hall RCAF from the Canadian unit was also hit. The pilot managed to nurse his damaged aircraft (EE663) as far as Riposto before he was obliged to bale out, and was rescued from the sea by a rowing boat. Next day saw the arrival of another Spitfire squadron in Sicily when 2SAAF led by Maj Tom Murray, which had only recently converted from Kittyhawks, landed at Pachino, as noted by Lt Barry Keyter:

> "I was flying a Spit IX and we followed a 3 Wing Boston to Pachino . . . the landing strip was in a terrible mess; it was like landing on a Free State mealie-field. However, the next afternoon we did a patrol over the Straits of Messina at 18,000 feet and although we were above cloud we could see the snout of Mount Etna, with an impressive pillar of black smoke sprouting from it. On the downwind leg before landing on our 'mealie-field' I could not get my landing gear down and had to use the emergency system, but bounced my Spit quite safely at the end of the strip." [18]

A lone Ju88 – 4U+DH of 1(F)/123 – set out from Frosinone at about 0630 on the morning of 22 August, with Knights Cross holder Uffz Heinz Krösing at the controls, he and his crew briefed to carry out a photo-reconnaissance of naval units in Malta's harbours and Allied shipping in Sicilian waters. On this occasion the aircraft carried no bombs and no rear gunner. Defence against fighter attack was provided by a machine-gun firing to the rear from the W/Op's position. The pilot set course over the toe of Italy to a point about 100 miles east-north-east of Malta and then turned west-south-west on a direct course to Grand Harbour. The aircraft climbed to 32,000 feet but its speed was no more than 200mph due to strong headwind. This allowed four Spitfire IXs of 249 Squadron to be scrambled to a correctly estimated height in good time, and these passed to the north of the approaching Ju88 before turning back on a reciprocal course. Time was running out for the German crew and, as the Junkers approached to within eight miles north of Grand Harbour at about 0830, the Spitfires closed in, as Krösing later recalled:

> "I was becoming aware of the presence of four fighters and a hurried oblique photograph of the Grand Harbour and coastline was taken. I then headed due west and then north in a wide sweep . . ."

One of the Spitfires, MA500/T-Z flown by Flt Lt Ken. Debenham, closed in from astern and below, as noted by Uffz Günther Lehmann, the W/Op:

> ". . . his first burst broke the pilot's arm and wounded him in the legs. The lower gun position and the boost lever were destroyed. The attack from underneath was sudden and unexpected. I was momentarily unsighted and no evasive action could be taken. The Observer officer (Lt Günther Wissel, a double Knights Cross recipient) ordered the crew to bale out .. ."

---

[18] see *From Wings to Jackboots* by Barry Keyter.

The Spitfires orbited the survivors until relieved by a section from 229 Squadron, which covered the rescue launch from Malta. All three airmen were rescued from the sea an hour later, the wounded pilot and W/Op being admitted to hospital.

The American ASR unit, the 1st Emergency Rescue Squadron, lost one of its OA-10s on 23 August when it fell victim to Oblt Franz Schiess of 8/JG53 for his 61st victory; survivors were later themselves rescued. A few days earlier one of the OA-10s had rescued 20 airmen from two downed B-17s south-west of Sardinia, and sometime later, another OA-10 alighted to pick up an injured Italian airman but came under fire from shore guns, and was then strafed three times by an Italian aircraft identified as a MC200 and set on fire. The flying boat's air gunner was killed and the rescued Italian pilot died of his injuries, although the remainder of the crew were rescued from their dinghy four hours later by a launch. By the end of August the 1st Emergency Rescue Squadron had rescued 40 Allied and five Axis airmen.

The inevitable spate of accidents continued as more and more Spitfires arrived in Sicily to operate from the various airstrips, many of which required urgent repair work. 417RCAF suffered another accident when EP957 overshot when landing at Lentini West, the aircraft overturning but without injuring the pilot, Plt Off S.A. Corbott RCAF. EP305 of newly arrived 2SAAF was written off when its engine caught fire on take-off from Lentini. 40SAAF Squadron lost another Spitfire on 24 August when ER482 ran out of fuel and force-landed on the island, Lt N.P. Prinsloo SAAF sustaining only slight injuries, as did Lt Johannes Kruger SAAF when he force-landed JK386 on a beach near Giarre next day. There occurred a rather bizarre incident concerning another 40SAAF machine, as remembered by Wg Cdr Duncan Smith:

"The grass runway area [at Gerbini] was extremely rough, so I ordered that aircraft taxying onto the runway were to carry an airman on the tail of each aircraft to insure against the pilot tipping up on his nose, and wrecking the propeller.

As the leading aircraft approached down the runway I noticed a peculiar bulge on the tail. It flashed past and the bulge turned into the shocked face of an airman peering down at me, his arms entwined across the sternpost of the Spitfire and with his legs gripping the leading edge of the tailplane. Already the wheels were up and the nose of the aircraft pointed heaven-wards. The South African pilot, having taxied onto the runway, had opened his throttle and taken off at once. He quite forgot about the wretched man sitting on his tail. My pilots came out to watch the fun, offering useless advice and taking bets as to whether the airman would fall or whether we would witness a nice, messy landing. Strange to relate, neither happened. The South African pilot [Lt E.G. Iles] flew his aircraft skilfully in for a landing. He had seen the man on his tail reflected in his rear-view mirror above his head as soon as he found the trim of his aircraft was haywire; being forewarned he was in a position to use caution tempered with skill. The Spitfire made a perfect three-point landing.

By the time I got to the startled airman [Air Mechanic Carter], now standing foolishly on the runway, the Spitfire had taken off again. His face had gone a peculiar greeny-yellow and his eyes stared into space. The next moment he pitched forward onto his arms and face in a dead faint. Half an hour later he was as good as new again, having had half a pint of tea and rum rammed down his throat." [19]

---

[19] see *Spitfire into Battle*.

Another Spitfire was written off coming into land at Lentini East when the pilot of ER533 of 1435 Squadron misjudged his approach and undershot; he survived unhurt. A second Spitfire was lost at Lentini East when one of the newly supplied 1437 Flight machines, ER532 flown by Sgt P.L. White, came into land, it clipped a wing and somersaulted six times and then burst into flames. Two airmen of 81 Squadron rushed over to the blazing machine and pulled the severely burned pilot from the wreck, thereby saving his life. Despite his injuries, Sgt White was more fortunate than a pilot from 244 Wing, as recalled by Grp Capt Kingcome:

> " . . . one of my Spitfire pilots crashed just inside the British lines after being shot up on a sweep over the island. He survived the crash but was trapped in the cockpit of his aircraft, which then caught fire. A group of soldiers did their best to free him until they were driven back by the flames, and the pilot, powerless to escape the agonising death he saw roaring implacably towards him, implored them to shoot him. Faced with the alternative of turning their backs and leaving him to burn, one finally levelled his rifle and fired. It was a horrible responsibility and an act of supreme moral courage. Even for a battle-hardened soldier inured to killing it must have left a lasting scar. It was also a tragic end for a promising pilot . . ." [20]

Another tragic incident occurred on 27 August when two US Spitfires of the 2nd FS flown by 1/Lt David W. Macmillan and 2/Lt John E. Fawcett were scrambled to investigate an unidentified aircraft over the Gulf of Castellamare, as recollected by the latter:

> "It was perhaps 11 o'clock in the morning when the white flare was fired from in front of the operations tent, and the readiness section pilots took off. As soon as we were airborne, Macmillan contacted the GCI Controller. We were given a vector that headed us west toward the Gulf of Castellamare. The Controller then told us he had a bandit heading north at high speed and that we would have a stern chase. Within the next five minutes he gave us two vector changes, each requiring about 20 or 30 degree turns to the right – toward the north. Within a matter of minutes the Controller called again, saying the bandit was straight ahead of us at a distance of about five miles, and that he appeared to be in a shallow dive. Mac and I sighted the bandit at the same time. Mac called the Controller that we were closing on it. We were running 'balls out' and in a shallow dive because the other aircraft was somewhat lower that we were. It was a twin-engine aircraft with a single vertical tailplane and going very fast. I was certain it was a Ju88.
>
> I believe the interception was made at about 10,000 feet, about 40-50 miles due north of Cape San Vito [and about 20 miles west of the island of Ustica]. As we got in close it was obvious that we were overhauling the aircraft quite rapidly. I was about 100 yards behind Mac, just to the right of his slipstream, and a bit above him. Mac got in very close before he fired – 50 to 75 yards, I would guess. I saw him fire, and immediately there was a great flash of orange flame and black smoke from the starboard engine of the target aircraft. Mac broke off by making a sharp turn to the right, and up. By then I was in the right position to fire, and very close, so it seemed. I fired about a two-second burst and broke right and up also. Then

---

[20] see *A Willingness to Die*.

I immediately lowered the left wing, to see the target – and there, perfectly clear, were the dull blue and red of British roundels on the target aircraft's wings. I immediately identified it as a Beaufighter." [21]

The Beaufighter was V8187 of the RDF Calibration Flight crewed by Flt Sgts Bob Waddell and Frank Noonan, both RAAF, and both natives of New South Wales, on detachment from 255 Squadron. Their task was to test the location and alertness of enemy radars along the western coastline of mainland Italy. Fawcett continued:

"Then Mac called, saying 'Johnnie, its a Beaufighter, its a Beaufighter.' And very quickly a British [sic] voice, calling his base or the Controller and saying, 'I'm being attacked by Spitfires, they've killed my observer and I've lost an engine. I'm heading back.' The Beaufighter was losing altitude as it headed back toward the middle of the Gulf of Castellamare and the right engine was smoking. I was overcome with shame and rage, and a feeling of helplessness; of wishing that I could reach out to hold the Beaufighter in the air. I think the pilot was trying to stretch his flight back to the island where he might find some open ground to make a belly landing. As we got to the middle of the Gulf it was obvious that the land all round the Gulf was high and very rugged, with no place for an emergency landing. The shoreline had no sandy beach, but was all strewn with boulders and fallen rock.
   When we were about two or three miles from the south shore of the Gulf, the Beaufighter was down to about 1,500 or 1,000 feet. He began a standard-rate turn to the right, into his dead engine. I think the pilot had decided that he would ditch in the water about a mile offshore and two or three miles south of Cape San Vito. Mac and I were weaving behind him and about 1,000 feet above. He was just straightening out of the turn, about 50 feet above the water, when his right wing dropped straight down, touched the water, and the aircraft cartwheeled into the sea in a great splash of foam and white water. We circled the area, line astern, for about five minutes looking for any signs of wreckage. Mac reported the circumstances to the Controller, who told us to return to base, which we did." [22]

Fawcett added:

"The mood around the Squadron was rather subdued for the next few days, and somewhat difficult for Mac and I. We continued to fly for the next six days, during which time I flew three more missions. Then we were told we had been taken off flying status and were to report to Lt Col Coward at Group right away. Mac and I felt crushed, beaten and humiliated. All I wanted to do was to go out and shoot myself, as an abject failure." [23]

The two unfortunate pilots were sent to USAAF 12th Air Force HQ in Algiers where they met, among others, Wg Cdr J.H. Player DFC, the CO of 255 Squadron:

"He showed great sensibility about our unhappiness and our feelings of guilt, which were verging on suicidal. He told us that these unfortunate things do happen and that we shouldn't let it throw us: the war went on and we were needed." [24]

[21/22/23/24] see *The American Beagle Squadron* by Lawrence G. Burke and Robert C. Curtis.

Following a requested interview with General Elwood R. Quesada, the Commanding General of the 12th Air Force, they were sent on an aircraft recognition course before being reassigned to the 31st Fighter Group.

Yet another reconnaissance Ju88 was lost to Malta's Spitfires during the afternoon of 27 August, when 4U+1H of 1(F)/123 flown by Fw Schwarz was intercepted 20 miles east of Kalafrana by 249 Squadron. The crew had already secured their photographs and the aircraft was on its return flight when the four IXs engaged. Flt Sgt A.R. Lifford was the first to sight the Junkers some 2,000 feet below, then the section leader, Flg Off Ken MacBain RCAF (EN256/T-B), yelled "Tally ho!" and dived to attack. The German machine dived away with MacBain following closely and, after three short bursts, both engines caught fire. The members of the crew were seen to bale out as it spiralled down to crash into the sea. Although Flt Sgt Lifford and Plt Off J.O. Gray RCAF also attacked and both reported strikes, the destruction of the Ju88 was credited to MacBain. The fourth member of the section had become separated and took no part in the action. Fw Schwarz was apparently lost with his aircraft, but the observer, Lt Karl-Otto Kluszmann, and the W/Op, Uffz Alfred Höpfner, were rescued from the sea, both slightly wounded.

During the late morning of 28 August, several groups of bombers each set out with their Spitfire escorts to attack various targets. Grp Capt Hugo led eight from 232 Squadron covering Mitchells which bombed the marshalling yards north-west of Lamezia, while eight from 81 Squadron, plus a further four from 232 Squadron swept the skies to the south-east of the bomber formation. A few Messerschmitts put in an appearance but no combats ensued. At about the same time, eight Spitfires of 152 Squadron provided escort to Baltimores which attacked the railway system north-west of Lamezia. Again Messerschmitts were seen but there were no engagements until six from I/JG53 attempted to bounce a dozen Bostons over the Gulf of Euphemia, these being escorted by eight Spitfires of 81 Squadron led by 322 Wing's new leader, Lt Colonel Laurie Wilmot DFC SAAF. The Messerschmitts were led by Obfw Rudolf Täschner, a 20-victory ace, who attempted to attack the bombers from height, accompanied by his wingman Uffz Rudi Kahlau. Another of the German pilots, Uffz Helmet Beck later reported that he saw two Spitfires climb to engage and that the other two members of the *Schwarm* executed a steep reversal to get behind the Spitfires, but he then lost sight of them. Both Täschner in White 4 (WkNr15222) and Kahlau in White 1 (WkNr18685) failed to return. Lt Col Wilmot (MA408) claimed one shot down for his fifth victory (one shared), Sgt Jim Robinson (MA402/FL-B) claiming two more, while Flt Sgt Alan Peart, another New Zealander (EN513/FL-J) claimed a fourth. Two Spitfires were hit, Plt Off H.M. Baker-Munson being obliged to crash-land JK373, although he survived unhurt. Another Messerschmitt was claimed late in the day when American Spitfire pilot 2/Lt Robert W. Hine of the 5th FS reported shooting down a Bf109G south of Naples. The identity and unit of his victim is unknown.

Up early on the morning of 29 August, Wg Cdr Duncan Smith decided to fly a dawn patrol between Augusta and Catania in an attempt to intercept FW190s which had been making early morning raids on shipping in the harbours. Taking off from the advance airstrip at Cassibile at 0605 in MA281, he was accompanied by Plt Off W.J. Steele (JP457) of 417RCAF Squadron. When at 16,000 feet they were informed that ten FW190s – aircraft from III/SKG10 – were approaching Catania from the south, and two formations of four fighter-bombers we soon observed flying in a south-westerly direction some 3,000 feet above. As the two Spitfires climbed to engage, the enemy aircraft rolled over and dived into cloud.

Wg Cdr Duncan Smith chased one and gave it a burst from long range:

> "Opening up to full power, I chased after the enemy and was immediately shot at by a second FW190, which dived in over my left shoulder. Tracers streaked past my port wing, and it shot past very close. The pilot unwisely straightened up giving me an excellent opportunity to open fire on him from slightly below on a fine quarter. I saw strikes on his wing root and the bottom of the cockpit, and with smoke trailing he disappeared into a thick cloud. We searched round the cloud then spiralled down below and had a look, but there was no sign of him." [25]

Meanwhile, Plt Off Steele had closed on another and followed it into cloud, firing two deflection bursts at extreme range, following which the FW190 dived to deck level and escaped. On returning to Lentini, Wg Cdr Duncan Smith was informed that two FW190s were down in the sea and that the pilot of one of them had been picked up by a rescue launch. This information was inaccurate, since only one FW190 failed to return, Lt Bruno Schäfer[26] of 9 Staffel being rescued from the sea and was clearly Duncan Smith's victim, his 17th victory of which two had been shared. Sometime later in the day, Wg Cdr Duncan Smith was scrambled when warned of the approach of a number of bombers, reported 15 miles north of Augusta, but these turned out to be Kittyhawks which were being fired on by Allied AA. He continued his patrol and shortly thereafter was ordered to engage 'enemy aircraft' in the same general area – which turned out to be a flight of American A-36As. However, another success was achieved by US Spitfires when 1/Lt Edwin J. Odom of the 5th FS reported shooting down a German twin-engine reconnaissance aircraft off the island of Ustica. This was possibly a Me410 of 2(F)/122 which crash-landed at Grottaglie, killing both members of the crew including Lt Heinrich Denker.

A patrol of Spitfires from 152 Squadron also had an engagement with enemy fighters, apparently Bf109Gs of 3/JG53, when flying near Pizzo. Two Messerschmitts were seen, the Spitfires pursuing them, Sqn Ldr Ingram and Flg Off Norman Jones each getting in long range bursts at one without observing any tangible results, while Sgt Len Smith fired at the second. As he did so, he saw his No2, Flt Sgt W.D. Sparkes (JK125) dive into the sea, apparently the victim of Uffz Bartel who claimed a Spitfire shot down. 682 Squadron lost its Commanding Officer, Wg Cdr Pat Ogilvie DSO DFC, during the morning when his aircraft EN427 failed to return from a sortie to Genoa. However, he managed to bale out safely and evaded capture. 682 Squadron lost another Spitfire (EN660) next day when Flg Off Stuart Woodhouse failed to return from a sortie to Foggia; he did not survive. As the month drew to an end, 43 Squadron suffered another loss when providing escort for a cruiser carrying out a bombardment off the Italian coast. A Ju88 was reported approaching at 33,000 feet and Flg Off Anthony Snell, who was leading the top cover, was vectored to intercept, but as the Spitfires climbed Snell's aircraft (MA572/FT-9) suddenly fell away into a dive and crashed into the sea, the pilot apparently the victim of oxygen failure. Two of the last sorties flown from Sicily on the last day of the month were undertaken by the dynamic AOC WDAF, Air Vice-Marshal Harry Broadhurst, and his deputy, Air Commodore C.B.R. Pelly

---

[25] see *Spitfire into Battle*.

[26] Lt Bruno Schäfer had shot down a Spitfire of 229 Squadron on 5 July 1943, shortly before the start of the invasion.

MC (won during WWI), when they borrowed two Spitfires (JF330 and ER848) from 145 Squadron at Lentini West, and set out for the Messina area to observe for themselves the state of play. They returned safely after 90 minutes, much to the relief of members of their HQ staff.

British and American troops now prepared themselves for the next move – across the Messina Straits to mainland Italy. Of this exciting and historic period, war correspondent Alan Moorehead later wrote:

> "The truth was that we were very tired. We were suspended in the very middle of the war at a point where we could neither remember the beginning nor see the end. Only lately, in the past year, had we grown used to advancing. Alamein, Tripoli, Tunis, Sicily. All victories, but the war seemed endless. No matter how far you advanced – a thousand, two thousand miles – there was always the enemy in front of you, always another thousand miles to go." [27]

The battle for Sicily had been won – the battle for Italy was about to begin.

---

[27] see *Eclipse* by Alan Moorehead.

A POTTED HISTORY OF GCII/7

1940-1945

GCII/7 had operated in the defence of France during the early days of WWII, when it flew D.520s, and between 3 September 1939 and 24 June 1940, when France capitulated, it was credited with about 50 victories for the loss of eight pilots killed and a dozen wounded. During the Vichy years, GCII/7 was based in North Africa and on occasion challenged RAF aircraft en route to the Middle East, at least one Blenheim falling to its pilots.

Following the Allied invasion of North-West Africa at the end of 1942, the reformed GCII/7, then based at Bou Saada airfield in Algeria under the command of Cmdt Adam, received it first Spitfire Vs from the British in March 1943. Initially 19 aircraft were received and two flights formed, a third (training) flight following when sufficient Spitfires and a few D.520s were made available. However, GCII/7 was not a unit the Allied Command felt it could entirely trust, since the majority of its pilots were pro-Vichy and some had fought against the Allies. Nonetheless, on 24 April 1943, GCII/7 moved to one of the newly captured Tunisian satellite airfields at Souk el-Khemis, where it was temporarily attached to the RAF's 324 Wing commanded by Wg Cdr G.K. Gilroy DSO DFC, apparently being renumbered 271 Squadron until it was realised that this number had already been allotted to one of the RAF's transport squadrons. Having reverted to its French nomenclature, GCII/7 flew its first operational mission on 7 May 1943 when it strafed three Me323s, a Bf109 and a FW190 at La Sebala airfield, and destroyed a number of MTBs seen near La Goulette harbour. Next day the French Spitfires attacked 14 Bf109s and MC202s at Korba airfield, destroying a number of these also. On 19 May it moved to Protville and became part of the RAF's 245 Coastal Wing, later in the month moving to Sidi Ahmed from where, on 11 June 1943, it flew to the forward airfield at Utique Bay for operations over Pantelleria.

On 6 August GCII/7, now under the command of Cmdt Papin, joined forces with the newly reformed, Spitfire-equipped GCI/3 at Bìne-les-Salines airfield in readiness for the invasion of Corsica, during which its pilots claimed several German aircraft shot down culminating in an action on 30 September when ten Do217s from KG100 equipped with Hs293 guided bombs, accompanied by a single Ju88, were intercepted by the French Spitfires. Four of the Dorniers plus the Ju88 were claimed shot down, with one probable and two damaged. In fact two of the Dorniers were lost and a third was damaged but it was able to land back at Istres. By the end of the month GCII/7 had flown 407 sorties in 19 days.

On 3 October 1943, GCII/7, with GCI/3, became part of the 1st Escadre of the Mediterranean Coastal Air Force, and was integrated into the RAF's 322 Wing. Now equipped with Spitfire Vs and IXs, it moved to Ajaccio in Corsica. On 1 December 1943 it was again renumbered and became 326 Squadron of the RAF. Bomber escorts and convoy patrols were its main duties with only the occasional opportunity for aerial combat, FW190s being claimed on 4 May and 14 June 1944. Armed with bombs, fighter-bomber sorties were undertaken against shipping and rail targets until September when it moved to southern France, where most of its time was spent on patrols and sweeps, flying bomber escorts and occasionally escorting spotter aircraft. Four more victories were claimed in October, with a further three in February 1945, two in March, and its final victories, two FW190s and two Bf109s, being claimed on 14 April 1945. By the time 326 Squadron was disbanded in November 1945, its CO was Capitaine Gabriel Gauthier, who had commanded one of the escadrilles when GCII/7 had reformed in March 1943.

MY FIRST DAY IN SICILY

Flg Off Gordon Wilson RCAF, 92 Squadron

Having force-landed his Spitfire near Pachino on 13 July 1943, Gordon Wilson later recalled his adventures:

"The field I picked looked fair, although it had irrigation ditches on two sides and a ploughed field at the end. It looked good enough. My confidence soared, so I put the wheels down and dropped to a perfect landing over the irrigation ditch and let it roll and roll and roll. Just before it came to a stop, I hit the ploughed field – just enough to put it on its nose – only a damaged prop. Finally, I climbed out, down the side, and to my horror saw about 30 people running toward me. I had landed a short distance from a Sicilian villa. Naturally, you think the worst. However, one man came up to me and offered me a drink of wine. I was suspicious and thought it was poisoned, but he laughed, took a drink and handed it over to me to drink, which I did. He said Mussolini was bad – King of Italy was good. I was on show all day.

It turned out these were Sicilians who had lived in the USA before the war, but at Mussolini's request came back to Sicily and were farming in a malaria-infested part of Sicily. They spoke fair English and were friendly and helpful. Naturally, I wanted to guard the Spitfire, so I asked a young man to get help from the British Army. The thought of retreating Italian or German soldiers never entered my mind. This young Sicilian was away for several hours, then came back, shrugged his shoulders, and said he couldn't find any help. My situation suddenly became serious, so I had him lead and show me the way to the Allies. After an hour's walk we came upon the Calgary Tanks [part of the 1st Canadian Division] coming forward but not prepared to stop. Finally, I was able to stop a jeep which took me to the Tanks' headquarters. I was given an MP escort and we made our way back to the Spitfire, still up on its nose. It was agreed with the MPs that we would take turns guarding the plane during the night. They cheated by letting me sleep all night as I was exhausted; I needed and appreciated it. I also gained a new respect for MPs.

The next morning a jeep took me and my parachute to a road junction and I was told to hitch a ride to Pachino. There was an American GI at this road junction who was also going back with a set of 'nerves'. His talk almost had me windy. He was sure that we could never stay in Sicily. However, a truck came along and I found my way to Pachino. I was in for a real shock; I had been away for over 18 hours with a Spitfire IX – and no one had missed me, including ground crew and other clots! My ego hit a new low. However, the newspaper people thought it was important, because I was the first pilot to force land in Sicily and walk back. It was a good omen that pilots could expect good treatment from the Sicilian citizens."

MALTA'S SPITFIRE IX – EN199

First flown at Eastleigh in Hampshire on 28 November 1942, EN199 reached the North African front at the end of January 1943, Wg Cdr Ronald Berry DFC, Wing Commander Flying of 322 Wing, selecting this aircraft as his personal mount on which he had his initials RB applied. Wg Cdr Berry claimed a Bf109G probably destroyed on 13 April 1943 whilst flying EN199, which was also flown on occasion by Sqn Ldr Colin Gray DFC of 81 Squadron. From North Africa, EN199 moved to Takali, Malta, having been transferred to 154 Squadron and it participated in the invasion of Sicily during which another Bf109G was claimed destroyed on 17 July 1943 when being flown by Flt Sgt Edward Artus, who also claimed a second as damaged (see Chapter VII). EN199 then moved to the Italian mainland, taking part in operations with 154 Squadron and later with 1435 Squadron before being transferred once again, at the end of 1944, this time joining 225 Squadron. Later that year, in October, EN199 was back on Malta, at Hal Far, taking part in Meteorological Flights and the following January (1946) it moved over to Luqa, joining 73 Squadron. On 23 December 1946 it was blown into a quarry during a gale and was finally struck off charge on 30 January 1947.

Following repairs, EN199 was presented to Malta's Air Scouts, within the Boy Scout Movement, and placed on display at their Headquarters in Floriana. Sadly, within a short while, the Spitfire fell into a very sorry state and was considered to be dangerous to the young scouts. As a consequence, it was then passed onto the Civil Defence Corps at the Gharghur Enclosure. Here it was used in several rescue training courses that were held during 1955. A further move to the new Rescue and Training Wing at Targa Battery, Mosta took place in April 1956. The aircraft was left purposely in a dismantled state to simulate as realistically as possible an air crash in open countryside. When its services were no longer required the Spitfire lay dismembered for several years, exposed to the elements and vandals which took their toll, leaving very little remains.

The newly established National War Museum Association collected the parts in 1974, but little progress was made and these were subsequently sent to a local scrapyard. By a stroke of luck, however, EN199's remains survived under tons of scrap and, in 1992, Ray Polidano of the NWMA extricated them and started a reconstruction in earnest. Sponsorship for the project was forthcoming from Mid-Med Bank plc (the main sponsor), the Museums' Department and the National War Museum Association. A number of aviation-minded friends, some from overseas, helped all along the reconstruction process until the aircraft was completed to static condition in time for the celebrations of the fiftieth anniversary of VE-Day, when it was displayed to the public on the Palace Square in Valetta. It now has pride of place in the Aviation Museum at Takali. [1]

Frederick R. Galea, Honorary Secretary
Malta National War Museum Association & Malta Aviation Museum Foundation

---

[1] see *A Brief History of Spitfire IX EN199* by Frederick R. Galea.

ITALIAN DOCUMENTATION RELATING TO THE LOSS OF FLT LT LES GOSLING DFC, RCAF, 229 SQUADRON

19 July 1943

C O P Y   33

C O M U N E   D I   L E T O J A N N I   G A L L O D O R O

P R O V I N C I A   D I   M E S S I N A

Subject : Tombe di Guerra.   To : AMGOT, TAORMINA.

17.11.43.

Referring to your request dated 14 November with regard to an Allied
Plane, after my enquiries I can communicate what follows :

  at 7.30 a.m. July 19th in the fraction Gallodoro a plane
precipitated ablaze. According to information ab results that it was
a Spitfire and that the targets (Marks) as well as the identification
discs were delivered to Allied Military Troops. One of these was an
uncommissioned officer. The things were handed over to them in
theparson's house. The pilots corpse was abandoned and laid for ten
days. Fascist authorities, commune and Carabinieri would not interest
themselves for giving an honourable burial to a soldier although even
if an enemy.

   The local authorities were :

   Cavallan Matteo - podesta in Letojanni.
   Pagini Carmelimo - vice podesta "

   The remains of the corpse were collected by :

   Micali Adolfo, Carpita Carmelo, Crisafulli Natale and
put into a wooden (oak) box; then they were taken to the church in
Gallodoro for the functions celebrated by the parson. After that the
remains were taken to the churchyard in Gallodoro and buried in a
special cemented grave. A machine gun was placed onto the grave as
a symbol (the machine gun belonged to the plane). The parson has a
rest of the plane in his habitation in Gallodoro. No documents was
found. No possibility of identification with regard to the pilot's
nationality. Lapi's Guiseppe verbally declares : the maresciallo of
the Carabinieri Pappalardo gave me instructions to collect the pilot's
remainders and to put them into a little grave (pit) I put no mark
on it.

      (Sgd) MARIO CRIVELLARO
        (The Mayor)

APPENDIX V

THE ADVENTURES OF
FLG OFF BRENDAN BAKER, 92 SQUADRON

Shot down by MC205Vs on 10 August 1943

Having been shot down, Flg Off Baker managed to bale out:

"Unfortunately, the cords of my parachute got entangled in my Mae West and I had to jettison both. I started to swim for the shore. I had covered half the distance when a rowing boat manned by Italians approached me. Probably to attract my attention, since they could easily have hit me had they wished, the Italians started firing in my direction. Eventually they picked me up. As they rowed to the shore they demanded such of my clothing as took their fancy and when I refused, set upon me, bludgeoning me with their fists and sticks, and wrenching a ring off my finger. This treatment was mild to that which awaited me when we reached the shore; for there was a crowd, consisting of many women, who surrounded me, striking me and spitting upon me, so that my chances would have been slim had not two German soldiers come along and intervened.

The Germans took me to a field hospital and I was eventually passed to another at Cosenza. I was well treated, and apart from a German sergeant who questioned me in broken English in a desultory way, no attempt was made to interrogate me. Shortly afterwards I and others were transferred to a large military hospital at Caserta. We went by road and arrived at Naples at night whilst an air raid was in progress. The German guards left us in the street; and without supervision of any sort we spent the night in a shelter until our escort located us in the morning.

One day in Caserta cheering was heard from the Italian quarters, and news trickled through that the Armistice had been signed. Shortly afterwards the Germans began moving the less serious cases to the north. My wound had almost healed, but since I had contracted malaria, and by pretending to be in much worse shape than I was, I succeeded in staying put. But I was not prepared to rely on my luck lasting, and was relieved when I heard from others of the existence of a remarkable hiding place. Just off the ward was a disused cupboard; this was locked, but the transom about it was broken, and the cupboard could be entered through this. A previous prisoner – a naval officer – had discovered this and on the other side had started to construct a tunnel, using an ordinary table fork to do it with. Unfortunately, he had come up against the foundations of a wall and had to abandon the project. But the tunnel now served me in very good stead, for whenever the guards came looking for me, I hid, with others, on the other side of the cupboard. Eventually, the Germans left, and shortly afterwards our own troops arrived. I was able to get aboard a C-47 which took me to Foggio, whence I was able to rejoin my unit."

Flg Off Baker was awarded the DFC.

APPENDIX VI

SPITFIRE PILOTS AERIAL COMBAT CLAIMS & CREDITS MALTA & SICILY

January-August 1943

3/1/43:	Sgt L.G. Barnes RCAF	126 Sqn EP205/MK-Y	He111 probable
6/1/43:	Flg Off H.F. Withy	185 Sqn EP791/GL-	MC202 probable
28/1/43:	Sqn Ldr J.R. Urwin Mann	126 Sqn EP330/MK-J	Me210 probable
7/2/43:	Flt Lt J.J. Lynch	249 Sqn BR373/T-N ⎫	Ju52/3m
	Plt Off I.F. Kennedy RCAF	249 Sqn EP519/T-C ⎭	
16/2/43:	Sqn Ldr W.A. Smith	1435 Sqn EP257/V-W ⎫	Z1007bis probable (crashed)
	Plt Off J.N. Kirkman	1435 Sqn EP915/V-U ⎬	(Plt Off Kirkman shot down and POW)
3/3/43:	Plt Off B.J. Oliver RNZAF	249 Sqn EP833/T-F ⎫	
	Plt Off I.F. Kennedy RCAF	249 Sqn EP343/T-V ⎬	Ju88
	Sgt W.J.B. Stark	249 Sqn EP706/T-U ⎭	
25/3/43:	Flg Off L.C. Gosling RCAF	229 Sqn EP606/X-P	Bf109
	Flg Off I.F. Kennedy RCAF	249 Sqn EP343/T-V ⎫	Ju88
	Flt Sgt E.D. Kelly RCAF	249 Sqn BR110/T-A ⎭	
6/4/43:	Flt Lt H.S. Jackson	126 Sqn EN142/MK-W	Bf109
7/4/43:	Sqn Ldr J.J. Lynch	249 Sqn EP829/T-N	Ju88
10/4/43:	Flt Lt H.F. Withy	185 Sqn EP791/GL- ⎫	Ju88
	Flg Off R.C. Shuren RCAF	185 Sqn BR375/GL- ⎭	
16/4/43:	Flg Off W.D. Idema	229 Sqn EP264/X-X ⎫	
	Plt Off K.B. Robinson	229 Sqn EP448/X-A	
	Plt Off J.A. Collis	229 Sqn EP305/X-Y	
	Sqn Ldr H.F. O'Neill	1435 Sqn EP658/V-F ⎬	Ju88
	Plt Off L.A. Stewart	1435 Sqn EP290/V-M	
	Sgt F.W. Thomson	1435 Sqn EP834/V-Q ⎭	
	Flg Off I.F. Kennedy RCAF	249 Sqn EP712/T-C ⎫	
	Plt Off B.J. Oliver RNZAF	249 Sqn EP188/T-Y ⎬	Ju88
	Plt Off M.J. Costello RNZAF	249 Sqn BR565/T-T ⎭	
19/4/43:	Plt Off J.M.W. Lloyd	229 Sqn EP842/X-D	SM82 (claimed as Ju52/3m)
	Sgt R.R. Salzman	229 Sqn EP790/X-K	Fiat G.12 (claimed as Ju52/3m)
	Flg Off L.C. Gosling RCAF	229 Sqn EP606/X-P	Ju88
	Flg Off L.C. Gosling RCAF	229 Sqn EP606/X-P ⎫	Ju88
	Sgt A.J. Clayton	229 Sqn EP955/X- ⎭	
22/4/43:	Flg Off I.F. Kennedy RCAF	249 Sqn AB535/T-Z	Ju52/3m, SM82 (claimed as two Ju52/3ms)
	Sqn Ldr J.J. Lynch	249 Sqn EP829/T-N	2 Ju52/3m
24/4/43:	Sqn Ldr J.J. Lynch	249 Sqn EP829/T-N	Ca313 (possibly Ca311)
28/4/43:	Sqn Ldr J.J. Lynch	249 Sqn EP829/T-N	Ju52/3m
	Sqn Ldr J.J. Lynch	249 Sqn EP829/T-N ⎫	Ju52/3m
	Plt Off A.F. Osborne	249 Sqn AB535/T-Z ⎭	
7/5/43:	Flg Off L.C. Gosling RCAF	229 Sqn EP720/X-E	Fi156
10/5/43:	Sqn Ldr J.J. Lynch	249 Sqn JK465/X	RS14, Z506B, Ju52/3m (claimed as two Z506Bs)
	Flg Off H.C. Holmes	249 Sqn AB535/T-Z	Z506B
21/5/43:	Flt Lt A.G. Russell	229 Sqn JK428/X-A	FW190
	Flt Sgt A. Williams	229 Sqn ES233/X-X	FW190

22/5/43:	Flt Lt J.D. Keynes	126 Sqn JK672/MK-E	Bf109
1/6/43:	Plt Off L.G. Barnes RCAF	126 Sqn EN532/MK-W	Bf109 probable
2/6/43:	Flg Off A.A. Vale	126 Sqn EN402/MK-R	Bf109 probable
3/6/43:	Sqn Ldr H.S. Jackson	126 Sqn EN402/MK-R	Bf109
	Plt Off G.G. White RNZAF	126 Sqn BS557/MK-C	Bf109
4/6/43:	Flt Lt H.A. Knight	185 Sqn EN533/GL-N	Bf109
	Sgt W.A. Cruickshank	185 Sqn EN404/GL-W	Bf109 probable
6/6/43:	Flt Sgt G.R. Nadon RCAF	185 Sqn EN404/GL-W	Bf109 probable
10/6/43:	Flg Off I.F. Kennedy RCAF	185 Sqn EN533/GL-N ⎫	Bf109
	Plt Off D. Sinclair RCAF	185 Sqn EN403/GL-A ⎭	
	Flg Off I.F. Kennedy RCAF	185 Sqn EN468/GL-J ⎫	MC202
	Flt Sgt A.L. Sinclair RCAF	185 Sqn EN349/GL-C ⎭	
13/6/43:	Plt Off D.E. Nicholson	249 Sqn JK879/T-B	Bf109 probable
	Sgt B.W. Sheehan RNZAF	249 Sqn ER811/T-J	MC202 (Sgt Sheehan also shot down and POW)
14/6/43:	Wg Cdr C.F. Gray	322 Wg EN350/CG	Bf109
	Flg Off P.G. Barber	81 Sqn EN181/FL-	Bf109 ⎫ both claimed as MC202s damaged but apparently
	Flt Sgt G.S. Hulse	81 Sqn EN478/FL-	Bf109 ⎬ both Bf109Gs of 6/JG53 (which crashed)
17/6/43:	Wg Cdr C.F. Gray	322 Wg EN534/EF-Y	MC202
18/6/43:	Flg Off G.N. Keith RCAF	72 Sqn JK429/RN-	Bf109
20/6/43:	Wt Off A.W. Gear	72 Sqn EN144/RN-	Bf109
23/6/43:	Plt Off W.I.H. Maguire	81 Sqn EN528/FL-S	Bf109
24/6/43:	Flt Sgt F. Mellor	111 Sqn EN518/JU-	Me410
26/6/43:	Wg Cdr W.G.G. Duncan Smith	Safi Wg JK611/MK-M	Bf109
29/6/43:	Sqn Ldr C.I.R. Arthur	232 Sqn JK656/EF- ⎫	Bf109
	Flt Sgt J.W. Patterson	232 Sqn JK708/EF- ⎭	
	Flt Lt W.A. Olmsted RCAF	232 Sqn JK274/EF-	Bf109 probable
	Flt Sgt G.R. Nadon RCAF	185 Sqn ES107/GL-	MC202
	Sgt G.H. Meager	185 Sqn EN523/GL-K	Bf109 probable
2/7/43:	Flg Off G.G. White RNZAF	126 Sqn JK672/MK-E	Bf109
	Plt Off T.G. Atkinson	1435 Sqn JK282/V-U ⎫	FW190
	Flt Sgt S.H. Benjamin	1435 Sqn JK139/V-X ⎭	
	Sqn Ldr B.E.G. White	229 Sqn JG838/X-W	Bf109 probable
	Flt Sgt G.F. Mercer RCAF	185 Sqn EN403/GL-A	Bf109 probable
3/7/43:	Sqn Ldr G.U. Hill RCAF	111 Sqn EN303/JU-	Bf109
	Sgt H.R. Hall	111 Sqn EN252/JU-	Bf109
4/7/43:	Sqn Ldr E.D. Mackie RNZAF	243 Sqn JK715/SN-A	Bf109
	Flg Off F.S. Banner	243 Sqn JK189/SN-L	Bf109
	Flt Lt K.F. MacDonald	243 Sqn EN148/SN-E	MC202 probable
	Wg Cdr H.S.L. Dundas	324 Wg JL122/HD ⎫	Bf109
	Flt Lt I.F. Crawford	111 Sqn JK643/JU- ⎭	
	Sgt J. Saphir RCAF	126 Sqn JK611/MK-M	2 Bf109
	Flt Lt G.J. Cox	43 Sqn JK612/FT-V	Bf109
5/7/43:	Sqn Ldr E.D. Mackie RNZAF	243 Sqn JK715/SN-A	Bf109
	Flg Off G.G. White RNZAF	126 Sqn JK611/MK-M	Bf109
	Flt Lt L.C. Gosling RCAF	229 Sqn LZ808/X-D	2 FW190
	Flt Sgt R.H. De Tourett RNZAF	229 Sqn ER494/X-H	FW190
6/7/43:	Plt Off J.S. Ekbery	232 Sqn JK365/EF-D	Bf109
7/7/43:	Wg Cdr B. Drake	Krendi Wg JK228/BD	MC202
8/7/43:	Plt Off R.J.H. Hussey	72 Sqn ES281/RN-	Bf109
	Sqn Ldr S.W. Daniel	72 Sqn JG793/RN-	Bf109
9/7/43:	Flt Sgt G.F. Mercer RCAF	185 Sqn EN403/GL-A	MC202 (probably Italian Bf109G)
	Sgt G.M. Buchanan RNZAF	185 Sqn EN349/GL-C	FW190
	Flt Lt L.M. McKee	185 Sqn EN533/GL-N	FW190 probable
10/7/43:	Sqn Ldr M.C.B. Boddington	242 Sqn JK260/LE-K	He111
	Sqn Ldr M.C.B. Boddington	242 Sqn JK260/LE-K ⎫	Bf109
	Flg Off C.W. Coulthard	242 Sqn /LE- ⎭	
	Flt Lt H.W. Chambers RNZAF	242 Sqn EN340/LE-D	MC200
	Flt Sgt W.J. Webster RNZAF	43 Sqn ES294/FT-	FW190
	Flt Lt J.A. Gray	93 Sqn JL323/HN-	MC202 probable
	Wg Cdr C.F. Gray	322 Wg EN350/CG	Bf109

	Pilot	Unit / Aircraft	Claim
	Flt Lt T.W. Savage	92 Sqn JL182/QJ-	Ju88 (Flt Lt Savage also shot down and KiA)
	Flg Off S.F. Browne RNZAF	93 Sqn LZ840/HN-	Ju88
	Wg Cdr A. Warburton	683 Sqn EN290/V-G	Bf109 probable
	Sqn Ldr G.J. Cox	229 Sqn LZ820/X-U	3 Re2002 (claimed as MC200)
	Flg Off O.C.H. Stanford-Smith	229 Sqn JK220/X-M	
	Flg Off R.H. Small	229 Sqn JK536/X-K	Re2002 probable (,,)
	Flt Sgt L.A. Taylor	229 Sqn LZ808/X-D	
11/7/43:	Wt Off P.J. Hedderwick RAAF	43 Sqn JG724/FT-H	Me210
	Wt Off R.W. Leeming RAAF	43 Sqn ES292/FT-	
	1/Lt Wright USAAF	309th FS /WZ-	Bf110 probable (claimed as Do217)
	Sqn Ldr M.C.B. Boddington	242 Sqn JK260/LE-K	
	Sgt E.S. Doherty RNZAF	242 Sqn /LE-	Ju88
	Flg Off J.A. Stock	242 Sqn /LE-	
	Capt John M. Winkler USAAF	307th FS /MX-	FW190
	Maj Frank A. Hill USAAF	309th FS /WZ-	Ju88
	Capt Berry Chandler USAAF	309th FS /WZ-	
	Sqn Ldr S.W. Daniel	72 Sqn JK173/RN-	G.50bis (claimed as MC200)
	Flt Lt M.V. Christopherson	72 Sqn JG793/RN-	
	Sgt K. Hermiston	72 Sqn JK275/RN-	G.50bis probable (claimed as MC200)
	Flg Off G.N. Keith RCAF	72 Sqn JK637/RN-	Ju88, G.50bis (claimed as MC200)
	Capt Jerry D. Collinsworth USAAF	307th FS /MX-	FW190
	Flg Off L.E. Hunt RCAF	93 Sqn JL219/HN-X	Bf109
	USAAF P-38 pilot	1st FG	
	Plt Off G.S. Richardson	93 Sqn EN140/HN-	Ju88
	Flg Off S.F. Browne RNZAF	93 Sqn LZ840/HN-	Ju88
	Plt Off R.G. Fisher RNZAF	93 Sqn BS553/HN-	
	Flg Off L.C. Gosling RCAF	229 Sqn LZ808/X-D	MC202
	Wg Cdr P. Olver	244 Wg EN448/PO	Ju88 (Wg Cdr Olver also shot down and POW)
	Flt Lt R.W. Richardson	92 Sqn ER470/QJ-	Ju88
	Flg Off M.E. Jowsey RCAF	92 Sqn EN188/QJ-6	Ju88
	Lt A. Sachs SAAF	92 Sqn ER871/QJ-	Ju88
	Wt Off S.R. Fry	92 Sqn EN152/QJ-	Ju88
	2/Lt J.E. Gasson SAAF	92 Sqn ES148/QJ-E	Ju88 probable
	Capt Carl W. Payne USAAF	309th FS /WZ-	Bf109
	Capt John H. Paulk USAAF	308th FS /HL-	Bf110 (claimed as Do217)
	1/Lt Alvin D. Callander USAAF	308th FS /HL-	Bf110 (claimed as Do217)
	1/Lt Wilfred L. Waltner USAAF	308th FS /HL-	Bf110 (claimed as Do217)
	Wg Cdr W.G.G. Duncan Smith	Safi Wg JK650/DS	MC202
	Flg Off G.G. White RNZAF	126 Sqn JK950/MK-H	MC202
	Flg Off B.W. Clarke	126 Sqn JK972/MK-L	MC202 probable
	Sgt H.S. Eccleston RAAF	111 Sqn JK728/JU-	2 Re2005 (claimed as Re2001)
	Flg Off F.A. Mellors	111 Sqn JK217/JU-	Re2005 (claimed as Re2001)
	Sqn Ldr G.U. Hill RCAF	111 Sqn EN518/JU-	Re2002 (claimed as FW190)
12/7/43:	Flt Lt A.H. Jupp	72 Sqn JG746/RN-	2 Bf109 probables (two sorties)
	Sgt K.E. Clarkson RAAF	72 Sqn EN309/RN-	Bf109
	Flg Off G.N. Keith RCAF	72 Sqn JK429/RN-	MC202 (first sortie)
		JK637/RN-	Bf109 probable (second sortie)
	Capt Harry L. Barr USAAF	307th FS /MX-	FW190
	Flg Off G.G. White RNZAF	126 Sqn JK672/MK-E	Bf109
	Flt Sgt N.H. Harrison RNZAF	1435 Sqn JK929/V-P	2 Bf109
	Plt Off R. Morris	1435 Sqn EP286/V-K	Bf109 probable
	Flt Lt L.C. Gosling RCAF	229 Sqn LZ808/X-D	2 Bf109 (two sorties)
	Flt Sgt F.R.M. Cook	229 Sqn ER533/X-R	Bf109
	Flt Sgt D. Andrew	229 Sqn JK811/X-F	Bf110
	Sqn Ldr F.W. Lister	152 Sqn ES112/UM-U	Bf109
	Sgt N.E.C. Dear	152 Sqn JK305/UM-	Bf110 (claimed as Do217)
	Plt Off B.J. Ingalls RCAF	72 Sqn EN358/RN-	Ju52
	Sqn Ldr S.W. Daniel	72 Sqn JK429/RN-	Bf109
	Flg Off T.B. Hughes	72 Sqn JG746/RN-	G.50 (claimed as MC200)

Flg Off J.F. King	72 Sqn JK468/RN-	G.50 (claimed as MC200)
Sgt A.M. Griffiths	72 Sqn EN309/RN-	2 G.50 (claimed as MC200s)
Flg Off R.D. Scrase	72 Sqn JK275/RN-	G.50 (claimed as MC200)
Flt Lt M. Johnston RCAF	72 Sqn JK990/RN-⎫	Bf109 probable
Sgt C.M. Scott	72 Sqn JK372/RN-⎭	(first sortie)
Sgt C.M. Scott	72 Sqn JK372/RN-	Bf109 (second sortie)
Sqn Ldr J.S. Taylor	601 Sqn EP966/UF-	Ju87 (Sqn Ldr Taylor also shot down and KiA)
Flg Off R.P.W. Sewell RCAF	601 Sqn ER566/UF-	Ju87 probable (crashed)
2/Lt M.A. Hagico Belg AF	601 Sqn ER181/UF-	Ju87 probable (crashed)
Sqn Ldr E.D. Mackie RNZAF	243 Sqn JK715/SN-A	MC202 probable
Plt Off R.J.H. Hussey	72 Sqn EN258/RN-B	Bf109
Plt Off E.J. Shaw RNZAF	72 Sqn JK450/RN-	MC202
Wg Cdr W.G.G. Duncan Smith	Safi Wg JK650/DS	MC202 probable
13/7/43: Sqn Ldr G.U. Hill RCAF	111 Sqn JK389/JU- JG937/JU-	Ju88 (two sorties) Re2002 (claimed variously as FW190 or MC200)
Flt Lt L. McIntosh RAAF	111 Sqn JK307/JU-U	Ju88
Sqn Ldr E.D. Mackie RNZAF	243 Sqn JK715/SN-A JK715/SN-A	2 Ju87 (first sortie) Re2002 (claimed as MC200; second sortie)
Flt Sgt H.C. Payne	243 Sqn JK614/SN-C	2 Ju87 (credited as one and one damaged)
Plt Off A.E. Lawrence	243 Sqn JK113/SN-B	Ju87
Sgt R. Jaques	243 Sqn JK642/SN-P	Ju87
Flg Off F.S. Banner	243 Sqn EN148/SN-E	Bf109 probable
Flg Off F.S. Banner	243 Sqn EN148/SN-E⎫	He111 (claimed as Do217)
Sgt P.J. Davoren RAAF	243 Sqn EN313/SN-D⎭	
Grp Capt G.K. Gilroy	324 Wg JK143/GK-G⎫	Ju88 probable (crashed)
Flt Lt J.A. Gray	93 Sqn JL232/HN-⎭	
Sgt J.R. Andrew	93 Sqn JK603/HN-	He111, Bf109
Sgt J.L. Liggett	93 Sqn JK606/HN-	2 He111 (claimed as damaged but both apparently crashed)
Flg Off S.F. Browne RNZAF	93 Sqn JK720/HN-⎫	Bf109
Flg Off P.E. Rivett RAAF	93 Sqn JK362/HN-⎭	
Flg Off C.S. Bamberger	243 Sqn JL219/HN-X	Ju87
Flt Lt G.F. Silvester	242 Sqn /LE-	Bf110
Flt Sgt E.R. Morgan	242 Sqn /LE-	Bf110
Flt Sgt J.J. Ronay	242 Sqn /LE-	Bf110
Flt Sgt L. Courtney	242 Sqn /LE-	Bf110
Sqn Ldr M.C.B. Boddington	242 Sqn JK260/LE-D	Bf110
Plt Off R.J.H. Hussey	72 Sqn EN258/RN-B	MC202
Plt Off R.J.H. Hussey	72 Sqn EN258/RN-B⎫	Bf109
Sgt A.M. Griffiths	72 Sqn EN144/RN- ⎭	
Sqn Ldr W.M. Sizer	93 Sqn JL219/HN-X	MC202
Flt Lt N.W. Lee	93 Sqn JK306/HN-⎫	MC202 probable
Flt Sgt R.H. Baxter	93 Sqn JK868/HN-H⎭	
Wg Cdr H.S.L. Dundas	324 Wg JL122/HD	Re2002 (claimed as MC200)
Sqn Ldr J.J. Lynch	249 Sqn JK465/X	FW190
14/7/43: Flg Off G.N. Keith RCAF	72 Sqn JK637/RN-	Bf109
Flg Off K. Smith	72 Sqn EN258/RN-B	Bf109
Flg Off G.N. Keith RCAF	72 Sqn JK637/RN-⎫	Bf109
Plt Off R.J.H. Hussey	72 Sqn JK372/RN-⎭	
Plt Off E.J. Shaw RNZAF	72 Sqn JK450/RN-	Bf109 probable
Sqn Ldr W.M. Whitamore	81 Sqn EN492/FL-E	Bf109 probable
Flg Off W.J. Goby	81 Sqn EN478/FL-	MC202
Flg Off M.E. Jowsey RCAF	92 Sqn EN333/QJ-7	MC202
Plt Off R.H. Probert RCAF	92 Sqn EN416/QJ-	MC202
16/7/43: Flg Off W.I.H. Maguire	81 Sqn EN492/FL-E	Bf109
Flt Sgt G.S. Hulse	81 Sqn ? /J	Bf109 probable
Sgt A.M. Griffiths	72 Sqn EN309/RN-	Bf109 (Sgt Griffiths also killed; aircraft hit by debris and crashed)
Sgt J.T. Connolly RAAF	72 Sqn JK826/RN-	Bf109

	Name	Squadron/Aircraft	Claim
	Plt Off J.S. Ekbery	232 Sqn EN365/EF-C	Bf109
	Plt Off C.H. McMinniman RCAF	232 Sqn EN464/EF-	Bf109
17/7/43:	Flt Lt A.F. Aikman RCAF	154 Sqn JK649/HT-	MC202
	Flg Off G.M. Haase	154 Sqn EN520/HT-	MC200 probable
	Flt Sgt E. Artus	154 Sqn EN199/HT-U	Bf109
	Flt Sgt J.W. Patterson	232 Sqn JG792/EF-	Bf109
18/7/43:	Flt Sgt N.H. Harrison RNZAF	1435 Sqn JK929/V-P	2 Bf110 probable
	Sgt C.R. Piper RNZAF	72 Sqn JK786/RN- ⎫	Bf110
	Plt Off R.J.H. Hussey	72 Sqn ES107/RN- ⎭	
	Flg Off W.I.H. Maguire	81 Sqn EN492/FL-E	FW190
	Flg Off R.W. Turkington	43 Sqn EF594/FT-	Bf109 (claimed as damaged; crashed)
19/7/43:	Sgt W.G. Downing	229 Sqn EP444/X-L	2 Bf110
	Flg Off N.G. Jones	152 Sqn JK829/UM-E	3 Re2002
	Flg Off R.S. Kingsford	152 Sqn JK327/UM-	Re2002
	Sgt L.A. Smith	152 Sqn ES308/UM-	Re2002
	Flg Off R.S. Kingsford	152 Sqn JK327/UM- ⎫	Re2002
	Sgt L.A. Smith	152 Sqn ES308/UM- ⎭	
	Lt S.W. van der Merwe SAAF	1SAAF Sqn /AX- ⎫	FW190
	Capt J.M. Faure SAAF	1SAAF Sqn /AX- ⎭	
	Lt W.D. Wikner SAAF	1SAAF Sqn /AX-	Bf109
25/7/43:	Wg Cdr C.F. Gray	322 Wg ES112/UM-U	2 Ju52
	Flg Off R.S. Kingsford	152 Sqn JK327/UM-	2 Ju52, Bf109 probable
	Sgt S.L. Bradbury	152 Sqn JG871/UM-	2 Ju52
	Flt Lt G.T. Baynham	152 Sqn JL240/UM-	Ju52
	Sgt L.A. Smith	152 Sqn LZ807/UM-V	Ju52
	Sgt R.O. Patterson	152 Sqn ER645/UM-	Ju52
	Flg Off E.R. Burrows	152 Sqn /UM- ⎫	Ju52
	Plt Off R.E.J. Macdonald	152 Sqn JG824/UM- ⎭	
	Flt Lt G.T. Baynham	152 Sqn JL240/UM- ⎫	
	Flg Off N.G. Jones	152 Sqn JK829/UM-E	
	Plt Off N.L. Myers	242 Sqn /LE- ⎬ Ju52	
	Plt Off K.A. Edwards	242 Sqn /LE- ⎭	
	Sgt E.S. Doherty RNZAF	242 Sqn /LE-A	3 Ju52
	Wt Off P. Gatley	242 Sqn /LE-	Ju52
	Flg Off J.H. Maxwell	242 Sqn /LE-	Ju52
	Flg Off W.J. Goby	81 Sqn EN565/FL-	Ju52
	Sgt W.E. Caldecott	81 Sqn JK322/FL-4	Ju52
	D.W. Rathwell RCAF	81 Sqn EN247/FL-	Ju52
	Sgt G.J. Whiteford RAAF	81 Sqn ER565/FL-	Ju52
	Flt Sgt L.F.M. Cronin RAAF	81 Sqn EN490/FL-	2 Bf109
	Sqn Ldr W.M. Whitamore	81 Sqn EN492/FL-E	Bf109
	Flg Off N.G. Jones	152 Sqn JK829/UM-	2 Bf109
	Sgt H.R. Kelly	242 Sqn /LE-	Bf109
	Flt Lt G.F. Silvester	242 Sqn /LE-	Bf109
27/7/43:	Plt Off W.H. Reid RCAF	43 Sqn JK782/FT- ⎫	Bf109
	Flt Sgt T.E. Johnson	43 Sqn LZ293/FT- ⎭	
28/7/43:	Flg Off E.S. Dicks-Sherwood	92 Sqn JL388/QJ-	Bf109
30/7/43:	2/Lt Frederick O. Trafton USAAF	309th FS /WZ-	Bf109 probable
	2/Lt Mutchler USAAF	309th FS /WZ-	Bf109 probable
1/8/43:	2/Lt Norman E. English USAAF	2nd FS	Do217
	Capt Norman L. McDonald USAAF	2nd FS	Do217
	1/Lt Charles R. Ramsey USAAF	308th FS /HL-	Bf109 probable
2/8/43:	Flg Off F.S. Banner	243 Sqn JL139/SN-J	Bf109
6/8/43:	1/Lt Leonard V. Helton USAAF	4th FS /WD-	Bf109
7/8/43:	Flt Lt L.S. Montgomerie RNZAF	81 Sqn EN478/FL- ⎫	
	Sgt W.E. Caldecott	81 Sqn JK399/FL- ⎬ Ca309	
	Sgt E.A. Carlisle	81 Sqn JK367/FL- ⎭	
8/8/43:	Capt John H. Paulk USAAF	308th FS /HL-	FW190
	1/Lt Charles R. Ramsey USAAF	308th FS /HL-	FW190
	2/Lt Richard F. Hurd USAAF	308th FS /HL-	FW190
10/8/43:	Capt J.T. Seccombe SAAF	1SAAF Sqn /AX-	FW190
11/8/43:	2/Lt Robert B. Chaddock USAAF	307th FS /MX-	MC202

	1/Lt Carroll A. Pryblo USAAF	307th FS /MX-⎫	
	2/Lt Delton G. Graham USAAF	307th FS /MX-⎬	FW190
	Capt Royal N. Baker USAAF	308th FS /HL-	FW190
12/8/43:	Wt Off J.W. Patterson	232 Sqn JK708/EF-	FW190
15/8/43:	Flt Lt W.J. Whitside RCAF	145 Sqn JF488/ZX-	FW190
	Flg Off J.K. Carswell RCAF	145 Sqn JF482/ZX-	FW190 (Flg Off Carswell FTR)
	Sqn Ldr P.W. Rabone RNZAF	23 Sqn Spitfire	Ju88
16/8/43:	Flg Off B.D. Baker	92 Sqn EN449/QJ-	2 MC202/MC205
			(Flg Off Baker also
			shot down, PoW)
20/8/43:	Sqn Ldr I.N. MacDougall	185 Sqn JK333/GL-⎫	
	Flt Lt T.W. Wilmot	185 Sqn JK521/GL-⎬	Z506B
	Flg Off S.V. Baxter RAAF	185 Sqn EE865/GL-	
	Plt Off W.E. Dunsmore RCAF	185 Sqn LZ809/GL-⎭	
22/8/43:	Flt Lt K.L.B. Debenham	249 Sqn MA500/T-Z	Ju88
27/8/43:	Flg Off K. MacBain RCAF	249 Sqn EN256/T-B	Ju88
28/8/43:	Lt Col L.A. Wilmot SAAF	322 Wg MA408/LW	Bf109
	Sgt W.J. Robinson RNZAF	81 Sqn MA402/FL-B	2 Bf109
	Flt Sgt A.McG. Peart RNZAF	81 Sqn EN513/FL-J	Bf109
	2/Lt Robert W. Hine USAAF	5th FS /VF-	Bf109
29/8/43:	Wg Cdr W.G.G. Duncan Smith	244 Wg MA281	FW190
	1/Lt Edwin J. Odom USAAF	5th FS /VF-	Me410

NB: Although every effort has been made to ensure accuracy of the serial numbers of Spitfires as recorded, almost inevitably there will be some inaccuracies.

APPENDIX VII

SPITFIRE OPERATIONAL LOSSES
AND PILOT CASUALTIES

Malta & Sicily: January-August 1943

6/1/43:	AB465/T-R	249 Sqn	Flg Off J.A.N. Dawkins	KiA (AA)
11/1/43:	BS500	69 Sqn	Flg Off J.A. Frazer RAAF	FTR (KiA)
17/1/43:	EP460/X-Z	229 Sqn	Sgt A. Williams	Baled out, rescued by Sunderland
	BR562/X-R	229 Sqn	Flt Lt A.R. Chaplin (SA)	FTR (drowned)
19/1/43:	EP701/GL-B	185 Sqn	Sub Lt E.F. Pratt RNZNVR	KiFA
28/1/43:	AB526/MK-P	126 Sqn	Flt Lt J.H. Long RCAF	KiA (AA)
	EP691/X-A	229 Sqn	Sgt D.W. Goodwin RCAF	Baled out, rescued by HSL107
29/1/43:	BR424	69 Sqn	Flt Lt R.C. Hill (SA)	FTR (Bf109) PoW
30/1/43:	AR561/V-I	1435 Sqn	Flt Lt P.W.E. Heppell DFC	Baled out, rescued by HSL166
4/2/43:	BR107/GL-	185 Sqn	Plt Off T. Nesbitt	Baled out, rescued by HSL166
8/2/43:	BR373/T-N	249 Sqn	Flg Off G. Newberry	FTR (AA) PoW
	EP473/GL-	185 Sqn	Flt Sgt C.J. Carmody RCAF	KiA (Bf109)
15/2/43:	EP641/X-J	229 Sqn	Flt Sgt S.H.K. Goodyear RCAF	KiA (AA)
16/2/43:	EP915/V-U	1435 Sqn	Plt Off J.N. Kirkman	FTR (Z1007bis) PoW
24/2/43:	AR559/T-W	249 Sqn	Sgt A. Notley	KiA (Bf109)
1/3/43:	BR534/GL-	185 Sqn	Flt Sgt J.N. Miller RCAF	Baled out (Bf109) rescued by HSL107
2/3/43:	BS496	683 Sqn	Flg Off P.L. Hanson-Lester	Baled out (burned) rescued by HSL128
3/3/43:	EP717/X-D	229 Sqn	Plt Off L. J. McDougall RCAF	KiA (Bf109)
	AR565/X-C	229 Sqn	Sgt E.E. Vine	Baled out (Bf109) PoW
	BR161/X-E	229 Sqn	Plt Off R.J. Taggart RCAF	Baled out (Bf109) rescued by HSL107
	EP706/T-U	249 Sqn	Sgt W.J.B. Stark	Baled out (Ju88) rescued by HSL107
	EP471/GL-	185 Sqn Flt	Sgt G.D. Billing RCAF	Baled out (Bf109) rescued by HSL166
	EP140/T-M	249 Sqn	Sgt J.R. Meadows	Crash-landed (injured)
9/3/43:	BS364	683 Sqn	Flt Sgt C.R. Peacock RCAF	FTR (KiA)
11/3/43:	EP519/T-C	249 Sqn	Sqn Ldr M.G. MacLeod RCAF	KiA (AA)
18/3/43:	AR556/V-C	1435 Sqn	Sgt W. Hart	KiA (AA)
20/3/43:	EP571/GL-	185 Sqn	Flt Lt H.F. Withy	Baled out (AA) rescued by Walrus W3012
	BR109/GL-W	185 Sqn Flt	Sgt J.N. Miller RCAF	KiA (Bf109)
	BP869/T-Z	249 Sqn	Sgt K. Browne	Baled out (Bf109) PoW
	BR345/T-W	249 Sqn	Flg Off W.J. Locke RCAF	KiA (Bf109)
25/3/43:	EN200/MK-Q	126 Sqn	Flg Off B. Stovel RCAF	Baled out (Bf109) rescued by fishing boat/transferred to HSL128
27/3/43:	EP122/V-C	1435 Sqn	Flt Sgt P. Stratford	Crash-landed (injured)
7/4/43:	EP567/MK-B	126 Sqn	Sgt T. Pennock	FTR (KiFA)
9/4/43:	BR130/T-O	249 Sqn	Flt Sgt W. Yaholnitsky RCAF	FTR (KiFA)
12/4/43:	EP716/X-A	229 Sqn	Sqn Ldr T. Smart DFC	KiA (Bf109)

215

13/4/43:	BR656	683 Sqn	Plt Off L.M. Gilchrist	}	Crashed, hit EN146 (injured)
	EN146/MK-X	126 Sqn	Sqn Ldr J.R. Urwin Mann		Hit by BR656 (injured)
29/4/43:	EP188/T-Y	249 Sqn	Flt Sgt D.E. Cruse		FTR (Bf109) PoW
6/5/43:	EP554/GL-	185 Sqn	Flt Sgt G.F. Mercer RCAF		Baled out, rescued by HSL107
11/5/43:	EP833/V-	1435 Sqn	Flg Off R.B. Martin		KiA (MC202)
12/5/43:	EP709/GL-	185 Sqn	Sgt J.S. Yates		KiA (AA)
14/5/43:	BR194/GL-	185 Sqn	Plt Off M.B. Zobell RCAF		Crashed (injured)
21/5/43:	EP842/X-D	229 Sqn	Plt Off J.A. Collis		Baled out (Bf109) safe on land
22/5/43:	EN142/MK-W	126 Sqn	Flg Off J. Hodges		Baled out (Bf109) rescued by HSL107
	JK816/MK-K	126 Sqn	Flt Sgt J. Rennolds		KiA (Bf109)
25/5/43:	JK463/GL-	185 Sqn	Flt Lt H.F. Withy		KiFA (oxygen failure)
1/6/43:	ES313/V-B	1435 Sqn	Plt Off K.G. Chandler RCAF		Baled out, rescued by HSL166
4/6/43:	EN532/MK-W	126 Sqn	Flt Lt J.D. Keynes		KiA (Bf109)
8/6/43:	JK646/X-V	229 Sqn	Sgt J.D. McKenzie		Baled out (Bf109), rescued by HSL107
10/6/43:	EN204/FL-	81 Sqn	Sgt M.J. O'Grady RAAF		Crashed on take-off (injured)
13/6/43:	JK308/JE	Krendi Wg	Wg Cdr J. Ellis DFC		Baled out (Bf109) PoW
	EF569/X-Z	229 Sqn	Sgt F. Davidson		Baled out (Bf109) PoW
	ER811/T-J	249 Sqn	Sgt B.W. Sheehan RNZAF		Baled out (Italian Bf109) PoW
	EF539/T-F	249 Sqn	Flt Sgt J.C. Hughes RCAF		Crash-landed (w/o)
	EE668/LE-	242 Sqn	Sgt F.L. Jones		Baled out, rescued by HSL107
18/6/43:	EN301/RN-	72 Sqn	Flt Lt D.J. Prytherch		Baled out (Bf109) drowned
	ES355/FT-S	43 Sqn	Flt Sgt M.K. Brown RNZAF		Baled out (Bf109) PoW
20/6/43:	EN298/RN-	72 Sqn	Flg Off G.C. Sharp RAAF		KiA (Bf109)
23/6/43:	JF352	Command EO Grp	Capt R.C. Jordan		Baled out, drowned
25/6/43:	BS557/MK-C	126 Sqn	Flt Sgt J.A. Leckie RCAF		KiFA
	EN257/AX-	1SAAF Sqn	Lt A. deL. Rossouw SAAF		KiA (Bf109)
29/6/43:	AR560/DS	1435 Sqn	Plt Off G.P. Bray RCAF		KiA (AA)
30/6/43:	? /HL-	308th FS	1/Lt George Stephens USAAF		KiFA
	ER165/HL-	308th FS	1/Lt Edward Fardella USAAF		Crashed (injured)
2/7/43:	EN404/GL-W	185 Sqn	Flt Sgt J. Lowry RCAF		KiA (AA)
3/7/43:	EN259/JU-	111 Sqn	Flt Sgt F. Mellor		Baled out, drowned (Bf109)
4/7/43:	AB459/ZX-	145 Sqn	Flt Sgt E.A. Daley RAAF		KiA (MC202)
	BR288/FT-F	43 Sqn	Flt Lt P.W.D. Reading		KiA (Bf109)
	JG928/FT-A	43 Sqn	Flg Off R.O. Barker		KiA (Bf109)
5/7/43:	JG838/X-W	229 Sqn	Sqn Ldr B.E.G. White		KiA (FW190)
	EF520/X-O	229 Sqn	Flt Sgt R.R. Salzman		KiA (FW190)
	JK124/X-G	229 Sqn	Plt Off G.W. Symons RNZAF		Baled out (FW190), rescued by ASR Pinnace 1254
	ER494/X-H	229 Sqn Flt	Sgt R.H. De Tourett RNZAF		Crash-landed (w/o)
6/7/43:	ER534/UF-	601 Sqn	Flg Off W.S. Seaman AFC		KiA (Bf109)
	? /HL-	308th FS	Capt Thomas B. Fleming USAAF		KiA (Bf109)
	? /HL-	308th FS	1/Lt Babcock USAAF		KiA (Bf109)
7/7/43:	LZ163/UM-	152 Sqn	Sgt T. Armstrong		Baled out (collision), rescued by ASR Pinnace 1244
10/7/43:	JL375/SL-Z	243 Sqn	Flg Off L.J. Connors RAAF		Ditched (out of fuel), drowned
	EP690/WR-	40SAAF Sqn	Capt G.C. le Roux DFC SAAF		KiA (MC202)[1]
	ER706/WR-	40SAAF Sqn	Lt E.C. Webb SAAF		Baled out (out of fuel), rescued by RN destroyer
	? /MX-	307th FS	1/Lt John E. Johnson USAAF		Crashed Sicily (USN AA), rescued by US troops
	? /MX-	307th FS	1/Lt John K. Conley USAAF		Baled out (USN AA), rescued by USN destroyer
	JL182/QJ-	92 Sqn	Flt Lt T.W. Savage		KiA (Allied AA/Bf109)
	EP440/QJ-	92 Sqn	Flg Off E.S. Dicks-Sherwood		Baled out (Allied AA/Bf109), rescued by Allied vessel
	EN466/HN-	93 Sqn	Flt Lt W.R. Daddo-Langlois		Crashed (Allied AA/Bf109), severly injured; lost when rescue LST sunk

[1] Capt le Roux's No2 (Lt E.C. Webb) believed another Spitfire shot down his No1.

	EN148/SN-E	243 Sqn	Flg Off G.B. Blunn	KiA (AA/Bf109)
	ER856/LE-S	242 Sqn	Flg Off A.N. Snell	Crash-landed (Bf109) PoW
	EN295/V-B	1435 Sqn	Flt Lt M.R. Rowland RNZAF	KiA (Bf109)
	JL361/V-N	1435 Sqn	Plt Off L.A. Stewart	Baled out (Bf109), rescued by HSL
11/7/43:	? /MX-	307th FS	1/Lt August Goldenberg USAAF	FTR (killed)
	EN448/PO	244 Wg	Wg Cdr P. Olver DFC	Baled out (Ju88) PoW
12/7/43:	JK233/X-X	229 Sqn	Plt Off A. Williams	KiA (BF109)
	JK305/UM-	152 Sqn	Sgt N.E.C. Dear	Baled out (Bf110) rescued
	JK511/UM-	152 Sqn	Sgt R. Quine RAAF	KiA (Bf109)
	JG751/UM-	152 Sqn	Flg Off J.A. Tooth	Crash-landed (Bf109)
	EP966/UF-	601 Sqn	Sqn Ldr J.A. Taylor DFC	KiA (Ju87)
	JK429/RN-	72 Sqn	Sgt J.B. King	FTR (Bf109) PoW
	? /WR-	40SAAF Sqn	Lt K. Robinson SAAF	Baled out (MC202) PoW
	EN287/V-F	1435 Sqn	Flt Sgt S.H. Benjamin	KiA (Bf109/MC202)
13/7/43:	ES282/HN-	93 Sqn	Sgt F.W. Bridger	Baled out (Bf109) returned
14/7/43:	EN300/AX-	1SAAF Sqn	Lt M.E. Robinson SAAF	Baled out (P-38) rescued by destroyer
	Seafire	807 Sqn	Lt de Vass. R.L.A. Claude (F)	KiA (Ju88)
16/7/43:	EN309/RN-	72 Sqn	Sgt A.M. Griffiths	KiA (hit by debris from Bf109 he had just shot down)
17/7/43:	JL125/EF-	232 Sqn	Sgt A.L. Frewer RNZAF	Baled out (Bf109) returned
	JK807/EF-	232 Sqn	Plt Off V. St John	Baled out (Bf109) returned
	? /AX-	1SAAF Sqn	Lt G.T. van der Veen SAAF	Crash-landed (AA) returned
	EN502/JU	111 Sqn	Sgt K.R. Allen	KiFA (crashed on take-off)
18/7/43:	JK394/X-Z	229 Sqn	Sgt D.E. Ripper RAAF	Crash-landed (Bf109) returned
	ES292/FT-	43 Sqn	Wt Off R.W. Leeming RAAF	Crash-landed (Bf109) w/o
	EN153	683 Sqn	Flt Sgt C.A. Tardiff	FTR PoW
19/7/43:	LZ808/X-D	229 Sqn	Flt Lt L.C. Gosling DFC RCAF	KiA (Bf110)
	EP444/X-L	229 Sqn	Sgt W.G. Downing	Baled out (Bf109) PoW
	EE785/AX-	1SAAF Sqn	Lt C.A. Halliday SAAF	KiA (Bf109)
25/7/43:	JL245/UM-	152 Sqn	Flg Off R.A. Marshall RNZAF	KiA (Bf109)
	JK461/HT-	154 Sqn	Flg Off E.D.M. Rippon	Baled out (Bf109) PoW
27/7/43:	/WZ-Z	309th FS	1/Lt Mehoff USAAF	Baled out, returned
28/7/43:	JK274/EF-	232 Sqn	Plt Off C.H. McMinniman RCAF	KiA (Bf110)
	/WZ-	309th FS	1/Lt Robert Heil USAAF	KiA (AA)
4/8/43:	JK637/RN-	72 Sqn	Flg Off G.N. Keith DFC RCAF	Baled out (AA) DoW
7/8/43:	ER163/HT-	154 Sqn	Flt Lt R. Thomson	Baled out, returned
	EN403/GL-A	185 Sqn	Plt Off A.A. Wyndham	Baled out (Ju88) rescued by Walrus
8/8/43:	/WR-	40SAAF Sqn	Lt D.S. Waugh SAAF	Baled out (AA) returned
11/8/43:	/HL-	308th FS	2/Lt Richard F. Hurd USAAF	Crash-landed w/o
night:		232 Sqn	Plt Off V. St John)	Killed on ground at Catania
		232 Sqn	Flt Sgt W.G. Atkinson RAAF }	by bombing
		232 Sqn	Flt Sgt P.E. King	Wounded in same raid
12/8/43:	EN520/HT-	154 Sqn	Sqn Ldr A.C.G. Wenman	Baled out (possibly Bf109), rescued by Walrus
13/8/43:	EF593/AN-	417RCAF Sqn	Plt Off J.T. Field RCAF	Baled out (MC202) PoW
	/WR-	40SAAF Sqn	Lt O.L. Dugmore SAAF	Baled out (AA) killed
15/8/43:	JF482/ZX-	145 Sqn	Flg Off J.F. Carswell RCAF	Baled out (FW190) killed
16/8/43:	EN449/QJ-	92 Sqn	Flg Off B.D. Baker	Baled out (MC205) PoW
17/8/43:	BR290/FT-	43 Sqn	Flt Lt N.W. Lee DFC	Baled out (Mustang) rescued by Walrus
18/8/43:	JK189/SN-L	243 Sqn	Flt Lt E. Gruwys	Baled out (Bf109) returned
	JK642/SN-P	243 Sqn	Sgt R. Jaques	KiA (Bf109)
21/8/43:	EE663/AN-	417RCAF Sqn	Flg Off L.A. Hall RCAF	Baled out (AA) rescued by rowing boat
24/8/43:	ER532	1437 Flt	Sgt P.L. White	Crashed (pilot burned)
28/8/43:	JK373/FL-	81 Sqn	Plt Off H.M. Baker-Munson	Crash-landed (Bf109) returned
29/8/43:	JK125/UM-	152 Sqn	Flt Sgt W.D. Sparkes	KiA (Bf109)
31/8/43:	MA572/FT-G	43 Sqn	Flg Off A.E. Snell	KiFA (oxygen failure)

SPITFIRE SQUADRON CODES

Malta/Sicily 1943

As at 1 July 1943:

244 WING

92 Squadron	QJ
145 Squadron	ZX
601 Squadron	UF
417 Squadron RCAF	AN
1 Squadron SAAF	AX
683 Squadron	No code
40 Squadron SAAF	WR

322 WING

81 Squadron	FL
152 Squadron	UM
154 Squadron	HT
232 Squadron	EF
242 Squadron	LE

324 WING

43 Squadron	FT
72 Squadron	RN
93 Squadron	HN
243 Squadron	SN

KRENDI WING

185 Squadron	GL
229 Squadron	X
249 Squadron	T

SAFI WING

111 Squadron	JU
126 Squadron	MK
1435 Squadron	V

GOZO WING

307th FS	MX
308th FS	HL
309th FS	WZ

NB: 249 Squadron reverted to its original GN codes at end of August 1943
    126 Squadron changed from MK to TD at end of August 1943

Group Captains' & Wing Commanders' Personal Codes:

Grp Capt G.K. Gilroy DSO DFC	GKG	(JK143)	OC 324 Wing
Grp Capt P.H. Hugo DSO DFC	PH	(EN240)	OC 322 Wing
Grp Capt C.B.F. Kingcome DSO DFC	BK		OC 244 Wing
Wg Cdr B. Drake DSO DFC	BD	(JK228)	Wing Leader, Krendi Wing
Wg Cdr W.G.G. Duncan Smith DSO DFC	DS	(AR560)	Wing Leader, Luqa Wing
	DS	(JK650)	Wing Leader, Safi & 244 Wings
Wg Cdr H.S.L. Dundas DSO DFC	HD	(JL122)	Wing Leader, 324 Wing
Wg Cdr J. Ellis DFC	JE	(JK533)	Wing Leader, Krendi Wing
Wg Cdr S.B. Grant DFC	SBG		Wing Leader, Takali Wing
Wg Cdr C.F. Gray DSO DFC	CG	(EN350)	Wing Leader, 322 Wing
Wg Cdr P.P. Hanks DSO DFC	PPH	(BR498)	Wing Leader, Luqa Wing
Wg Cdr A.V.R. Johnstone DFC	AVRJ		Wing Leader, Krendi Wing
Wg Cdr A.D.J. Lovell DSO DFC	ADJL		Wing Leader, Krendi & Safi Wings
Wg Cdr P. Olver DFC	PO	(EN448)	Wing Leader, 244 Wing
Wg Cdr M.M. Stephens DSO DFC	MMS		Wing Leader, Hal Far Wing
Wg Cdr J.M. Thompson DSO DFC	JMT	(AR560)	Wing Leader, Luqa Wing
Lt Col L.A. Wilmot DFC SAAF	LW	(MA408)	Wing Leader, 322 Wing
Lt Col Fred M. Dean USAAF	FMD		OC 31st Fighter Group USAAF

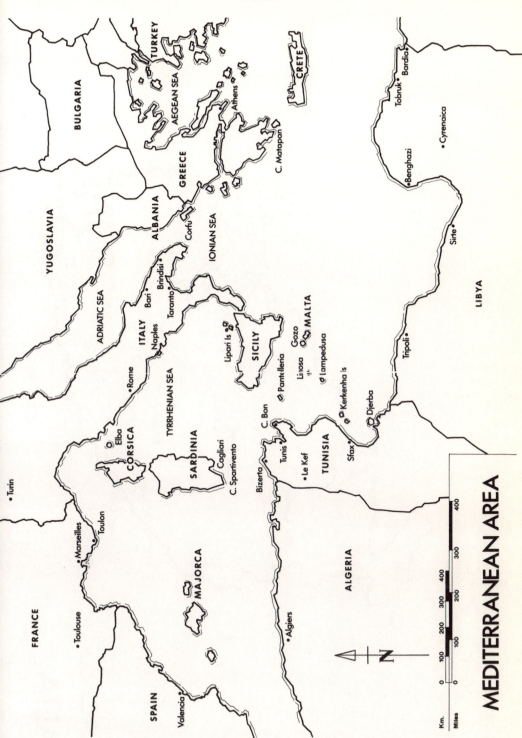

MEDITERRANEAN AREA

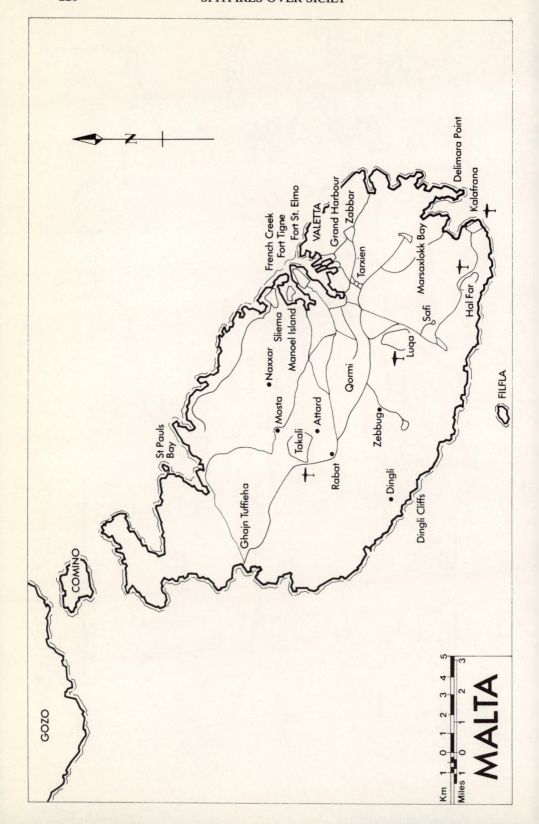

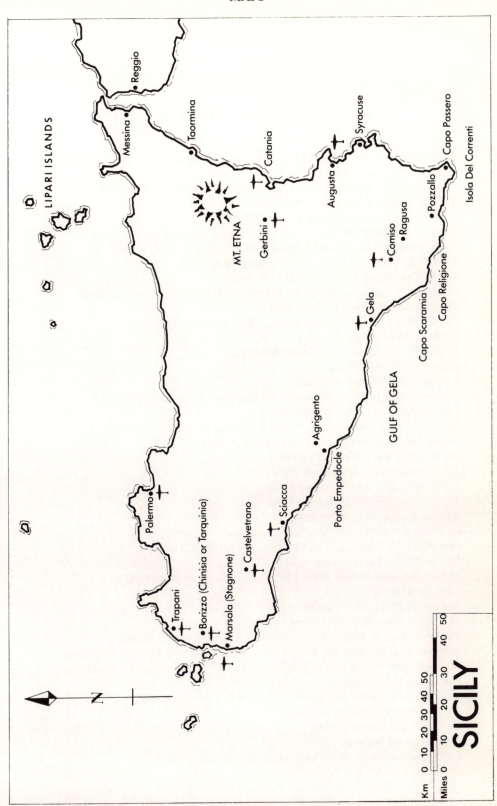

SICILY

Km 0 10 20 30 40 50
Miles 0   10   20   30   40   50

LIPARI ISLANDS

Reggio

Messina

Taormina

Catania

MT. ETNA

Gerbini

Syracuse

Augusta

Capo Passero

Isola Del Correnti

Pozzallo

Ragusa

Comiso

Capo Religione

Capo Scaramia

GULF OF GELA

Gela

Agrigento

Porto Empedocle

Sciacca

Castelvetrano

Marsala (Stagnone)

Borizzo (Chinisia or Tarquinia)

Trapani

Palermo

N

SELECT AND BRIEF BIBLIOGRAPHY

A Brief History of Spitfire IX EN199: Frederick R. Galea
A Few of the Many: Dilip Sarkar
A History of the RAF Servicing Commandos: J.P. Kellett & J. Davies
A Knave Amongst Knights in their Spitfires: Jerry Billing
A Mouse in My Pocket: Hedley Everard DFC
A Sailor's Odyssey: Admiral of the Fleet Lord Cunningham
A Willingness to Die: Group Captain Brian Kingcome DSO DFC
Aces High, Volumes One & Two: Christopher Shores
All the Fine Young Eagles: David L. Bashow
American Beagle Squadron, The: Lawrence G. Burke & Robert C. Curtis
Bitter Victory: Colonel Carlo D'Este
Black Crosses off my Wingtip: Sqn Ldr Hap Kennedy DFC
Courage Alone: Chris Dunning
Eagles Victorious: H.J. Martin & Neil Orpen
Eclipse: Alan Moorehead
Escape – or Die: Paul Brickhill
Fighters over Tunisia: Christopher Shores, Hans Ring & William Hess
First and the Last, The: Adolf Galland
Fleet Air Arm Aircraft 1939-1945: Ray Sturtivant with Mick Burrow
Flying Start: Group Captain Hugh Dundas CBE DSO DFC
Focke Wulf 190 at War: Alfred Price
Jagdgeschwader 3: Dr Jochen Prien
Jagdgeschwader 53: Dr Jochen Prien
Jagdgeschwader 77: Dr Jochen Prien
Heaven & Hell: Martin Pöppel
In A Now Forgotten Sky: Dennis C. Kucera
Lest We Forget: John A. Agius MBE & Frederick R. Galea
Malta; Blitzed But Not Beaten: Philip Vella
Malta: The Spitfire Year 1942: Christopher Shores & Brian Cull with
   Nicola Malizia
Maltese Penguin, The: Frank Cockett
Man Who Never Was, The: Ewen Montague
Mediterranean & Middle East Volume V: Brigadier C.J.C. Malony
Memoirs of Field-Marshal Kesselring, The: Feldmarschall Albert Kesselring
Messerschmitt 109 in Italian Service 1943-1945, The: Ferdinando D'Amico
   & Gabriele Valentini
Monty: Master of the Battlefield, 1942-1944: Nigel Hamilton
Mountbatten: Philip Ziegler
On Y Va!: Constantin Feldzer
Seafire: David Brown
Sicily-Salerno-Anzio: Admiral Samuel Eliot Morison USN
Slaughter over Sicily: Charles Whiting

Spitfire into Battle: Group Captain Duncan Smith DSO DFC
Spitfire Leader: Max Avery with Christopher Shores
Spitfire Patrol: Wing Commander Colin Gray DSO DFC
Spitfires over Israel: Brian Cull & Shlomo Aloni with David Nicolle
Stars & Bars: Frank Olynyk
Straits of Messina, The: Johannes Steinhoff
Victory in the Air: Richard Caruana
War at Sea, The, Volume III: Capt S.W. Roskill DSC RN
Warburton's War: Tony Spooner DSO DFC
We Happy Few: Edited by Lloyd Hunt
Where No Angels Dwell: Air Vice-Marshal Sandy Johnstone CBE DFC
Wings of Pegasus, The: George Chatterton
43 Squadron: J. Beedle
73 Squadron Part Two: Don Minterne
249 at War: Brian Cull

Italian language publications, including articles, consulted by Nico Malizia and Gianandrea Bussi included:
Bf109 – Storia del Caccia Messerschmitt: Nino Arena
Dal RE2002 al RE2005 Storia degli aerei Reggiane – Gruppo Caproni:
    Sergio Govi
Da Bir-Hackeim and Augusta 1942-1943: Ferdinando Pedriali
Gli Stuka della Regia Aeronautica 1940-1945: A. Borgiotti & C. Gori
La Ballata dell'Aviatore: General Alberto Mainini
Na Storia Nostra: Aldo Barbaglio
Quarant'anni due Idroscali: Tullio Marcon
Quelli del Cavallino Rampante: Antonio Duma
50°Stormo d'Assalto: Nino Arena
Il 150°, 151°, 153° Gruppo Caccia: Eugenio Tarantola
Il 5°Stormo – Il 51°Stormo Caccia: Nicola Malizia
101°Gruppo Tuffatori: Giuseppe Pesce

Few books of this nature would be complete without reference to the excellent Air-Britain Serial Registers series, while primary PRO documents consulted included Air 22/393 (Air Intelligence Summaries), Air 22/6787 (*RAF Review* produced by AHB), Air 23/5554 (Air Intelligence Claims and Losses), Air 26/328, Air 26/425, and Air 26/429 (Wing ORBs) Air 27 series (Squadron ORBs), Air 29/869 (Flight ORBs), Air 40/1864 (POW Interrogation Reports), and Air 41/42 (AHB Summary of Operation *Husky*).

HURRICANES OVER TOBRUK

Addenda

Since the publication of the first volume in this series – *Hurricanes over Tobruk* – further information has come to light regarding one of the Free French pilots who flew with 73 Squadron in the defence of Tobruk in April 1941, Sous-Lt Louis Ferrant. His son Yves has sent me a photocopy of a page from his father's logbook, together with a translation of an article which contained an interview with Sous-Lt James Denis, who commanded the Free French Flight at Tobruk:

> "April 14th. I started the first flight with Sous-Lt Ferrant. It was Easter Monday. I was on alert when a formation of dive-bombers, firmly escorted by fighters, appeared far off over the airfield. A patrol of three British aircraft took off. I gained altitude. I reached 6,500 feet. At 5,000 feet I saw a patrol of twelve aircraft passing. But at 8,000 feet some Messerschmitt 110s weaved above me. Suddenly a Ju88 appeared in my line of fire. I fired with all my machine-guns. Did I hit it? I think so, but a Stuka that I pursued and shot down within a few seconds prevented me from seeing the result of my previous action. In the meantime, Sous-Lt Ferrant remained at the base of the clouds and shot down successively, with great coolness, three German aircraft just as they started their dives . . ."

Sous-Lt Ferrant's logbook confirms a 30-minute flight in Hurricane V7856 during which he claimed two Ju87s in flames, with a third last seen trailing smoke. On page 116 of *Hurricanes over Tobruk*, and again on page 204, I attributed these victories to Sous-Lt Albert Littolf, another of the Free French pilots.

73 Squadron's ORB fails to record any flights for Sous-Lt Ferrant on either 13 or 14 April, whereas his logbook clearly shows he participated in two flights on each of those days. The 73 Squadron diarist had entered the name of Sous-Lt Littolf as the pilot of V7856 on the morning of 14 April and therefore he was assumed to have been Sous-Lt Denis' companion on the sortie in question. This is evidently incorrect, hence the inaccurate statements in *Hurricanes over Tobruk*. Confusion reigned at Tobruk at this time, and accurate recording of flights was not maintained. Sous-Lt Ferrant was flown out of Tobruk aboard a Blenheim on 25 April, and three days later was awarded a Citation by Général d'Armée Catroux, Commander-in-Chief of Free French Forces in the Middle East, which cited his three victories, including one probable, on 14 April.

Brian Cull
Author of *Hurricanes over Tobruk*

PERSONNEL INDEX

BRITISH & COMMONWEALTH PERSONNEL

Adams, Sgt A.J. 111 Sqn 156
Aikman, Flt Lt A.F. RCAF 154 Sqn 166, 213
Alexander, Gen Sir Harold C-in-C North Africa 2, 178, 179, 192
Allen, Sgt K.R. 111 Sqn 139, 140, 167, 217
Anderson, Plt Off T.G. 1435 Sqn 131
Andrew, Flt Sgt D. 229 Sqn 145, 211
Andrew, Sgt J.R. 93 Sqn 154, 212
Armstrong, Sgt T. 152 Sqn 108, 216
Arthur, Sqn Ldr C.I.R. 232 Sqn 65, 88, 93, 166, 188, 189, 210
Artus, Flt Sgt E. 154 Sqn 166, 206, 213
Ashton, Sqn Ldr J.D. 185 Sqn 15, 18
Askey, Flt Sgt M.W.H. RCAF 92 Sqn 127, 163, 181
Atkinson, Flt Lt R.E. 185 Sqn 7, 14
Atkinson, Sgt/Plt Off T.G. 1435 Sqn 38, 75, 95, 131, 210
Atkinson, Flt Sgt W.G. RAAF 232 Sqn 187, 217

Bage, Flt Sgt N. 249 Sqn 8
Baker, Flg Off B.D. 92 Sqn 97, 99, 190, 208, 214, 217
Baker, Plt Off K. ASRU 19
Baker-Munson, Plt Off H.M. 81 Sqn 200, 217
Bamberger, Flg Off C.S. 93 Sqn 155, 212
Banner, Flg Off F.S. 243 Sqn 98, 153, 154, 179, 210, 212, 213
Barber, Flg Off P.G. 81 Sqn 79, 210
Barker, Flg Off R.O. 43 Sqn 100, 216
Barnes, Sgt/Plt Off L.G. RCAF 126 Sqn 7, 60, 63, 209, 210
Baxter, Flt Sgt R.H. 93 Sqn v, vi, 123, 127-128, 157, 212
Baxter, Flg Off S.V. RAAF 185 Sqn 195, 214
Baynham, Flt Lt G.T. 152 Sqn 173, 213
Beatson, Flg Off J. RAAF 249 Sqn 60, 77, 89
Benjamin, Flt Sgt S.H. 1435 Sqn 95, 149, 210, 217
Berry, Flt Sgt J.R. RNZAF 284 Sqn 192
Berry, Wg Cdr R. 322 Wing 206
Billing, Flt Sgt G.D. RCAF 185 Sqn 9, 18, 26, 30, 34, 55, 215
Bingham, Flt Sgt A. 126 Sqn 96, 139
Bisdee, Wg Cdr J.D. Military Governor Lampedusa 76
Blaauw, Lt Col J.D.P. SAAF 40SAAF Sqn 83, 93
Blumer, Flg Off A.G. RAAF 601 Sqn 147
Blunn, Flg Off G.B. 243 Sqn 129, 217
Boddington, Sqn Ldr M.C.B. 242 Sqn 93, 106, 121, 125, 129, 134, 156, 210-212
Bosch, Lt P.H. SAAF 185 Sqn 86
Bowring, Sgt L.J. 232 Sqn 175
Bradbury, Sgt S.L. 152 Sqn 173, 213
Bradley, Flt Sgt J. 284 Sqn 180
Bramley, Flt Sgt E.F. 73 Sqn 119
Bray, Plt Off G.P. RCAF 1435 Sqn 87, 216
Bridger, Sgt F.W. 93 Sqn 154, 217
Brister, Sgt T.E. 92 Sqn 161
Broadhurst, AVM H. AOC WDAF 147, 174, 175, 181, 201

Bromhead, Flt Sgt W.G. 229 Sqn 145
Brooks, Flg Off B.B. 1435 Sqn 83
Brown, Flt Lt M.G. RCAF 683 Sqn 53
Brown, Flt Sgt M.K. RNZAF 43 Sqn 81, 216
Brown, Flt Lt R. 229 Sqn 45, 49
Browne, Sgt K. 249 Sqn 37-39, 215
Browne, Flg Off S.F. RNZAF 93 Sqn 127, 136, 154, 211, 212
Bruce, Flt Lt E.A.C.G. 92/417RCAF Sqns 186, 187, 194, 195
Buchanan, Sgt G.M. RNZAF 185 Sqn 110, 210
Burrows, Flg Off E.R. 152 Sqn 173, 213
Butler, Flt Sgt S. 1435 Sqn 144

Caldecott, Sgt W.E. 81 Sqn 173, 183, 213
Caldwell, Wt Off T.R. 72 Sqn 146
Cam, Plt Off E.K. 232 Sqn 66
Cameron, Sgt G.A. RCAF 1435 Sqn 19
Cameron, Flg Off W.J. 72 Sqn 146
Campbell, Sgt K. 242 Sqn 144
Carmody, Flt Sgt C.J. RCAF 185 Sqn 16, 24, 34, 215
Carpenter, Flt Lt J.M.V. 92 Sqn 187
Carswell, Flg Off J.F. RCAF 145 Sqn 180, 189, 190, 214, 217
Carter, Air Mech SAAF 40SAAF Sqn 197
Carver, Lt Cdr(A) R.H.P. RN 885 Sqn 115
Cattermoul, Flg Off F. 126 Sqn 61
Chambers, Flt Lt H.W. RNZAF 242 Sqn 122, 210
Chandler, Plt Off K.G. RCAF 1435 Sqn 63, 103, 216
Chaplin, Flt Lt A.R. 229 Sqn 13, 215
Chappell, Flt Lt C.G. 185 Sqn 183
Chatterton, Col G. Glider Pilot Regt 116, 117
Cheek, Flg Off L. 185 Sqn 10, 21
Christopherson, Flt Lt M.V. 72 Sqn 135, 211
Churchill, The Hon Winston Prime Minister 2, 192
Clarence, Lt B.V. SAAF 40SAAF Sqn 148, 162
Clarke, Flg Off B.W. 126 Sqn 139, 211
Clarkson, Sgt K.E. RAAF 72 Sqn 80, 143, 148, 211
Clay, Sgt C. 126 Sqn 64
Clayton, Sgt A.J. 229 Sqn 49, 209
Cleverly, Plt Off/Flt Lt W.J. 249 Sqn 10, 24, 36
Clifford, Alex Daily Mail 73, 74
Cockett, Plt Off F. RAF MO 117-118
Cohen, Sgt S. ASRU 75, 76
Collis, Plt Off J.A. 229 Sqn 46, 59, 209, 216
Colvin, Flg Off D.A.S. 249 Sqn 38
Coningham, Air Marshal Sir Arthur AOC NWATAF 142, 181
Connolly, Sgt J.T. RAAF 72 Sqn 165, 212
Connors, Flg Off L.J. RAAF 243 Sqn 124, 216
Cook, Flt Sgt F.R.M. 229 Sqn 145, 211
Cooper, Flt Sgt M.R. RNZAF 601 Sqn 183
Cooper, Wt Off S.F. 154 Sqn 126
Corbott, Plt Off S.A. RCAF 417RCAF Sqn 197
Costain, Plt Off H.D. 154 Sqn 126
Costello, Plt Off W.J. RNZAF 249 Sqn 41, 47, 209
Coulthard, Flg Off C.W. 242 Sqn 129, 194, 210
Courtney, Flt Sgt L. 242 Sqn 156, 212
Cox, Flt Lt/Sqn Ldr G.J. 43, 229 Sqns 100, 101, 108,

131, 160, 170, 210, 211
Crafts, Sqn Ldr H.C. RNZAF 185 Sqn 26, 28, 61, 65
Craig, Plt Off G. 683 Sqn 58
Crawford, Flt Lt I.K. 111 Sqn 100, 210
Crockett, Flt Lt G.R. ASRU 32, 85
Cronin, Flt Sgt L.F. RAAF 81 Sqn 173, 213
Cross, Sgt C. 185 Sqn 47
Cruickshank, Sgt W.A. 185 Sqn 65, 210
Cruse, Flt Sgt D.E. 249 Sqn 33, 50, 52, 216
Cunningham, Adm Sir Andrew C-in-C Allied Naval
   Forces 2, 116, 120, 192

Daddo-Langlois, Flt Lt W.R. 93 Sqn 128, 216
Daley, Flt Sgt E.A. RAAF 145 Sqn 100, 216
Dalrymple, Flg Off S.I. 243 Sqn 98, 153
Daniel, Sqn Ldr S.W. 72 Sqn 75, 93, 94, 108, 134,
   135, 145, 146, 148, 168, 210, 211
Darwen, Grp Capt J. OC 239 Wing 135
Davidson, Sgt F. 126 Sqn 64, 76, 77, 216
Davidson, Sgt J.S. 126 Sqn 139
Davies, Sgt E.R. 229 Sqn 59, 60
Davies, Flg Off M. 154 Sqn 166
Davison, Sgt S.J. 232 Sqn 189
Davoren, Sgt P.J. RAAF 243 Sqn 154, 212
Dawkins, Flg Off J.A.N. 249 Sqn 8, 9, 215
Dear, Sgt N.E.C. 152 Sqn 145, 211, 217
Debenham, Flt Lt K.B.L. 249 Sqn 35, 41, 196, 214
de Guingand, Maj Gen F. CoS Eighth Army 174
De Tourett, Flt Sgt R.H. RNZAF 229 Sqn 103, 104,
   107, 210, 216
Dicks-Sherwood, Flt Lt E.S. 92 Sqn 127, 175, 213,
   216
Divers, Sgt A. RNZAF 283 Sqn 187
Doherty, Sgt E.S. RNZAF 242 Sqn 107, 108, 134,
   173, 211, 213
Donnelly, Lt P.H. SAAF 40SAAF Sqn 87
Downing, Sgt W.G. 229 Sqn 145, 169, 213, 217
Drake, Wg Cdr B. WCF Krendi Wing 80, 81, 83, 89,
   94, 107, 159, 210, 218
Dugmore, Lt O.L. SAAF 40SAAF Sqn 188, 217
Duncan Smith, Wg Cdr W.G.G. WCF Luqa, Safi & 244
   Wings 64, 66, 67, 74, 75, 86, 87, 94, 128, 130, 131,
   134, 139, 147, 149, 171, 175, 196, 197, 200, 201,
   210-212, 214, 218
Dundas, Wg Cdr H.S.L. WCF 324 Wing 75, 80, 82,
   93, 96, 97, 100, 124, 157, 158, 210, 212, 218
Dunsmore, Plt Off W.E. RCAF 185 Sqn 195, 214
du Plessis, 2/Lt J.P. SAAF 40SAAF Sqn 184
Durbidge, Plt Off K. 683 Sqn 169
Dutton, Plt Off W.N. 242 Sqn 122

Eaton, Sqn Ldr B.A. RAAF 3RAAF Sqn 189
Eccleston, Sgt H.S. RAAF 111 Sqn 139, 211
Edwards, Flt Sgt C. RNZAF 73 Sqn 119-120
Edwards, Flg Off K.A. 242 Sqn 108, 173, 213
Einhorn, Plt Off M.D. 243 Sqn 153
Ekbery, Plt Off J.S. 232 Sqn 106, 165, 210, 213
Ellis, Wg Cdr J. WCF Krendi Wing 43, 45, 50, 66, 76,
   77, 216, 218
Everard, Flg Off H.J. RCAF 417RCAF Sqn 104, 161,
   182, 186

Fakhry, Plt Off M.J. RAAF 92 Sqn 109
Faure, Capt J.M. SAAF 1SAAF Sqn 170, 213
Field, Plt Off J.T. RCAF 417RCAF Sqn 188, 217
Filson, Plt Off J. 1435 Sqn 82
Firth, Lt Cdr(A) K. RNVR 807 Sqn 115
Fisher, Plt Off R.G. RNZAF 93 Sqn 136, 154, 211
Fowler, Flt Lt F.E. 249 Sqn 10
Frazer, Plt Off J.A. RAAF 69 Sqn 11, 215
Frewer, Flt Sgt A.V. RNZAF 232 Sqn 79, 166, 217

Frith, Plt Off M.W. 229 Sqn 28
Fry, Wt Off S.R. 92 Sqn 137, 211
Furniss, Flg Off P. 154 Sqn 174

Gabbutt, Flt Sgt W. 683 Sqn 171, 184
Garrett-Reed, L/Air P. ASRU 37
Garwood, Flg Off H.G. RCAF 417RCAF Sqn 184
Gasson, 2/Lt J.E. SAAF 92 Sqn 127, 137, 175, 211
Gatley, Wt Off P. 242 Sqn 122, 173, 213
Gear, Wt Off A.W. 72 Sqn 80, 82, 210
Gilchrist, Plt Off L.M. 683 Sqn 46, 216
Gilliland, Flg Off W.H. 1437 Flight 192
Gilroy, Grp Capt G.K. OC 324 Wing 75, 80, 93, 123,
   124, 129, 134, 154, 203, 212, 218
Goby, Flg Off W.J. 81 Sqn 161, 173, 212, 213
Goodwin, Sgt D.W. RCAF 229 Sqn 19, 215
Goodyear, Flt Sgt S.H.K. RCAF 229 Sqn 25, 26, 215
Gort, Lord Governor of Malta 90
Gosling, Flg Off/Flt Lt L.C. RCAF 229 Sqn 25, 38,
   45, 49, 55, 62, 66, 76, 89, 103, 136, 145, 148, 160,
   169, 170, 207, 209-211, 217
Grant, Wg Cdr S.B. WCF Takali Wing 4, 8, 218
Gray, Wg Cdr C.F. WCF 322 Wing 65, 79-81, 88, 93,
   124, 126, 160, 172, 183, 206, 210, 213, 218
Gray, Flt Lt J.A. 93 Sqn 125, 154, 210, 212
Gray, Plt Off J.O. RCAF 249 Sqn 200
Green, Flg Off/Flt Lt R.E. 126 Sqn 18, 35, 54, 61, 76,
   96
Greenwood, Sgt A.J. RAAF 126 Sqn 35, 55, 171
Gregory, Plt Off L.E. 243 Sqn 153
Griffith, Flg Off J.L. 1437 Flt 147, 179, 184, 192
Griffiths, Sgt A.M. 72 Sqn 146, 148, 156, 160, 165,
   212, 217
Gruwys, Flt Lt G.E. 243 Sqn 157, 193, 217

Haase, Flg Off G.M. 154 Sqn 166, 213
Hackett, Brig 1st Airborne Division 117
Hagico, 2/Lt M.A. Belg AF 601 Sqn 147, 212
Halcombe, Flt Sgt F.K. 1435 Sqn 103
Hall, Sgt H.R. 111 Sqn 96, 210
Hall, Wt Off K.G. 284 Sqn 192
Hall, Flg Off L.A. RCAF 417RCAF Sqn 196, 217
Halliday, Lt C.A. SAAF 1SAAF Sqn 158, 170, 217
Hanks, Wg Cdr P.P. OC RAF Hal Far 4, 9, 11, 14, 21,
   138, 218
Hanson-Lester, Flg Off P.L. 683 Sqn 32, 215
Hards, Flt Lt M.S. 601 Sqn 147, 174
Harris, Sgt G. 185 Sqn 86
Harrison, Sgt N.H. RNZAF 1435 Sqn 144, 168, 211,
   213
Harrison, Sgt W.N. 1435 Sqn 45
Hart, Sgt W. 1435 Sqn 23, 36, 215
Hawkins, Plt Off/Flg Off D.J. 1435 Sqn 15, 83, 144
Head, Flt Sgt L.G. ASRU 45, 55
Hedderwick, Wt Off P.J. RAAF 43 Sqn 101, 134, 211
Henderson, Capt J.D. HQ Eighth Army 174
Henderson, Sgt K.R. 185 Sqn 89
Hendry, Sgt R.B. RNZAF 126 Sqn 18
Heppell, Flt Lt/Sqn Ldr P.W.E. 1435, 229 Sqns 19, 20,
   24, 25, 35, 38, 46, 47, 215
Hermiston, Flt Sgt K. 72 Sqn 108, 135, 211
Hibbert, Plt Off W.J. RCAF 126 Sqn 8
Hicks, Brig P.H.W. 1st Airborne Brigade 117
Higgo, Lt A. SAAF 1SAAF Sqn 85
Hill, Sqn Ldr G.U. RCAF 111 Sqn 75, 94, 96, 97,
   139, 140, 152, 156, 210-212
Hill, Flt Lt R.C. 69 Sqn 20, 215
Hillary, Lt G.W. SAAF 1SAAF Sqn 171
Hind, Wt Off R. 185 Sqn 21, 22
Hoare, Wt Off P.J.N. 1435 Sqn 159
Hockey, Sgt F.W. 93 Sqn 157

Hodges, Plt Off/Flg Off J.   126 Sqn   17, 52, 60, 216
Holmes, Flg Off H.C.   249 Sqn   56, 209
Holt, Flt Lt   92 Sqn MO   186
Hopkinson, Maj Gen G.F.   1st Airborne Division   117, 119
Hopkinson, Flt Lt H.   229 Sqn   95
Horbaczewski, Flt Lt E.   43 Sqn   174
Horricks, Plt Off G.E. RCAF   417RCAF Sqn   195
Houle, Flt Lt A.U. RCAF   417RCAF Sqn   182
Howarth, Lt Cdr(A) R.B. RNVR   899 Sqn   115
Hughes, Flt Sgt J.C. RCAF   249 Sqn   26, 38, 77, 216
Hughes, Flg Off T.B.   72 Sqn   101, 146, 182, 211
Hugo, Grp Capt P.H.   OC 322 Wing   65, 68, 74, 80, 88, 93, 172, 200, 218
Hulse, Flt Sgt G.S.   81 Sqn   79, 165, 210, 212
Humphreys, Sqn Ldr P.H.   92 Sqn   79, 82, 93, 103, 172, 181
Hunt, Flg Off L.E. RCAF   93 Sqn   136, 193, 211
Hussey, Plt Off R.J.H.   72 Sqn   108, 135, 148, 156, 160, 168, 210, 212, 213

Idema, Flg Off W.D.   229 Sqn   44, 46, 59, 89, 104, 209
Iles, Lt E.G. SAAF   40SAAF Sqn   197
Ingalls, Plt Off B.J. RCAF   72 Sqn   145, 211
Ingram, Flt Lt/Sqn Ldr M.R.B. RNZAF   243/152 Sqns   179, 191, 201

Jackson, Flt Lt/Sqn Ldr H.S.   126 Sqn   17, 26, 28, 42, 43, 46, 49, 50, 58, 61, 64, 67, 68, 86, 87, 94, 209, 210
Jaques, Sgt R.   243 Sqn   153, 193, 212, 217
Jennings, Sgt P.S.   229 Sqn   59, 60
Johnson, Flt Sgt T.E.   43 Sqn   174, 213
Johnston, Flt Lt M. RCAF   72 Sqn   146, 212
Johnstone, Wg Cdr A.V.R.   WCF Krendi Wing   4, 7, 8, 12, 25, 35, 218
Jones, Sgt F.L.   242 Sqn   78, 216
Jones, Flg Off N.G.   152 Sqn   170, 173, 201, 213
Jones, Flg Off R.M.C.   1437 Flt   175, 189
Jordan, Grp Capt R.C.   Command E.O.   83, 216
Jowsey, Flg Off M.E. RCAF   92 Sqn   127, 137, 161, 163, 181, 194, 211, 212
Jupp, Flt Lt A.H.   72 Sqn   143, 147, 148, 165, 170, 211

Keating, Sgt R.   249 Sqn   60
Keith, Flg Off G.N. RCAF   72 Sqn   80, 81, 135, 140, 143, 148, 160, 180, 210-212, 217
Kelley, Flt Lt P.   683 Sqn   122, 130, 184
Kelly, Flt Sgt E.D. RCAF   249 Sqn   39, 52, 209
Kelly, Flt Sgt H.R.   242 Sqn   173, 213
Kennedy, Plt Off/Flt Lt I.F. RCAF   249/185/111 Sqns   9, 24, 33, 39, 46-50, 68, 69, 195, 209, 210
Keynes, Flt Lt J.D.   126 Sqn   55, 60, 65, 210, 216
Keyter, Lt B. SAAF   2SAAF Sqn   196
King, Sgt J.B.   72 Sqn   148, 217
King, Flg Off J.F.   72 Sqn   146, 148, 170, 212
King, Flt Sgt P.E.   232 Sqn   187, 217
Kingcome, Grp Capt C.B.F.   OC 244 Wing   93, 106, 151, 165, 170, 176, 186, 198, 218
Kingsford, Flg Off R.S.   152 Sqn   170, 173, 213
Kirkman, Plt Off J.N.   1435 Sqn   27, 209, 215
Kleimeyer, Plt Off/Flt Lt RCAF   1435 Sqn   23, 36, 86
Knight, Flg Off/Flt Lt H.A.   185 Sqn   11, 15, 16, 24, 31, 42, 49, 65, 210
Kruger, Lt J.H. SAAF   40SAAF Sqn   162, 197
Kuhlman, Capt K.C. SAAF   185 Sqn   10, 11

Lambert, Sgt W.S.   283 Sqn   143
Langerman, Capt W.M. SAAF   1SAAF Sqn   170, 182
Lapp, Flg Off E.G. RCAF   185 Sqn   16
Laubscher, Maj C.J. SAAF   attached 242 Sqn   125
Lawrence, Plt Off E.A.   243 Sqn   153, 212

Lea, Flg Off H.   43 Sqn   140
Leckie, Flt Sgt J.A. RCAF   126 Sqn   85, 216
Lee, Cpl J.   Royal Signals   123
Lee, Flt Lt N.W.   93 Sqn   125, 148, 157, 192, 193, 212, 217
Leeming, Wt Off R.W. RAAF   43 Sqn   134, 169, 211, 217
Leggo, Wt Off H.M.   1437 Flight   179, 184
Leguerrier, Plt Off J.H.G. RCAF   417RCAF Sqn   188
Le Jeune, Plt Off J.R.   126 Sqn   52, 59
Le May, Grp Capt W.K.   OC RAF Luqa   4
Le Roux, Capt G.C. SAAF   40SAAF Sqn   125, 216
Lewis, Flt Sgt W.S.   683 Sqn   39, 67
Lifford, Flt Sgt A.R.   249 Sqn   200
Liggett, Sgt J.L.   93 Sqn   154, 212
Lindner, Flg Off W.S.   242 Sqn   121
Lindsay, Flg Off W.R.M.   242 Sqn   122
Lister, Sqn Ldr F.W.   152 Sqn   65, 66, 93, 145, 179, 211
Lloyd, Plt Off J.   229 Sqn   45, 48, 209
Locke, Flg Off W.J. RCAF   249 Sqn   38, 215
Long, Flt Lt J.H. RCAF   126 Sqn   14, 18, 215
Louden, Wg Cdr M.J.   WCF 239 Wing   147, 158
Lovell, Wg Cdr A.D.J.   WCF Krendi Wing   35, 36, 218
Lowther, Flg Off J.L.   242 Sqn   194
Lowry, Flt Sgt J. RCAF   185 Sqn   95, 216
Lunn, Sgt D.J.   284 Sqn   180
Lynch, Flt Lt/Sqn Ldr J.J.   249 Sqn   10, 24, 35, 43, 50, 51, 56, 94, 158, 209, 212

MacBain, Flg Off K. RCAF   249 Sqn   200, 214
MacDonald, Flt Lt K.F.   243 Sqn   98, 210
Macdonald, Plt Off R.E.J.   152 Sqn   88, 108, 173, 213
MacDougall, Sqn Ldr I.N.   185 Sqn   65, 87, 89, 94, 95, 108, 195, 214
Mackay, Sqn Ldr R.C.   69 Sqn   4
Mackie, Sqn Ldr E.D. RNZAF   243 Sqn   75, 81, 93, 98, 99, 101, 124, 138, 143, 147, 153, 157, 210, 212
MacLeod, Sqn Ldr M.G. RCAF   249 Sqn   10, 22, 25, 27, 35, 215
Maffre, Flt Sgt J.M.   185 Sqn   30
Maguire, Plt Off/Flg Off W.I.H.   81 Sqn   83, 165, 168, 181, 210, 212, 213
Mahoney, Flg Off G.H.E. RCAF   683 Sqn   44
Marshall, Flg Off R.A. RNZAF   152 Sqn   173, 217
Martin, Flg Off R.B.   1435 Sqn   57, 216
Martyn, Lt Cdr(A) W.H. RNVR   880 Sqn   115
Mattingley, Wg Cdr   OC RAF Kalafrana   91
Maxwell, Flg Off J.H.   242 Sqn   173, 213
May, Wg Cdr P.R.   38 Group   151
McCall, Flg Off R.M.   1437 Flight   191
McCann, Flt Sgt E.A.   232 Sqn   165
McConnell, Plt Off P.M.   126 Sqn   87
McDougall, Plt Off L.J. RCAF   229 Sqn   32, 215
McIntosh, Flt Lt L. RAAF   111 Sqn   152, 212
McKee, Plt Off/Flt Lt L.M.   185 Sqn   47, 66, 86, 110, 210
McKenzie, Sgt J.D.   229 Sqn   67, 95, 216
McLaren, Wt Off I.N.   243 Sqn   153
McLaren, Lt P.D.L. SAAF   1437 Flight   180
McMinniman, Plt Off C.H. RCAF   232 Sqn   165, 175, 213, 217
Meadows, Sgt J.R.   249 Sqn   34, 215
Meagher, Sgt G.H.   185 Sqn   89, 210
Mellor, Flt Sgt F.   111 Sqn   83, 96, 97, 210, 216
Mellors, Flg Off F.A.   111 Sqn   139, 211
Melville, Sgt G.T.   243 Sqn   157
Mercer, Flt Sgt G.F. RCAF   185 Sqn   35, 54, 86, 95, 110, 210, 216
Merton, Grp Capt W.H.   OC RAF Luqa   4
Miller, Flt Sgt A.W.   1435 Sqn   168

Miller, Flt Sgt J.N. RCAF   185 Sqn   30, 31, 37, 215
Mills, Flt Lt J.P.   73 Sqn   109
Montgomerie, Flt Lt L.J. RNZAF   81 Sqn   183, 213
Montgomery, Gen Sir Bernard   OC Eighth Army   2, 3, 93, 119, 121, 133, 174, 175, 192
Moodie, Maj D.D. SAAF   1SAAF Sqn   79, 85, 93, 158
Moore, Flt Sgt H.H.S. RNZAF   242 Sqn   185
Moorehead, Alan   War Correspondent   202
Morgan, Flt Sgt E.R.   242 Sqn   156, 212
Moribito, Flt Sgt A.B. RCAF   283 Sqn   187
Morris, Sgt J.B.   72 Sqn   143
Morris, Plt Off R.   1435 Sqn   144, 211
Mountbatten, Vice-Adm Lord Louis   133
Murray, Maj T.B. SAAF   2SAAF Sqn   196
Myers, Plt Off N.L.   242 Sqn   173, 213
Mygind, Sgt W. RNZAF   73 Sqn   141

Nadon, Flt Sgt G.R. RCAF   185 Sqn   66, 89, 210
Nesbitt, Plt Off T.   185 Sqn   23, 55, 215
Newberry, Flg Off G.   249 Sqn   24, 215
Nicholson, Sgt/Plt Off D.E.   249 Sqn   12, 38, 77, 210
Noonan, Flt Sgt F.A. RAAF   255 Sqn   199
Norton, Sqn Ldr G.H.   112 Sqn   159
Notley, Sgt A.   249 Sqn   28, 215
Nuttall, LAC E.   3231 SCU   91

O'Brien, Flg Off P.A.J.   185 Sqn   7, 9-11, 16
Ogilvie, Wg Cdr P.B.   682 Sqn   201
O'Grady, Sgt M.J. RAAF   81 Sqn   68, 216
Oliver, Plt Off B.J. RNZAF   249 Sqn   33, 47, 209
Olmsted, Flt Lt W.A. RCAF   232 Sqn   79, 88, 210
Olver, Wg Cdr P.   WCF 244 Wing   66, 82, 93, 136-138, 140, 211, 217, 218
O'Neill, Sqn Ldr H.F.   1435 Sqn   38, 44-47, 50, 60, 64, 87, 94, 130, 131, 209
Osborne, Plt Off A.F.   249 Sqn   51, 209

Park, AVM Sir Keith   AOC Malta   21, 25, 48, 49, 51, 57, 90, 148, 167, 168
Patterson, Flt Sgt/Wt Off J.W.   232 Sqn   88, 166, 188, 210, 213, 214
Patterson, Sgt R.O.   152 Sqn   173, 213
Payne, Flt Sgt H.C.   243 Sqn   153, 212
Peacock, Flt Sgt C. RCAF   683 Sqn   35, 215
Pearce, Plt Off R.H.   126 Sqn   60
Pearson, Sgt R.C.   72 Sqn   135, 148
Peart, Plt Off A.McG. RNZAF   81 Sqn   165, 200, 214
Pelly, Air Commodore C.B.R.   HQWDAF   201
Penn, Sgt D.   682 Sqn   78
Pennock, Sgt T.   126 Sqn   43, 215
Peppler, Flt Lt C. RCAF   232 Sqn   165
Philpotts, Flg Off L.F.   683 Sqn   36
Pickles, Wt Off N.   284 Sqn   180
Piper, Sgt C.R. RNZAF   72 Sqn   168, 213
Player, Wg Cdr J.H.   255 Sqn   199
Pratt, Sub Lt E.F. RNZNVR   RNAS   14, 215
Price, Flt Lt E.G.   ASRU   33, 54
Prinsloo, Lt N.P. SAAF   40SAAF Sqn   197
Probert, Plt Off R.H. RCAF   92 Sqn   161, 194, 212
Proud, Flt Sgt H.H.   1437 Sqn   180
Prytherch, Flt Lt D.J.   72 Sqn   80, 216
Pugh, Sgt K.R.   283 Sqn   143
Pursall, Lt(A) R.D. RNVR   ASRU   37, 48

Quine, Sgt R. RAAF   152 Sqn   145, 217

Rabone, Sqn Ldr P.W. RNZAF   23 Sqn   190, 214
Ramsay, Adm Sir Bertram   OC Eastern Task Force   3
Ramsey, Flt Lt N.H.D.   1435 Sqn   23
Rathwell, Sgt D.W. RCAF   154/81 Sqns   126, 173, 213
Rayner, Flg Off R.   43 Sqn   152

Reading, Flt Lt P.W.D.   43 Sqn   100, 216
Reece, Sub Lt G. RNZNVR   885 Sqn   162
Reed, Plt Off/Flg Off M.J. RCAF   185 Sqn   10, 66
Reid, Plt Off W.H. RCAF   43 Sqn   174, 213
Rennolds, Flt Sgt J.   126 Sqn   60, 216
Richards, Lt S.J. SAAF   1SAAF Sqn   185
Richardson, Plt Off G.S.   93 Sqn   136, 157, 158, 211
Richardson, Flt Lt R.W.   92 Sqn   137, 169, 211
Ripper, Sgt D.E. RAAF   229 Sqn   168, 217
Rippon, Flg Off E.D.M.   154 Sqn   173, 217
Riseley, Sgt E.A.   126 Sqn   65
Rivett, Flg Off P.E. RAAF   93 Sqn   154, 158, 212
Roberts, Sgt P.H.P. RAAF   185 Sqn   69, 171
Robinson, Lt K. SAAF   40SAAF Sqn   148, 217
Robinson, Plt Off K.B.   229 Sqn   44, 46, 47, 209
Robinson, Lt M.E. SAAF   1SAAF Sqn   161, 217
Robinson, Sgt W.J. RNZAF   81 Sqn   158, 181, 200, 214
Rogan, Lt D.S. SAAF   1SAAF Sqn   85, 103, 167
Rogers, Capt R.H. SAAF   40SAAF Sqn   187
Ronay, Flt Sgt J.J.   242 Sqn   156, 212
Rook, Sqn Ldr M.   43 Sqn   75, 93, 124
Rossouw, Lt A. deL. SAAF   1SAAF Sqn   85, 216
Rowland, Flg Off M.R. RNZAF   1435 Sqn   131, 217
Russell, Flt Lt A.G.   229 Sqn   59, 209

Sachs, Lt A. SAAF   92 Sqn   137, 211
Salzman, Sgt R.R.   229 Sqn   48, 49, 64, 104, 209, 216
Saphir, Sgt J. RCAF   126 Sqn   100, 210
Satchell, Grp Capt W.A.J.   OC RAF Takali   4
Savage, Flt Lt T.W.   92 Sqn   85, 105, 127, 211, 216
Schmitz, Sgt D.J. RCAF   243 Sqn   99, 143
Schrader, Plt Off W.E. RNZAF   1435 Sqn   82
Scott, Sgt C.M.   72 Sqn   108, 146, 148, 212
Scrase, Flg Off R.D.   72 Sqn   146, 212
Seaman, Flg Off W.S.   601 Sqn   106, 216
Seccombe, Capt J.T. SAAF   1SAAF Sqn   182, 185, 213
Seed, Flt Lt R.   249 Sqn   10, 11, 14
Sewell, Flg Off R.P.W. RCAF   601 Sqn   147, 171, 212
Shapiro, Lionel   War Correspondent   192
Sharp, Flg Off G.S. RAAF   72 Sqn   82, 216
Sharun, Sgt M.R. RCAF   1435 Sqn   19, 25
Shaw, Plt Off E.J. RNZAF   72 Sqn   148, 160, 212
Sheehan, Sgt B.W. RNZAF   249 Sqn   76, 77, 210, 216
Shuren, Flg Off R.C. RCAF   185 Sqn   44, 209
Shute, Flt Sgt F.E.   ASRU   55, 91
Silvester, Flt Lt G.F.   242 Sqn   65, 155, 173, 212, 213
Sinclair, Sir Archibald   Air Minister   83
Sinclair, Flt Sgt A.L. RCAF   185 Sqn   69, 86, 210
Sinclair, Plt Off D. RCAF   185 Sqn   69, 210
Sizer, Sqn Ldr W.M.   93 Sqn   75, 93, 127, 128, 136, 148, 157, 212
Skalski, Sqn Ldr S.   601 Sqn   171
Small, Flg Off R.H.   229 Sqn   131, 211
Smart, Sqn Ldr T.   229 Sqn   4, 22, 25, 27, 28, 42, 43, 45, 215
Smith, Flt Sgt A.W.   1435 Sqn   149
Smith, Flg Off K.   72 Sqn   160, 212
Smith, Sgt L.A.   152 Sqn   170, 173, 201, 213
Smith, Flt Sgt M. RNZAF   43 Sqn   110
Smith, Sqn Ldr W.A.   1435 Sqn   4, 27, 30, 32, 209
Snell, Flg Off A.E.   43 Sqn   201, 207
Snell, Flg Off A.N.   242 Sqn   129, 130, 217
Snowden, Sgt/Flt Sgt R.M.   683 Sqn   36, 52, 53
Sparkes, Flt Sgt W.D.   152 Sqn   201, 217
Spiers, Plt Off J.R.   1435 Sqn   144
St John, Plt Off V.   232 Sqn   166, 187, 217
Stanford-Smith, Flg Off O.C.H.   229 Sqn   131, 211
Staniforth, Plt Off J.M.   93 Sqn   123
Stanley, Flt Sgt K.C.B.   1437 Flt   175
Staples, Flt Sgt J.E.   126 Sqn   65

Stark, Sgt W.J.B. 249 Sqn 33, 34, 209, 215
Steele, Plt Off W.J. RCAF 417RCAF Sqn 200, 201
Stephens, Wg Cdr M.M. WCF Hal Far Wing 4, 9, 14, 15, 218
Stevenson, Sgt F. 229 Sqn 55
Stewart, Flt Lt A.R. 1435 Sqn 15
Stewart, Plt Off/Flg Off L.A. 1435 Sqn 46, 95, 131, 209, 217
Stock, Flg Off J.A. 242 Sqn 134, 156, 211
Stovel, Flg Off B. RCAF 126 Sqn 38, 215
Stratford, Flt Sgt P.S. 1435 Sqn 40, 215
Susans, Flt Lt R.T. RAAF 3RAAF Sqn 189
Symons, Plt Off G.W. RNZAF 229 Sqn 104, 105, 216

Taggart, Plt Off R.J. RCAF 1435 Sqn 23, 32, 33, 215
Tarbuck, Plt Off J. 185 Sqn 31
Tardiff, Flt Sgt C.A. 683 Sqn 169, 217
Tayleur, Flg Off J.L. 232 Sqn 94
Taylor, LAC J. 3231 SCU 91
Taylor, Sqn Ldr J.S. 601 Sqn 66, 93, 147, 212, 217
Taylor, Sgt/Flt Sgt L.A. 229 Sqn 28, 59, 131, 211
Tedder, Air Chief Marshal Sir Arthur C-in-C Med Air Command 2, 192
te Kloot, Flg Off J. RAAF 229 Sqn 104
Theobald, Sgt H.L. 81 Sqn 67
Thompson, Wg Cdr J.M. WCF Luqa Wing 4, 14, 15, 17, 22, 23, 27, 28, 30, 36, 39, 49, 60, 64, 218
Thomson, Sgt F.W. 1435 Sqn 24, 46, 209
Thomson, Flt Lt R. 154 Sqn 166, 183, 217
Thorogood, Sgt J.D. 185 Sqn 10, 86
Tighe, Desmond *Reuters* 122
Todd, Flt Lt A.M. 230 Sqn 13
Tooth, Flg Off J.A. 152 Sqn 145, 217
Torney, Flg Off J.G. 1435 Sqn 12
Towgood, Flt Sgt D.J. 243 Sqn 101, 138, 158
Trotter, Lt B. SAAF 1SAAF Sqn 165
Trowbridge, Sgt R.H. RAAF 111 Sqn 100
Turkington, Flg Off R.W. 43 Sqn 130, 143, 169, 213
Turner, Sqn Ldr P.S. 417RCAF Sqn 79, 93, 182
Tyrrell, Grp Capt G.Y. OC RAF Takali 4
Tyson, Wg Cdr F.H. OC RAF Krendi 4, 8, 28, 159

Urwin Mann, Sqn Ldr J.R. 126 Sqn 4, 13, 16, 18, 28, 30, 36, 41, 43, 46, 209, 216

Vale, Flg Off A.A. 126 Sqn 25, 45, 52, 58, 64, 210
Vance, Flt Sgt/Wt Off F.R. RCAF 185/112 Sqns 16, 159
van Nus, Lt J. SAAF 1SAAF Sqn 167
van der Merwe, Lt S.W. SAAF 1SAAF Sqn 144, 165, 170, 213
van der Veen, Lt G.T. SAAF 1SAAF Sqn 167, 217
Vine, Sgt E.E. 229 Sqn 32, 215

Waddell, Flt Sgt R.R. RAAF 255 Sqn 199
Wade, Sqn Ldr L.C. 145 Sqn 66, 82, 93, 125, 151, 174
Walker, Flt Lt R.E. 682 Sqn 109
Walton, Flt Lt W.C. 1435 Sqn 14
Warburton, Wg Cdr A. 683 Sqn 22, 25, 41, 42, 56, 64, 93, 94, 122, 130, 131, 171, 196, 211
Warcup, Sgt G.C. 185 Sqn 21
Warr, Sgt D.H. 185 Sqn 40
Warren, Sgt K. 92 Sqn 127
Waugh, Lt D.S. SAAF 40SAAF Sqn 184, 217
Webb, Lt E.C. SAAF 40SAAF Sqn 125, 216
Webster, Flt Sgt W.J. RNZAF 43 Sqn 104, 124, 210
Wells, Lt H.E. SAAF 145 Sqn 106
Wells, Flt Sgt H.S. 229 Sqn 59
Welshman, Sqn Ldr S.G. 1437 Flt 147, 191
Wenman, Sqn Ldr A.C.G. 154 Sqn 65, 93, 173, 187, 217

Westmacott, Wg Cdr I.B. OC RAF Safi 27, 70, 126
Whitamore, Sqn Ldr W.M. 81 Sqn 65, 93, 158, 161, 173, 181, 212, 213
White, Sqn Ldr B.E.G. 185, 229 Sqns 4, 9, 11, 14, 15, 55, 65, 94, 95, 104, 210, 216
White, Plt Off/Flg Off G.G. White RNZAF 126 Sqn 43, 58, 59, 61, 64, 95, 103, 139, 144, 210, 211
White, Sgt P.L. 1437 Flight 198, 217
Whiteford, Sgt G.J. RAAF 81 Sqn 83, 173, 213
Whitney, Plt Off R.K. 111 Sqn 100
Whitside, Flt Lt W.J. RCAF 145 Sqn 189, 190, 214
Wikner, Lt W.D. SAAF 1SAAF Sqn 171, 213
Williams, Sgt/Plt Off A. 229 Sqn 13, 59, 145, 209, 215, 217
Williams, Plt Off S.S. 185 Sqn 16, 32
Wilmot, Lt Col L.A. SAAF attached 242 Sqn, OC 322 Wing 125, 129, 200, 214, 218
Wilmot, Flt Lt T.W. 185 Sqn 66, 110, 171, 195, 214
Wilson, Flg Off G.A. RCAF 92 Sqn 158, 187, 190, 205
Wilson, Sgt R.F.G. 111 Sqn 140
Withy, Flg Off/Flt Lt H.F. 185 Sqn 9, 30, 31, 37, 43, 44, 47, 61, 209, 215, 216
Wood, Plt Off R.L. 1435 Sqn 20, 35
Woodhill, Flg Off J.G. 232 Sqn 94
Woodhouse, Flg Off S.H. 682 Sqn 201
Woods, Sqn Ldr E.N. 249 Sqn 4, 8, 10
Wyndham, Plt Off A.A. RAAF 185 Sqn 183, 217

Yaholnitsky, Flt Sgt W. RCAF 249 Sqn 44, 215
Yates, Sgt J.S. 185 Sqn 57, 216
Young, Flg Off W. 111 Sqn 104

Zobell, Plt Off M.B. RCAF 185 Sqn 58, 216

MALTESE PERSONNEL

Attard, Vincent Civilian 174
Bezzina family Civilians 89
Carabott, Vincent Civilian 58
Gonzi, Bishop Bishop of Gozo 90
Mifsud, Carmelo Civilian 58
Testa, Joseph Civilian 58
Vella, Catherine Civilian 89

AMERICAN PERSONNEL

Adams, 1/Lt Albert C. Jr 2 FS 76
Armstrong, 1/Lt Robert E. Jr 4th FS 72, 76
Ashley, 1/Lt Willie 99th FS 71

Babcock, 1/Lt 308th FS 106, 216
Baker, 1/Lt-Capt Royal N. 308th FS 71, 72, 184, 185, 214
Barr, Capt Harry L. 307th FS 143, 211
Bryson, Capt William C. 307th FS 71, 72
Burnett, 2/Lt Robert L. III 4 FS 76

Callender, 1/Lt Alvin D. 308th FS 71, 138, 211
Chaddock, 2/Lt Robert B. 307th FS 185, 213
Chandler, Capt Berry 309th FS 72, 135, 211
Collinsworth, 1/Lt/Capt Jerry D. 307th FS 71, 72, 136, 211
Conley, 1/Lt John K. 307th FS 71, 127, 216
Coward, Lt Col James S. 52nd FG 175, 199

Dalrymple, 1/Lt Edwin 308th FS 71
Davis, 1/Lt Adrian A. 308th FS 71
Davis, Maj Mercer P. 307th FS 94
Dean, Lt Col Fred M. 31st FG 70, 91, 94, 218
Dunn, Col Air Transport Command 116, 117, 119

Eisenhower, Gen Dwight Supreme Commander 2, 142, 167
English, 2/Lt Norman E. 2nd FS 178, 213
Everett, 1/Lt Franklin A. 5th FS 143

Fardella, 1/Lt Edward 308th FS 91, 216
Fawcett, 2/Lt John E. 2nd FS 198, 199
Feld, 1/Lt Sylvan 52nd FG 70
Fischette, 1/Lt Charles F. 307th FS 71, 72
Fleming, Capt Thomas B. 308th FS 71, 94, 106, 216

Goldenberg, 1/Lt August 307th FS 135, 217
Gooding, 1/Lt George 307th FS 72
Gottlieb, 2/Lt Irwin 5th FS 143
Graham, 2/Lt Delton G. 307th FS 185, 214

Hall, 1/Lt Charles B. 99th FS 71, 96
Heil, 1/Lt Robert 309th FS 175, 217
Helton, 1/Lt Leonard V. 4th FS 183, 213
Hewitt, Vice-Adm H. Kent OC Western Task Force 3
Hill, Maj Frank A. 309th FS 72, 94, 135, 211
Hine, 2/Lt Robert W. 5th FS 200, 214
Hurd, 2/Lt Richard F. 308th FS 184, 185, 213, 217

Jenkins, 1/Lt Everett K. Jr 5th FS 143
Johnson, 1/Lt John E. 307th FS 127, 216

Keith, 1/Lt Donald J. 309th FS 72

Lewis, Lt C.G. USN USS *Boise* 126
Lupton, 1/Lt Robert M. Jr 309th FS 70

Macmillan, 1/Lt Donald W. 2nd FS 198, 199
McDonald, Capt Norman L. 2nd FS 178, 213
McMann, 1/Lt 308th FS 70
Mehroff, 1/Lt 309th FS 174, 217
Meldeau, 2/Lt Leonard H. 309th FS 72
Mutchler, 2/Lt 309th FS 175, 213

Odom, 1/Lt Edwin J. 5th FS 201, 214
Overend, 1/Lt Walter J. 308th FS 71

Patton, Gen George OC Seventh Army 2, 142
Paulk, Capt John H. 309th FS 72, 138, 184, 211, 213
Payne, Capt Carl W. 309th FS 72, 134, 138, 211
Pryblo, 1/Lt Carroll 307th FS 185, 214

Quesada, Gen Elwood R. 12th AF 200

Rahn, 1/Lt Robert O. 309th FS 72
Ramsey, 1/Lt Charles R. 308th FS 178, 184, 213
Rich, 1/Lt Gordon 308th FS 71
Roosevelt, President Franklin US President 2, 192

Shafer, 1/Lt Dale R. Jr 309th FS 72
Smith, 1/Lt Derwood K. 308th FS 72
Smith, 1/Lt Monroe P. 31st FG 72
Stephens, 1/Lt George 308th FS 91, 216
Strickland, Brig-Gen A.C. Military Governor Pantelleria 76
Swiger, 1/Lt James R. 309th FS 72

Trafton, 2/Lt Frederick O. 308th FS 70, 175, 213
Tyler, 1/Lt James O. 4th FS 76

Van Ausdell, 1/Lt P. Dixon 308th FS 109

Waltner, 1/Lt Wilfred L. 308th FS 138, 211
Watson, 1/Lt Spann 99th FS 71
West, Lt Col George W. 52nd FG 70
Weynandt, F/O Louis M. 5th FS 143
White, 1/Lt John H. 307th FS 71, 72
Williams, Capt 308th FS 184, 185
Winkler, Capt John M. 307th FS 134, 135, 211
Wolfe, 1/Lt Merritt C. 308th FS 71
Woodrich, 1/Lt 308th FS 138
Wootten, 1/Lt Roland F. Jr 307th FS 71, 136
Wright, 1/Lt 309th FS 134, 211

FRENCH PERSONNEL

Adam, Cmdt GCII/7 73, 203
Claude, Lt de Vass R.L.A. 807 Sqn 162, 217
Feldzer, Adjt Constantin GCII/7 72-73
Gauthier, Cne Gabriel GCII/7/326 Sqn 204
Kann, Sgt-Chef Louis GCII/7 72
Papin, Cmdt GCII/7/326 Sqn 203

GERMAN PERSONNEL

Abendroth, Obfw Alexander 7/SKG10 136
Achter, Fw Arno 6/SKG10 178
Adolph, Uffz Martin 6/KG1 153

Bahnsen, Uffz Jens 8/JG53 97
Bär, Maj Heinz I/JG77 112
Bartel, Uffz 3/JG53 201
Barten, Lt Franz 7/JG53 112, 143, 149
Barth, Uffz Heinz-August 7/JG53 143
Bartusch, Obfw 1/JG53 101
Beck, Uffz Helmut I/JG53 200
Becker, Uffz Helmut 3/KG6 138
Berger, Oblt Helmut IV/SKG10 135
Berres, Oblt Heinz-Edgar I/JG77 78, 94, 95, 112, 173
Beyer, Hptm Franz IV/JG3 112, 140, 170
Bickel, Lt Heinz 3/KG26 169
Blind, Uffz Richard 5/ZG1 138
Bonin, Gen Bogislaw von CoS XIV Panzer Korps 191
Börngen, Hptm Ernst 5/JG27 127, 158, 165
Bosch, Uffz Georg 2(F)/122 134
Braasch, Fw Kurt 3/JG53 145
Brändle, Fw Josef II/JG27 52
Breiling, Uffz 2/JG53 60
Bregtschneider, Lt 6/KG76 162
Brönnle, Lt Herbert 2/JG53 100
Brücker, Hptm Heinrich Stab SchG2 112
Bründl, Obfw Willi 9/ZG26 168
Brunn, Lt von 8/KG54 138
Bürckle, Lt Werner III/KG100 178
Buschek, Lt Erich 4/JG27 71

Christl, Hptm Georg III/ZG26 6
Chucholowius, Fw Herbert 11/JG3 148
Clade, Obfw Emile 5/JG27 32
Claus, Obfw Martin 6/SKG10 190
Conrade, Fw Herbert 5/SchG2 60
Cozclack, Obgfr Werner II/SKG10 188
Cziossek, Uffz Friedrich 6/JG27 71

Daspelgruber, Oblt Fritz 10/JG3 163
Daum, Uffz Rolf 3/JG77 106, 185

Deicke, Oblt Joachim 6/JG77 112
Denker, Lt Heinrich 2(F)/122 201
Dinger, Oblt Fritz 4/JG53 65, 106, 111, 168
Dömbrack, Hptm Werner III/SchG2 112
Dörffer, Fw Albin 6/JG27 70
Dörn, Hptm 2/KG6 162
Dreher, Oblt Wilhelm 5/ZG1 138
Dreyer, Uffz Erich 9/JG27 43
Dritthuber, Lt Josef 3/JG77 155
Dudeck, Oblt Heinz 4/JG77 112

Eckert, Hptm Klaus Stab JG53 101, 102
Ellers, Uffz Hans-Wilhelm 1/JG53 65
Esser, Lt Wilhelm Stab JG53 129
Ettel, Oblt Wolf 8/JG27 163, 165, 167
Eward, Uffz Hans 4/JG53 131

Feyerlein, Fw Hans 6/JG53 79, 88
Fischer, Fw Arno 1/JG53 150, 157
Flink, Oblt Theodor 3/JG53 157
Fowé, Lt Werner 5/SchG2 60
Franke, Fw Herbert 3/JG53 157
Frey, Lt Harry 7/KG6 135
Freytag, Hptm Siegfried II/JG77 78, 99, 112, 150
Friedrichs, Lt 2/LG2 128
Frielinghaus, Oblt Gustav 11/JG3 146, 159

Galland, GenMaj Adolf General of Fighters 84, 157
Gerdes, Fw Hermann 5/ZG1 138
Gettinger, Uffz Franz II/SKG10 184
Glanz, Oblt Ferdinand III/ZG1 56
Göring, Reichsmarschall Hermann C-in-C Luftwaffe
    63, 84, 133, 140, 166, 171, 181
Götz, Maj Franz III/JG53 6, 57, 112
Gräff, Uffz 1/JG77 99
Gröber, Uffz Reinhold 3/JG53 101
Grundt, Fw Bernhard II/ZG1 169
Gugelberger, Uffz Robert 4/JG53 168

Hache, Uffz Gerhard 8/JG27 165
Hagedorn, Obgfr Reinhard 11/JG3 171
Hammer, Lt Alfred 4/JG53 129
Hannak, Oblt Günther 7/JG27 41, 45, 53
Harder, Lt Jürgen 8/JG53 17, 24
Harnisch, Uffz Hermann 8/JG53 89
Hartmann, Oblt Willi II/ZG1 169
Haschke, Lt Rudolf I/KG6 138
Hauenschild, Hptm Hans-Jobst II/SKG10 112
Hauer, Uffz Karl 3/JG77 86
Hefter, Uffz Helmut 6/JG27 71
Heilmann, Obstlt Ludwig FJR3 150
Heinig, Uffz Ferry pilot 30
Heiss, Fw Hermann Stab SKG10 143
Hennig, Oblt Heinz-Günther 3/JG53 65
Hettler, Uffz Karl-Eugen 1/JG77 175
Heuser, Uffz Gerhard 2/LG2 128
Hilbert, Fw KGrzbV.25 155
Hillmann, Uffz Franz 5/ZG1 138, 169
Hissbach, Hptm 5/NJG2 112
Hitler, Adolf Chancellor 78, 176, 177
Hoffmann, Uffz Kurt 2/LG2 128
Hoffmann, Uffz Oswald IV/JG3 187
Hofmann, Fw Engelbert 6/JG53 79
Hofmann, Lt Walter II/JG53 72
Holstein, Uffz Hermann 2/JG53 129, 138, 145
Holzapfel, Oblt Fritz 13/SKG10 170
Holzenburg, Gfr Günther 6/KG1 153
Homeier, Uffz Georg 2(F)/122 134
Höpfner, Uffz Alfred 1(F)/123 200
Hötzender, Lt Walter 6/KG77 136
Hrdlicka, Oblt Franz 5/JG77 78, 99, 112, 178

Hube, Gen Hans Valentin XIV Panzer Korps 164
Hueschens, Hptm 4/NJG2 112

Iffland, Lt Hans IV/JG3 159, 166, 167
Irps, Hptm Erich Stab JG53 55

Jakubik, Uffz Adolf 11/JG3 148
Janusch, Gfr Georg III/ZG26 156
Jegg, Uffz Hans 9/JG53 100
Jost, Lt Klaus II/SKG10 185
Jürgens, Uffz Hans 5/JG27 31, 85

Kahlau, Uffz Rudi I/JG53 200
Kaldenburg, Maj Gerhard von 14/SKG10 130
Kampmann, Lt Walter-Karl TG1 173
Kapp, Lt Heinz-Karl 4/JG27 129
Karlsböck, Uffz Robert 6/JG27 71
Kesselring, Feldmarschall Albert C-in-C Fliegerkorps II
    (Süd) 112, 150, 164, 176
Kientsch, Lt Willy 6/JG27 71, 127, 158
Kissel, Lt Helmut 8/KG54 138
Klammer, Uffz Oskar 2(F)/122 134
Klein, Oblt Wilhelm 1/JG53 72, 101, 102
Kluszmann, Lt Karl-Otto 1(F)/123 200
Knepler, Lt Gerhard 3/KG6 174
Kobele, Obfw Walter III/ZG26 156
Koch, Fw Walter 6/SchG2 71
Kögler, Lt Hans-Joachim 1/JG53 138
Köhler, Lt Armin I/JG77 78, 84, 112, 166, 179
Körn, Gfr Wolfgang II/JG27 38
Kornstädt, Lt Hans-Ulrich 4/JG27 70
Krais, Fw 10/JG3 166
Krösing, Uffz Heinz 1(F)/123 196
Kuetgens, Lt Wilhelm 6/JG27 71
Kühdorf, StFw Karl I/JG77 179
Kulla, Uffz Karl II/JG77 55
Kutscha, Lt Herbert 12/JG3 146, 159
Kuttner, Lt Johann 4/JG27 30

Laube, Oblt Ernst 3/JG77 78, 112
Laube, Oblt Martin 5/JG53 111, 131
Laue, Uffz Ludwig 7/JG53 13
Lehmann, Uffz Günther 1(F)/123 196
Lehmann, Hptm Kurt 9/KG54 138
Lenk, Uffz Kurt 6/KG1 153
Leonhard, Oblt Karl 8/JG53 6
Lewes, Lt Hans 5/JG27 71
Licha, Lt Ludwig 3/JG77 106, 179
Liedtke, Lt Arthur 5/SchG2 72
Luftkampf, Lt Behrendt I/JG77 179
Lutter, Uffz August 7/SchG2 71
Lux, Lt Peter II/JG27 169

Mackmüller, Lt Hans 4/KG1 154
Madaun, Uffz 1/JG77 173
Mäder, Lt Labert TG1 173
Maltzahn, Obstlt Baron Günther von Stab JG53 57,
    111
Marten, Obfw Karl 5/JG53 60
Mayer, Uffz Gustav 2/LG2 128
Mazurek, Fw Marian 1/JG53 71
Meikstat, Obfw Fritz 5/JG77 173
Merden, Oblt Hans III/KG76 43
Messer, Lt Karl-Heinz 2/JG53 138
Michalski, Maj Gerhard II/JG53 57, 67, 77, 81
Mint, Fw Peter 6/KG76 162
Minuth, Uffz Werner 2/SchG2 110
Missbach, Uffz KGrzbV.25 155
Mittenhuber, Fw Hans IV/JG3 187
Möller, Fw Willi 2(F)/122 134
Mondry, Uffz Meinhard 4/JG27 71

Mrwik, Uffz Ernst 1/JG53 145
Müller, Fw Alfred 4/JG27 165
Müller, Hptm Friedrich-Karl I/JG53 57, 61, 77, 112
Müller, Fw Paul-Heinz 2/LG2 128
Müller, Oblt II/KG1 152

Nauck, Oblt Ulrich 2(F)/122 83
Neu, Gfr Erwin 3/KG6 174
Niederhagen, Obfw Kurt 1/JG77 160
Niese, Oblt Erhard 7/JG77 154
Nitzsche, Lt Hans 6/JG27 70
Nolte-Ernsting, Uffz Rolf 1/JG77 88

Oldendorf, Hptm Heinrich 8/KG76 46
Öser, Fw I/LLG2 155
Ostermann, Uffz Helmut II/SKG10 184
Ostermeyer, Uffz Alfred 4/JG53 100

Paashaus, Lt Karl 5/JG53 77, 88
Patuschka, Hptm Dr Horst II/NJG1 6
Philipp, Uffz 6/JG77 183
Pichler, Obfw Johann 7/JG77 159, 161
Pohl, Fw Otto I/JG77 78, 94
Polowiec, Lt Alexander 4/KG1 152
Pöppel, Lt Martin FJR3 155
Potjans, Oblt Leo 6/JG53 82, 111
Prellwitz, Lt Jürgen 2(F)/122 134
Pufahl, Hptm Winfried 7/JG53 6, 17

Rademacher, Uffz Hans II/SKG10 185
Rammelt, Maj Karl II/JG51 112
Rapp, StFw Paul II/ZG1 134
Rather, Uffz Walter I/KG26 121
Rehwoldt, Obfw Ernst 6/SKG10 189
Reinert, Lt Ernst-Wilhelm II/JG77 78, 183, 187, 193
Reinicke, Uffz Walter 7/JG53 96, 97
Reiter, Fw Theo 5/JG53 60, 64, 67, 68, 77, 81, 87
Riedelberger, Oblt I/NJG2 142
Riepelsiep, Obfw Rudi 6/SKG10 178
Rödel, Maj Gustav II/JG27 30, 57
Röhrig, Oblt Hans 9/JG53 6, 106, 112, 131, 156
Rollwage, Obfw Herbert 5/JG53 60, 68, 77, 99
Roth, Lt Stab JG77 193
Rott, Hptm Frank-Werner III/JG27 40
Russ, Fw Otto 4/JG53 82
Ruth, Fw Josef III/ZG26 156
Ryll, Fw 2/JG77 96, 179

Salgert, Uffz Peter 2(F)/122 134
Salzer, Uffz Albert 4/JG77 173
Sareiter, Uffz Georg Stab I/KG54 33
Sartory, Lt Karl 2(F)/122 134
Sauer, Uffz 2/JG77 179
Schäfer, Lt Bruno 9/SKG10 104, 201
Schäfer, Uffz Hans 10/JG3 144, 148, 166
Scheer, Uffz Friedrich 8/JG53 20, 24
Scheid, Fw Günther II/SKG10 185
Schenk, Lt Silvio III/KG100 178
Scherbaum, Fw Josef 9/ZG26 175
Scherber, Uffz Horst 7/JG27 165
Schiess, Oblt Franz 8/JG53 28, 40, 72, 112, 197
Schimhof, Fw Helmut III/ZG26 156
Schlechter, Lt Heinz 6/JG27 31, 35
"Scholl, Uffz Erich" 2/JG53 180
Schlösser, Lt Günther 9/SKG10 104
Schmidt, Uff Franz 3/JG77 143
Schmidt, Uffz Kurt 11/JG3 144
Schneider, Fw Bernhard 6/JG27 32, 35, 37
Schnell, Maj Karl-Heinz II/JG53 111, 129
Schragow, Uffz Hans 3/SchG2 124
Schroer, Hptm Werner II/JG27 57, 71, 112

Schröter, Hptm Fritz 9/SKG10 103, 104, 112
Schumann, Maj Heinz IV/SKG10 78, 112
Schwarz, Fw 1(F)/123 200
Seeger, Obfw Günther 7/JG53 106, 131
Seiffert, Lt Ulrich 8/JG53 89
Senger, Gen Fridolin von (und Etterlin) XIV Panzer
   Korps 150
Sielaff, Obfw Heinz III/ZG26 156
Sinnwell, Fw Erwin 6/JG27 71
Skrizipczuk, Uffz Helmut III/ZG26 156
Sommer, Hptm Paul II/JG27 38
Sorg, Obfw Otto 5/SchG2 60
Stangelmeier, Uffz Dagobert 4/JG27 165
Steinhoff, Maj Johannes JG77 78, 84, 102, 107, 111,
   112
Steis, Fw Heinrich 4/JG27 70, 71, 149, 173
Stigler, Obfw Franz 6/JG27 166
Stöhr, Uffz Friedrich II/SKG10 184
Stracke, Uffz Herbert 5/JG53 64
Strasen, Oblt Gerhard Stab JG77 173
Stretz, Uffz 10/JG3 166, 167
Stumpf, Uffz Franz 4/JG27 71

Täschner, Obfw Rudolf I/JG53 200
Tenner, Uffz Rudolf 12/JG3 148
Tonne, Maj Günther Stab SKG10 112, 163
Tonne, Hptm Wolfgang 3/JG53 6, 38
Trager, Lt Josef 2(F)/122 80

Ubben, Maj Kurt III/JG77 112
Unterecker, Uffz Klaus Stab I/KG54 33
Untermark, Uffz Helmut 5/KG77 136

Vacano, Fw Martin von 8/JG53 72, 156
Vietinghoff, Gen Heinrich von 15th Army 191
Vogel, Fw Hans-Dieter 1/JG77 160
Vögl, Oblt Anton Stab I/KG54 33
Vögl, Hptm Ferdinand II/JG27 30
Voss, Lt Fritz 11/JG3 146

Waag, Uffz Gerhard 6/JG53 88
Wagenknecht, Fw Klaus 4/JG53 82
Wagner, Uffz Emil 1/JG53 101, 145
Weber, Uffz Willi 2(F)/122 83
Weinert, Oblt Gerhard 2(H)/14 174
Wenk, Obfhr Helmut 6/SKG10 174, 178
Wessels, Uffz Hermann Stab I/KG54 33
Wessling, Lt Otto 10/JG3 144, 146, 148
Weyrauch, Oblt Ernst von 2(H)/14 112, 140
Wicht, Lt Erhardt 9/SKG10 104
Wilde, Fw I/LLG2 155
Wissel, Lt Günther 1(F)/123 196
Witt, Uffz Hermann 5/JG53 60, 67, 79, 88, 99, 106
Wöffen, Fw Anton II/JG27 169
Wolfsteiner, Fw Hans 9/ZG26 168
Woltering, Uffz August II/SKG10 185
Wulff, Uffz Hermann 4/JG27 165
Wurzer, Uffz KGrzbV.25 155

Zander, Lt Friedrich 2(H)/14 68, 69
Zantropp, Lt Joachim III/KG100 187
Zielke, Uffz Revi 8/JG53 97
Zimmermann, Uffz Hans 2/JG77 171-172
Zimmermann, Uffz Reinhold 6/JG53 79
Zinser, Obfw KGrzbV.25 155
Zuck, Fw Herbert 3/JG77 95

ITALIAN PERSONNEL

Agnati, TenCol Giorgio 25°Gruppo Aut BT 5
Agnello, Cap Edoardo 173^Sqd 6
Aiello, Col Ciro 53°Stormo CT 4
Alessandrini, Magg/TenCol Aldo 3°Gruppo Aut CT 5, 62, 113
Alessandrini, Cap Bruno 155^Sqd 113
Alula' Av/Radio Angelo 186^Sqd 56
Ambrosio, Gen D.A. Vittorio Comando Supremo 113
Annoni, Cap Emanuele 96^Sqd 113, 139, 189
Arduini, M.llo Tullio 362^Sqd 139

Badoglio, Marshal Pietro Prime Minister 3, 176
Baldini, Cap Edoardo 79^Sqd 5
Banfi, Serg Luigi 239^Sqd 131
Barbaglio, Serg Aldo 160^Sqd 47
Barcaro, Ten Giovanni 97^Sqd 99, 113
Baroni, Sottoten Renalto 4°Stormo CT 188, 191
Barroni, Av/Mot Alberto 170^Sqd 56
Bartolucchi, Sottoten Dante 208^Sqd 157
Baruffi, Magg Pericle 17°Gruppo CT 5
Beggiato, Cap Guido 81^Sqd 5
Bellagambi, Cap Mario 363^Sqd 62, 113, 148
Bergami, Serg Antonio 170^Sqd 56
Bertolaso, Ten Giorgio 91^Sqd 159
Bettuzzi, Av/Mot Antonio 186^Sqd 56
Beverina, Ten Renalto 239^Sqd 131
Bevilacqua, Cap Domenico 153°Gruppo CT 72
Bianchelli, M.llo Gianni 97^Sqd 102, 125
Blengini, Cap Antonio 186^Sqd 56
Bombardini, Serg Alfredo 97^Sqd 99, 189
Borrelli, Serg Onofrio 216^Sqd 153
Boselli, Sottoten Leo 4°Stormo CT 100
Bragè, Serg 208/238^Sqd 170
Buffarini, M.llo Guido 209^Sqd 140
Burroni, Cap Mario 163^Sqd 114
Bussola, Serg Gianfranco 388^Sqd 146

Calistri, Cap Pietro 76^Sqd 5
Calvi, Av/Sc 216^Sqd 153
Calzoni, Sottoten Arrigo 216^Sqd 153
Canfora, Ten Antonio 97^Sqd 125
Capitani, Magg Carlo Alberto 32°Gruppo Aut BT 5
Capponi, Ten Vascello 186^Sqd 56
Carboni, Gen 3
Carillo, Ten 150°Gruppo CT 148
Carlini, Serg 216^Sqd 153
Carotti, Cap Trento 386^Sqd 113
Castello, Gen 3
Cavaglia, Marshal 3
Cavagliano, Serg Magg Carlo 153^Sqd 78, 106
Cavatore, Ten 150°Gruppo Aut CT 110
Celle, Ten Giancarlo 151°Gruppo CT 72
Cenni, Magg Giuseppe 5°Stormo CT 136, 140
Ceoletta, Serg Magg 9°Gruppo CT 181
Cesari, M.llo Elio 151°Gruppo CT 70
Chiale, Ten Giovanni 150°Gruppo Aut CT 71, 148
Chiarello, Av.Sc 216^Sqd 153
Cima, Sottoten Ferdinando 4°Stormo CT 189
Clauser, Sottoten Fabio 96^Sqd 110, 139, 191
Commini, Ten Giorgio 202^Sqd 6
Constantini, Cap Giuseppe 367^Sqd 5
Cori, Serg 216^Sqd 153
Corte, Ten Aldo della 159°Gruppo Ass 135
Cosconati, Av/Sc 216^Sqd 153
Crabbia, Sottoten Antonio 151°Gruppo CT 71
Cracco, Serg Ruggero 237^Sqd 146

Daffara, Sottoten Vittorino 97^Sqd 101, 110, 191
D'Alanno, Serg Magg Carlo 159°Gruppo Ass 146

Dallari, Sottoten Enrico 4°Stormo CT 188
Dal Molin, Sottoten Arnaldo 4°Stormo CT 125, 189
D'Arrigo, Sottoten Salvatore 239^Sqd 140
De Francesco, Magg Silvio 159°Gruppo Ass 132, 145
dell'Innocenti, Ten Giovanni 150°Gruppo Aut CT 96
De Nicola, Cap Genesio 162^Sqd 114
De Rosa, Serg Magg Federico 208/238^Sqd 170
Di Bernardo, Magg Luigi 6°Gruppo CT 5
D'onta, Av/Sc Enrico 216^Sqd 153
Drago, Ten Ugo 363^Sqd 70, 71
Duke of Acquarone 3

Falchi, Ten Giorgio 88^Sqd 5
Favini, Magg Andrea 153°Gruppo CT 4
Felici, Cap Aldo 71^Sqd 5
Ferrero, Cap Mario 368^Sqd 5, 70
Ferrazzani, Ten 4°Stormo CT 188
Ferrigolo, M.llo Silvio 391^Sqd 146
Ferrulli, Sottoten Leonardo 91^Sqd 103
Fiacchino, Magg Elio 157°Gruppo Aut CT 5
Filippi, Ten Fausto 365^Sqd 62, 113
Fiorillo, Sottoten Amedeo 186^Sqd 56
Fornalé, Serg Magg Giulio 4°Stormo CT 188
Fornoncini, Ten Angelo 150°Gruppo Aut CT 110
Foschini, Magg Ettore 21°Gruppo Aut CT 113
Franchi, M.llo Paolo 151°Gruppo CT 72
Franchini, Cap Giovanni 351^Sqd 125
Francois, TenCol Armando 4°Stormo CT 113
Fratini, Ten Flavio 96^Sqd 108

Gaspari, Serg Magg 9°Gruppo CT 181
Gay, Sottoten Luigi 186^Sqd 56
Gennari, Sottoten Germano 386^Sqd 136
Gensini, Ten Otello 96^Sqd 139
Giachino, TenCol Antonio 151°Gruppo CT 5
Giannella, Sottoten Luigi 84^Sqd 100, 113
Giannelli, Ten Giuseppe 364^Sqd 62, 113
Giordano, M.llo Vittorio 391^Sqd 146
Gobbato, Sottoten Piero 4°Stormo CT 189
Grandi, Count Dino 3
Greco, Cap Filippo 159°Gruppo Ass 135
Guza, Cap Rodolfo 371^Sqd 114
Guzzoni, Gen D.A. Alfredo C-in-C Sicily 115, 164

Keller, Serg Magg 159°Gruppo Ass 135

La Ferla, Cap Germano 362^Sqd 114, 139
Lanna, Av/Arm Angelo 186^Sqd 56
Leoncini, Cap Francesco 361^Sqd 113, 146
Libera, Sottoten Sforza 90^Sqd 100
Li Greci, Cap Aldo 356^Sqd 113
Lionello, Sottoten Gino 361^Sqd 148
Liso, 1°Av/Radio Emanuele 186^Sqd 56
Lorenzi, Ten Lorenzo 209^Sqd 140
Lucchini, Cap Franco 10°Gruppo CT 102
Lucifora, M.llo Antonio 238^Sqd 170

Magri, Sottoten Simone 91^Sqd 107
Maiorani, Magg Ugo 83°Gruppo RM 6
Mancini, Serg 216^Sqd 153
Marazio, Ten Giuseppe 161°Gruppo CT 72
Marchesi, Cap Cesare 373^Sqd 5
Marcocci, Ten Vincenzo 237^Sqd 146
Marcolin, Cap Luciano 377^Sqd 5
Mariotti, Cap Luigi 9°Gruppo CT 113, 181, 188, 191
Martinoli, Serg Teresio 73^Sqd 125, 189
Massaro, Ten Nicola 3°Gruppo Aut CT 89
Masetti, Serg Alessandro 351^Sqd 163
Melotti, Serg Magg Bruno 239^Sqd 140
Mecatti, Ten/Cap Mario 91^Sqd 100, 113, 159, 190
Moglia, Ten Renalto 102°Gruppo 148

Molteni, Serg Magg Natale 90^Sqd 99
Mondo, Cap Federico ASRU 167
Monesi, Cap Olivio 153^Sqd 113
Monti, Gen S.A. Adriano OC Aeronautica della Sicilia 113
Mussolini, Benito Fascist Dictator 3, 78, 151, 176, 177

Necatti, Ten 9°Gruppo CT 181
Naccari, Serg Magg Oberdan 237^Sqd 146
Nava, Serg Rino 151°Gruppo CT 72
Nioi, Cap Clizio 80^Sqd 5
Nitoglia, Ten Luigi 362^Sqd 139
Nobili, TenCol Guido 5°Stormo CT 131
Noziglia, Magg Giuseppe 30°Gruppo Aut BT 5

Orlandini, Magg Luciano 121°Gruppo Tuff 114, 146

Parodi, Cap Mario 208/238^Sqd 170
Pasquinelli, Col Ettore 10°Stormo BT 5
Patrizi, Serg Corrado 84^Sqd 99, 103
Pavesi, Adm Gino NOC Pantelleria 74
Pecoroni, Cap Annibale ASRU 167
Pellegrino, Av/Arm Simone 56
Pergoli, Cap Piero 216^Sqd 153
Perozzi, M.llo Zaccaria 239^Sqd 131
Piccolomini, Cap Ranieri 10°Gruppo CT 113
Poggioli, Sottoten 237^Sqd 146
Porcu, Cap Adriano 164^Sqd 5, 114
Pozzoli, Ten Virginio 363^Sqd 106
Pozzoli, Sottoten 160^Sqd 47
Priolo, Cap Gino 208^Sqd 170
Prosperpio, Ten Mario 374^Sqn 9

Ravasio, M.llo Giuseppe 161°Gruppo CT 72
Reale, Sottoten 216^Sqd 153
Reglieri, Col Alfredo 1°Stormo CT 5
Reiner, Cap Giulio 73^Sqd 113
Residori, Serg Magg Sergio 170^Sqd 56
Rimoldi, Av Vittorio 237^Sqd 146, 147
Romano, Magg Francesco 85°Gruppo RM 6
Rossano, Av/Mot Pasquale 186^Sqd 56
Ruzzin, Sottoten Giuseppe 154^Sqd 88, 89, 106

Salvatore, Serg Magg Massimo 4°Stormo CT 188
Salvi, Ten Enrico 362^Sqd 139, 148
Santini, Ten Plinio 154^Sqd 99
Savi, TenCol Ercole 33°Gruppo Aut BT 5
Serini, Magg Pietro 161°Gruppo CT 84
Sodi, Cap Mario 208/238^Sqd 170
Soligo, Serg Olindo 150°Gruppo Aut CT 91
Soprani, Sottoten Iolando 161°Gruppo CT 72
Squarcia, Ten Vittorio 73^Sqd 125, 189
Storti, Av/Sc Renato 216^Sqd 153

Tani, Av/Sc Vinicio 216^Sqd 153
Tarantini, Av/Sc 216^Sqd 153
Tarini, Ten Gino 208^Sqd 170
Tomaselli, Cap Pio 72^Sqd 5
Tondi, Col Angelo Test & Research Centre, Guidonia 185
Torresi, Ten Giulio 362^Sqd 139, 148
Torselli, Ten 160^Sqd 47
Tovazzi, Cap Giuseppe 154^Sqd 5, 113
Trapani, Av/Arm Giuseppe 186^Sqd 56

Vaghi, Ten Edoardo 362^Sqd 139, 148
Veneziani, Ten Piero 366^Sqd 5
Veronesi, Cap Bruno 151°Gruppo CT 71
Veronesi, Cap Natale 374^Sqd 5
Victor Emmanuel III King of Italy 3, 176

Vidulis, Sottoten Arduino 208^Sqd 157
Vincenzetti, M.llo Pasquale 186^Sqd 56
Vizzotto, Magg Antonio 150°Gruppo Aut CT 62, 113
Voltan, Ten Paolo 4°Stormo CT 188

Zacco, Av/Radio Giovanni 170^Sqd 56
Zavadlal, Cap Bruno 372^Sqd 4